W9-BEO-339

THINGS OLD AND NEW

Catholic Social Teaching Revisited

Editors

Francis P. McHugh
Samuel M. Natale

Assistant Editors

John Schachinger
Brian Rothschild

UNIVERSITY
PRESS OF
AMERICA

Lanham • New York • London

OXFORD
PHILOSOPHY
TRUST

Copyright © 1993 by
University Press of America,® Inc.
4720 Boston Way
Lanham, Maryland 20706

3 Henrietta Street
London WC2E 8LU England

All rights reserved
Printed in the United States of America
British Cataloging in Publication Information Available

Copublished by arrangement with
Oxford Philosophy Trust

Library of Congress Cataloging-in-Publication Data

Things old and new : Catholic social teaching revisited / editors,
Francis P. McHugh . . . [et al.].
p.   cm.
Papers presented at a conference.
1. Sociology, Christian (Catholic)—Congresses.   2. Sociology,
Christian (Catholic)—History of doctrines—19th century—Congresses.
3. Sociology, Christian (Catholic)—History of doctrines—20th
century—Congresses.   4. Catholic Church—Doctrines—Congresses.
5. Catholic Church—Doctrines—History—19th century—Congresses.
6. Catholic Church—Doctrines—History—20th century—Congresses.
I. McHugh, Francis P.
BX1753.T54   1992   261.8—dc20   92–27123 CIP

ISBN 0–8191–8901–4 (cloth : alk. paper)
ISBN 0–8191–8902–2 (pbk. : alk. paper)

 The paper used in this publication meets the minimum requirements of
American National Standard for Information Sciences—Permanence
of Paper for Printed Library Materials, ANSI Z39.48–1984.

CONTENTS

Page

INTRODUCTION

Francis P. McHugh
Samuel M. Natale

Things old and new: Catholic social teaching re-visited

There are two errors about Catholic social teaching which bedevil almost all writing on the subject.[1] The first is that there is virtually no substantive encyclical social teaching before *Rerum novarum*; and the second is that *Rerum novarum* may be taken as some self-contained form of socio-ethical teaching able to be applied as a solution to all successive historical problems. The first error, exhibiting a lack of awareness that Leo's encyclical was the culmination of a century of papal letters which reacted to European social and cultural developments, has encouraged a Catholic tendency to accord to *Rerum novarum* a status of unique and privileged knowledge.[2] The second error has fostered the idea that there is only one model of Catholic social teaching.

The tradition of encyclical social teaching should be viewed, in fact, as a response, dating from the beginning of the nineteenth century, to modernity, if we define that term as 'the development of massive social and cultural changes which began to occur in the seventeenth century and which were bound up with the emergence of industrial capitalist society as a revolutionary break with social formations and social stability in the preceding age. Indeed, the title of Leo XIII's 1891 encyclical may be translated, not inaccurately, as "about modernity", dealing, as it did, with recent revolutionary changes and with some tragic consequences of the development, in Europe, of industrialisation and capitalism.

As a response to modernity, then, encyclical social teaching is older than *Rerum novarum* and may be dated back to 1832[3], when Pope Gregory XVI issued Mirari vos, an unsympathetic reaction against new freedoms commended by the French Revolution and espoused, on the one hand by radical secular political economists, and, on the other, by Charles de Coux and his journal, *L'Avenir*, which was recommending proletarian freedoms viewed, from Rome, as threatening to the established order.[4] In the seventy or so encyclicals written before Leo XIII, the popes did not accord separate treatment, after our fashion of a division of academic labour, to moral, liturgical and social matters. They treated, in a unified form, over-arching ideas about God, humanity and the world and also specific questions about religious, family, economic, political and cultural life. One may begin to detect, for example, a communitarian conception of the self and society in these early writings, but it is not a separate social category so much as part of a moral conception of interdependence. Or, when Pius XI, in *Quanto conficiamur moerore*, attacked individualism, he was more concerned with the moral foundation of the disorder than with its political manifestations.

> We are referring, he wrote, to that un-
> bridled self-love and self-interest that drive
> many to seek their own advantage and profit
> with clearly no regard for their neighbour.
> We mean that thoroughly insati- able passion
> for power and possession that overrides all
> rules of justice and honesty and never ceases
> by every means possible to amass and
> greedily heap up wealth. Com- pletely
> absorbed in the things of earth, forgetful of
> God, religion and their souls, they
> wrongfully place all their happiness in
> procuring riches and money.

The emphasis which encyclicals placed on the moral dimension of individualism was not so different from that of contemporary secular literature. The Oxford English Dictionary gives as Sense 1 of 'individualism', "self-centred feeling or conduct as a principle; a mode of life in which the individual pursues his own ends or follows out his own ideas; free and independent individual action or thought; egoism." It was not until the 1880s that Sense 2 became common:

> The social theory which advocates the free
> and independent action of the individual as

opposed to communistic methods of action
and state interference; opposed to Collectivism and Socialism.

While admitting that encyclical writing in the pre-Leonine period
stressed the underlying moral themes, it is interesting to note that the
teaching did swing, at a theoretical and practical level, between the moral
sense and political manifestations. Individualism and liberty are connected
to foundations in atheism, naturalism and rationalism; and allusions are
made to their social manifestations in liberal capitalism and in socialism,
as can be studied in Pius IX's *Qui pluribus* (1846), *Nostis et nobiscum*
(1840) and in *Quanta cura*, with its celebrated appendix, *The Syllabus of
Errors* (1864). Catholic social teaching was making a public appearance
well before 1891.[5] Still, there is a common agreement that Pope Leo
XIII's *Rerum novarum* inaugurated a special period of encyclical social
teaching which acquired a remarkable and monolithic continuity from
1891 until the death of Pius XII, in 1958. Later popes, in order to mark
the importance of this document, have often revisited *Rerum novarum* on
its anniversary to reiterate its principles and to update its teaching in the
light of changing conditions. This has left a legacy: *Quadragesimo anno*
(1931), *Mater et Magistra* (1961), *Octagesimo adveniens* (1971),
Laborem exercens (1981) and, to mark the centenary, *Centesimus annus*
(1991).

The papers presented here are a selection from 54 contributions to
a conference held in Cambridge in the summer of 1991 to mark the
centenary of *Rerum novarum*. The conference title was "Four
Revolutions: an unfinished agenda." The revolutions referred to were
the industrial, the liberal capitalist, the socialist and the one which has not
yet taken place, the, Christian social revolution.[6] The presenters of
papers at the Cambridge conference were challenged to revisit the
tradition of Catholic social teaching with a view to assessing historical
developments in the light of social teaching and to assessing the corpus
of teaching in the light of historical developments. Broadly speaking, the
papers fell into five categories, and the selection presented here is
representative:

1. Social philosophy
2. The historical context of *Rerum novarum*
3. Social sciences and ethics/theology
4. Political thought and the theory of the state
5. Economics in a modern advanced economy.

The clearest entrant in the "social philosophy" category is J.E. Kelly's contribution on natural law. While recognising that it was not a part of pre-Leonine encyclical social teaching and that it may have receded sufficiently in the post-Vatican II period to make Catholic social teaching less one-dimensional, natural law has been and continues to be an important element in the Catholic tradition. The return of corporatism to the debate, a topic touched on also by Milbank (and by other contributors to the conference) is noted by Kelly. It is difficult to confine the rich offerings of Milbank, Novak, Knight, Keightley, and Wall to any one section, but all, from different points of view, challenge, either to query or support, the foundations of the Catholic tradition. The debates between right and left, between male dominated and female challenged ethical and theological territory are examined in these essays.

At the conference, a number of contributors dealt specifically with the historical context of *Rerum novarum*, and most writers in this collection refer to it in one way or another. But Peter Hebblethwaite's essay, "A new theme for Catholic social doctrine: Europe" draws out the significance of that context for the origins and development of the tradition. In the whole corpus of writing on Catholic social teaching, it is noticeable that some commentators pass directly from *Rerum novarum* to contemporary problems, while others pay detailed attention to how the tradition is mediated historically. Hebblethwaite's piece locates the historical importance of Europe to the whole nature of Catholic social teaching over the past one hundred years.

Categories 4 and 5 deal with the relationship of political theory and science and economics to Catholic social teaching. In all of these contributions there is a mediation between moral ideas and historical realities. In his contribution on solidarity, Jonathan Boswell goes some way towards combatting the second error mentioned in paragraph one of this editorial, when he makes suggestions for a new model. Chaplin introduces a welcome ecumenical dimension in his comparison of subsidiarity and sphere sovereignty, a topic which has interesting connections with Boswell's comments on economic communitarianism. Some specific applications of these ideas are made by Charles O'Donnell in his essay on, "The social encyclicals and social security," an important use of the concept of distributive justice, which is basic to Catholic social teaching.

In a way that is different from other areas of theology, Catholic social teaching exhibits a sense of reality by reason of its openness to history and to new data. This aspect comes out clearly in the papers on economics. Brady, Goodpaster and Kennedy show the significance of Catholic social teaching for contemporary discussions of business ethics. Sora and Natale, identifying a theme in *Centesimus annus*, take up the challenge to moral thinking constituted by modern developments in information technology. In a wide-ranging review of the whole tradition, Joseph Ford draws out the implications of radical concepts for contemporary economic practice. The complex world of international economics is used by Professor Stephen Frowen to probe the adequacy of Catholic moral thinking.

The essays of Margaret Archer and Philip Blond were selected to represent category 3, social sciences and Catholic social teaching because they include the challenge of post-modern thought to this tradition. There are reasons for saying that the period of 'modern' Catholic social teaching was brought to an end at the death of Pius XII, and that we have not yet sufficiently absorbed the nature of post-modern thought to meet the challenge which it constitutes for Catholic social teaching. This challenge is being set out in recent works like John Milbank's *Theology and Social Theory: beyond secular reason* (Oxford: Blackwell, 1990) and Gillian Rose's, *The Broken Middle* (Oxford: Blackwell, February 1992). Archer and Blond show that the challenge must not be made too easy.

In a way that distinguishes it from secular writing in the field of social values, encyclicals always end with a discussion of the role of virtues and holiness in social reconstruction. This selection of essays, in similar fashion, concludes with a contribution by John G Driscoll, President of Iona College, on the subject of rest in a high-stress modern advanced economy: "A modest proposal: keep holy the Sabbath."

ENDNOTES

1.   Notable exceptions with regard to the first error are: Misner, P. *Social Catholicism in Europe from the outset of industrialisation to the First World War*. London: DLT, 1991. Schuck, M.J., *That They Be One: the social teaching of the papal encyclicals 1790-1989*. Washington, D.C.: Georgetown University Press, 1991.

2.   Leo XIII himself was aware of preceding work. In a reply to his private secretary, who wanted him to take a position on a pressing social problem, Leo replied, "A pastoral letter ought to prepare the ground; an encyclical ought to find it already tilled." Utz, A.F., *La Doctrine Sociale de L'Eglise à travers les Siècles*. Paris: Beauchesne. 4 vols. p. xxix.

3.   There is a case for dating Catholic social teaching back to 1745, the year of publication of Benedict XIV's encyclical, *Vix pervenit*, on usury. This encyclical dealt with usury in specific terms such that tension was sustained between church doctrine and the world of commerce and finance, and so as to disturb respectable business people. But it was specific to this topic rather than the beginning of a genre of social teaching.

4.   Misner, P. *op. cit.*, pp. 40-55.

5.   Part 1 of Collini, S. *Liberalism and Sociology: L.T. Hobhouse and political argument in England 1880-1914*, is interesting on this topic, through lacking any consideration of the point being made here about the contribution of 'religious sociology' to the definition of terms.

6.   The complete *Proceedings* of the conference were published in 1991: Editors: Natale & McHugh: New Rochelle, NY: Iona College.

Against the Resignations of the Age

John Milbank

1891 to 1991........the distance of the twentieth century, almost. Or perhaps not. If one is to believe the Italian Marxist, Antonio Negri, the twentieth century has only just begun with nine years to go, for up to now it has been abortive, the mere outworking of the ideological projects of the century that preceded it.[1] There have been three such projects, all characterised by a refusal to be 'resigned' to the unrestrained rule of the capitalist market: fascist corporatism, state socialism and social democracy. Only since 1989 has the failure and termination of all these projects become fully apparent; only since that new revolutionary date have the historical entanglements engendered by these three programmes finally come unravelled.

In one respect it would seem that the verdict of Antonio Negri is endorsed by Karol Wojtyla. According to *Centesimus annus*, the papal encyclical issued to commemorate one hundred years of Catholic social teaching since *Rerum novarum*, the twentieth century measures the distance of a failure which is the inevitable result of a refusal to attend to the wisdom of papal social doctrine.[2] The failure is that of state socialism, Marxist socialism, or indeed socialism tout court, for the pope allows no such subtle discriminations. However, this failure by no means betokens his simple resignation to a 'postmodern' reign of the market; on the contrary, unrestrained capitalism is still to be characterised, as it has been by popes for a century, as a surrender of justice to power and of truth, to opinion.[3] In place of discredited Marxism, Wojtyla offers to workers' movements the relatively untapped theoretical capital of 'Catholic social doctrine'; this, he proposes, will provide the necessary corrective.

However, the Polish Pope is interested in only one third of the story: he has little to say, first of all, about the demise of social democracy (in the sense of 'reformed capitalism,' or 'welfare capitalism') and the evidence that sufficient state welfare provision and trade union rights are predicated upon capitalist growth, and therefore will succumb

1

to periodic downturns in market cycles, and periodically renewed efforts to maximize profits by reducing the proportion deducted in wages and taxes. Witness Britain since the seventies, and more especially Norway and Sweden. Secondly, the pope has nothing to say about fascism, not simply a long-ago banished spectre, for its shadow today hovers once more over eastern Europe, not least in Wojtyla's own country. This, one might allege, is a subject that has to be avoided out of embarrassment, because it embraces instances where the capital of Catholic social doctrine has already before been invested in practice, with a yield of terror and tragic chaos no less patent than in the case of East European state socialism.[4] Of course many will here protest that fascism and nazism distorted the themes of Catholic social teaching out of all recognition, substituting pagan cults of collective force for a Christian respect for 'subjectivity' at every level. However, I shall argue that, albeit against its apparent 'intentions', the fascist tendency of all non-socialist corporatist thought is inevitable. Moreover I shall also contend that the same tendencies, albeit more muted, are contained in Wojtyla's own economic philosophy, which appears to lean somewhat towards the notion of the 'social market'.

Do these remarks imply that I wish to join an already existing chorus of protest against John Paul II's revival of the notion of a substantive Catholic social doctrine, a chorus consisting of M-D Chenu, liberation theologians and others?[5] Not precisely. Here I want to make certain observations intended to re-orientate our perspectives on the current fissure in Catholic social and political thought, between 'Church social teaching' on the one hand, and 'liberation theology' on the other.

Most of all it must be stressed that in comparing these two things one is not comparing like with like. In the first case one has an ahistorical, prescriptive social vision: here is the general pattern for the well-ordered human society, time and place will supply unprescribed but legitmate variations. In the second case one finds little concrete prescription (economic, political or social), but instead an attempt to give a positive theological construal to certain temporal processes which supposedly characterise modernity—the releasing of humanity's rational and political autonomy from religious tutelage, and the gradual flowering of human freedom and genuine sociality. This process is apprehended as

2

being still under way, and as furthered by revolutionary socialism. Since free human practice and the logic of history will 'of their nature' deliver the liberated future, imaginings of future ideal space are relatively inappropriate. Utopianism and specifically Christian social prescriptions are both ruled out by a single gesture which entrusts emancipation to a negative casting-off of mystifying shackles, and the formalism of a truly self-legislating humanity.

On the one hand: space, and sublimely confident authorization. On the other hand: time, and a modest celebration of the human endeavour to be human. Surely the former approach is manifestly conservative and pernicious, the latter radical and enlightened? I want to suggest that things are nothing like so simple, and in particular that in their obsessively temporal concerns and dislike of any direct association of Christian doctrine with socialist vision, liberation theologians are not, on the whole, in continuity with the main lines of Christian and Jewish 'religious socialism'.[6] If one takes here as an example the case of Simone Weil, one finds someone who articulated a sophisticated suspicion of the more teleological and totalizing aspects of Marxism, and endeavoured to imagine patterns of spatial distribution that would eliminate or drastically reduce the instance of, coercive power and arbitrary domination.[7] Weil was no slower to prescribe than Wojtyla, yet her prescriptions were radical, egalitarian, anarchic. Was she guilty of 'deductivism'? Of extracting social norms from a priori religious principles in abstraction from all lived actuality? The answer is surely 'no', and the tendency of liberation theologians to brand as 'deductivist' any account of the derivation of norms other than that contained in their own 'priority of praxis' model, disguises from view the degree to which the latter is a fusion of a teleological historicism with a mystical activism which fetishizes outcomes.[8] By contrast, the attempt to envision, as a sort of 'general topos', a universally normative human society, may represent not so much a deduction from metaphysical or theological first principles, as rather an attempt to more exactly articulate or concretely envision in what those principles consist, such that one is not here talking about any merely secondary 'entailment.' Moreover, this envisioning will always draw upon a chain of historical enactments which are irreplacably exemplary in their performance—and thereby more exact envisioning of—the continuously hovering vision itself.

This co-belonging of deed with vision is somehow missed in both Papal deduction from theoretical principles of natural law (although this is really only an intermittently present feature of encyclical exposition), and the liberationists equally is naturalist verifications of doctrine within the text of practice, which grants to the event as event the unwarrented status of disclosure or revelation.

It is no accident that what I have dubbed the 'temporal' obsession of liberation theology stems not from Christian socialism, nor even in the first place from Marxism, but rather from the somewhat whiggish spirit of John XXIII and the second Vatican council. Not content with a belated recognition of certain positive features within modernity, which would have remained selective and discriminating, John and the council had a tendency to baptize modernity wholesale, as the manifestation of a providentially ordained process of increasing liberation and socialisation. The 'general direction' is perceived as upwards and progressive. Within this perspective, capitalism was explicitly or implicitly endorsed,[9] and liberation theology merely adds a dialectical twist to this endorsement. That is to say, whereas, on the whole, earlier Christian and Jewish socialists followed the perspectives of anarcho-socialists like Pirre-Joseph Proudhon and Gustav Landauer according to whom capitalism is not a necessary stage in the passage to socialism,[10] liberation theologians appear to endorse the Marxist view that proletarianization and concentration of the means of production are necessary stages on the way to liberation and a 'co-operative' society, and must be enforced under state guidance in the case of a 'premature' revolution. (One can have more Maoist, less industrializing, versions of this.) It is true that one finds a certain commendable distancing from this position in the celebration of the poor in general, not just the proletariat, as subjects to be emancipated; nonetheless, this distancing is largely rhetorical and not fully co-ordinated at a theoretical level with the undergirding Marxist metanarrative.[11]

I have said that earlier Christian socialists were readier to prescribe, to articulate the outlines of redeemed human space. But more strikingly, these articulations frequently contain themes much more stressed by papal social teaching than by liberation theology. I am

4

thinking of the notes of personalism, distributism, solidarism, subsidiarity, household independence, free association, balance between the rural and the urban environments. Linking all these is the repeated refrain of 'intermediate associations' which variegate the monotonous harmony of sovereign state and sovereign individual. Together, all these themes belong to what I want to call 'the advocacy of complex space', which seems to me to be the key distinguishing mark of Christian social teaching in the nineteenth and twentieth centuries—whether Catholic, Calvinist or Anglican (the Lutheran case is less certain)—in so far as it in any significant way distances itself from modern social reality. What is more, a somewhat similar advocacy seems to be now once more surfacing to view amongst secular radicals.

The disastrous failure of the Marxist experiment in the east has forced most socialists to realize that Marx was simply too cavalier in entrusting the emergence of a socialist society to the logic of history, and moreover to see that his advocacy of a necessary phase of expropriation and centralization, along with a permanent element of central 'scientific' direction of society, itself contained the germs of totalitarianism. (This is not to say that in Marx's writings one finds the entire and single source of Stalinist terror). Thus contemporary socialists increasingly realize that one must marry checks and balances, and a democratic distribution of power, to the simultaneous socialization of human economic endeavour. Likewise they realize that a workable and authentic socialism cannot replace the operation of the market with exhaustive central planning. Instead it must discover a way of ensuring that market exchanges are also democratically or freely assented-to transactions—the outcomes of processees of free and equal negotiation—which repeatedly seek to preserve or extend a distribution of resources held to be 'just'. (Note this is not the same thing as so-called 'market socialism,' since it accords no place to pure market forces of supply and demand regarded as essentially indifferent to the pursuit of justice and the presence of collective democratic and individual unconstrained agreement. This rules out the exploitation of scarcity and necessity for profit, and the automatic legitimacy of any expressed 'need,' while not at all trying to inhibit the free proliferation of needs that can be judged legitmate and beneficial).[12]

5

However, in coming to these new realizations about the need for distribution of power, and the necessity to actively institute a socialist market, contemporary socialists know that they are abandoning pure Marxism and attempting to integrate with the Marxist analysis of capitalist economy the programmatic visions of other nineteenth century socialists like Buchez, Proudhon and Kropotkin. It is also being noted that the 'late Marx' of the Critique of the Gotha programme made certain concessions to the anarchist and socialist critique of his thought, or at least made clearer the ways in which this applied more to Lassalle than to himself: thus he stresses that peasants and petty producers do not constitute 'one reactionary mass,' that land as well as labour is a source of wealth, that collectively held capital reserves for the future and taxes for welfare provision must still be deducted from the product of labour (although this only applies to the 'socialist' interval before the advent of 'communist' superabundance), and that the organs of the liberal sovereign state cannot simply be 'taken over' untransformed.[13] In the case of the new eclectic socialism, or else Marxism modified in a socialist direction, we are not then talking about a watered-down socialism, but rather, perhaps, about the recovery of socialism and anarchism after the demise of communism.

I hope, with these indications, to have convinced you that the 'spatial' preoccupations of Catholic social teaching, and in particular its advocacy of 'complex space,' are not necessarily the property of the political right. (It is indeed arguable that these themes first emerged most distinctly within a left-orientated romanticism in France before 1848).[14] Contrariwise, a certain whiggish historicism, perhaps especially in its dialectical version, can also—as much as any spatial fixation—be a source of totalitarian oppression.

However, in the case of papal social teaching, it is obvious that the 'advocacy of complex space' has become detached from socialism. This reflects a more general tendency of the twentieth century, whereby at least up to as far as the 1960's, the themes of regionalism, ecologism, rural romanticism and the craft association or corporation were mostly colonised by the political right. By contrast, the left has allied itself with science, progress, and positive certainty, failing to realize that claims to possess a universal, manifest truth can be the masks of a domineering authority. (And indeed can be used to legitimate racist, eugenicist, imperialist and genocidal policies which have frequently found 'progressivist' advocates on the left as well as the right.) Here we have the outlines of competing totalitarianisms: on the one hand complex space hierarchized, and recruited to the service of crude mythologies, whose quasi-religious, yet essentially secular, imaginings of untrammelled energy obliquely disclose that corporatist fantasy has not really obliterated the formal emptiness of the modern state and market. On the other hand, simple space articulated between the controlling centre and the controlled individuals, an articulation whose supposedly 'social' character barely disguises the fact that this is still the simple space of liberal modernity.

In this migration of the theme of complex space from left to right one has, therefore, arguably one source of the tragedies of the twentieth century. But one can claim something further: this migration was already underway after 1848, and was at least mightily assisted, perhaps even primarily promoted, by the increasing stand-off between the Catholic Church on the one hand, and socialism on the other, in France, Germany and Austria. Before 1848 most French socialism had a religious, sometimes even an orthodox Catholic character: the primacy of association was connected with the idea of a mystical, religious bonding that would correct the one-sidedness and secularity of enlightenment individualism. But after the revolution of that year, even most erstwhile sympathetic Catholics took fright at socialism, and meanwhile the all-important German social democratic party developed under the aegis of Lassalle and Marx, who were both more positivist, secularist, statist, amoralist and straightforwardly collectivist than the French socialist tradition.[15] The caricatures of socialism presented by *Rerum novarum*—that it abolishes all private property and threatens the institution of the family—are indeed caricatures even in the case of German social democracy, yet could be applied to the latter with somewhat more plausibility. (It should be added that much papal suspicion of socialism had the character of dislike of a quasi-religious grouping—which socialism was, as much as a political organization—outside the aegis of the official church: hence the desire for explicitly Catholic trade unions etc. more subject to hierarchical control.)

Because of the stand-off between an increasingly atheist socialism, and an increasingly conservative Church—a stand-off which had, I am

7

suggesting, the most momentous, and disastrous consequences—Catholic criticism of liberalism now had to give a reactionary twist to the advocacy of complex space, which had hitherto just as frequently been given a socialist or else a liberal expression (for example, La Mennais and De Tocqueville). The fortunes of the word 'solidarity' illustrate this point dramatically. The term was first used with political import by Mirabeau during the French revolution to designate the idea that 'the faith of each is the faith of all'—meaning, of course, republican faith.[16] This notion was then conceptualised by the socialist Pierre Leroux, for whom it denotes a kind of Leibnizian pre-established harmony between individuals, constituted not through the imposition of any universal rule, but rather through the unique but perfect reflection of the—otherwise transcendental and unrepresentable—whole in each singular person.[17] What matters here are not the metaphysical details, but the attempt to combine the principle of association with that of free independence, in terms of the idea of self-realization achieved in collective harmony with others. This combination is characteristic of French socialism in general, which was therfore already 'solidarist' in character, although it must be noted that the idea receives its most famous expression in The Communist Manifesto, when Marx and Engels declare that 'The free development of each is the pre-condition for the free development of all.'[18] It is arguable that this inherited slogan is nonetheless betrayed by communist proposals for centralised direction of what is deemed economically 'essential,' which cancel the earlier Leibnizian insight that the essential and universal is infinitely dispersed amongst the free creative judgement of individuals and the constantly re-emergent event of their collaboration.

The concept of 'solidarity' is taken up again in Germany in the second half of the century by Heinrich Pesch: it now evolves into a doctrine of 'solidarism' put forwards as an alternative to socialism, since it advocates 'solidarity' between persons, regardless of the fact that some may be owners of capital, and others dispossessed workers.[19] The question of how equal 'free development' is possible under conditions of such extreme and violently engendered disparity has now been repressed. And so to Lech Walesa....

The rough gist of my thesis should by now be apparent. Unlike others on the Christian left, I don't altogether object to the prescriptive

8

tone of Catholic social teaching, nor its claim (as a project) to be an integral part of evangelization (for if it isn't, as for the liberationists, then Christianity is paradoxically desocialised), nor to the 'spatiality' of its content. However, much of this content is territory stolen, long ago, from socialists. If Wojtyla is really interested in unravelling the tragedy of the twentieth century, and wishes to prevent farcical and tragical repetitions of earlier acts of the tragedy in the east, then he should think back to 1848, he should reconsider the complex historical relationship of Christianity and Marxism and socialism, and should consider entertaining a specifically socialist variant of 'complex space.' Only in this way can one sustain a 'non-resignation' to liberal capitalism without lapsing into the dangerous illusions of state socialism, fascism and social democracy.

But why, it may be asked, do I claim that the right-wing versions are necessarily perverse and pernicious 'displacements'? Why, moreover, do I appear to insist that John Paul II's mixture of social democracy and social market must be classified as right-wing and even incipiently fascistic? Before answering these questions I must say more about just what I entertain by the phrase 'complex space.'

So far, for the sake of simplicity, I've contrasted spatial with temporal emphases. Actually this is only a cipher standing for a more complex contrast of different co-articulations of both space and time. Relatively 'utopian' thinkers don't just dream eternal complex simulataneity; they also envisage history as radically contingent and open-ended. This is not at all to say that they ignore questions of necessary preconditions and achievability: for example, while the anarcho-socialists Gustav Landauer and Simone Weil contended that the industrial proletariat were in no absolute sense 'nearer' socialism than rebelling Roman slaves or mediaeval peasants, they also claimed that a condition of general proletarianisation of both manual and intellectual workers would actually inhibit a transition to socialism (the argument being that proletarianization would diminish independence, and make them more open to coercive and propagandistic manipulation).[20] On the other hand, more Marxist thinkers don't just espouse a theory of necessary historical stages, they also and concomitantly envisage the ultimately emergent utopian space as a clearly revealed, transparent and so 'simple' space, where every person is in his proper place as a 'producer'—albeit that 'proper' now means, as it

9

properly should, etymologically speaking—self-defined. (The self-definition involved here is both of humanity as a whole, as represented by a 'scientific' central direction of society, and of individuals simply 'realizing' unproblematic productive potentials. In either case the 'complexity' that interrupts autonomous space is denied: the irreplacability of individual vantage-points for the making of judgements is disregarded from the centre, while the formation of our capacities and preferences by evolving cultural standards of judgement is disregarded from the peripheries).

Such co-articulations of space and time can be dubbed, following Michael Bakhtin, 'chronotopes.'[21] What I want to do now is characterize the chronotope firstly of enlightenment social thought, and secondly that of those nineteenth century thinkers from left to right of the political spectrum who espoused in reaction a 'complex space,' which I am now going to re-name 'gothic space.'

First, the chronotope of enlightenment. Here the temporal figure of human growth from infancy to maturity is coordinated with the spatial figure of organic coherence.[22] The past is represented as a time of illusion and confusion dominated by the power of the imagination. Yet imagination is also seen as a surrogate for reason, even as the necessarily confused beginnings of reason, which is only fully exercised in the clarity of the present. Now it becomes apparent, after the decay of complex and exotic mythical hierarchies, that political reality is a 'simple space' suspended between the mass of atomic individuals on the one hand, and an absolutely sovereign centre on the other. Despite the merely contractual origins of the state, its actual functioning demands an organic, bodily coordination of the centre and the individual components. There are two divergent ways of conceiving this body: either it is essentially artificial, the result of a subsumption of the atomistic particulars under the ordered judgement of the sovereign head, or else it is 'natural,' the unplanned and providential co-ordination of individual desires and choices in the agonistic harmony of a market economy. In either case, bodies intermediate between the state and the individual—guilds, religious associations, universities—tend to suffer reduced autonomy, or else total extirpation. Their corporateness, in line with the traditions of mediaeval Roman law, and its links with papal absolutism, is reduced to the condition of persona

10

ficta, which as a mere convention cannot accordingly be authorised by pre-given community, but must be a privilege bestowed by the one self-legitimating community, namely the state—whose own fictive personhood is somewhat glossed over.[23]

This enlightenment chronotope can modulate into a romantic variant, with two distinguishing features, the first of which may, however, be found without the second. First, the whole is mystically elevated as greater than the parts, in such a fashion that the totality is held to transcend the grasp of reason and must be regarded as the work of an unfathomable nature or providence. Accordingly 'growth' ceases to be the smooth and predictable realisation of reason and becomes instead more arborescent, something whose upshots 'reason' must patiently attend. Such an outlook is present in the work of the 'historical' school of jurists, like Savigny. The latter, however, remained wedded to the Roman civil law, and accordingly to statism and the most fundamental features of 'simple space'; his organicism is accordingly focused primarily upon the political whole. By contrast, the 'Germanists' within the historical school, for example Grimm, exhibit also a second feature, which more genuinely marks the transition to 'complex space.' For these jurists, as also for many French romantic liberals and socialists, there can also be inter-mediate organisms, with their own 'group personality', between the in-dividual and state bodies; these organisms have a 'natural' function in-dependent of the fictive creativity of an absolute sovereign rule. Both these modulations interpose the theme of a complex, revived gothic space.[24] In its espousal of intermediate associations, this 'gothicism' clearly escapes the confines of a sub-personalist organicism more typical of the enlightenment, which would deprive the 'parts'—individual or collective—of any independent subjective standing. Moreover, corporatism could sometimes escape Hegelian statist restrictions, in which corporate bodies still 'mediate' within a space that retains its essentially enlightenment character of suspension between sovereign whole and individual subjective parts. (One thinks here especially of Otto von Gierke and his often more radical followers, such as the historian and Anglo-Catholic theologian, John Neville Figgis, in whose spirit I hope the present essay is written). In fact, in so far as gothicism remained a mere nostalgia for Gemeinschaft—neglecting the 'free' component in its

11

advocacy of 'free associations'—it also paradoxically failed to escape the conditions of a specifically modern organicism proper to Gesellchaft. The interest in 'complex bodies' wherein parts are in turn wholes, and not simply subordinate to the greater whole (the model for this being, according to Gierke, ultimately the Pauline concept of the church as 'body of Christ),[25] by contrast exhibits a way in which mediaeval exemplars were thought to manifest a crucial aspect of freedom—the freedom of groups—that modernity tends to obliterate. In many ways, this interest transcended the terms of the usual 'sociological' contrasts of ancient organicism and modern contractualism. (It is notable that the perspectives of the historian-jurists, with their strong focus on 'discourse,' appears in many ways more congenial in a post-structuralist climate than those of the sociologists, who perhaps distorted their work).

The less statist gothicism tends in the direction of qualifying the importance of the whole/part ratio (affirmed in pre-modernity, but accentuated by the modern 'rule of reason'), with that of the unit of relation (taken as essential to the identity of its components) whether between persons, or different groups of persons regarded as possessing collective identity. In this manner the second romantic modulation is partially wrenched free from organicism, such that multiple associations cease to 'mediate' between part and whole, but become themselves a new sort of context, a never 'completed' and complexly ramifying 'network,' involving 'confused,' overlapping jurisdictions, which disperses and dissolves political sovereignty.[26] An analogy can be made here with the gothic cathedral: it is a building which can be endlessly added to, either extensively through new additions, or intensively through the filling in of detail. This condition embodies a constant recognition of imperfection, of the fragmentary and therefore always-already 'ruined' character of the gothic structure, which, as John Ruskin argued, expresses the Christian imperative of straining for the ultimate at the risk of thereby more comprehensively exhibiting one's finite and fallen insufficiency.[27]

The first modulation also now escapes the organicist major key: not only does the whole exceed the sum of the parts, also the parts escape the totalizing grasp of the whole. For Gierke, this double excess had been initiated in the Middle Ages and was explicitly the result of a reconstrual of space as Christ's body.[28] The church as a whole was not an enclosed, defensible terrain like the antique polis, but in its unity with the heavenly city and Christ its head, infinitely surpassed the scope of the state, and the grasp of human reason. At the same time, what was fundamentally the same excess could be glimpsed in the single person and the Christian association (monastery or guild) whose activities are legitimised by the quest for salvation, not by human law. Like the English historian F.W. Maitland, whom he influenced, Gierke appears to have recognised, against the sociologists, a certain prevailing individualism in pre-mediaeval ancient society—whether manifest in the land-ownership of the Germanic village, or in Roman law which recognised only the literal person on the one hand, and the unlimited state power on the other, which was conceived as containing persons as functional parts, as they in turn were thought to contain different faculties in their souls and bodies. By contrast, 'organicism' in Gierke's sense, transcends through 'double excess' this part/whole fixation which undergirds individualism and occludes the primacy of social relation. Although it has for Gierke certain roots in primitive 'Germanic' community, it is fundamentally a sophisticated attainment, arriving at its zenith in mediaeval boroughs, not villages, and assisted through the evolution of legal 'realist' notions of 'corporate personality.'[29] The Gemeinschaft of Gierke, therefore, unlike that of Tonnies and Weber, in no sense belongs to an inevitably 'prior' phase, nor indeed to any necessary phase whatsoever, but is rather a thoroughly contingent product—to such a degree instigated by the Christian 'interruption' of history that his contrast of the 'mediaeval' with the 'antique-modern' (as he puts it) appears to echo Augustine's metahistorical account of 'two cities.'[30]

In Gierke, the note of 'excess' belies expectations that Gothic organicism simply respects foreordained 'position.' This is still more the case with Ruskin's gothic aesthetics. In 'The Nature of Gothic,' Ruskin claims that 'redundant' ornamentation is precisely the essential characteristic of the gothic building, which veers in the direction of being nothing but the piling up of extraneous detail, although were it to reach this decadent extreme (exemplified for Ruskin in certain aspects of the 'flamboyant') then a balancing sense of unifying form (the whole exceeding the parts) would be lost sight of, such that extreme refinement of decoration would revert to the condition of mere 'heap,' mere accidental juxtaposition.[31]   Nonetheless, it is only the principle of redundancy which is able to mediate between style and function: thus a practical need for light may dictate the cutting of an extra window, irregularly positioned. In a gothic structure this intrusion can still be rendered unobtrusive.[32] Applying these principles to 'social space' (as Ruskin of course envisaged), one finds that redundancy implies respect for the inviolability of personal assent, whether of individuals or corporations; Wojtyla has recently dubbed this 'the principle of subjectivity.'[33]   In a 'complex space,' there is always room to adjust to the innovations made by free subjects, without thereby surrendering the quest for harmonic coherence.

To fully grasp this spatial conception however, one needs to transcend the idea of a mere structural homology between aesthetic and social space, in a 'geographic' direction.[34]   Since human life is both material and social, human work performed, on cathedrals and other physical constructs, does not just 'reflect' a given social order, but also builds it as the space which directs our respective visions, displays exemplary roles, and distributes our routes and circulations, our goings-out and comings-in. Variegated space has to have literal embodiment. Inversely, the diversity of this space is a function of the role given to many subjects, as for example the many craftsmen and many craft-guilds operating with relative autonomy (though this should not be exaggerated, remembering the 'excess of the whole,' and the now admitted role of mediaeval architects), in the building of a gothic cathedral, or more importantly in the making of a gothic town.

The spatial-aesthetic and the social do not mirror each other, but are jointly generated through property distribution and productive labour. Thus in the case of 'gothic' respect for subjectivity, the person is granted her own property, or a sufficient space for use and creative self-development which is the material condition for her free participation in society; the household unit is in itself—as it was not for pagan antiquity—a fully constituted and in principle self-sufficient political society, conjoined to wider society in the first place by association for mutual benefit, not by a contractual surrendering of supposed 'natural rights.' Just as in gothic architecture, the basic structural unit—for example the arch—is multi-functional, such that it can be infinitely enlarged or infinitely

14

diminished, itself the total context, or linked with similar features to form a wider context, so also the social unit, which at every level marries 'female' household care with 'male' political excellence can be very small or very large, self-standing or conjoined with other such entities. (This 'gothic' respect for personality embodied in property, and for the independence of the household, is clearly maintained in papal social teaching right up to the present day) In the gothic vision, association is paradoxically enabled by the constant reserve of a free-standing space which 'exceeds' its own entanglements; this is a concomitant of the primacy of 'relation,' or of the 'horizontal.' As regards the inescapable dimension of the vertical and hierarchical, the upwardly aspiring building is simultaneously 'deconstructed,' or subordinated to the function of sheltering the many altars, many depictions, many procedures, enacted within its frame.

This is the principle which Catholic social thought will later dub 'subsidiarity,' but I should like to mention here that this principle is abused if it is taken to inhibit the intervention of a higher, or indeed merely other authority to protect the individual or institution abused by an intermediate one: for example the child mistreated within the family. On the contrary, the gothic perspective implies also—this is the essence of 'solidarity —that as the individual exceeds the association (or a smaller association exceeds a larger one) it has the right to appeal to others beyond that association, and others may appeal on his behalf.

The above paragraphs give the 'topic' aspect of the gothic chronotope. What of its 'chronos'? Instead of an enlightenment teleogical vision of gradual necessary evolution, one has a dramatic sense of history as ceaseless loss and gain: the enlightenment has gained for us the formal principles of individual liberty and equality, but at the same time we have lost certain practices of free association for common purposes. Socialists and liberals who partook of the gothic fascination in the nineteenth century (remembering this includes even J.S. Mill) were clearly not simply subject to romantic nostalgia: their mediaeval interests were selective, and what mainly concerned them was not hierarchical authority, but rather a pervasive legal constitutionalism orientated to consensus beyond mere mutual expediency or contractual obligation; to the diversification of sources of power, and to a guild organisation permitting a measure of economic democracy and collective preservation of standards of excellence. Obviously these concerns were not always free from the taint of anachronistic whiggery (and in England 'whig gothicism', derived in part from the common law tradition, was already fully articulated in the eighteenth century), but it is notable that while, in reaction, twentieth century mediaeval historiography has tended to stress the alien and vertical characteritics of mediaeval society, more recent writers have again started to point out its horizontal, associative, consensual aspects.[35]

In a sense, however, the question of how far such features were ever a reality in the Middle Ages was not decisive for nineteenth century gothicism. Ruskin, for example, was far from supposing either that the mediaeval cathedral perfectly embodied egalitarian features, such that its particular style of 'redundancy' should be copied today, after the fashion of Pugin, or that its genuinely 'utopian' features exactly mirrored the society which built it. On the contrary, his protestant love for mediaeval Catholic art led him to regard the latter as a kind of 'heterotopic' space, foreshadowing later actual or hoped—for developments in other spheres.[36] Similarly, mediaeval corporatism and 'free association' could be regarded as heterotopic in relation to the more feudal and nakedly hierarchic features of mediaeval society, (and also in relation to certain 'proto-modern' features of burgeoning papal and royal absolutism.[37] As indeed barely escaping these, and yet in this very 'ruined' condition as disclosing certain yet-to-be-attained possibilities.[38]

One last decisive element of contrast between enlightenment simple space, and gothic complex space, must be mentioned. The former is 'secular,' the latter 'sacred.' In the first case religious authorisation or providential intervention is moved to the margins: God commands the absolute sovereign, who then imposes rule according to an a priori rational logic of subsumption of parts under wholes. Or else God/Nature coordinates coordinates our desires behind our backs, through the operation of the capitalist market.[39] But in the second, gothic case, every act of association, every act of economic exchange, involves a mutual judgement about what is right, true and beautiful, about the order we are to have in common. It is no longer a matter of 'transparent' principles of reason, nor of mere diversification of desire, regardless of what that desire may be for. Instead one must distil order out of an irreducible diversity, one must

16

find a measure between diverse things which are, as Aristotle said, inherently incommensurable. The order so discovered, so assented to, tends to be imbued with a 'sacred' character because it cannot be defined, and is always being repeated with a same yet different character, such that, according to the social Christology indicated above, the excess perpetrated ever-anew by the individual is the only possible 'representation' of an infinite excess always beyond our reach (We are that body of Christ we can never yet see; a kind of 'sublimed' micro/macrocosmic relation is involved here). The assent which such an order commands must clearly have the character of an allegiance of faith rather than that of a rational conviction.[40]

The gothic vision therefore acknowledges sublime indeterminacy and the inescapability of an aesthetic judgement—of both unity and distinction—which is an imprescribable 'event,' not the subsumption of new instances under a pre-given formula, nor a mere 'accurate' empirical observation. Without this binding by pre-given rules, or by what is 'manifestly' observable, the Kantian sway of a self-sufficient immanence is undone; in complex space every judgement 'exceeds,' and if it wishes to anchor itself beyond mere 'preference,' must seek again the harbour of transcendence. (Though now transcendence secures, not, as in the middle ages, a hierarchy of 'given' essential identities, but rather, in this 'neo-gothic' space, the possible truthfulness of the human imagination.)[41]

To envisage the possibility of judging objectively, without rules, is to envisage the reality of God, and the inevitably religious character of the just society. This must apply also and even especially to socialism, which seeks to surpass the essentially secular formal justice of capitalism (grounded only in consensus and legalised coercion) and yet cannot escape the predicament of judging without precedent. For even a fully free, democratic and participatory society would still have to judge issues not adjudicable through appeal to the principles of freedom, democracy and participation themselves. For example, collective priorities for achievement and use of resources; patterns of distribution of space, time, goods and skills, which inevitably involve 'equalizing the unequal,' given that people can never possess exactly the same resources (and this of course would not be just or even 'equal').[42] This space of judgement is the space of morality, aesthetics and 'religion.' It is a space which

17

communism (which was invented in the eighteenth century by atheist priests, whereas socialism was invented in the nineteenth by religious but laypersons) thought would be abolished with the emergence of a simplified and now specifically economic space, suspended between a 'scientific' organisation of industry on the one hand, and a supposedly unproblematic realisation of individual human capacities on the other. As Jacques Ranciere and others have argued, Marxism preserves the classical idea that 'the worker' (as opposed, for the classical schema, to the ruler and the warrior) is properly confined to the realm of work and animal desires.[43] In classical antiquity the manual worker simply imposed pre-existing ideal forms upon matter; his work in itself was not subject to considerations of 'virtue,' or the attainment of socially recognised excellence. Likewise the household, the site of productive provision, was not an arena of 'politics' and dialectical disputation, but of unquestioned paternal control. The Christian gothic 'merging' of oikos and polis, which as Ruskin in particular grasped, opened the question of virtue exercised within the material sphere of work,[44] is really occluded by Marx. This is because Marx considers that religion, morality and politics will vanish with the arrival of communism, since communism embodies a purely economic social reality, and he still thinks of this enlarged oikos on the model of the little antique household as a 'transparent' realm outside the problematic indeterminacy of political association between free citizens. This economic realm is, indeed, no longer managed by the patrician representation of the laws of the polis from above, but is instead 'self-managed' according to immanent criteria, and yet Marx's characterisation of this realm still echoes the negative exclusions of Platonic and Aristotelian philosophy: work lies outside the sphere of idealizing reason, virtue and aesthetic judgement. Paradoxically, it is only the Platonic exclusion of work from this sphere which engenders the Marxist suspicion that the sphere itself has only illusory existence. That this suspicion is metaphysically, and not critically materialist, is demonstrated by the evident fact that the material realm is not rendered transparent once the veil of idealist mystification is lifted. On the contrary, it is idealism which seeks to impose arbitrary fixations, and our material life which remains constantly open to question: what to produce?

18

Where to live? How to measure exchanges, how to pattern collective space and time?

Contemporary socialists are capable of recognising that a materialist perspective by no means removes the necessity for ethical judgement, yet they tend to halt at the point of declaring that collective judgements must be made democratically, and that the ultimate aims are better fulfilment of basic needs and the promotion of individual choice and autonomy. This is still to remain with enlightenment simple space, since it does not allow that our life in common might transcend the imperatives of self-preservation and self-emancipation. It does in fact always point beyond these imperatives, because complex space has a certain natural, ontological priority, and simple space remains by comparison merely an abstracting, idealizing project. (In this sense Christological space discovers a certain 'natural' legality; however, the construal of this space as harmonious, and the refusal of the simplifying venture, are existential choices, not recognitions of universal rational exigencies). This is the case because there is no such thing as absolute non-interference; no action can be perfectly self-contained, but always impinges upon other people, so that spaces will always in some degree 'complexly' overlap, jurisdictions always in some measure be competing, loyalties remain (perhaps benignly) divided. It follows that the decisions of freedom which escape the mere provision of 'necessities' (itself an area difficult to enclose) do not easily remain the decisions of isolated individuals or groups alone: the issue of the common good most pointedly surfaces, not in the more abstract deliberations of governments, where, on the contrary, its reduction to utilitarian calculus or promotion of free choice will seem most seductively plausible, but rather in the ever re-encountered 'boundary disputes' and occasions for collective action in the everyday lives of citizens. These disputes and occasions have somehow to be mediated, and where the reality of 'community' fades, the attempt is made to more and more do so by the extension of merely formal regulation of human transactions (with its utilitarian and more predominantly liberal indi-vidualist presuppositions). More of life becomes economized and legali-zed, as legislation seeks—hopelessly—to catch up with every instance of 'overlap,' and institute more detailed rules of absolute ownership, whether by individuals, or legally incorporated groups: so much and no more for you; so far and no further for you. Since it can never catch up, and since also it will be bound to regard non-formalised mediations as merely arbitrary, this explains exactly why the most capitalist and litigious society in the world—the United States—is also subject to endemic lawlessness and civil violence at every level.

Without 'community,' without its self-sustaining affirmation of objective justice, 'excellence,' and transcendental truth, goodness and beauty, one must remain resigned to capitalism and bureaucracy. This, I think, has often been a 'socialist' (less frequently a 'communist') claim,[45] and it is clearly an inherently religious one. And by that I mean that it is inescapably Platonic, Judaic and Christian.

However, it is absolutely crucial to distinguish this socialist advocacy of 'just measures' and 'proportionate harmony' from its pre-modern variant. That depended upon a Platonic or Aristotelian idealism, on founding justice upon fixed, 'natural' positions and social roles. It is for this reason, presumably, that Aristotle can say that 'need' is a measure for comparing the incomparable in exchange.[46] Needs are natural, because they belong to the various social classes according to their fixed, hierarchic positions: preservation of these positions is what undergirds 'just prices' and supposedly 'natural' exchange (it might be thought that initially 'equal' positions could also support these things; however, equal positions cannot be fixed and definitely specifiable in the same manner as hierarchic ones, as I shall shortly argue). Given prior 'natural' distribution, exchange is relatively unproblematic, and this is why Aristotelian 'need as the measure of exchange' can later modulate into the rule of 'demand' for the political economists. Although demand is now, under capitalism, changing and inexhaustible, in accord with a newly fluid society, it is still conceived as a 'natural' and empirical reality. By contrast, for socialism, need cannot be the measure of comparison between the incomparable, for two reasons. First, there is a recognition of the social production of need, so that it is deprived of its 'natural right', and the 'meeting of needs' is no longer superior to the judgement of socially desirable goals. Second, a condition of equality is only formally specifiable, unless one were to suppose the nonsense of everyone doing and possessing the 'same' things. Unlike hierarchy, it dictates no fixed distribution of roles, and therefore no normal, proper,

20

desires. As with capitalism, new and unexpected demands will constantly arise, but to conserve social equality these demands themselves will have to be measured, to see whether or not their fulfilment, and in what degree, upsets or promotes the social balance. Hence the Aristotelian distinction between initially distributive and later rectifying justice is considerably muted, for corrective or economic justice can no longer appeal to a once-and-for-all given order of distribution, but instead distribution remains always in question, and is constantly being re-enacted. In fact, the just order persistently remains to be recognised within the very productive—and no longer merely rectifying or exchanging —acts of bringing it about. In this way economic transactions now come more under the sway of 'political' phronesis than Aristotle perhaps presupposed, and indeed become the site for the exercise of 'aesthetic' judgements of the kind described by Kant in the third critique: judgements where we enact no subsumptions, appeal to no certain rules, and yet make a social bid for the assent of others.

In line with the above one can suggest that in upholding the reality of justice, the possibility of human harmony, socialism need not retreat to a premodern contemplation of eternal positions and pre-given hierarchies, although it cannot remain content with a modernist negative unravelling of illusion and contradiction to finally unveil a consensus about the unproblematic, á la Habermas. Instead it should embrace Lyotard's postmodern, defined as the post/modus, the 'future anterior,' insofar as socialism has to take a wager on justice, on the possibility that we live in a universe where we can be the vehicles for just acts, whose 'characteristic' shape we will continuously come to know.[47]

This distinction of the post from the pre-modern (with the implication that socialism, as the left-wing advocate of 'gothic space,' has always had a postmodern character) leads me back, finally, to the issue of papal social teaching. The latter has constantly given a centrist or right-wing version of the themes—often originally socialist—of gothic space. Where this is done, I want to argue, one has incipient fascism. Why? For two overriding reasons. First of all, the legacy of traditionalism, and to a lesser degree of scholastic ahistoricism, has led Catholics again and again to assume that a 'natural' social order must still in some fashion be in place ('surely providence cannot have abandoned us?' seems

21

to be the unspoken thought). Thereby one runs into the contradiction of thinking both that liberal capitalism subverts the natural order, and yet that it in some sense still discloses it. Catholic social teaching becomes in consequence a grotesque hybrid: liberal, Lockean understandings of property rights, and Smithian construals of the supposed 'contribution' of capital to production are freely incorporated, and yet upon them is superimposed an organicist, patriarchal vision of society. Capital and labour are constantly conceived as belonging to a natural hierarchy, such that they should ideally be united in corporate harmony: this is of course to disguise the initially rawly coercive and quite unpatriarchal origins of this specifically modern power structure. Once one has combined modern formal emptiness and de facto rule of coercive power with paternalist sentiment, then what one has is kitsch, and a doctrine that in the end will only give a sentimental colouring to, and also emotionally reinforce, a culture of violence.

It is of course clear that John Paul II has not returned to a full-scale endorsement of corporatism, but exactly the same misapprehension and sickly false-consciousness informs also the vaguely social market philosophy he seems to espouse, and is capable of engendering a kind of 'soft fascism.'[48] For where a certain practice and ethos of 'welfare' and supposed promotion of the worker's 'humanity' infuse the capitalist firm (though these elements are really strictly functional for capitalist purposes) the encouragement given by a more 'openly' liberal system to workers generating their own autonomous counter-authorities, and wresting certain rights and benefits that are guaranteed by political powers, tends to be reduced. One approximates that fearful mixture of constant 'concern' and exhaustive reduction of humanity to economic purposes, characteristic of the capitalist far east (and admired by Walesa; it seems also significant that the pope now apparently mistrusts a possible 'culture of dependency' generated by state welfare provision).[49]

Through his acquiescence in his own 'marketing', Wojtyla has become somewhat of a 'kitsch' Pope, and he teaches a somewhat kitsch social philosophy. Nowhere is this more exemplified than in his writings on the family—where, knowing that he is talking about the modern, bourgeouis, nuclear family, he yet tries to embue it with the self-sufficient qualities of the traditional household: it is to be a 'school of work,' the father should be able to provide the full means of subsistence to his children etc. etc.[50] One could indeed argue that some sort of reversal of capitalist expropriation would be desirable, but this would involve a massive upheaval such as the pope clearly does not contemplate.

This brings me to my second point. From *Rerum novarum* until now, papal fear of socialism has been fear of diminution of patriarchal authority. The power of the father in the family is the ultimate basis of all authority: here is a doctrine with, perhaps, traditionalist rather than scholastic roots, which has never been rescinded, and which Wojtyla covertly seeks to re-emphasise. The nuclear family, with father in charge, mother at home, is coyly described in his most recent encyclical as the 'natural home environment,' which states have a duty to preserve, along with a sound ecology.[51] It is clear that the pope thinks the state should systematically encourage paternal supremacy, female subordination and sexual 'normality' in all the received Catholic senses. He may be content —unlike his corporatist predecessor, Pius IX—to accept modern erosion of secular paternal hierarchies above and beyond the sphere of the family, but this after all leaves the male, clerical hierarchy intact and still more distinctive. However, its authority would truly be eroded if its isomorphism with secular society at the point of paternal authority in the family were lost sight of.

Clearly this sort of sexual politics, pursued in the modern context, could only assume an authoritarian character. Moreover it is based, as I am afraid is virtually the entire current official Catholic teaching about sex and gender, in a pre-modern tying of what is objectively 'right' to fixed places and inviolable taboos. There is a failure to 'go beyond the law.' (As long as this remains the case, then what remains true and necessarily corrective in a Christian attitude to sex, namely that here the fulfilment of desire is dependent upon grace, the grant of the other, and by no means a matter of 'right', will go unheard). If a first source, therefore, of papal resistance to socialism, and substitution of a fascist-tending amalgam, is a certain prevalent ahistoricism, then a second source is resistance to feminism, with a concomitant ecclesiastical and political suppression of all opposition to the family-based power of the adult male. What is tragic here, is that valuable insights (and Wojtyla's encyclicals contain not a few) about subsidiarity and the independence of the household as the most

23

'fundamental' intermediate association, are betrayed by the ethically unnecessary contention that the household must assume a conventional and patriarchal shape.

The same sort of tragedy engulfs Catholic social teaching as a whole. Its 'advocacy of complex space' desperately needs to be heard in an age when those last surviving corporate bodies, still at times 'religiously' held together by the pursuit of collectively acknowledged excellence—namely the 'universities,' bearers still of the latin name for what is more than a mere contractual societas—are being subverted and effectively extirpated. Not to mention in a country—Britain—which has recently fulfilled the logic of its 'common law's non-recognition of political as opposed to voluntary and economic corporations.'[52] The tradition also poses topical questions: if Europe is to be once again a communitas communitarum, then should the stress be upon direct parliamentary democracy, or upon a 'corporatist' higher representation of many bodies at a lesser level? (Perhaps genuine subsidiarity and solidarity demands that the former should qualify the latter, and help to prevent a fascistic degeneration). However, where modernist elements, rooted in modern natural law doctrines which ground right in the self-preserving impulse of the individual or political whole—absolute, self-alienable property rights as the norm, the fiction that capital constitutes a real motive force, endorsement of political sovereignty at the centre—are smuggled into the corporatist or quasi-corporatist vision, then a violently welded together Leviathan is secretly baptised as the *Corpus Christi*, and the path of fascistic terror is opened once more.

That the papacy should repeatedly be in danger of perpetrating this insidious hybrid, is, moreover, by no means historically accidental. On the contrary, ever since the mediaeval Pope Innocent IV, its power has always basked in an ambiguity: on the one hand it flourishes by according recognition to already constituted manifestations of supra-political complex space—the manifold varieties of religious and semi-religious association —on the other hand, thanks to the originally canonical device of persona ficta, it annihilates the integrity of the association through the very act of recognition, by alienating to its own sovereign power, the right of group creation.[53] Papal advocacy of complex space is therefore always likely to be flawed, since the ecclesiastical structure it upholds itself exhibits

24

troublingly hybrid features. Against mere 'political' power, the papacy discovers and recognises his own dispersed corporate troops (the hosts of Israel, whom we may indeed applaud), yet by converting discovery into authorisation it perfects its own, and more absolutist imperium, devouring lesser bodies, while digesting their substance as the fiction of the papacy's own single, undying body, which supposedly knows no stunted or abortive growths, but only infallible accretions. No mediaeval relic this ontology, perfected only yesterday: on the contrary, here is ideal modernist absolutism, just as the smooth additive 'development' of Papal doctrine is sublime whiggery. In this fashion, Papal institutions themselves provide a soil for the eugenic nurturing of fascistic hybrids, whereas a truly Catholic critique of modernity, if it is not to be perverted, must include an element of self-critique, especially of the undemocratic and non-participatory character of current ecclesial (and not just Roman Catholic) institutions. One can agree with Pope John Paul II: democracy risks surrender to propaganda, and the forgetting of the primacy of truth[54], yet the antidote to this cannot be merely the entrusting of truth to a sovereign power or clerical/clericist caste. In the end, the only security for excellence resides in a republican but complex dispersal of guardianship and trusteeship. How to replace manipulation with education (the development of genuinely desirable human life) in the space of popular culture? Only in theoretical and practical answers to this question, do we discover again the Church, the 'doubly exceeding' body of Christ,' the Other Space of our history.

With Catholic social teaching (and writing as an 'Anglican Catholic'), I refuse to be resigned to the present age. I endorse its advocacy of a complex, gothic space. But the non-socialist version of this advocacy belongs to the history of attempts to overcome or recast capitalism that have gone tragically wrong (and one must remember how much of initial fascist ideology could look benign and congenial). If we wish, in the nine years of a century that remain to us, both to face up to the postmodern predicament and yet not succumb to resignation, then I suggest we must re-think the sources of twentieth century disaster along the lines I have proposed, and consider again the claims of the 'gothic vision' in its radical, socialist variant.

Footnotes and References

1. Antonio Negri, 'The end of the century,' in *The Politics of Subversion*, trans. James Newell (Polity, Cambridge, 1989) 61-74.

2. *Centesimus annus* (Catholic Truth Society, London, 1991) paras. 12-21, 26.

3. *Centesimus annus* 30-43.

4. See Donal Dorr, Option for the Poor: *A Hundred Years of Vatican Social Teaching* (Gill/Orbis, Dublin/New York, 1987) 57-76, on Pius XI's 1931 encyclical *Quadragesimo anno*. For the latter see Selected Papal Encyclicals and Letters, Vol I ed. P.E. Hallett (CTS, London, 1932). See also, Michael Novak, *Catholic Social Thought and Liberal Institutions* (Transaction, New Brunswick/ Oxford 1989) 69-110; Edgar Alexander, 'Church and society in Germany', in *Church and Society* (Arts Inc. New York, 1953) 325-583, on German and Austrian Catholic sources of right-wing corporatism, often including a racist component.

5. See Paul A. Lakeland, 'Does Papal Social Teaching have a Place in our World' in *Cross Currents*, Vol XXXV, number four, 393-407.

6. See my *Theology and Social Theory: Beyond Secular Reason* (Blackwell, Oxford 1990) 177-259. Also my article 'Were the Christian Socialists Socialist?' in *Papers of the Nineteenth Century Working Group* (eds.) Jack Forstman and Joseph Pickle, Vol. XIV, 86-95.

7. Simone Weil, *Oppression et Liberté* (Gallimard, Paris, 1955) esp. 194- 204.

8. *Theology and Social Theory*, 249-252.

9.   See Dorr, 104-138.

10.   Gustav Landauer, *For Socialism*, trans. David J. Parent (Telos, St. Louis, 1978) 29-46; P-J Proudhon, *Selected Writings* (Macmillan, London, 1969).

11.   See Gustavo Gutierrez, *A Theology of Liberation*, trans. Sister Carrida Inda and John Eagleson (Orbis/SCM, Maryknoll NY/ London, 1973) 29-30, 236-237; *The Power of the Poor in History* trans. Robert R. Barr (Orbis/SCM, Maryknoll NY/London, 1983) 125-160; J-L Segundo, *Faith and Ideologies*, trans. John Drury (Orbis, Maryknoll NY, 1984) 200-218, 251- 253, 255, 259, 262-263. In the latter pages Segundo does indeed begin to express reservations about revolutionary expropriation of land, but provides no sufficiently thoroughgoing critique of what is inevitably sinister in the specifically communist programme.

12.   On socialism and the market see Pat Devine, *Democracy and Economic Planning* (Polity, Cambridge, 1988); John Keane, 'What's left of the left' in *TLS*, June 21 1991, 7-8; Robin Blackburn, 'Fin de siècle: socialism after the crash' in *New Left Review* 185, 5-66.

13.   Karl Marx, 'Critique of the Gotha Programme,' in *The First International and After* ed. David Fernbach (Penguin, London, 1981) 339- 359. On Marxism and anarcho-socialism see also Robin Blackburn, *Fin de Siècle*, and Christopher Knight, 'Christians and the Politics of Liberty' in *Theology* XCIII, 1990, 191-197.

14. *Theology and Social Theory*, 195-202; 'Were the Christian socialists socialist?' Weil, 194-197; Joseph N. Moody, 'Catholicism and Society in France' in Moody, *Church and Society* pp 95-187; Jean Bruhat, 'Le Socialisme Franceais de 1815 a 1848' in *Histoire Générale du Socialisme*, Tome I, ed. Jacques Droz (PUF, Paris, 1972); Armand Cuvillier, P.J.B. *Buchez et les Origines du Socialisme Chrétien* (PUF, Paris, 1948); K. Steven Vincent, *Pierre-Joseph Proudhon and the rise of French Republican Socialism* (OUP, Oxford, 1984); David Owen Evans, *Le Socialisme Romantique: Pierre Leroux et ses Contemporains* (Marcel Riviere, Paris, 1948); Jean-Baptiste Duroselle, Débuts du Catholicisme Sociale en France 1822-1870 (PUF, Paris, 1951)

15. Moody notes that the 1848 revolution in France was uniquely not anti-clerical; modern French anti-clericalism arguably post-dating that event: Moody, 130, while G.D.H. Cole records the continuing shock of French socialists at the atheism of their German comrades: Cole, *Socialist Thought: Marxism and Anarchism 1850-1890*, (MacMillan, London, 1964) 11, 261-264; *Socialist Thought: The Forerunners 1789-1850* (MacMillan, London, 1967) 179.

16. Evans, *Le Socialisme Romantique* 69.

17. Evans, 60-69.

18. Karl Marx and Friedrich Engels, 'The Communist Manifesto,' in Marx, *The Revolutions of 1848* (Penguin, London, 1981) 87.

19. Novak, *Catholic Social thought and liberal Institutions* 69-81.

20.   Landauer, *For Socialism*, 16, 123. Weil, *Oppression et Liberté*, 211. Those who assume that 'mediaevalism' is just the preserve of the right should attend to the words of Landauer, the assassinated leader of the Bavarian soviet: '[Marx assumes that] when capitalism has gained complete victory over the remains of the Middle Ages, progress is sealed and socialism is practically here' (160; whereas one needs to awaken the 'spirit of just exchange and joyous work' as known in the 'Christian and pre-Christian era of the Teutonic nations' (17) (though at times Landauer compares Germans unfavourably to Latins and Celts, 62). Marxists are said to prefer 'a new machine for the transportation of men' to 'the living Jesus on the cross'(64). And finally: 'something like a mediaeval republic of cities or a village mark...cannot for him [Marx] bear the least similarity with socialism, but a broad, centralized state already resembles his state of the future quite closely.' (61) Landauer critically rebuts the idea that capitalist concentration of industry, trade and credit, along with proletarianisation of the masses in any way provide necessary conditions for socialism; on the contrary, the loss of mediaeval 'dispersal' ensures more adverse conditions for socialist revolution.

21.   See Ken Hirschkop, 'Introduction: Bakhtin and cultural theory,' in *Bakhtin and Cultural Theory*, ed. Ken Hirschkop and David Shepherd (Manchester UP, Manchester, 1989) 4-5, 13, 30.

22.   See Otto Gierke, *Natural Law and the Theory of Society: 1500-1800*, trans. Ernest Barker (CUP, Cambridge, 1958) 50ff.

23.   See Howard Caygill, *Art of Judgement* (Blackwell, Oxford, 1989) 38- 189. For a shorter summary, 'Post-Modernism and Judgement' in *Economy and Society*, Vol 17, No 1, 1-21; Steven Shapin and Simon Schaffer, *Leviathan and the Air-Pump* (Princeton UP, Princeton NJ, 1985) 80-110, 283-345.

24.   See F.W. Maitland, 'Introduction,' in Otto Gierke, *Political Theories of the Middle Ages*, trans. F.W. Maitland, (CUP, Cambridge, 1987) xii-xviii. In another essay Maitland vividly describes the nineteenth century's resuscitation of 'gothic space': 'You know that classical distribution of private law under three grand rubrics—persons, things, actions. Half a century ago the first of these three titles seemed to be almost vanishing from civilized jurisprudence. No longer was there much, if anything, to be said of exceptional classes, of nobles, clerics, monks, serfs, slaves, excommunicates or outlaws. Children there must always be, and lunatics, but women had been freed from tutelage. The march of the progressive society was, as we all know, from status to contract. And now? And now that forlorn old title is wont to introduce to us ever new species and new genera of persons to vivacious controversy, to teeming life, and there are many to tell us that the line of advance is no longer from status to contract, but through contract to something contract cannot explain, and for which our best, if an inadequate name, is the personality of the organised group'. Maitland, 'Moral Personality and Legal Personality' in *Selected Essays* (CUP, Cambridge, 1936) 233. (Note that the shift Maitland refers to, occurred on the whole rather later in England than on the continent). This exactly captures the demise of a hierarchical and role-determinate gothic, and the return of a horizontal gothic together with 'persons' who are again substantively differentiated, and therefore cannot be treated with justice as formally the same. At the same time they are not arranged hierarchically, are not readily locatable in specific individuals, and possess a more shifting and self-determined identity than their mediaeval equivalents. The 'return of persons' embraces the rising importance of joint-stock companies, trade unions, universities, leisure and educational associations, clubs, non-established religious bodies, and even revived religious communities. It should be noted that one germ of a right-wing corporatism lay in the legal incorporation of capitalist firms on the one hand, often involving semi-official monopoly, and even a quasi-governmental status, and the non-recognition of trade unions

30

and the immunity of its individual members from personal responsibility for acts of the association, on the other.

Another description of the shift from simple to complex chronotope, including the Romanist and Germanist phases, is provided by Paul Vinogradoff, writing in 1892. Before the French Revolution, he says, scholars were 'not sufficiently aware of the differences between epochs; they were too ready with explanations drawn from conscious plans and arrangements. The shock of revolution and reaction taught people to look deeper for the laws of social and political organism...speaking broadly, the field of conscious change was narrowed, the field of organic development and unconscious tradition widened. On this basis, Savigny's school demonstrated the influence of Roman civilisation in the Middle Ages, started the inquiry as to national characteristics...[then] the Germanist school arose to show the extent to which modern constitutional ideas were connected with mediaeval facts.' Paul Vinogradoff, *Villainage in England* (OUP, Oxford, 1892) 'Introduction,' 35-6.

I am grateful to Professor David Sugarman, of the Department of Law, Lancaster University, for discussions and suggestions concerning the corporations debate.

25. Otto Gierke, *Political Theories of the Middle Age*, 22f; *Associations and Law: the Classical and Early Christian Stages*, trans, George Heinrich (Toronto UP, Toronto/Buffalo, 1977) 143-160.

26. See Gierke, *Political Theories of the Middle Age*, 1-100; *Associations and Law*, 67, 151ff, 155-156.

27. See John Ruskin, 'The Nature of Gothic' in *The Stones of Venice, Works* X ed. E.T. Cook and Alex Wedderburn (George Allen, London, 1904) 191, for the injunction to repect 'shattered majesty', and 'not to set the meaner thing in its narrow accomplishment, above the nobler thing in its mighty progress'.

Likewise we are to respect deficiencies, irregularities and 'wild and wayward' work (188), since 'the law of human life may be Effort, and that of human judgement, Mercy'(203). This is not, however, to say that Ruskin simply devalues the spatial and static in favour of temporal striving; on the contrary, the point is that one must take the risk of embodiment, and only in the very 'failure' of concrete fixation, can striving be apparent. Thus for Ruskin gothic exhibits an oxymoronic 'active rigidity'; its unbending, unyielding, stiff, prickly spikiness, also permits its energetic flow, which depends upon tension (239ff). (The possibility of psychoanalytic glosses requires no underlining!). In this way Ruskin discovers in gothic space a property resistant to totalisation, and a constant 'confession' of its embodiment of human productivity, which is never fully 'realized'; this tends to prevent any alienation or political fetishisation of the edifice.

Considering the fashion in which French mediaeval gothic in particular, sought to (almost) dissolve solidity into decoration, and empty space for the reception of light and colour (likewise three dimensions almost into a flat, readable surface, and the surface in turn almost into the flowing line, as celebrated by Ruskin and discussed by Proust), thereby 'denaturing' architecture, and considering also the direct influence of the writings of Pseudo-Dionysius on the first gothic ventures, it is tempting to regard it as 'negative architecture,' akin to 'negative theology.'
I am grateful to discussions with Alison Milbank on the subject of Ruskin, and gothicism in general.

28. Gierke, *Political Theories*, 22ff; *Associations and Law*, 155-7; Ernst H. Kantorowicz, *The King's Two Bodies: A Study in Mediaeval Political Theology* (Princeton UP, Princeton NJ, 1957) 42-87, 273-314.

29. F.W. Maitland, 'Introduction' to Gierke, *Political Theories*, *vii-xiv and xxviii*: '[Gierke] has incurred the dissent of some of his fellow Germanists for refusing to carry back to the remotest time the

distinction between co-ownership and corporate ownership,' whereas (xxvii) for Gierke it is in the borough of the later Middle Ages that 'the group is first abstracted by thought and law from the plurality.' More especially, see Maitland, 'The Village Community' in *Domesday Book and Beyond* (Fontana, London, 1960) 398-415, for his account of the 'individualism' inherent in the primitive Germanic system of landholding. In the age of Kripke and Lyotard, we ourselves are scarcely able to read with a grave face Maitland's contention here that 'No one who has paid any attention to the history of law is likely to maintain with a grave face that the ownership of land was attributed to fictitious persons before it was attributed to men' (398). And we are likely to recall Marcel Mauss's famous contention (which only reiterates the view of Vico in the eighteenth century) that the persona was originally the transferable mask, not the distinguished individual: Marcel Mauss, 'A Category of the Human Mind: the Notion of Person; the Notion of Self,' trans. W.D. Halls, in *The Category of the Person*, ed. Michael Carrithers et al (CUP, Cambridge, 1985) 1-26. However, the mask is not the legal or philosophic collective personality without definite location in either individual or political ruler or place. Hence the mask must be definitely appropriated by the single individual, and can be acquired through inheritance, or violent seizure. For this ancient mode of individualism, identity itself as mask can be alienated, though property cannot be (through free transaction), as in modern individualism. Yet 'individualism,' it still, arguably, is.

32.   Gierke, *Political Theories*, 3ff.

31.   Ruskin, 'The Nature of Gothic,' 243, 262-3

32.   'The Nature of Gothic,' 212.

33.   *Centesimus annus*, 46, 49.

34. For the new geographical interest see Tony Pinkney, 'Space: the Final Frontier' in *News From Nowhere*, No 8, Autumn 1990, 10-27; Edward Soja, *Postmodern Geographies: the Reassertion of Space in Critical Social Theory* (Routledge, London, 1988).

I am grateful to Tony Pinkney, of the Department of English, Lancaster University, for discussions on this topic.

35. See Susan Reynolds, *Country, Kingdom and Community in Western Europe: 900-1500* (OUP, Oxford, 1984) 1-11. She notes that one finds many groups 'acting on their own initiative and with a relatively small amount of formal regulation and physical coercion' (2), citing, for example, the proliferation of parishes more on the initiative of the laity than the ecclesiastical hierarchy (5-7), in addition to the proliferation of guilds modelled on monastic organisation, celebrating feast days, and assembled for charitable, economic and religious purposes (75ff). She thereby implies, and indeed explicitly confirms, Gierke's view of the predominantly Christian context for this practice of voluntary association (7), and qualifies Maitland's judgements that local political-juridical institutions (as opposed to economic ones) derived from the royal centre, and that the frequent instance of freedom with respect to small property ownership and ability to choose overlords, necessarily suggests 'individualism.' Rather, this for Reynolds indicates plurality of allegiance and associative bonds, such that 'community' keeps pace with 'freedom.'

Her stress on the prevalence of consultation and consensus appears to be at variance with Alan Macfarlane's version of a return to the 'horizontal' dimensions of the Middle Ages, which stresses individualism as always characteristic of England: Alan MacFarlane, *The Origins of English Individualism* (CUP, Cambridge, 1979); see also the Review by Barbara J. Harris in the *Journal of Social History*, Fall 1980, Vol 14, No 1.

However, his reading of Maitland may be one-sided and insular; unlike the Edwardian historian-jurist he generalises too easily from formal legality and formally free economic conditions, and appears to ignore the crucial Gierke/Maitland contention (which Reynolds' rectifications do not undermine) that the individualist independence of the small property owner in Germanic villages is 'primitive' (albeit persisting, with long-term consequences in western Europe), whereas the Middle Ages witnessed an increase of complex corporate bonds.

In all these arguments, it is obvious that the very idea of a 'free association' permits a certain latitude as to whether one lays the stress on 'collectivism' (i.e., individualism, to be juristically precise), or 'organicism'.

I am grateful for discussions with Professor Jeffery Richards, of the Department of History, Lancaster University, on Mediaeval communities.

36. Ruskin, 'The Nature of Gothic,' 237: 'and every discriminating touch of the chisel, as it rounds the petal or gilds the branch, is a prophecy of the development of the entire body of the national society, beginning with that of medicine, of the recovery of literature, and the establishment of the most necessary processes of domestic wisdom and national peace.' Also: 'We don't want either the life or the decorations of the thirteenth century back again...all that gorgeousness of the Middle Ages had for foundation or end, nothing but the pride of life—the pride of the so-called superior classes; a pride which supported itself by violence and robbery, and led in the end to the destruction both of the arts themselves and the states in which they flourished,' from 'Modern Manufacture and Design,' Lecture III of The Two Paths (1892) in *Works* Vol. XVI. This despite the fact that he is talking about Pisa, and always primaily celebrated secular mediaeval art in the context of the Italian free city republics.

For heterotopia, see Michel Foucault, 'Of Other Spaces,' *Diacritics*, Vol. 16, Spring 1986, and Tony Pinkney, 'The Gothic as Heterotopia,' unpublished paper on Ruskin.

37.   *Theology and Social Theory*, 432-434.

38.   See F.W. Maitland, 'The Village Community,' 412: 'throughout the Middle Ages there were here and there groups of freeholders, and even of customary tenants, who were managing agrarian affairs in a manner which feudalism could not explain, and our English law would not warrant, for they were behaving as members of a landowning corporation.' Fragments of Utopia?

39.   Caygill, *Art of Judgement*, 38-189.

40.   Slavoj Zizek argues that such 'ineffable' identity can only be the upshot of a non-acknowledgement that we worship an empty site X, which merely stands for the inherent non-attainability of our desire. But that the 'exceeding' dimension of desire is a factor of its nullity, rather than its transcendent guidance, cannot be shown. Without the latter assumption one is left with a choice between an atavistic and mystifying right-wing corporatism on the one-hand, which suppresses indeterminacy from our view, and the pure instigation of infinitely proliferating individual desires in pursuit of the unattainable void, on the other.

Apparently it is on the latter—capitalism—that Zizek pins his hopes for the future of Slovenia and Eastern Europe. Though he knows this is hope in the end of hope…and claims that this last necessity discloses just why history and philosophy have arrived at their Hegelian terminus. See Zizek, 'Eastern Europe's Republics of Gilead' in *New Left Review*, 183, 1990, 50-62. His essay is also relevant to other parts of my paper.

41.   See Caygill, *Art of Judgement*, 367-396.

42. See Cornelius Castoriadis, 'Value, equality, justice, politics: from Marx to Aristotle and from Aristotle to ourselves' in *Crossroads in the Labyrinth*, trans. Kate Soper and Martin H. Ryle (Harvester, Brighton, 1984) 260-330.

43. Jacques Ranciere, *Le Philosophe et Ses Pauvres* (Fayard, Paris, 1983).

44. Ruskin, 'Time and Tide by Wear and Tyne' in *Works*, Vol XVII, 379,384: 'all political economy, as well as all higher virtue, depends first on sound work.' On the antique household, see Xenophon, *Oeconomicus*, IV.24 - V.18.

45. One must distinguish between the 'Icarian communists,' followers of Cabet, and the atheist successors of Gracchus Babeuf, of whom alone Marx really approved. On mainly socio-political grounds, or because they were grounded in an immanentist, natural rights tradition, focused on unproblematic 'needs?' See Droz, *Histoire Générale du Socialisme*, 383- 395; Marx and Engels, 'Manifesto' 86-96 (where they also make clear their preference for 'industrial armies' over 'corporate guilds' and fail to explain why the latter are necessarily 'reactionary'); Marx, 'Critique of the Gotha Programme', 353-4.

46. Aristotle, *Politics* trans. A.T. Sinclair, (Penguin, London, 1970) Book One, Chapter 8, section 9.

47. J-F. Lyotard, 'Defining the Postmodern' and 'Complexity and the Sublime' in *Postmodernism: ICA documents*, ed. Lisa Appignanesi, 7-10, 19- 26. Here Lyotard correctly links the eighteenth century sublime in general with the idea of imprescribable judgement which bids for a collective assent containing in consequence a 'promise' of community. This, however, appears inconsistent with the more agonistic emphasis of his major writings, and in Kantian terms seems to make more room for 'the beautiful.' (Before Burke

and Kant the sublime and the beautiful were not so clearly distinguished: this being the whole—mistaken?—point of Burke's thesis. In fact, by turning the non-representable into 'event,' Lyotard seems to 'incarnate' the sublime while preserving its elusiveness, so making it cover again the whole sphere of the aesthetic (perhaps preceeded by Hegel here). In which case there might be an opening for a more consensual (but not Habermasian formalistic) construal of judgement and community than Lyotard seems (mostly) to allow. See also Lyotard, 'What is Postmodernism' in *The Postmodern Condition* (Manchester UP, Manchester, 1986) 71-82.

The present essay would also question Lyotard's association of 'complexity' with modernity. (Lyotard doesn't really approve of cultural postmodernism in the sense of eclecticism and pastiche). His complex space is only the filling in of simple space with more and more 'indifferent'—it might as well be this way—detail. Only constant indifference (the 'whole' context) and constant variation (the 'individuals') have ontological security, whereas for gothic complexity this 'ultimacy' is accorded to intermediate and contingent formations. They don't just 'fill in' a void, they 'represent,' in their flux, infinite transcendence.

48.   Regarding entitlement to property there have, however, been many oscillations: see Dorr, *Option for the Poor*, 48 and passim. Also Novak, *Catholic Social Thought*, 69-81, 62-80, on Pesch and von Ketteler's fusions of corporatism with Smithian economic liberalism. It was their tradition which had the greatest influence on papal teaching up to *Quadragesimo anno*.

49.   *Centesimus annus*, 48.

50.   *Centesimus annus* 6; *Laborem exercens* (CTS, London, 1984) para 43. Kitsch also is the statement that 'consumer choices, savings and investments' should be directed by the quest for 'truth, beauty, goodness and communion with others' *Centesimus annus*, 36.

51. *Rerum novarum* in *The Pope and the People* (CTS, London, 1950) 138-139; *Laborem exercens*, 91-92; *Centesimus annus*, 38-40. In paragraph 47 the pope appears to confine rights of sexual self-expression to 'the right freely to establish a family, to have and to rear children through the responsible use of one's sexuality' (More kitsch combining of liberal terminology and patriarchal tradition here). Certain oblique remarks later in this paragraph could, it seems to me, very well be referring disparagingly to the emancipation of homosexuals.

I am grateful to Andrew Shanks, Reckitt teaching fellow elect in the Department of Religious Studies, University of Lancaster, for drawing my attention to the political importance of 'kitsch.'

52. See F.W Maitland, 'Introduction' to Gierke, *Political Theories*, xxxiv-xxxv.

53. Maitland, 'Introduction,' xiv, xix.

54. *Centesimus annus*, 44.

Transforming the Democratic/ Capitalist Revolution

Michael Novak

In announcing one of the many worldwide conferences convoked in 1991 to mark the centenary of Pope Leo XIII's social encyclical *Rerum novarum*, a brochure from St. Edmund's College in Cambridge, England spoke of "Four Revolutions": the industrial revolution, the liberal-capitalist revolution, the socialist revolution, and a yet-to-be-seen "Christian transformation of society." The same brochure contained the following description of the present situation:

> In the century since [1891], capitalism seemed to go into decline, while socialism was in the ascendancy. In the last 20 years, however, capitalism has regrouped and risen again; now Marxism and socialism seem to be in decline.[1]

This thumbnail sketch of recent history, while broadly acceptable, raises certain serious questions.

First, why did Marxism and socialism fail? Correlatively, as the American Marxist Robert Heilbroner recently asked, why did so few intellectuals or academics, particularly of the center and the left, predict this failure?[2] On these points, much can be learned today from those who have lived under Marxist and socialist systems. Their accounts stunningly confirm the predictions made by Leo XIII in 1891.

Second, how are we to understand the capacity of the "liberal-capitalist revolution" to renew itself? Part of the answer to that question may lie in the marriage of capitalism to a democratic political system, and thus in its openness to the religious and humanistic ideals, habits, and aspirations of a Jewish and a Christian people. Besides that, though, what exactly constitutes the inner dynamic of capitalism and its openness to change? The dictionary definitions of capitalism and the descriptions of it proffered by its ideological opponents seem oddly wide of the mark.

Third, supposing that, as the most practical and liberating social ideal, most of the human race will now be "stuck" with the capitalist model for the foreseeable future, how can these capitalistic societies be brought into closer accord with Jewish, Christian, and humanistic criteria?

Each of these questions must be faced in turn.

1. WHY DID SOCIALISM FAIL?

The *Socialists*, therefore, in endeavoring to transfer the possessions of individuals to the community, strike at the interests of every wage earner, for they deprive him of the liberty of disposing of his wages, and thus of all hope and possibility of increasing his stock and of bettering his condition in life.

What is of still greater importance, however, is that the remedy they propose is manifestly against justice. For every man has by nature the right to possess property as his own. This is one of the *chief points of distinction* between man and the animal creation. —*Rerum novarum* (3)

We are talking here about "real existing socialism," meaning Eastern European and Soviet socialism and the socialism of those elsewhere who admired and supported it. Socialism in this sense has a broader meaning than is intended today by Western social democrats and democratic socialists. The Pope in 1891 was using the term "socialism" in this very broad sense, easily understood by ordinary Catholic parishioners throughout Europe and elsewhere, who were being proselytized by socialist labor unions and parties, sometimes under the name of socialism, sometimes under the name of communism.[3]

In *Rerum novarum*, Leo XIII listed at least ten reasons why the program of socialism would prove futile. After one hundred years, his words seem remarkably prescient. At the same time, Pope Leo was sharply critical of many of the beliefs, customs, and abuses that he observed in the practices of liberal capitalist nations (then relatively few in number). He criticized capitalism severely, although not by that name, which never occurs in the encyclical. His approach to socialism was not at all symmetrical. He did not criticize socialism or recommend its

41

reform. He condemned it. He condemned it because it is against natural justice, against nature, against liberty, and against common sense. In order to get beyond the liberalism of the day and to reconstruct the social order, the pope judged it especially necessary to distinguish his own ideal of a reconstructed order from that of the socialists.

Among the good factors in capitalist and pre-capitalist societies that Leo XIII judged to be violated by socialism were the principles of private property, personal initiative, and natural inequality. On *private property*, the Pope writes: "Nature confers on man the right to possess things privately as his own" (10). And he adds: "In seeking help for the masses this principle before all is to be considered as basic, namely, that private ownership must be preserved inviolate" (23). "To own goods privately is a right natural to man, and to exercise this right, especially in life in society, is not only lawful but clearly necessary" (36).[4]

On *personal initiative*, *Rerum novarum* supplies these texts: "Clearly the essential reason why those who engage in any gainful occupation undertake labor, and at the same time the end to which workers immediately look, is to procure property for themselves and to retain it by individual right as theirs and as their very own" (9). "Would justice permit anyone to own and enjoy that upon which another has toiled? As effects follow the cause producing them, so it is just that the fruit of labor belongs precisely to those who have performed the labor" (16). "If incentives to ingenuity and skill in individual persons were to be abolished, the very fountains of wealth would necessarily dry up; and the equality conjured up by the socialist imagination would, in reality, be nothing but uniform wretchedness and meanness for one and all, without distinction" (22).

On *natural inequality*, Leo XIII writes: Therefore, let it be laid down in the first place that in civil society the lowest cannot be made equal with the highest. Socialists, of course, agitate the contrary, but all struggling against nature is vain. There are truly very great and very many natural differences among men. Neither the talents, nor the skill, nor the health, nor the capacities of all are the same, and unequal fortune follows of itself upon necessary inequality in respect to these endowments. And clearly this condition of things is adapted to benefit both individuals and the community; for to carry on its affairs community life requires varied aptitudes and diverse services, and to perform these diverse services men are impelled most by differences in individual property holdings. (26).

To which he later adds: "While justice does not oppose our striving for better things, it does forbid anyone to take from another what is his and, in the name of a certain absurd equality, to seize forcibly the property of others; nor does the interest of the common good permit this" (55).

Among the nearly one dozen serious charges that Leo XIII then leveled against socialism (in paragraphs 8-23) are the following: Socialism "violates the rights of lawful owners"; "perverts the functions of the State"; and "throws governments into utter confusion" (8). Socialism is "openly in conflict with justice inasmuch as nature confers on man the right to possess things as his own," and its partisans "abolish the freedom to dispose of wages" (10). Socialists injure the farmer inasmuch as they "absolutely deny him the right to hold as owner either the ground on which he has built or the farm he has cultivated" (16). Further, "inasmuch as the Socialists disregard care by parents and in its place introduce care by the State, they act *against natural justice* and dissolve the structure of the home" (21). Socialism abolishes "incentives to ingenuity and skill in individual persons," which causes "the very fountains of wealth" to dry up (22). Socialism "contravenes the natural rights of individual persons" and "throws the function of the State and public peace into confusion" (23).

This is a pretty devastating list, and it is not hard to match it against the testimony of those who have lived under socialism in the USSR and Eastern Europe for the last several decades. Kevin Acker compiled a list of such testimony in *Policy Review*,[5] and many others have also been collecting quotations. (Someone ought to do a book of them.) From Acker we glean the following:

> Several German intellectuals and politicians
> had hard words for the fellow citizens who
> flung themselves on the West German shops
> as soon as they could . . . These could only
> be the words of people who have forgotten,

or never knew, the personal humiliation inflicted by the permanent lack of the most elementary consumer goods: the humiliation of silent and hostile lines, the humiliation inflicted upon you by sales people who seem angry to see you standing there, the humiliation of always having to buy what there is, not what you need. The systematic penury of material goods strikes a blow at the moral dignity of the individual.—Bulgaria[6]

For 50 years it was said that this was public property and belonged to everyone, but no way was ever found to make workers feel they were the co-owners and masters of the factories, farms and enterprises. They felt themselves to be cogs in a gigantic machine. —USSR[7]

We cannot talk of freedom unless we have private property.—USSR.[8]

How can you say you have a motherland when you don't own a single square meter of land which you can leave to your grandchildren?—USSR[9]

We are consciously limiting the role of the state in the economy. It is no longer the supermanager of a superfactory, the main boss and the main controller, the main storekeeper and the main distributor of goods and services. Several dozen years of costly experience have shown that the state cannot do this well, and, in particular, cannot inspire energy in people so that they may work productively, efficiently, and economically.—Poland[10]

When people are compelled to look only one way, when they are deprived of information and the possibility to compare things, they stop thinking. Well-informed people, ones who have access to versatile information, inevitably begin to think. The very system invites lies.—USSR[11]

We categorically favor the concept of private initiative. The economic foundation of totalitarianism has been the absolute power derived from the monopoly on property. We shall never have political pluralism without economic pluralism. But some of those who still have Communist leanings try to equate private initiative with "exploitation" and maintain that the emergence of rich entrepreneurs would be a catastrophe. In the same way they try to play on the feelings of those who are lazy and would therefore envy the wealthy, and those who—having once enjoyed the privileges of the Communist system—are afraid of the effort of working.—Romania[12]

The totalitarian system has a special bacterial property. The system is strong not only in its repressive police methods but, more, in the fact that it poisons people's souls and demoralizes them.—Czecho-slovakia[13]

In a totalitarian situation people conform outwardly to the prevailing morals and isolate themselves in microsocieties where they live, work, and die. People act according to moral double standards, an unwritten social contract that everyone knows. Workers are allowed to idle and steal, as long as they come to party meetings and applaud. Only a small mafia of party bosses and enterprise bosses took it seriously; the rest of the people cut themselves off. —Czechoslovakia[14]

Listen again, with these texts in mind, to two of Leo XIII's extended predictions about socialism:

the *Socialists*, working on the poor man's envy of the rich, endeavor to destroy private property, and maintain that individual possessions should become the common property of all, to be administered by the State or by municipal bodies. They hold that, by thus transferring property from private persons to the community, the present evil state of things will be set to rights, because each citizen will then have his equal share of whatever there is to enjoy. But their proposals are so clearly futile for all practical purposes, that if they were carried out the working man himself would be among the first to suffer. Moreover they are emphatically unjust, because they would rob the lawful possessor, bring the State into a sphere that is not its own, and cause complete confusion in the community (4-5).

A few paragraphs later, after some further jabs, the pope once again opens up with both fists:

> The Socialists, therefore, in setting aside the parent and introducing the providence of the State, act *against natural justice*, and threaten the very existence of family life. And such interference is not only unjust, but is quite certain to harass and disturb all classes of citizens, and to subject them to odious and intolerable slavery. It would open the door to envy, to evil speaking, and to quarreling; the sources of wealth would themselves run dry, for no one would have any interest in exerting his talents or industry; and that ideal equality of which so much is said would, in reality, be the leveling down of all to the same condition of misery and dishonor. Thus it is clear *that the main tenet of Socialism, the community of goods, must be utterly rejected*; for it would injure those whom it is intended to benefit, it would be contrary to the natural rights of mankind, and it would introduce confusion, and disorder into the commonwealth (11-12).

This prediction, one hundred years later, seems inspired.

Nonetheless, there is one major criticism of socialism which Leo XIII did not make; Ludwig von Mises discerned it only some 30 years later.[15] Perhaps the most important function of a market system is to communicate information vital to everyone. Without market systems, economic actors are blind. They cannot know what people want, or how much of it they want, or how much they are willing to pay for it; and they cannot know the costs that lie behind raw materials, labor, and goods or services. A "planned" system is an exercise in pretense. Its prices are arbitrary; someone just makes them up. In the Soviet economy, Professor Heilbroner reports, the State Committee on Prices had responsibility for setting prices on more than 24 million items.[16] A person assigned as a "planner" to set prices on a certain sector of goods could carry in his briefcase papers concerning hundreds of items on which he must decide each day. It proved impossible to deal with so many prices even monthly, let alone instantaneously. Individual planners or functionaries were reduced to blind guesswork. Nothing related rationally to anything else, except in the mind of the planner. And even this relation left out of account the sweat, the desires, and the effort that real human beings were interested in investing in their purchases or sales. The joke was: "We pretend to work, and they pretend to pay us." The whole economy was based on make-believe, pursued in the name of "rationality."

As Hayek has pointed out, the "fatal conceit" of socialism lies in its mistaken view of reason.[17] In the name of rationality, socialism misconstrues the nature of practical intelligence as it actually operates in society. Socialism imagines that society works from the top down, like a pyramid, and through a more or less geometric form of reason, as if from a few goals (which operate as premises) a planner can deduce practical directives, which in turn will guide every individual action. This indeed is a form of rationality. But, as Aristotle remarked, there are several kinds of rationality, and it is a sign of wisdom to choose an appropriate kind for each field of inquiry. In the practical affairs of society, one must allow for the contingency inherent in temporal events and also for the liberty of individual human agents. In such a field, the appropriate form of rationality is prudence (practical wisdom, *phronesis*), not geometry. This is why so many writers rebelling against socialist rule, such as Dostoevsky, Orwell, and Zamyatin, protested against the "2 x 2 = 4 man."[18]

Freedom is a necessary condition for the exercise of practical wisdom, since individuals must activate their own capacities for practical reasoning and make their own choices. Regarding ideas, individuals need freedom of inquiry and discourse. Regarding economic choices, they require a free market. Reflections of this sort lay behind Leo XIII's arguments in favor of private property, long-term family incentives, and the limited state.

Leo XIII neither defended nor attacked the free market. He neither described its many important functions nor pointed out why it is necessary to a free society governed by practical wisdom and charity. As Professor Waterman has pointed out, the Catholic environment in which Leo XIII worked missed out on the argument for market systems that had agitated British intellectual life for a century prior to 1891; its main points had simply not been considered.[19] Thus, Leo was especially concerned about the condition of workers and the poor, but did not seem to grasp how much they suffered from the lack of competition in markets. He saw the excessive power of a relatively few employers, but saw no cure for such monopoly except in government.

While he dwelt little upon markets, Leo's grasp of the fundamental importance of private property to the free society was admirable. A regime of private property is, as Eastern European reformers see clearly, indispensable to limiting the power of the state. But so also is a regime based on market exchange. For the alternative to market exchange is an authoritarianism so vast that it overpowers every exchange of private property. Indeed, most Eastern Europeans have learned to dread total political control over free markets. Thus Vaclav Klaus, Finance Minister of Czechoslovakia, in 1989: "We want a market economy without any adjectives. Any compromises will only fuzzy up the problems we have. To pursue a so-called third way is foolish. We had our experience with this in the 1960s when we looked for socialism with a human face. It did not work, and we must be explicit when we say that we are not aiming for a more efficient version of a system that has failed. The market is indivisible; it cannot be an instrument in the hands of central planning."[20]

A market economy is important not only for political freedom; it is also important for morals. A market economy inculcates a type of mentality quite different from that of a command economy. In place of passivity and obedience, it awakens the life of active virtue. The mayor of Leningrad in 1990 put the alternative quite clearly:

49

> For decades in our country, we have
> fostered a beggar/consumer mentality: the
> state will provide and decide everything for
> you—poorly, perhaps, but provide equally
> for everyone, give you all the basic
> necessities. And this parasitic mentality is
> very widespread here. Yet a market
> economy, in order to function, requires a
> very different type of mentality: enterprise,
> initiative, responsibility, every person
> solving his own problems. The government
> does nothing more than create the conditions
> in which one can employ one's initiative and
> enterprise; the rest is up to the individual.[21]

If markets are to serve liberty and morality in this way, competition within each market area needs to be insisted upon, not narrowed. Access to markets must be universal, legally accessible to all. Not fully exploring the ways in which markets may be used as tools, especially for the amelioration of the lot of the poor, Leo XIII deprived himself of an important argument against socialism, one whose force in history would prove decisive.

Concerning Professor Heilbroner's question, why writers of the left and center were so remiss in failing to see the impending failure of socialism, the most direct answer is that most have shared in the rationalistic conceit. To many it once seemed almost intuitively obvious that an economy under political control from above would be more "rational" than one in which every person simply thinks and chooses for himself. There would be, so it was thought, less duplication, less wastage, less concern with (by someone's standards) trivialities and more concern with basic needs. And intellectuals were especially tempted by the proposition that members of their own class, given authority, would fashion a more rational and more moral social order than would free citizens alone, left to their own choices. Once theoreticians of the left and center succumbed to this conceit (particularly in an intellectual environment driven by the left, in which the center merely moves more

50

slowly than the left but in the same direction), it was exceedingly difficult for them to predict their own failures. Those who rejected this conceit root and branch, by contrast, were more likely to spot the inevitability of failure.

But why were such persons, the scholars of the "right" named by Heilbroner (Hayek, von Mises, Friedman, and others), treated so dismissively by their leftward peers? Those who knew which way history was moving—toward greater rationality from above—could dismiss such dissenters as malcontents, who preposterously wanted "to set the clock back" (as if history moves forward as rigidly as a clock's inner mechanical wheels). In other words, the rationalistic conceit disallowed challenge from outside. Those who embraced it claimed to have rationality all to themselves. Their consciences were not uneasy, therefore, when they accused those to their right of irrational and unworthy motives (protecting the interests of the rich, for example). They never imagined that their own motives might be suspect, and that they might be protecting the interests of the politically powerful. Their consciences were clean, and their core conceit was untroubled by doubt. That is why the sudden collapse of the moral prestige of socialism surprised them. One must credit Heilbroner for the honesty to admit it.

2. THE RESURGENCE OF LIBERAL CAPITALISM

It is a paradox that in the 20th century the ideas of socialism have not been realized in the socialist countries, but in other countries, the capitalist countries. In the countries which call themselves socialist, socialism has been distorted to the degree where it causes disgust.
— USSR[22]

The reasons for the failure of socialism are many. What are the reasons for the success of capitalism in reforming and refashioning itself from within? "Progressives" are not the only ones who hold capitalism in low regard. Down through the ages, aristocrats have shown considerable contempt for persons of commerce.[23] Aristocrats could afford to be concerned with things "for their own sake," and could look down on grubby utilitarian efforts requiring sweat. More generally, especially in Latin cultures, traditionalists have thought of capitalism as crass, vulgar, and uncivilized. In Latin America, there is even a saying,

51

"liberalism is sin." From both the left and the right, there were many reasons for misjudging capitalism.

From the point of view of *Rerum novarum*, by contrast, the European economy of 1891 had two or three saving features, even though it was in need of reconstruction. The saving features were these: at least liberal capitalism allowed for private property, the *sine qua non* of a society of personal self-determination; it allowed for, even insisted on, the limited state; and it created a significant degree of "civic space" within which free associations could thrive. Nonetheless, Leo XIII judged that the liberal-capitalist society of 1891 was founded on at least two serious errors. Liberalism misconceived the human person, thinking each to be radically individual and isolated from others, except through artificial social contract. Second, it assumed that all human beings are equal, without paying sufficient heed to the weakness and helplessness of many, who could not be expected to compete with others on equal terms. In this respect, the new liberal order left too many at the mercy of too few: "The present age handed over the workers, each alone and defenseless, to the inhumanity of employers and the unbridled greed of competitors" (6).

Karl Marx reached the concept of exploitation through his theory of class conflict, his labor theory of value, and his theory of the expropriation by capitalist owners of the "surplus value" of the labor of workers. In a more subtle way, as Stephen T. Worland has demonstrated,[24] Leo XIII also worked from a theory of "exploitation" different from and deeper than that of Marx. Leo XIII rejected the theory of class conflict, the labor theory of value, and the theory of surplus labor. In his view, each class "needs the other completely: neither capital can do without labor, nor labor without capital" (28). The exploitation Leo feared was of a different order. He feared that the concrete pragmatism required by capitalism would inculcate habits of instrumentalist thinking at the expense of other habits, from the religious to the aesthetic, necessary for full human development. Everything might come to be judged according to a calculus of profit and loss, which would induce hardheartedness among powerful persons in society, truncate their humanity, and warp their souls. In one sense, such tendencies in humans are an old story; the Bible recounts many tales of hardheartedness, callousness, and cruelty. In another sense, though, liberal capitalism might inculcate such habits more systemically and more broadly throughout the population.

This was a serious charge. It rested, however, on a hidden premise; viz., that liberal capitalism is a one-sided system, subject to no internal checks and balances (from the political and moral cultural system, for example). This premise, be it noted, does hold for pre-modern regimes and also for socialist regimes. The rationalistic conceit at the heart of socialism leads to social structures that are at least authoritarian and certainly monistic. All three powers—moral, political and economic—are concentrated in one set of institutions and one set of hands. The economy is under political control, as both are under ideological (moral) control. In the classic texts of Marxism and socialism, accordingly, there is little or no discussion of the separation of systems, the separation of powers, checks and balances, and the "auxiliary precautions" of which, at the very founding of the American constitutional order, James Madison spoke so eloquently.[25] The socialist vision in most of its forms has been caught up with the vision of shaping "the new man," a man perfect in justice and thoroughly imbued with the spirit of equality and comradeship. This rationalistic conceit led to considerable optimism concerning man, once the evil structures of capitalism could be removed. No such illusion is likely under democratic and capitalist presuppositions.[26] For the liberal capitalist order was brought to birth (at least in the United States) within an ethos thoroughly penetrated with a clear awareness of human weakness, fallibility and vice, that is, of what in Christian theology is called original sin. So it was, for example, in the work of James Madison and Alexander Hamilton, as in the Puritan divines.

In this respect, these two contrasting social visions, socialism and capitalism, are not symmetrical. Socialism is a unitary system. It *intends* to concentrate all powers in the hands of those who control the apparatus of the state. Even in its more moderate forms, the impulse of socialism is to bring the economy under political control and, in general, to strengthen the hand and to enlarge the reach of big government. By contrast, liberal theory, even in its most secular forms, retains a healthy fear of Leviathan, a worry about torture and tyranny flowing from the concentrated power of the state.

The constant liberal purpose, therefore, is to divide social systems, to divide the powers of the state, to divide offices and functions from top to bottom as thoroughly as possible, and to establish checks and balances. One purpose of this pervasive concern to limit and to divide government is to retain as large a civic space as possible for the voluntary action of individuals and their associations. The reason for this is the profound conviction that the most creative sources of virtue, intellect, and moral progress lie in spheres of private life [27] protected from state control. The state is granted no right to make any laws restricting the free exercise of religion. Neither is it permitted to restrict the generation or the dissemination of information and ideas. The life of the spirit—of religion, science, the arts, morals, and culture—is kept free of state control.

The resulting moral and cultural vigor, in turn, has provided a decisive check and balance to the economic system. Citizens are regarded as moral and cultural agents first and as economic agents only secondly. They are regarded as having moral and religious responsibilities that, at crucial places, take precedence over their economic projects. In the hot blood of its youth, of course, the new capitalist order often ran roughshod over religious and moral energies. But these quietly gathered their force and over the generations have tamed the wildness of capitalism's youth. They could not have done so if they had not been ceded the important role of counterweight throughout the social system as a whole. Through the observance of the Sabbath, through the encouragement of philanthropy and compassion for the poor, through the "social gospel," through activism, and in many other ways the churches continually and steadily disciplined the raw economic passions with which they were confronted. This process took time. But whole generations of clergymen, university professors, social workers, writers, and reformers gradually made their presence felt in the world of public opinion.

They did not have to rely on moral and cultural persuasion alone. For a second counterweight was also built into the system: the political power of the democratic state. In a democracy, farmers, workers, and the poor outnumber the rich owners of factories and the captains of commerce by large numerical proportions. Moreover, in a highly diversified society,

54

the interests of citizens cannot be confined solely within the narrow banks of class analysis; this was Madison's point in *Federalist* Nos. 10 and 51.[28] The many have effective means of bringing about the slow but steady transformation of the institutions of the social order, until the latter produce measurable progress that meets their pleasure. As a whole, working people and the poor tend to be socially conservative, not nearly as radical as intellectuals and middle class reformers. Ordinary people seldom want revolution, since they fear disruption in the patterns of their daily lives which are already hard enough. What pleases them best, therefore, is steady but measurable progress, which a pluralistic, democratic order is well suited to provide.

Thus, from two different directions, one moral-cultural and the other political, notable creative energies have arisen in the slow but steady transformation of liberal capitalism. From its founding in the late eighteenth century, to the late twentieth century, the social system as a whole (composed of three relatively independent parts—political, economic, and moral-cultural) has demonstrated a remarkable capacity for self-reform and internal transformation. Slavery was abolished; a civil rights revolution was conducted. By practically every measure available, the conditions of daily life were quite considerably transformed from decade to decade. Even in the seventeenth century, John Locke had noted that "a king of a large fruitful territory [in a primitive land] feeds, lodges, and is clad worse than a day laborer in England."[29] As liberal capitalist countries experienced further material progress, their standards for the life and health of the poor also rose, and their sense of compassion and civil responsibility grew exponentially. Medical care improved dramatically. So did wages, housing conditions, educational opportunity, and other facets of life. Associations of "middle class reformers" of all sorts flourished. The churches used the available civic space to develop a remarkable proliferation of institutions in the social sphere: schools, orphanages, hospitals, musical societies, domestic clubs, athletic leagues, and discussion groups. It may be doubted if any century excelled the nineteenth in the reach of its social reform, civic responsibility, and voluntarism. Millions who came to America poor soon were poor no longer, just as in Western Europe standards of living reached by 1991 exceeded the wildest fantasies of the Depression of 1931, let alone of 1891.[30]

So today we take for granted much that to John Locke and Adam Smith would have seemed astonishing. This is certainly true regarding the condition of the poor. Consider such things as welfare benefits (which are not counted in calculating who is below the poverty line); the fact that 38 percent of the American *poor* own their own homes; that the average poor American is more likely to own his own car than the average Western European; that 95 percent of the poor have television sets;[31] that the elderly among them are eligible for Medicare and the younger for Medicaid; and even such trivial indicators as the Reeboks worn by poor youngsters on schoolyard basketball courts. Boris Yeltsin astringently pointed out: "Some of what are, in the United States, called 'slums' would pass for pretty decent housing in the Soviet Union."[32]

Never in the history of the North Atlantic peoples have so many been so free and so prosperous. Thus, Marx wrongly predicted that under capitalism we should see the accelerating immiseration of the poor. (If anyone had collected a nickel from every Marxist and socialist who predicted the collapse of the capitalist order, that person would today be rich.) Instead, the liberal capitalist order has experienced one resurgence after another.

The fundamental reason for the capacity for self-reform in democratic capitalism lies in the independence of its moral-cultural order and its political order, which operate effectively upon its economic system. Each of these three systems represents a different aspect of reality, and each of them is moved by certain organic laws that, when violated, exact considerable costs. Thus, the system as a whole comes under three quite different reality checks. This tension places the system regularly in crisis. Each crisis becomes an opportunity for fresh restructuring.

Underlying this three-fold system is a considerable faith in the creative capacity of the human person. Theologically, this faith is well placed. Each person is made in the image of God, the Creator; each is called to be a co-creator and is given the vocation to act creatively and responsibly as a free citizen. Each is expected to show initiative, and to assume responsibility.

Thus, a new moral virtue is summoned up among such citizens, who are no longer merely subjects of king or emperor, but sovereigns in their own right: I mean the virtue of enterprise. Enterprise in this sense is a moral and intellectual virtue that prompts them to be alert, noticing, and discerning with respect to projects to be launched and goods and services to be provided.[33] Such citizens are taught to act for themselves, rather than to look to the state for the things they want and need. They themselves must set in motion procedures to bring about the goals they desire. They are taught to live as free men and women, responsible for their own destiny.

This image of free men and free women in a free society is compatible with the vision of Leo XIII. *Rerum novarum* encouraged Christians around the world to take up their own responsibilities for the reconstruction of the social order and played a significant role in the transformation of liberal capitalism.

Moreover, internal to capitalism itself lies another source of regeneration: its innovative spirit. Schumpeter discerned that the dynamism of capitalism lies in the impulse of creativity.[34] Hayek showed that this creativity appears in practice as enterprise.[35] Israel Kirzner showed that at the heart of enterprise is the act of discovery.[36] In brief, capitalism is a system rooted in mind. The characteristic signs of its presence are innovation, discovery, and invention. In this respect, capitalism goes beyond all preceding economic systems. It is constituted by much more than (1) private property, (2) market exchange, and (3) profit (or accumulation), the three characteristics which formed the spine of earlier, traditional economies. These are preconditions of capitalism, but they do not identify its specific difference (although they figure in most dictionary definitions).[37] Such dictionary definitions seem to distinguish capitalism from Marx's idea of socialism, but not from traditional (pre-capitalist) market systems. They fail to identify the dynamic and creative element that distinguishes capitalism from prior systems of the traditional market type. It is ironic that Mikhail Gorbachev should grasp the point that so many Westerners miss:

> The Soviet Union is suffering from a spiritual decline. We were among the last

to understand that in the age of information technology the most valuable asset is knowledge, which springs from individual imagination and creativity. We will pay for our mistakes for many years to come.[38]

Capitalism has its origin in the human capacity for invention and innovation—the human capacity to create. For that reason, it has a profound interest in freedom of thought and expression. As any visitor to a trade fair may observe, a market functions as an efficient disseminator of information, skills, methods, and new possibilities. In addition, a market is an efficient instrument for taking useful goods and services from the research laboratory into immediate public use. The USSR was not scientifically backward; still, lacking a vital marketplace, it succeeded poorly in bringing its research into the service of the common people. Similarly, the public success of the industrial revolution depended on the spirit of enterprise and the openness of the marketplace. Abraham Lincoln, who saw in the Patent and Copyright Clause of the U.S. Constitution one of the decisive turning points in the history of liberty, was aware of this dependence,[39] but it has received too little attention from economic historians.

In summary, capitalism is resurgent for two main reasons. First, a capitalist order was early embedded in a powerful moral-cultural system and a democratic political system, which together were able to direct it into fruitful channels and eventually to curb many abuses, real and potential. Second, the dynamic agency at the heart of capitalism is the creative capacity of the human mind, which a capitalist order nourishes by means of a distinctive set of institutions. Among these institutions are universal education, patent and copyright laws, research facilities, and associations for raising venture capital.

3. WHAT'S LEFT?

I have been to the West and have become convinced that we can use many things from the Western democracies, including the

58

> attitude to property, the parliamentary
> system, and much more. There is no reason
> to renounce all this because it is capitalist.
> Why should we do that if it is rational and
> useful?—Boris Yeltsin, 1989.[40]

For many years after *Rerum novarum*, interpreters of Catholic social thought suggested that since Leo XIII had condemned socialism and was critical of capitalism, the Catholic Church must be propounding a "middle way." But this way of thinking overlooked the asymmetry between capitalism and socialism. Socialism fuses a moral, economic, and political system into one; capitalism is the name only of an economic system, which for its full and free development requires a democratic polity and a humanistic and pluralist culture. Thus, in a sense, the threefold combination of democracy, capitalism, and religious liberty *is* the middle way between socialism and capitalism, narrowly considered. Just the same, after praising institutions of democracy, personal economic initiative, and religious liberty, Pope John II said emphatically in *Sollicitudo rei socialis* that the Catholic Church is *not* seeking a middle way.[41] No doubt the pope also recognized that in Central Europe these days, the term "middle way" is spoken of disdainfully. Thus Leszek Balcerowicz, Finance Minister of Poland, in 1989: "We don't want to try out a third way. We will leave it to the richer countries to try out a third way and if they succeed maybe we will follow."[42] The Finance Minister of Czechoslovakia spoke in terms as clear as Bohemian crystal: "We want the market economy without any adjectives. Any compromises will only fuzzy up the problems we have. To pursue a so-called third way is foolish. We had our experience with this in the 1960s when we looked for socialism with a human face. It did not work."[43] The future president of Bulgaria went further: "To speak of any future for socialism in this country is nonsense. . . .Our goal now is to lead Bulgaria to a modern, democratic capitalism."[44]

There are some persons in the church, particularly in Latin countries, who reluctantly accept the fact that papal social thinking proposes neither a socialist way nor a middle way; but they are reluctant to draw the conclusion that that leaves only one alternative, democratic capitalism--and that an incarnational strategy must begin with the best materials available, however poor these are. Democratic capitalism is a poor system, but the known human alternatives are worse. For Catholic social thought, the perfect is not the enemy of the good. The ethic proper to political economy is an ethic of prudence, suffused with charity;[45] of justice, tempered with mercy.[46] Nonetheless, Catholic social thought does insist on one principle that some erroneously regard as contrary to the spirit of democratic capitalism.

Pope John Paul II stated "the characteristic principle of Christian social doctrine" quite simply in a single sentence in *Sollicitudo rei socialis* (42): "The goods of this world are *originally meant for all.*" In the footnote accompanying this text, the Pope cites as background Vatican II's decree *Gaudium et spes* (69), Paul VI's encyclical Populorum progressio (22), and St. Thomas Aquinas, *Summa Theologiae* (I-II.66.2). This principle is formally known as "the universal destination of created goods." Vatican II affirms this principle in these words: "God intended the earth and all that it contains for the use of every human being and people. Thus, as men follow justice and unite in charity, created goods should abound for them on a reasonable basis."[47]

"Created goods should abound"—this modern treatment of the ancient principle includes two modern assumptions: first, that the goods of creation do abound in support of human life; second, that human economic creativity can keep ahead of population growth. These assumptions clash with premodern views, which stress scarcity, hardship, poverty, and the persistent threat of famine, plague, and demographic decline. In 1776 the earth supported only 735 million persons, for example. Yet, after experiencing the inventiveness of democratic capitalism (especially in the fields of medicine and agriculture), the earth by 1990 supported 5.3 billion persons. Thus, the assumption that human inventiveness and economic creativity can keep ahead of population to provide abundance "on a reasonable basis" turns out to have been a sound assumption, but only on one condition: the smooth functioning of democratic capitalist institutions. In the non-capitalist countries of the world poverty and scarcity still prevail.

The modern statement of the "universal destination" in *Gaudium et spes* and *Populorum progressio*, then, assumes that in the human

60

condition, abundance may be taken for granted. But in socialist and pre-capitalist (Third World) nations, this assumption does not hold. It does hold in democratic capitalist nations, and one reason this is so (but only one reason among many) is that within them rights to private property are respected by a regime of law. Yet here these documents take a curious turn. Since ancient times—in the Bible, in Aristotle, in Cicero, in St. Augustine, and consistently in the Catholic tradition—a statement about the universal destination as final end has led to an unambiguous statement about the necessary means to its fulfillment: a regime of private property. Traditional, pre-capitalist moral reasoning highly commended private property. By contrast, appearing near the high tide of Eurosocialism in 1967, *Populorum progressio* sounded a troubled note about private property: "Private property does not constitute for anyone an absolute and unconditional right. No one is justified in keeping for his exclusive use what he does not need, when others lack necessities" (23). This affirmation is found in St. Thomas Aquinas, it is true, but his main argument ran in exactly the opposite direction.

The issue that confronted Aquinas (cited by Pope John Paul II in *Sollicitudo*) was this: "Whether it is lawful for a man to possess a thing as his own" (S.T. I-II.66.2). St. Thomas took the principle of universal destination for granted. Over against it, he saw the urgent need for a regime of private property. By contrast, recent Vatican passages attempt the reverse--to take the principle of private property for granted, and seek to limit its sweep. St. Thomas argued against extreme communitarians; some recent Vatican statements seem to argue on their behalf. This shift in emphasis is altogether legitimate, but it should be noted.

Aquinas begins with three objections against the legitimacy of private property, as raised by the communitarians. The first objection he faced was this: "According to the natural law all things are common property." The second was a criticism by St. Basil of "the rich who deem as their own property the goods that they have seized." The third was from St. Ambrose, who had written, "Let no man call his own that which is common property."

St. Thomas replies to these objections by distinguishing between two powers of humans over material goods: The power to procure and distribute material goods, and the power to use them. Regarding the

61

second of these, the *use* of material goods, he says that a man "ought to possess external things, not as his own, but as common, so that he is ready to communicate them to others in their need." Aquinas seems to hold this principle as a matter of Christian belief. In support of it, he quotes from St. Paul's first Epistle to Timothy (6: 17-18), St. Basil, and St. Ambrose. Regarding the *production* and *distribution* of material goods, however, Aquinas gives three reasons why a regime of private property is "necessary." On the necessity of a regime of private property, Aquinas cites one argument from faith (from St. Augustine), then three based on natural reason. A regime of private property, he writes,

> is necessary to human life for three reasons. First because every man is more careful to procure what is for himself alone than that which is common to many or to all: since each one would shirk the labor and leave to another that which concerns the community, as happens where there is a great number of servants. Secondly, because human affairs are conducted in more orderly fashion if each man is charged with taking care of some particular thing himself, whereas there would be confusion if everyone had to look after any one thing indeterminately. Thirdly, because a more peaceful state is ensured to man if each one is contented with his own. Hence it is to be observed that quarrels arise more frequently where there is no division of the things possessed.

To those who have lived through the 70-year experiment with socialism in our time, this threefold reasoning about the necessity of private property must seem painfully vindicated by modern experience. If men were angels, the common ownership of the means of production might work, but human experience has taught us that private property is a practical necessity. Indeed, Pope John Paul II himself, having experienced "real existing socialism" at first hand, has taken pains to spell out the commonsense reasoning of St. Thomas on property, much as Leo XIII did.[48]

Clearly enough, a regime of private property is taken for granted by the Ten Commandments. Neither "Thou shall not steal" nor "Thou shall not covet" makes sense apart from the right to personal property. Beyond this, the arguments of Aquinas underline the social functions of private property. A regime of private property serves social peace, good order, and positive personal incentives. Without peace, order, and incentives, the raw goods of creation could not be transmuted by human labor into usable goods and services. Creation left to itself does not supply for human needs. If a man wants to eat, he must work "by the sweat of his brow."[49] As Leo XIII emphasized, in undercutting family-centered incentives, socialism severs the arteries of economic growth. The resource-rich Soviet Union is a living lesson in the damage done to itself by a nation that abandons private property. The situation in the Third World is nearly as bad.

In few places on earth today are property rights practiced as natural rights (in the sense of "natural rights" intended by Madison and Jefferson). In most of Latin America, for example, property rights are insecure, even where in principle respected. Since the property even of the wealthiest has often been subjected to arbitrary confiscations, nationalization, and unlawful seizures, how can the property of the lowliest be guaranteed? Title to property is often uncertain and virtually unverifiable; and huge majorities of the population are propertyless with respect to land or home. Wherever rights to property are protected for the families of farmers and other laborers across the generations, they find incentives to improve it. Wherever they do not, stagnation or even decline is visible.

This traditional Catholic reasoning on the universal destination of created goods as the end and property rights as the means, is not exactly identical to that of John Locke and the Anglo-American tradition; but neither is it wholly different. Locke, too, held that by nature all earthly goods belong to the entire human race.[50] He held that abandoned to itself and without human labor, the earth would hardly support human life, and that the use of human wit and human labor is indispensable for the improvement and cultivation of nature. Left to nature alone, a field might yield a harvest only one-tenth to one one-hundredth as large as the same field under human care and cultivation.[51] In this respect, the cause of the wealth of nations is human creativity. From experience, Locke concluded (like the ancients) that the most practical means of drawing usable wealth out of nature—of improving the land, for example—is a system of laws which would secure man's natural right to private property. Human creativity needs many social supports, including limited government, the rule of law, a regime of private property, monogamous marriage and the family, and systems of transport and markets. A regime of private property is, therefore, a social institution, designed for social purposes whose benefits redound on all. Indeed, John Stuart Mill even allowed that an owner of land who did not improve property by his labor would lose his claim to private ownership, since the justification for private property is its service to the common good.[52] This principle cuts two ways: A society that arbitrarily abridges private property will destroy incentives; but individuals who do not use private property to improve the public good undercut their claim to ownership.

In general, it appears that since *Gaudium et spes* papal statements on "the universal destination of goods" have been directed toward persuading rich nations and rich persons to give of their abundance to poor nations and poor persons. They have done less well in persuading the citizens of socialist and pre-capitalist states to reconstruct their inadequate social systems. But this task is also important. Self-reliance—within nations and among nations—is a crucial concept for Catholic social thought, as the Vatican Institute for Justice and Peace has emphasized for many years;[53] dependency is not honored. In commending the welfare programs of highly developed (i.e., democratic capitalist) nations, for example, *Gaudium et spes* also includes a prescient warning about problems that would become apparent in all welfare states three decades later:

> In highly developed nations a body of social
> institutions dealing with insurance and
> security can, for its part, make the common
> purpose of earthly goods effective. Family

64

and social services, especially those which provide for culture and education, should be further promoted. Still, care must be taken lest, as a result of all these provisions, the citizenry fall into a kind of sluggishness toward society, and reject the burdens of office and of public service (69).

In recent years, papal social teaching has also spoken metaphorically of a "gap" between the affluent (democratic capitalist) nations and the pre-capitalist and socialist nations. This "gap" is not to be understood arithmetically, of course. Even though a poor country should grow by ten percent while a wealthy one grew by only one percent, the base on which the one percent is calculated might be so much larger than the base on which the ten percent is calculated that at the end the absolute difference between the two GDPs might be larger, not smaller. Ten percent of a $50 billion economy is only $5 billion, for example, but one percent of a $5 trillion economy is $50 billion. Thus, the situation of poorer countries might be improving at a faster rate even though the "gap" did not seem to be diminishing; it is not the "gap" that is the moral point, but rapid improvement in the lot of the poor.

Moreover, the inability of some Third World nations to pay their debts indicates that their economies do not use borrowed money creatively enough to make a profit on it, from which interest could be paid. Instead, the money seems simply to vanish, sometimes with little to show for it. This fact indicates that even massive infusions of grants from other countries might also be of little lasting benefit. Moneys paid into the coffers of governments, bankers, industrialists, and other members of local power elites do not always find their way into use for the benefit of ordinary people or even into productive investments at home. On the contrary, amounts equal to half or more of the total debt of Latin America have actually been reinvested in Switzerland, North America, and elsewhere, in the phenomenon known as "capital flight."[54] For such reasons, many scholars are opposed to "foreign aid," on the ground that it encourages an irresponsible use of the money of others for which those who receive it feel little responsibility or obligation.[55] They are particularly opposed to foreign aid granted by one government to another, on the grounds that the corruption of political elites in Third World countries is virtually uncontrollable. By contrast, such aid should be given directly to ordinary people, not in the form of welfare benefits but, rather, in the form of education, training, and small amounts of carefully supervised credit, for the launching of small local businesses. "Better than to give a man a fish is to teach him how to fish."

A serious Jewish or Christian conscience (even the conscience of a serious humanist) feels the bite of this principle; *viz.*, that the material goods of this world have as their rightful destination the benefit of all human beings. A human society is judged morally by how well it cares for the most vulnerable in its midst and for the most vulnerable on the planet. But how best to do this? By outright grants? By loans? By the transmission of basic skills and assistance? By training in the laws and practices of a sound and growing economy? By good counsel regarding how to establish the basic institutions of a productive system? By opening the markets of Europe, Japan, North America, and other centers of dynamic economic growth to the products and services of the poorer nations? It is not enough to say that citizens of the commercially successful nations have an obligation to help their less fortunate brothers and sisters. It is crucial to begin to say *how* this obligation can be fruitfully acquitted. Few tasks in life are more difficult than giving truly useful help to the needy, without reducing the latter to servile dependence on their donors.

One of the most urgent needs of democratic capitalist societies, therefore, is to invent practical working methods for helping other nations to experience fruitful institutional development. It is clear that even nations with enormous material resources, such as Brazil and the USSR, violate the principle of the universal destination of material goods (or created goods) by failing to develop for the good of the whole race even such resources as they have. When we speak of "material things" or "created goods," therefore, we need to see that many of God's precious gifts to the human race are not being developed for the benefit of humankind, but are lying neglected or abused for want of creative, productive systems of political economy.

66

Being saddled with a defective system, furthermore, frustrates even a virtuous people, whereas getting the system right helps them mightily. That is why it is crucial for Jewish, Christian and humanistic thinkers to inquire carefully into which sorts of systems best serve the potentialities of our human nature, such as God has made us in all our cultural variety. For it does the poor no good to entrap them further into defective, illiberal, and inhumane systems.

4. TRANSFORMING DEMOCRATIC CAPITALISM

In this respect, one great advantage of democratic capitalist systems is that they are capable of self-reform. Well, then, how shall we go about trying to improve democratic and capitalist societies, in order to bring them more into harmony with Jewish, Christian, and humanistic ideals? There are many directions that such reforms could take. Since no temporal system ever enters into the fullness of "the Kingdom of God," a good and realistic conscience and a strong social imagination will always bring to light useful reforms. The continuing Jewish and Christian self-admonition is "not yet." *Societas semper reformanda*. For purposes of brevity, I limit myself in this brief conclusion to two urgent reforms: first, in the cultural and moral sphere; and, second, with regard to the poor.

(a.) *Moral and intellectual reforms.* The moral-cultural system is at once crucial to the health of democratic capitalism and easily overlooked. The moral-cultural system is crucial because the primary form of capital is the human spirit, which moves forward by inquiry, enterprise, discovery, and action. The moral-cultural system is too easily taken for granted because the habits of the heart are learned in childhood, supplying reasons that reason has forgotten. Each generation lives off the spiritual capital of its inheritance, and may not even notice when it is squandering this treasure. By dint of habits of hard work and attentiveness, for example, men sometimes grow successful only to indulge themselves and to leave their children barren of spiritual instruction. The moral and spiritual life of nations depends, therefore, on sequences of at least three generations. The habits inculcated by the first generation may be significantly abandoned by the second, and almost nonexistent in the third. Conversely, we do not always understand the treasures that, all

67

unknowing, we have inherited from the hard experience of several faithful generations. In any one generation, the moral life runs deeper than is discernible to the conscious mind.

Thus, tragedy always haunts the free society. Precisely because it is free it is rife with alluring temptations. A generation may not grasp the full implications of altering the traditions of the past, not at least until too late. Forgetting the principles on which their society has been constructed—even a single generation may be afflicted with such forgetfulness—its citizens may slide into behaviors and ways of thinking that set in motion its destruction. For example, the founders of the American experiment announced, "We hold these truths to be self-evident," and took as a model Republican Rome with its civic virtue. But later generations may brush aside this model, forget the truths once held to be self-evident and the daily practices that kneaded such truths into civic virtues. A people that abandons the intellectual and moral habits that hold its social system together must fly apart.

The specific moral challenges to democratic capitalist systems today are perhaps too obvious to need elaboration. Especially through the new technology of television, the solicitations of popular culture have come to occupy unprecedented space in the inner lives of the young—rock video, films of violence, sexual license, and the cultivation of passion and desire. Although counterbalanced by abiding moral seriousness on the part of many, there is, nonetheless, considerable evidence of mounting behavioral dysfunction among us: drugs, crime, births out of wedlock, children disoriented by divorce, teenage pregnancy, and a truly staggering number of abortions. Many of these behavioral dysfunctions result in various forms of social dependency. Thus, a widespread loss of moral virtue creates larger and larger numbers of clients claiming to be supported by society, on the one hand, and of uncivic-minded hedonists, on the other.

In addition, a profound disorientation of intellectual habits undermines the truths a people once held to be self-evident, until such truths can no longer be intellectually defended. Thus, Professor Richard Rorty has propounded a "cheerful nihilism," in which any claim to "truth" independent of social preference is to be joshingly brushed aside,[56] while Arthur M. Schlesinger, Jr., argues that America was founded on "relativism."[57]   Professor Rorty would have us be kind and tolerant to one another, while happily refusing to offer an intellectual ("metaphysical") defense of our system.

By contrast, the conception of "inalienable rights" on which the American experiment rests is intelligible only in terms of truth, nature, and nature's God.   Against a background of "cheerful nihilism," this experiment makes no sense at all; it is only an assertion of arbitrary will. Cheerful nihilism would render the American experiment philosophically vulnerable to any adversarial will armed with superior power.

Quite unlike Professor Rorty, others have argued that the philosophical background in which the American experiment was historically placed is congenial to the traditions of Christian philosophy and Christian belief; among these are John Courtney Murray, S.J., and Jacques Maritain.[58]   Indeed, a large majority of American citizens share these traditions still today and understand the American experiment in their light.   Rooted in a sense of transcendence, what Walter Lippmann has called "the public philosophy"[59] gives individual citizens an intellectual basis for resisting public expressions of arbitrary will, and for vindicating their rights against aggression from any quarter.   They believe these rights to be rooted not in human preference, will, or custom but in the intellect and will of God.   Parallel to the task of renewing the moral foundation of modern societies, therefore, is a further task of deepening the intellectual foundations of the free society.   It may even be the case that liberal institutions cannot be defended on the basis of the secular philosophies of the Enlightenment, but must be recast in more ancient terms, consistent with Jewish and Christian intellectual traditions.[60]

Finally, since democratic capitalist societies bring to the fore a new set of moral and intellectual virtues to complement the classical virtues, some new Aristotle should describe their phenomenology as they are actually practiced today.   Fresh thinking is needed on a whole range of traditional moral concepts, whose concrete embodiment is now quite different than in the past.   For example, such concepts as person, community, dignity, equality, rights, responsibilities, and common good are today enfleshed in new settings.   Thus individuals today are citizens rather than (or in Britain, in addition to being) subjects; they are expected to act for themselves, with initiative and enterprise, and not simply to wait for orders. Again, large and broad markets work through voluntary choice, consent, and cooperation to achieve beneficial outcomes too complex for any one agency to direct, a form of common good quite unlike the simple common good defined by a tribal chief of yore. From infancy, our young children—erroneously described as suffering from excessive individualism—are immersed in social practices, group activities, cooperative projects, and group memberships of so many sorts that scarcely any human beings in history have been so thoroughly and complexly socialized. Reflection on these and other characteristics of moral life today suggests significant additions to the understanding of basic concepts worked out by scholars in earlier contexts.

Thus, the work to be done in reform of the moral and cultural sphere is quite immense.[61] It is not unconnected to a new way of thinking about the principle of helping the poor and a new approach in practice.

(b.) *The poor*. Among the 165 or so nations of the world, the nations most conspicuous for their poverty lie either in the pre-capitalist, traditionalist parts of the world (Africa, Latin America, and South Asia) or in the socialist world. We have learned recently, indeed, that the "second world" did not exist except as a more heavily armed part of the third world, since the crumbling economy of the USSR more resembles the economy of India or China than that of West Germany, and even in the newly united Germany, the economic inferiority of its Eastern portion is quite pronounced. Thus the promise of economic development, which originated in Adam Smith's *Inquiry into the Nature and Causes of the Wealth of Nations*, seems to have been realized almost exclusively among the relatively few capitalist nations of the world. The economic plight of the poor is harsh in socialist and in traditionalist economies; put otherwise, the standard of living of the poor is certainly higher in capitalist economies than in either of the latter. As a system, capitalism is better for the poor than any other existing system.

In Latin America, for example, there are today some 90 million youngsters under the age of 15 who will be entering the workforce each year for the next fifteen years. But scores of millions of older adults in Latin America are also unemployed or underemployed. Moreover, by the year 2000 fewer Latin Americans than today will almost certainly be working in agriculture, since the flight from farm to city is virtually universal; and it is nearly as certain that fewer will be working for transnational corporations. This vast pool of the unemployed contrasts vividly with the enormous amounts of work that need to be done to improve the conditions of daily life among the poor. By what mechanism shall these two factors—work to be done and workers needing employment—be brought together, if not by the rapid generation of tens of millions of small businesses engaged in manufacturing and services? However, large proportions of the poor of Latin America are not only excluded from participation in employment; they are also excluded from access to the legal incorporation of small businesses. Notwithstanding this disability, 43 percent of the houses in Peru have been constructed by *illegals*, and 93 percent of public transport is provided by them.[62]

Further, two-thirds of all the poor in Peru are neither peasants nor factory workers (proletarians); they are entrepreneurs. Not only is their work considered illegal and even criminalized; no legitimate institutions exist to extend credit (the mother's milk of enterprise) to the poor. All these exclusions—from employment, incorporation, and credit—are unjust. So also is the exclusion of the poor from property ownership, whether in land or home or business. Property titles in Peru are in extreme disarray and exceedingly unstable.

Much the same situation, *mutatis mutandis*, obtains throughout Latin America: *There is no capitalism for the poor of Latin America.* Nearly all the economies of Latin America are in the grip of the state, and the state in turn is typically bent to the service of a relatively few elite families. Neither in Cuba nor in Nicaragua, nor in any other socialist experiment, has socialism proved to be an answer to the longings of the poor for material progress, creative opportunity, and civic liberty.

In this sense, Robert Heilbroner's famous sentence is true: "Less than seventy-five years after it officially began, the contest between capitalism and socialism is over: capitalism has won."[63] The reason for this victory (surprising to so many) appears to be twofold. First, as a system capitalism is constituted by a set of institutions nourishing invention, innovation, and enterprise. These are the primary cause of economic development. Second, market systems better recognize the dignity of individuals and respect their choices, better reward cooperation

71

and mutual adjustment, and attain ever higher levels of progress. Both in creativity and in cooperative voluntary activities the capitalist order attains a progressively higher standard of the common good.[64] Nonetheless, the question remains: *Within* capitalist nations, how may the good of the poor be better served?

On this matter, perhaps, I may refer to a long study of poverty in the U.S. undertaken by the Working Seminar on Family and American Welfare Policy.[65] This study examines both the successes and the failures of the so-called War on Poverty launched by President Lyndon Johnson in March, 1964. It found that after 20 years, the welfare of the elderly had been dramatically improved, and both medical and other noncash benefits had substantially bettered the economic plight of nearly all the poor. By contrast with this success, however, considerable evidence showed that the condition of younger cohorts among the poor, particularly children and single parents, had deteriorated. There were far more births out of wedlock in 1985 than there had been in 1965, and far more single parents (especially young parents). In addition, especially in urban areas morale among the poor seemed to be worse.

Undeniably, there was more money in poor areas of the inner city than ever before, but also far more social dysfunction. Drug use and crime rates were higher than ever; a certain pall of despondency had become visible. Many households seemed trapped in a cycle of welfare, unmarried pregnancy, unemployment (or even unemployability), and inability to cope. Even though schooling through high school is free, many drop out. Even though books are more widely available than ever, many do not learn to read. Even though jobs are so plentiful that immigrants from abroad flock to them, many remain out of the work force, neither finding nor even seeking gainful employment. Material circumstances in 1985 were at far higher levels than in 1965; indeed beyond their relatively high levels of reported income, the poor (in a separate survey) reported spending three times as much money as they reported in income.[66] Despite this, levels of dependency, behavioral dysfunction, and inability to cope were higher than in 1965.

Nor is this pattern unique to the United States. Other social welfare states face analogous problems. Indeed, a radical dilemma has appeared at the heart of the welfare state. Rates of out-of-wedlock

72

pregnancy in Sweden are even higher than in the U.S., and are growing rapidly in most welfare states.[67]   In the U.S., the granting of material benefits traps a significant proportion of able-bodied adults between the ages of 18-64 in more or less permanent dependency upon the public purse, not merely financial dependency, but also behavioral dependency. Many (not all) recipients remain on-and-off, if not continuous, wards of the state.[68]   The results of their behaviors on their children are not difficult to trace. Having children out of wedlock dramatically increases the chances of infant mortality, and children of such unions have a higher likelihood of poor health, difficulties in school, truancy, unemployment, crime, and involvement in drugs.

From a year's study of the evidence, the Working Seminar decided that the radical problem of the poor in the United States is no longer monetary; indeed, the urban poor often have considerably more disposable income than did the immigrant poor of any preceding generation (or even today). Rather, the radical problem has a far thicker human dimension, and it requires humane solutions far more complex than can be reached by monetary grants alone. Many of the poor suffer far too much self-destruction. The rest of the human community has to reach out to the most injured among them, helping them to restore behaviors, motivations, outlooks, and habits to healthier modes and to restructure the small and vital "little platoons" of healthy social life. Civic life has broken down among some of the poor, and needs to be rebuilt from within, with the assistance of sympathetic helping hands. Perhaps the Christian community will respond, as it has historically, by inspiring new religious congregations to undertake this civilizing mission.

The heart of this problem has come to be identified under the unpleasant name "underclass," a term that in the U.S. has been applied to some four million poor persons concentrated in poverty areas of the nation's 100 largest cities.[69]   Unlike the large majority of the poor, whose poverty is primarily monetary and temporary, the "underclass" exhibits many self-destructive habits that keep them in perpetual dependency on others. Instead of living as free and independent citizens in a free society, they live almost as serfs, dependent on the state. Instead of contributing to the common good, they take from it and, in some cases, prey upon it. Moreover, it is the quasi-permanency of their dependent

73

condition and the probability of their passing it on to their children that most inspires in observers dread and horror.

In fairly sharp contrast, those poor Americans who perform well three traditional and relatively simple accomplishments have almost no probability of remaining long in poverty. Some 97 percent of those who complete high school, stay married (even if not on the first try), and work full-time year-round (even at the minimum wage) are not poor; nearly all poverty is associated with the absence of one or more of these basic accomplishments.[70] Indeed, the vast majority of the more than 12 million immigrants, mostly non-white, who entered the U.S. in the 1970s and 1980s swiftly moved out of poverty chiefly by strong family life and diligent work; not even inadequacy in the English language held them back. Lacking a high school education or its equivalent, they made up for this by reliable work, commending themselves to employers by the soundness of their moral habits.

Within capitalist countries, however, the residual poverty left behind by this generally rapid *embourgeoisement* of the "proletariat" seems resistant to traditional anti-poverty techniques. Economic growth alone does not cure this form of poverty, since so many afflicted with it work not at all or only for brief stints.[71] Some commentators stress that, in every society, some percentage of persons will suffer from physical, emotional, or moral disabilities which prevent them from achieving the levels of independence and self-reliance that others do. With the right sort of assistance, some of these less fortunate persons may be brought into the mainstream. However, care must be taken lest programs of assistance seduce even the able-bodied into self-destructive dependency. That this often happens is a powerful accusation against democratic capitalist societies.

To return to the worldwide perspective, there is much to be done in the non-capitalist world in order to construct institutions favorable to economic development from the bottom up. Among these desperately needed institutions are universal education, institutions of credit and venture capital designed especially for the aspiring poor, the easy incorporation of small businesses, an ethos of enterprise, and other crucial social supports tailored especially for the poor. Guy Sorman calls this "barefoot capitalism,"[72] and others call it "popular" or "people's capitalism." This emphasis upon enterprise and creativity is consistent with credit unions, cooperatives, workers' ownership, employee stock options (ESOPs), and other techniques. But such an emphasis is more important than any other single factor.

5. SUMMARY

In *Rerum novarum*, Leo XIII predicted with remarkable accuracy the futility of socialism. By his criticism of visible faults in liberal capitalist societies he set in motion currents of reform that ultimately contributed to social reconstruction. Nonetheless, for various historical and cultural reasons, neither Leo XIII nor his successors until John Paul II thoroughly analyzed the sources of regeneration and invention in democratic capitalist societies. These sources notably include the separation of systems (precisely the economic, political, cultural systems that are mirrored in the threefold structure of *Gaudium et spes*). These sources also include the internal constitution of capitalism itself, specifically those institutions that add invention, innovation, and enterprise to traditional market economies. They include as well the institutional protection of religious liberty and private property. (The latter is the *sine qua non* of free civic life and family-based incentives.)

Even though the best hope of the poor on earth lies in the universal spread and deeper development of democratic capitalist systems, much fresh thinking is needed to deepen the present intellectual and moral foundations of democratic capitalist societies. Clear thinking is also needed if we are to bring swift and effective assistance to the poor.

Within a Jewish and Christian horizon, the road toward an earthly approximation of the kingdom of God stretches very far into the future. There is no danger of confusing the sin, imperfection and suffering that characterize democratic capitalist societies with the kingdom of God. For humans, given their liberty, do often what they should not do, and do not do what they should. What can at least be said, though, is that no existing alternative offers better systemic promise, and none seems more adequately suited both to eliciting human creativity and to deflecting human weakness into watchfulness, by assigning private interest to be a sentinel to public good.

NOTE

The author is grateful to Kenneth R. Craycraft, Jr., for the execution of the endnotes, and to Derek Cross for significant editorial and research assistance.

ENDNOTES

1. Brochure for "A Conference to Mark the Centenary of Pope Leo XIII's Social Encyclical *Rerum novarum*," Von Hügel Institute, St. Edmund's College, Cambridge, England.

2. "What I find startling and disconcerting is that these massive historical trends [towards capitalism] have been largely unanticipated. The conventional wisdom with respect to socialism has been that it was, or would be, a success and that the future very likely belonged to it. The same wisdom with respect to capitalism was that its future was clouded.

   "But what voice of the present generation has anticipated the demise of socialism and the 'triumph of capitalism'? Not a single writer in the Marxian tradition! Are there any in the left-centrist group? None that I can think of, including myself. As for the center itself—the Samuelsons, Solows, Glazers, Lipsets, Bells, and so on—I believe that many expected capitalism to experience serious and mounting, if not fatal, problems and anticipated some form of socialism to be the organizing force for the twenty-first century.

   "That leaves the right. Here is the part that's hard to swallow. It has been the Friedmans, Hayeks, von Mises, *e tutte quanti* who have maintained that capitalism would flourish and that socialism would develop incurable ailments. All three have regarded capitalism as the 'natural' system of free men; all have maintained that left to its own devices capitalism would achieve material growth more successfully than any other system.

"From this admittedly impressionistic and incomplete sampling I draw the following discomforting generalization: *The farther to the right one looks, the more prescient has been the historical foresight; the farther to the left, the less so*" (emphasis his). Robert Heilbroner, "Was the Right Right All Along?" *Harper's*, Vol. 282, No. 1688 (January, 1991): 18-22. Reprinted from *Dissent* (Fall, 1990).

3. In his first use of the term, the pope says, "Socialists, exciting the envy of the poor toward the rich, contend that it is necessary to do away with private possession of goods and in its place to make the goods of individuals common to all, and that the men who preside over a municipality or who direct the entire State should act as administrators of these goods. They hold that, by such transfer of private goods from private individuals to the community, they can cure the present evil through dividing wealth and benefits equally among the citizens." Pope Leo XIII, *Rerum novarum* (Boston: Daughters of St. Paul), No. 7. All paragraph numbers in the text refer to this edition of *Rerum novarum*, the authorized translation of the Holy See.

4. "The fact that God gave the whole human race the earth to use and enjoy cannot indeed in any manner serve as an objection against private possessions. For God is said to have given the earth to mankind in common, not because He intended indiscriminate ownership of it by all, but because He assigned no part to anyone in ownership, leaving the limits of private possessions to be fixed by the industry of men and the institutions of peoples" (14).

5. "'Poisoning the Soul', New Leaders of Russia and Central Europe Talk about the Evil Empire," compiled by Kevin Acker in *Policy Review*, No. 55 (Winter 1991): 60-65. Notes 5 through 14 are from this compilation.

6. Tzvetan Todorov, Bulgarian author, *The New Republic* (June 25, 1990).

7. Tatyana Zaslavskaya, Soviet sociologist, in *Voices of Glasnost*.

8. Gavrii Popov, Mayor of Moscow, Cato Institute/Soviet Academy of Sciences, September 10, 1990.

9. Suyatoslav Fyodorov, Soviet laser scientist, *New York Times* (March 11, 1990).

10. Tadeusz Mazowiecki, Prime Minister of Poland, before the *Sejm* (Polish Parliament), January 18, 1990.

11. Oleg Kalugin, former KGB Major-General and USSR People's Deputy, *Moscow News* (July 1, 1990).

12. Timisoara Declaration, Romania, March 11, 1990.

13. Vaclav Havel, President of Czechoslovakia, *Izvestia* (February 23, 1990).

14. Valtr Komarek, Deputy Prime Minister of Czechoslovakia, *NRC Handelsblad* (Rotterdam), February 6, 1990.

15. "Under a system based upon private ownership in the means of production, the scale of values is the outcome of the actions of every independent member of society. Everyone plays a twofold part in its establishment first as a consumer, secondly, as a producer. As consumer, he establishes the valuation of goods ready for consumption. As a producer, he guides the production-goods into those uses in which they yield the highest product. . . . And in this way, arises the exactly graded system of prices which enables everyone to frame his demand on economic lines.
"Under Socialism, all this must necessarily be lacking. The economic administration may indeed know exactly what

commodities are needed most urgently. But this is only half the problem. The other half, the valuation of the means of production, it cannot solve. It can ascertain the value of the totality of such instruments. That is obviously equal to the value of the satisfactions they afford. If it calculates the loss that would be incurred by withdrawing them, it can also ascertain the value of single instruments of production. But it cannot assimilate them to a common price denominator, as can be done under a system of economic freedom and money prices.

"The problem of economic calculation is the fundamental problem of Socialism. That for decades people could write and talk about Socialism without touching this problem only shows how devastating were the effects of the Marxian prohibition on scientific scrutiny of the nature and working of a socialist economy.

"To prove that economic calculation would be impossible in the socialist community is to prove also that Socialism is impracticable.

"The discovery of this fact is clearly most inconvenient for the socialist parties. . . . Nothing has shaken the proof that under Socialism economic calculation is impossible." Ludwig von Mises, *Socialism*, tr. J. Kahane from 2d ed. of 1932 (Indianapolis: Liberty Classics, 1981), 103-104; 116-17.

16.   "In the nineteen-thirties, when I was studying economics, a few economists had already expressed doubts about the feasibility of centrally planned socialism. One of them was Ludwig von Mises, an Austrian of extremely conservative views, who had written of the 'impossibility' of socialism, arguing that no Central Planning Board could ever gather the enormous amount of information needed to create a workable economic system. . . . Our skepticism [of Mises's views] was fortified when Oskar Lange, a brilliant young Polish economist, . . . wrote two dazzling articles showing that a Board would not need all the information that Mises said it couldn't collect. All that such a Board would have to do, Lange wrote, was watch the levels of inventories in its

warehouses: if inventories rose, the obvious thing to do was to lower prices, so that goods would move out more rapidly; and if inventories were too rapidly depleted, to raise prices to discourage sales. Fifty years ago, it was felt that Lange had decisively won the argument for socialist planning. . . .

"It turns out, of course, that Mises was right. The Soviet system has long been dogged by a method of pricing that produced grotesque misallocations of effort. The difficulties were not so visible in the early days of Soviet industrialization or in the post-Second World War reconstruction period. The dams and mills and entire new cities of the 1930s astonished the world, as did the Chinese Great Leap Forward of the 1950s, which performed similar miracles from a still lower base. But those undertakings, like the building of the Pyramids or the Great Wall, depended less on economic coordination than on the political capacity for marshalling vast labor forces. Inefficiency set in when projects had to be joined into a complex whole—a process that required knowing how much things should cost. Then, as Mises foresaw, setting prices became a hopeless problem because the economy never stood still long enough for anyone to decide anything correctly." Robert Heilbroner, "After Communism," *The New Yorker* (September 10, 1990), 92. For a discussion of the famous debate between Lange and Mises (including the original articles), see Tyrgve J.B. Hoff, *Economic Calculation and the Socialist Society* (Indianapolis: Liberty Press, 1981 [1938]).

17.   "The main point of my argument is . . . that the conflict between, on one hand, advocates of the spontaneous extended human order created by a competitive market, and on the other hand, those who demand a deliberate arrangement of human interaction by central authority based on collective command over available resources is due to a factual error by the latter about how knowledge of these resources is and can be generated and utilized. As a question of fact, this conflict must be settled by scientific study. Such study shows that, by following the spontaneously generated moral traditions underlying the competitive market order (traditions

which do not satisfy the canons or norms of rationality embraced by most socialists), we generate and garner greater knowledge and wealth than could ever be obtained or utilized in a centrally-directed economy whose adherents claim to proceed strictly in accordance with 'reason.' Thus, socialist aims and programs are factually impossible to achieve or execute; and they also happen into the bargain as it were, to be logically impossible." F.A. Hayek, *The Fatal Conceit* (Chicago: University of Chicago Press, 1988), 7.

18. From Zamyatin's novel *We*:
"The state poet wrote a poem,
> Eternally enamored two times two
> Eternally united in the passionate four,
> Most ardent lovers in the world—
> Inseparable two times two. . . .
The state newspapers stated: You are perfect. You are machinelike. The road to one hundred percent happiness is free. . ." Mihajlo Mihajlov, "Life = Freedom: The Symbolism of 2 x 2 = 4 in Dostoevsky, Zamyatin and Orwell," *Catholicism in Crisis*, Vol. 3, No. 10 (October 1985): 20-24.

19. "Between 1798 and 1832 the new science of political economy was fully integrated into contemporary Christian social theory by a profoundly influential group of British economists. The ethical implications of a market economy had been rigorously analyzed from the standpoint of trinitarian orthodoxy, and a fairly robust theodicy constructed in order to account for the poverty and inequality inevitable in a world ruled by scarcity. 'Christian political economy' passed into the mainstream of English-speaking culture and formed political attitudes down to the late 1970s.

"So far as the Church of Rome knew or cared, however, all this might have happened on another planet. After 1789 its attention, or at any rate that of the Curia, was engrossed by more pressing matters. When Leo XIII turned belatedly to economic matters in 1891 he issued an anti-socialist tract that steered well

clear of any recognition of market forces in the social order."
Waterman discusses the "three most important elements of this
explanation: a misunderstanding of classical political economy, a
misperception of the European economy in the nineteenth century,
and philosophical commitment to a purely Scholastic understanding
of liberty." A.E.C. Waterman, "The Intellectual Context of
Rerum novarum," (first draft of unpublished paper, December
1990), 1, 7. To appear in *Review of Social Economy*.

20. Vaclav Klaus, Finance Minister of Czechoslovakia, in Acker, 64-
64. Original citation from *Reason* (June 1990).

21. Anatoly Sobchak, Mayor of Leningrad, in Acker, 63. Original
citation from Cato Institute/Soviet Academy of Sciences,
September 11, 1990.

22. Yuri Afanasyev, USSR People's Deputy and Rector of the
Moscow Historical Archival Institute, in Acker, 64. Original
citation from *Dagens Nyheter* (Stockholm), (January 3, 1990).

23. St. Ambrose, for example: "In general, Ambrose
apparently believes that almost all methods of acquiring wealth are
unjust. That is certainly true of trade, which he regards with the
abhorrence of a Roman aristocrat brought up in traditional values.
Trade is based on lying and cunning, for the seller tries to make
the merchandise appear more valuable than it is, and the buyer
does the exact opposite. He goes so far as to declare that to use
the sea for commerce is to twist its purpose, for the sea was given
in order to produce fish and not in order to be sailed. . . . For
Ambrose, travel to distant lands to procure what is not available
locally is one more consequence of greed, of not being content
with what is really at hand.
"The only source of wealth of which Ambrose occasionally
approves is agriculture. As a true Roman aristocrat, he stands in
the tradition of Columella and Cato. He can well understand and
approve of Naboth's reluctance to give up his inheritance.

Agriculture is also commendable in that it produces wealth without taking it away from another, which is more than can be said of other means of acquiring wealth." Justo L. Gonzalez, *Faith and Wealth: A History of Early Christian Ideas on the Origin, Significance, and Use of Money* (New York: Harper & Row, 1990), 189. Gonzalez cites St. Ambrose, De Officiis 3.37, 57, 65-66, 71-72, in *Nicene and Post Nicene Fathers*, 2d series.

24.   ". . . the ideal of a liberal society could be fully achieved--that is, there could be universal compliance with the demands of contractual justice—and yet, according to the Scholastic view, widespread injustice and exploitation could still occur in the economic system. . . .

"Reflection on the Scholastic procedure for distributive justice helps clarify the conception of exploitation implicit in the Pope's condemnation of the evils of capitalism. In the transition to a new mode of production, with the proletarization of the labor force, one whole class in society was deprived of that share of the community's property income proportionate to the *dignitas* of its members, with the result that capitalism, in the words of Leo XIII, 'handed over the workers, each alone and defenseless, to the inhumanity of employers and the greed of competitors'. . . .

"According to the Scholastic division between the 'parts' of justice, justice in distribution requires first and foremost that there be a community identified by a common desire to share in the exemplification of complementary personal excellences—a community characterized by what Aristotle, in *Ethics* IX, refers to as civic friendship. It is the communal perception of complementary excellences that provides the ground for judgment as to the relative *dignitas* of a society's members. Capitalism, so the great social encyclicals of Leo XIII and Pius XI indicate, has destroyed the sense of community and obliterated the moral vision required to establish distributive justice. Such destruction and obliteration . . . might very well originate in that *demotion of reason* whereby the technical means-end rationality characteristic of capitalism has displaced that *ontological* kind of reason mankind needs in order to perceive the good and the beautiful. When such demotion of reason occurs, perceptions of value cannot be articulated and distributive justice, therefore, can have no solid base. In a society afflicted by such a *malaise*, there is sure to be widespread alienation and a tendency, relying upon instrumental reasoning as the ground for social relationships, for members of society to use one another as instrumental means for the achievement of arbitrary egoistic ends. In such a society, it might very well happen, as Pius XI said of capitalism, that 'dead matter comes forth from the factory ennobled while men are corrupted and degraded'. . . .

"[This is] exploitation derived from the demotion of reason, whereby a community is deprived of the vision required to perceive and appreciate instantiations of the good and the beautiful." Stephen T. Worland, "Exploitative Capitalism: The Natural-Law Perspective," *Social Research*, Vol. 48, No. 2 (Summer 1981): 294-95; 299; 304-305.

25.   "Ambition must be made to counteract ambition. The interest of the man must be connected with the constitutional rights of the place. It may be a reflection on human nature that such devices should be necessary to control the abuses of government. But what is government itself but the greatest of all reflections on human nature? If men were angels, no government would be necessary. If angels were to govern men, neither external nor internal controls on government would be necessary. In framing a government which is to be administered by men over men, the great difficulty lies in this: you must first enable the government to control the governed; and in the next place to oblige it to control itself. A dependence on the people is, no doubt, the primary control on the government; but experience has taught mankind the necessity of auxiliary precautions.

"This policy of supplying, by opposite and rival interests, the defect of better motives, might be traced through the whole system of human affairs, private as well as public. We see it particularly displayed in all the subordinate distributions of power, where the constant aim is to divide and arrange the several offices in such a manner as that each may be a check on the other--that the private interest of every individual may be a sentinel over the public rights.   These inventions of prudence cannot be less requisite in the distribution of the supreme powers of the State." *The Federalist Papers*, No. 51, ed. Clinton Rossiter (New York: New American Library, 1961), 322.

26.   Heilbroner has lately noticed this: "Radical views are inherently more optimistic than conservative ones. Through radical glasses society always appears to fall far short of its potential, whereas through conservative ones it always expresses inescapable and insistent needs of abiding human nature. Conversely, the conservative view is always darker than the radical. It is more concerned with avoiding catastrophe than with achieving unrealized possibilities. It cannot be progress-oriented or teleological in the way that radical thought must be." Heilbroner, "Was the Right Right All Along?" 20.   Compare the words of Vaclav Klaus, Finance Minister of Czechoslovakia: "We wanted to create a new man, with only unselfish thoughts. I am afraid it is not possible." Acker, 62.

27.   Such "private life," of course, can be socially organized and publicly active; some forms of it (unions, associations, nonprofit organization) may be legally incorporated and thus, in a sense, "public." We should not confine the word "public" only to the action of the state.

28.   Long before Marx was on the scene, Madison stated the problem in *Federalist* 10: "The most common and durable source of factions has been the various and unequal distribution of property. Those who hold and those who are without property have ever formed distinct interests in society. Those who are creditors, and those who are debtors, fall under a like discrimination. A landed interest, a manufacturing interest, a mercantile interest, a moneyed interest, with many lesser interests,

grow up of necessity in civilized nations, and divide them into different classes, actuated by different sentiments and views. The regulation of those various and interfering interests forms the principal task of modern legislation, and involves the spirit of party and faction in the necessary operations of the government. . . . The apportionment of taxes on the various descriptions of property is an act which seems to require the most exact impartiality; yet there is, perhaps, no legislative act in which greater opportunity and temptation are given to a predominant party to trample on the rules of justice. Every shilling with which they overburden the inferior number, is a shilling saved to their own pockets.

"It is vain to say that enlightened statesmen will be able to adjust these clashing interests, and render them all subservient to the public good. Enlightened statesmen will not always be at the helm."

Then Madison suggests the solution in No. 51: "It is of great importance in a republic not only to guard the society against the oppression of its rulers, but to guard one part of the society against the injustice of the other part. Different interests necessarily exist in different classes of citizens. If a majority be united by a common interest, the rights of the minority will be insecure." The method of providing "against this evil. . .will be exemplified in the federal republic of the United States. Whilst all authority in it will be derived from and dependent on society, the society itself will be broken into so many parts, interests and classes of citizens, that the rights of individuals, or of the minority, will be in little danger from interested combinations of the majority."

29.   John Locke, *Two Treatises of Government*, Second Treatise, sec. 41, ed. Peter Laslett, rev. ed. (New York: New American Library, 1965), 339.

30. "As a result of . . . steady and tireless efforts, there has arisen a new branch of jurisprudence unknown to earlier times, whose aim is the energetic defense of those sacred rights of the workingman which proceed from his dignity as a man and as a Christian. These laws concern the soul, the health, the strength, the housing, workshops, wages, dangerous employments, in a word, all that concerns the wage earners, with particular regard to women and children. Even though these regulations do not agree always and in every detail with the recommendations of Pope Leo, it is none the less certain that much which they contain is strongly suggestive of *Rerum novarum*, to which in large measure must be attributed the improved condition of the workingmen." Pius XI, *Quadragesimo anno*, sec. 28, in *Seven Great Encyclicals*, ed. William J. Gibbons, S.J. (Glen Rock, NJ: Paulist Press, 1963), 132.

31. "How 'Poor' are America's Poor?" *Heritage Foundation Backgrounder*, No. 791 (September 21, 1990).

32. Boris Yeltsin, speech at Columbia University, cited in Acker, 64.

33. Michael Novak, *This Hemisphere of Liberty: A Philosophy of the Americas* (Washington, D.C.: The AEI Press, 1990), 25-35.

34. "The fundamental impulse that sets and keeps the capitalist engine in motion comes from new consumers' goods, the new methods of production or transportation, the new markets, the new forms of industrial organization that capitalist enterprise creates. . . . This process of Creative Destruction is the essential fact about capitalism," Joseph Schumpeter, *Capitalism, Socialism and Democracy* (New York: Harper & Row, 1950), 83.

35. See Friedrich A. Hayek, "The Use of Knowledge in Society," in *Individualism and the Economic Order* (Chicago: Henry Regnery, 1972).

36.   Kirzner sees "market capitalism not simply as a set of institutions governing exchanges . . . but as an ongoing process of creative discovery. What one witnesses in a market economy, at any point in time, are nothing but attempts by market participants to take advantage of newly discovered or created possibilities. . . . The process of creative discovery is never completed, nor is it ever arrested." Israel Kirzner, *Discovery and the Market Process* (Chicago: University of Chicago Press, 1985), ix-x.

37.   For example, *The American Heritage Dictionary* (1976) defines capitalism as "An economic system characterized by freedom of the market with increasing concentration of private and corporate ownership of production and distribution means, proportionate to increasing accumulation and reinvestment of profits." For others see Michael Novak, *The Spirit of Democratic Capitalism* 4, 2d ed. (Lanham, Md.: Madison Books, 1991), 430 (new Afterword).

38.   George Gilder quoting Mikhail Gorbachev, "Freedom and the High Tech Revolution," *Imprimis*, Vol. 19, No. 11 (November 1990): 1.

39.   "It is . . . a curious fact that a new country is most favorable—almost necessary—to the immancipation [sic] of thought, and consequent advancement of civilization and the arts. . . . I have mentioned the discovery of America as an event greatly favoring and facilitating useful discoveries and inventions.
        "Next came the Patent laws. These began in England in 1624; and, in this country, with the adoption of our constitution [sic]. Before then, any man might instantly use what another had invented; so that the inventor had no special advantage from his own invention. The patent system changed this; secured the inventor, for a limited time, the exclusive use of his invention; and thereby added the fuel of *interest* to the *fire* of genius, in the discovery and production of new and useful things." Abraham Lincoln, *Abraham Lincoln: Speeches and Writings 1859-1865* (New York, Library of America, 1989), 10-11.

See also Nathan Rosenberg & L.E. Birdzell, Jr., *How the West Grew Rich* (New York: Basic, 1986): "Competition also became involved in innovation. The market rewards of innovation depended largely on the innovator's ability to charge a high price for a unique product or service until such time as it could be imitated or superseded by others. The rewards depended, in other words, on the innovator's margin of priority in time over imitators and successors. This was even true of patents, which go to the first inventor, and whose economic life is measured by the time it takes to find a better alternative. Given the multiplicity of Western enterprises, the possibility of forming new ones, and the possibility that old ones could shift to new activities, the process of gaining the rewards of innovative ideas takes on the characteristics of a race, informal but still competitive. The competitive nature of the process was intensified by the Western practice of leaving the losers to bear their own losses, which were often substantial. This use of a competitive spur to stimulate change was a marked departure from tradition, for societies and their rulers have almost always strongly resisted change unless it enhanced the ruler's own power and well-being" 23.

40.   Acker, 64. Original citation from *Det Fri Aktuelt* (Copenhagen), (December 2, 1989).

41.   "The Church's social doctrine *is not* a 'third way' between *liberal capitalism* and *Marxist collectivism*, nor even a possible alternative to other solutions less radically opposed to one another: rather, it constitutes a *category of its own*. Nor is it an *ideology*, but rather the *accurate formulation* of the results of a careful reflection on the complex realities of human existence, in society and in the international order, in the light of faith and of the Church's tradition. Its main aim is to *interpret* these realities, determining their conformity with or divergence from the lines of the Gospel teaching on man and his vocation, a vocation which is at once earthly and transcendent; its aim is thus *to guide* Christian

behavior. It therefore belongs to the field, not of *ideology*, but of *theology* and particularly of moral theology" (#41).

Further, Pope John Paul II insists that the "right of economic initiative" is essential to economic development. "It is a right which is important not only for the individual but also for the common good. Experience shows us that the denial of this right, or its limitation in the name of an alleged 'equality' of everyone in society, diminishes, or in practice absolutely destroys the spirit of initiative, that is to say, *the creative subjectivity of the citizen.*" *Sollicitudo rei socialis*, Vatican Translation, sec. 15.

42. Acker, 63. Original citation from *The Washington Post*, (November 30, 1989).

43. Acker, 63. From a speech of December 18, 1989.

44. Zhelyo Zhelev, cited in Acker, 64.

45. St. Thomas Aquinas writes, "Our will can reach higher than can our intelligence when we are confronted by things that are above us. Whereas our notions about moral matters, which are below man, are enlightened by a cognitive habit—for prudence informs the other moral virtues—when it comes to the divine virtues about God, a will-virtue, namely charity, informs the mind-virtue, namely faith." Disputations, *de Caritate* 3, *ad* 13, cited in *St. Thomas Aquinas: Philosophical Texts*, tr. and ed. Thomas Gilby (New York: Oxford University Press, 1960), p. 285.

46. "Mercy is supremely God's effectively rather than affectively. . . .The work of divine justice always presupposes the work of mercy and is founded thereon. Creatures have no rights except because of something pre-existing or pre-considered in them, and since we cannot go back and back, we must come to something founded on the sole generosity of the divine will, which is the ultimate end. . . .Mercy is the root in each and every divine work, and its virtue persists in everything that grows out of that, and even more

90

vehemently flourishes there. . . .the order of justice would be served by much less than in fact is granted by divine generosity, which far exceeds what is owing." St. Thomas Aquinas, *Summa Theologica*, I-I.21.3-4, cited in Gilby, pp. 116-117.

47.   The document goes on to say, "Whatever the forms of ownership may be, as adapted to the legitimate institutions of people according to diverse and changeable circumstances, attention must always be paid to the universal purpose for which created goods are meant. In using them, therefore, a man should regard his lawful possessions not merely as his own but also as a common property in the sense that they should accrue to the benefit of not only himself but of others." *Gaudium et spes*, sec. 69 in Joseph Gremillion, ed., *The Gospel of Peace and Justice* (Maryknoll, Orbis, 1976), p. 305.

48.   "The person who works desires not only due renumeration for his work; he also wishes that within the production process provision be made for him to be able to know that in his work, even on something that is owned in common, he is working 'for himself.' This awareness is extinguished within him in a system of excessive bureaucratic centralization, which makes the worker feel that he is just a cog in a huge machine moved from above, that he is for more reasons than one a mere production instrument rather than a true subject of work with an initiative of his own. . . . In the mind of St. Thomas Aquinas, this is the principal reason in favor of private ownership of the means of production. . . . The personalist argument still holds good both on the level of principles and on the practical level. If it is to be rational and fruitful, any socialization of the means of production must be made to ensure that in this kind of system also the human person can preserve his awareness of working 'for himself.'" *Laborem exercens*, sec. 15 in *Origins*, Vol. 11, No. 15 (September 24, 1981), p. 236. Compare Leo XIII in *Rerum novarum*: "Private possessions are clearly in accord with nature" sec. 15. "To own goods privately. . . is a right natural to man, and to exercise this right, especially in life in society, is not

only lawful, but clearly necessary" sec. 36. Pope Leo then quotes St. Thomas Aquinas: "It is lawful for man to own his own things. It is even necessary for human life." *Summa Theologica*, II-II.66.2.

49.　　Genesis 3:19.

50.　　"Whether we consider natural *Reason*, which tells us, that Men, being once born, have a right to their Preservation and consequently to Meat and Drink, and such other things, as Nature affords for their subsistence: or *Revelation*, which gives us an account of those Grants God made of the World to *Adam*, and to *Noah*, and his Sons, 'tis very clear, that God, as King *David* says, *Psal. CXV. xvi. has given the Earth to the Children of Men*, given it to Mankind in common." John Locke, *Two Treatises of Government*, ed. Peter Laslett (New York: New American Library, 1965), *Second Treatise*, sec. 25, 327. For an analysis of chapter 5 of Locke's *Second Treatise*, see Robert A. Goldwin, "A Reading of Locke's Chapter 'Of Property,'" in *Why Blacks, Women, and Jews are not Mentioned in the Constitution, and Other Unorthodox Views* (Washington, D.C.: The AEI Press, 1990), 99-109.

51.　　". . . he who appropriates land to himself by his labour, does not lessen but increase the common stock of mankind. For the provisions serving to the support of humane life, produced by one acre of inclosed and cultivated land, are (to speak much within compasse) ten times more, than those, which are yielded by an acre of land, of an equal richness, lying waste in common. . . .I have here rated the improved land very low in making its product but as ten to one, when it is much nearer an hundred to one." Locke, *Two Treatises*, 336.

52.　　"Whenever, in any country, the proprietor, generally speaking, ceases to be the improver, political economy has nothing to say in defense of private property, as there established. . . . When the 'sacredness of property' is talked of, it should always be remembered that any such sacredness does not belong in the same degree to landed property. No man made the land. It is the original inheritance of the whole species. Its appropriation is wholly a question of general expediency. When private property in land is not expedient, it is unjust. . . . Even in the case of cultivated land, a man whom, though only one among millions, the law permits to hold thousands of acres as his single share, is not entitled to think that all this is given to him to use and abuse, and deal with as if it concerned nobody but himself. . . . The rents of profits which he can obtain for it are at his sole disposal; but with regard to the land, in everything which he does with it, and in everything which he abstains from doing, he is morally bound, and should whenever the case admits, be legally compelled to make his interest and pleasure consistent with the public good." Mill, *Principles of Political Economy*, ed. Sir William Ashley (New York: Augustus M. Kelley, 1969), 231; 233-235.

53.   See Rev. Roger Heckel, S.J., *Self Reliance* (Vatican City: Pontifical Commission Justice and Peace, 1978): "Self-reliance does not project the idea of 'falling back upon oneself' or of isolation, but rather of a genuine return to the living subject and his/her dynamism. The connotation, therefore, is of an eminently positive nature. The full meaning of the concept appears less in the *noun* (self-reliance) and more in the *adjective* (self-reliant) coupled to the word *development* with which it finds its full meaning. . . .[Self-reliance] is of the same order as *freedom*. It is through voluntary and reasoned action that a people becomes aware of its own law of development and implements it as a vital capacity or power. Self-reliance would therefore be an internal vital principle which manifests its presence under the guise of a power. It is the ever-increasing capacity of a people to assume its past, decide upon its future, and, on a level of equality, contribute to the shaping of humankind and the universe of which it is part" (pp. 4-5).

54. According to a 1989 report by the Morgan Guarantee Trust Company, at the end of 1987 Latin American foreign investment was as follows: Brazil, $31 billion; Mexico, $84 billion; Venezuela, $58 billion; Argentina, $46 billion. According to Mark Falcoff, these amounts would cover the following percentages of foreign debt for each country if invested at home: Brazil, 30-40%; Mexico, 60%; and for Argentina and Venezuela, 100%.

55. "Foreign aid does not in fact go to the pitiable figures we see on aid posters, in aid advertisements, and in other aid propaganda in the media. It goes to the governments, that is to the rulers, and the policies of the rulers who receive aid are sometimes directly responsible for conditions such as those depicted. But even in less extreme instances, it is still the case that aid goes to the rulers; and their policies, including the pattern of public spending, are determined by their own personal and political interests, among which the position of the poorest has a very low priority." P.T. Bauer, *Reality and Rhetoric: Studies in the Economics of Development* (Cambridge, Massachusetts: Harvard University Press, 1984), p. 50.

56. Of one of his intellectual predecessors, Rorty approvingly notes, "Wittgenstein . . . cheerfully tosses out half-a-dozen incompatible metaphilosophical views in the course of the *Investigations."* *Consequences of Pragmatism* (Minneapolis: University of Minnesota Press, 1982), 23. Rorty draws an explicitly historicist consequence from this: "We Deweyan historicists. . .think that 'first principles' are abbreviations of, rather than justifications for a set of beliefs about the desirability of certain concrete alternatives over others; the source of those beliefs is not 'reason' or 'nature', but rather the prevalence of certain institutions or modes of life in the past." Richard Rorty, "That Old-Time Philosophy," *The New Republic* (April 4, 1988), 30. See also: "No specific doctrine is much of a danger, but the idea that democracy depends on adhesion to some such doctrine is."

Richard Rorty, "Taking Philosophy Seriously," *The New Republic* (April 11, 1988), 33.

57.   Schlesinger writes that "the American mind is by nature and tradition skeptical, irreverent, pluralistic and relativistic. . . .Our relative values are not matters of whim and happenstance. History has given them to us. They are anchored in our national experience, in our great national documents, in our national heroes, in our folkways, traditions, standards. Some of these values seem to us so self-evident that even relativists think they have, or ought to have, universal application: the right to life, liberty and the pursuit of happiness, for example; the duty to treat persons as ends in themselves; the prohibition of slavery, torture, genocide. People with different history will have different values. But we believe that our own are better for us. They work for us; and, for that reason, we live and die by them." Arthur Schlesinger, Jr., "The Opening of the American Mind," *New York Times Book Review* (July 23, 1989), 26. See my reply, "Relativism or Absolutes: Which is the American Way?" in *National Catholic Register* (October 29, 1989).

58.   Murray wrote, "The Catholic community faces the task of making itself intellectually aware of the conditions of its own co-existence within the American pluralistic scene. We have behind us a lengthy historical tradition of acceptance of the special situation of the church in America, in all its differences from the situations in which the Church elsewhere finds herself. But it is a question here of pursuing the subject, not in the horizontal dimension of history but in the vertical dimension of theory.

"The argument readily falls into two parts. The first part is an analysis of the American Proposition with regard to political unity. The effort is to make a statement . . . of the essential contents of the American consensus, whereby we are made '*e pluribus unum*,' one society subsisting amid multiple pluralisms. Simply to make this statement is to show why American Catholics participate with ready conviction in the American consensus. The

95

second part of the argument . . . is an analysis of the American Proposition with regard to religious pluralism, especially as the proposition is embodied in our fundamental law. Again, simply to make this analysis is to lay bare the reasons why American Catholics accept on principle the unique American solution to the age-old problem." John Courtney Murray, S.J., *We Hold These Truths* (New York: Sheed & Ward, 1960), 27-28.

And Maritain writes, "Not only does the democratic state of mind stem from the inspiration of the Gospel, but it cannot exist without it. To keep faith in the forward march of humanity despite all the temptations to despair of man that are furnished by history, and particularly contemporary history; to have faith in the dignity of the person and of common humanity, in human rights and in justice—that is, in essentially spiritual values; to have, not in formulas but in reality, the sense of and respect for the dignity of the people, which is a spiritual dignity and is revealed to whoever knows how to love it; to sustain and revive the sense of equality without sinking into egalitarianism; to respect authority, knowing that its wielders are only men, like those they rule, and derive their trust from the consent or the will of the people whose vicars or representatives they are; to believe in the sanctity of law and in the efficacious virtue—efficacious at long range—of political justice in face of the scandalous triumphs of falsehood and violence; to have faith in liberty and in fraternity, and heroical inspiration and an heroical belief are needed which fortify and vivify reason, and which none other than Jesus of Nazareth brought forth in the world." Jacques Maritain, Christianity and Democracy (New York: Charles Scribner's Sons, 1950), 59-60.

59.   "Freedom of religion and of thought and of speech were achieved by denying both to the state and to the established church a sovereign monopoly in the field of religion, philosophy, morals, science, learning, opinion and conscience. The liberal constitutions, with their bills of rights, fixed the boundaries past which the sovereign—the King, the Parliament, the Congress, the voters—were forbidden to go.

"Yet the men of the seventeenth and eighteenth centuries who established these great salutary rules would certainly have denied that a community could do without a general public philosophy. They were themselves the adherents of a public philosophy—of the doctrine of natural law, which held that there was law 'above the ruler and the sovereign people . . . above the whole community of morals'." Walter Lippmann, *The Public Philosophy* (New York: New American Library, 1956), 76; 77-78.

60. For example, contrast these two views: Prof. David Hollenbach, S.J. writes, "The thesis proposed here is that Catholic teaching on human rights today presupposes a reconstruction of the classical liberal understanding of what these rights are. The pivot on which this reconstruction turns is the traditional natural law conviction that the human person is an essentially social being. Catholic thought and action in the human rights sphere, in other words, are rooted in a communitarian alternative to classical liberal human rights theory. At the same time, by adopting certain key ideas about constitutional democracy originally developed by classical liberalism, recent Catholic thought has brought about a notable new development of the longer tradition of the church while simultaneously offering an alternative to the standard liberal theory of democratic government." David Hollenbach, S.J., "A Communitarian Reconstruction of Human Rights: Contributions from Catholic Tradition," (unpublished paper prepared for a project on "Liberalism, Catholicism, and American Public Philosophy," at the Woodstock Theological Center, Georgetown University, forthcoming in a book published by Fr. Hollenbach), 2.

Cf. Prof. Ernest Fortin, A.A.: "For centuries, the cornerstone of Catholic moral theology was not the natural or human *rights* doctrine but something quite different, called the natural *law*. Rights, to the extent that they were mentioned at least by implication, were contingent on the fulfillment of prior duties.

. . . Simply stated, what the church taught and tried to inculcate was an ethic of virtue as distinct from an ethic of rights. . . .

"The bishops may have confused some of their readers by using language that looks in two different directions at once: that of rights or freedom on the one hand, and of virtue, character formation, and the common good on the other. They would certainly be ill-advised to give up their vigorous defense of rights, especially since the pseudomorphic collapse of Neo-Thomism in the wake of Vatican II has left them without any alternative on which to fall back; but they have yet to tell us, or tell us more clearly, how the two ends are supposed to meet." Ernest L. Fortin, A.A., "The Trouble with Catholic Social Thought," *Boston College Magazine* (Summer 1988): 38; 42.

61.   Even so, Jacques Maritain reminds us that we need not be completely despairing. Every age sees itself as falling off in morals (*"O Tempora, O Mores"*). Yet in a chapter called "The Old Tag of American Materialism," Maritain says, "The American people are the least materialist among the modern peoples which have attained the industrial stage. . . .

"Americans like to give. . . . Not only the great foundations, but the ordinary course of activity of American institutions and the innumerable American private groups show us that the ancient Greek and Roman idea of the *civis praeclarus*, the dedicated citizen who spends his money in the service of the common good, plays an essential part in American consciousness. And let me observe that more often than not the gifts in question are made for the sake of education and knowledge. Frequently people who were unable to have a college education make large gifts to universities.

"There is no materialism, I think, in the astonishing countless initiatives of fraternal help which are the daily bread of the American people, or in the profound feeling of obligation toward others which exists in them, especially toward any people abroad who are in distress. . . .

"There is no materialism in the fact that the American charities, drawing money from every purse, and notably to assist people abroad, run every year into such enormous sums that charity ranks among the largest American industries, the second or third in size, according to statisticians. . . . Let us not forget what an immense amount of personal attention to one's neighbor and what personal effort is unceasingly put forth in all the groups which exist in this country, and which spring up every day, to meet some particular human misfortune or some particular social maladjustment. . . .

"There is a perpetual self-examination and self-criticism going on everywhere and in every sphere of American life; a phenomenon incomprehensible without a quest for truth of which a materialist cast of mind is incapable." Jacques Maritain, *Reflections on America* (New York: Charles Scribner's Sons, 1958), 29-30; 34-35; 36; 38.

62. See Hernando de Soto, *The Other Path* (New York: Harper & Row, 1989), 13. In Peru, "48 percent of the economically active population and 61.2 percent of work hours are devoted to informal activities which contribute 38.9 percent of the gross domestic product recorded in the national accounts" (12). "Informals have managed to gain control of 93 percent of the urban transport fleet" (13).

63. Heilbroner goes on to write, "The Soviet Union, China and Eastern Europe have given us the clearest possible proof that capitalism organizes the material affairs of humankind more satisfactorily than socialism: that however inequitably or irresponsibly the marketplace may deliver the goods, it does so better than the queues of a planned economy. . . . Indeed, it is difficult to observe the changes taking place in the world today and not conclude that the nose of the capitalist camel has been pushed so far under the socialist tent that the great question now seems how rapid will be the transformation of socialism into capitalism, and not the other way around as things looked only a half century

ago." Robert Heilbroner, "Reflections: The Triumph of Capitalism," *The New Yorker* (January 23, 1989), 98.

64.   As I have said elsewhere, "The market, then, is a social device for achieving the common good. Alone, the market cannot attain the *whole* common good. It is a device chiefly of the economic order, which is, in turn, only a part of political economy. Many constituent parts of the common good can only be supplied outside of markets. More than markets can accomplish cannot be asked of them. On the other hand, matched with institutions of invention and innovation, no economic institution has ever succeeded better in raising up so many of the poor. None has generated a higher standard of living, brought about a more regular and swifter circulation of elites, or inspired more extensive creativity. Its founders intended a market order based upon invention and patents to excel in its achievement of the common good. That was the experiment. In promoting the general welfare, measured empirically against what has been achieved by other systems, the market system based upon creative invention has no peer. In that respect, the common good has been a basic underlying criterion for measuring both its successes and its failures. The new concept of the common good does not require intentions, but it does require achievements. It does not require the perfect, but only the greater, good. Its essence is to establish an order promoting the free cooperation of all, for the benefit of all, among those who are not saints. . . .

"If we had to prove that markets are perfect instruments of the common good, we could not. But we do not have to do so. All that is required is to show that markets, however imperfect, are better social instruments for their limited purposes than any other known alternatives, traditionalist or socialist; and that their deficiencies may be made up through supplementary agencies of the polity and culture." Michael Novak, *Free Persons and the Common Good* (Lanham, Md.: Madison Books, 1989), 108-109.

100

65. See Michael Novak, *The New Consensus on Family and Welfare* (Milwaukee: Marquette University, 1987).

66. "The 1984 survey by the Bureau of Labor Statistics, based on complete income figures submitted by several thousand nationally representative households, shows that the poorest 20 percent of households had average reported income before taxes of $3,200 and annual expenditures of $10,800. U.S. Department of Labor, Bureau of Labor Statistics, *1984 Consumer Expenditure Survey* (pamphlet)." *New Consensus*, 70.

67. David Popenoe has recently written, "The Swedish marriage rate is now the lowest in the industrialized world, and the average age at first marriage is probably the highest. The rate of nonmarital cohabitation, or consensual unions, outranks that of all other advanced nations; such unions, rather than being a mere prelude to marriage (as is more often the case in the United States now), have become a parallel institution alongside legal marriage. About 25 percent of all couples in Sweden today are living in consensual unions (up from 1 percent in 1960), compared with about 5 percent in the United States. The growth of nonmarital cohabitation among childbearing couples has given Sweden one of the highest percentages of children born out of wedlock in the industrial world—over 50 percent of all children, compared with about 22 percent in the United States."

Popenoe adds, "There is one thing about growing up in Sweden today that should give pause even to those sympathetic to the welfare state. There is a strong likelihood that the family has grown weaker there than anywhere else in the world. What has happened to the family in Sweden over the past few decades lends strong support to the proposition that as the welfare state advances, the family declines. If unchecked, this decline could eventually undermine the very welfare that the state seeks to promote.

"The modern welfare state was founded with the goal of helping families to function better as decentralized welfare agencies. It sought to strengthen families, not to weaken them.

101

Over time, however, welfare states have increasingly tended not so much to assist families as to replace them; people's dependence on the state has grown while their reliance on families has weakened. In a classic illustration of the law of unintended consequences, the family under the welfare state is gradually losing both the ability and the will to care for itself." David Popenoe, "Family Decline in the Swedish Welfare State," in *The Public Interest* No. 102 (Winter 1991): 66; 65-66.

68.   "Today a significant population of able, nonelderly adults stay on welfare for more than two years (and sometimes for more than one intermittent spell). Rather than supporting the elderly and the young [who cannot enter the labor force], they themselves are long-term dependents." *New Consensus*, 58-59. This is based on data presented by Mary Jo Bane and David Ellwood in a paper prepared for the assistant secretary for planning and evaluation, Department of Health and Human Services. They say, "Fewer than half the women who go onto AFDC are off within two years. Of those who remain into the third year, 60 percent will be on at least six years." *New Consensus*, 68.

69.   "The dependency of the 5 million or so who are in that situation [both poor and concentrated in cities in which 20 percent of the population is also poor], is of a depth not exhausted by the catch-all phrase 'below the poverty line.' *New Consensus*, 25-26. This is based on data presented by Richard P. Nathan, in "The Underclass: Will It Always Be With Us?" (Presented at the New School for Social Research, November 14, 1986). On the underclass in Britain, Charles Murray explains, "'Underclass' is an ugly word, with its whiff of Marx and the lumpenproletariat. Perhaps because it is ugly, 'underclass' as used in Britain tends to be sanitised, a sort of synonym for people who are not just poor, but especially poor. So let us get it straight from the outset: the 'underclass' does not refer to degree of poverty, but to type of poverty.

102

"It is not a new concept. I grew up knowing what the underclass was; we just didn't call it that in those days. In the small Iowa town where I lived, I was taught by my middle-class parents that there were two kinds of poor people. One class of poor people was never even called 'poor.' I came to understand that they simply lived with low incomes, as my own parents had done when they were young. Then there was another set of poor people, just a handful of them. These poor people didn't lack just money. They were defined by their behaviour. Their homes were littered and unkept. The men in the family were unable to hold a job for more than a few weeks at a time. Drunkenness was common. The children grew up ill-schooled and ill-behaved and contributed a disproportionate share of the local juvenile delinquents." Charles Murray, *The Emerging British Underclass* (London: The IEA Health and Welfare Unit, 1990), p. 1.

70. See Charles Murray with Deborah Laren, "According to Age: Longitudinal Profiles of AFDC Recipients and the Poor by Age Group," (paper presented at the Working Seminar on the Family and American Welfare Policy, Washington, D.C., September 23, 1986). Murray cites a Michigan study which shows that of all men ages 20 to 64 who had completed high school—with no more education—less than 1 percent are poor.

71. Larry Mead, "The Work Problem in Workfare," (paper presented at the Working Seminary on the Family and American Welfare Policy). "For example, the poverty rate for black families with no workers, is 69 percent; with one worker, 35 percent; with two workers, 8 percent. Clearly, work is an effective path out of poverty, and the number of workers per family matters a great deal." *New Consensus*, 59.

72. Guy Sorman, *Barefoot Capitalism: A Solution for India* (New Delhi: Vikas Publishing [Distributed by Advent Books, New York], 1989).

The Influence of Aquinas' Natural Law Theory on the Principle of "Corporatism" in the Thought of Leo XIII and Pius XI

John E. Kelly

Through a close attention to a relatively succinct set of texts in St. Thomas' *Summa Theologiae* pertaining to private ownership, it can be shown that there is found there a more radical approach to private property than is commonly appreciated. In addition, it can be demonstrated that, Leo XIII, and especially Pius XI, were able to draw upon the insights of Aquinas in an attempt to forge organic links and common bonds at every level of industry. Their encouragement of mutual interrelatedness was meant to foster a more holistic view of labor, man and the state. Pius pursued the theme more fully than Leo. What Pius envisioned above all else from the state and from its citizens, was that men should see beyond class conflict and create and foster harmony between "vocational groups." He employed this term to encourage a sense of calling and common allegiance through every level of industry to promote the common welfare.

In his reflections on the occasion of the tenth anniversary of the encyclical *Pacem in terris*, Cardinal Maurice Roy raises this question: Is the term and concept "natural law" still valid and useful for today's social teaching? "For today," Roy asserts, "this idea of nature is very much questioned, if not rejected." Also, use of the term can erroneously lead to "a strict parallel between man and his morality and biological laws and behavior." In fact, the very content of "nature" as forbidding or permitting human acts, presents problems.

> This concept seems too "essentialist" to the people of our time, who challenge as being a relic of Greek philosophy, the term "Natural Law," which they consider

anachronistic, conservative and defensive. They object further that the expression was defined arbitrarily and once and for all in a subjective and Western manner, and is therefore one-sided and lacking in any moral authority for the universal conscience.[1]

According to the school of thought that considers this term "essentialist" and defined "once and for all," "natural law" seems to have meant an objective moral code complete in all details and needing merely to be discovered by the human mind.

Roy's remarks reflect the view of many contemporary writers both within and outside the tradition that the Second Vatican Council marks, perhaps, the end of the period in which Thomistic natural law theories served as the central guiding thread of Catholic social thought. Paul Sigmund, for example, notes the negative response of Jacques Maritain in *The Peasant of the Garone* to the new theology of the 1960's. Further still, by the time of Pope Paul VI's writing of *Populorum progressio*, one is struck by the absence of the vocabulary of natural law employed in earlier papal documents. A case might also be made for the thesis that "the ecumenism which was encouraged by the Council also resulted in an increased attention to the bases of Catholic social thought in scripture and the early church which echoed Protestant criticisms of the corruption of the Christian message resulting from the introduction of Greco-Roman elements."[2]

Yet a careful reading of St. Thomas on this subject indicates that he viewed the natural law as not of itself a complete and completely detailed rule of human action. Aquinas writes:

> The end is fixed for man by nature. But the means to the end are not determined for us by nature but are to be investigated by reason (*Finis autem determinatus est homini a natura... Ea autem quae sunt ad finem non sunt nobis determinata a natura sed per rationem investiganda*).[3]

105

According to Aristotle and St. Thomas, the subject matter is such that we cannot deduce detailed, specific conclusions with certitude.[4] St. Thomas recommends that we examine the nature of practical knowledge by contrasting it with analytical reasoning. Mathematics, mathematical reasoning, is the best example of analytic reasoning. In contrast with mathematics, both metaphysics and moral philosophy must proceed from the things that are most known to us, the sensible things of experience.[5]

In spite of texts that do more than suggest that Aquinas laid down the principles of a synthesis between deduction and experience, both Thomistic theory and practice in the field of ethics still appear to many Thomists and non Thomists alike to be "essentialist," in the sense of analytico - deductive. For example, Monsignor Joseph Gremillion, in his anthology of Catholic social teaching since Pope John XXIII argues that the aggiornamento moves "from a relatively *static* (emphasis mine) view of man's nature and reason toward human rights and fulfillment of human capacities promoted by man's innate worth."[6]

Cardinal Roy in his study of *Pacem in terris* emphasizes, however, that John XXIII loses nothing of the authentic spirit of Thomistic natural law theory and is not a party to the caricature of this doctrine on the part of so many critics. He writes:

> Although the term 'nature' does in fact lend itself to serious misunderstanding, the reality intended has lost nothing of its forcefulness when it is replaced by modern synonyms (almost all of which are to be found in the Encyclical). Such synonyms are: man, human being, conscience, humaneness (in conduct), the struggle for justice, and more recently, the duty of being, the quality of life.[7]

The words used, Roy concludes, can be left aside. What continues to remain relevant is that "in this nature individuals and peoples all have a common denominator, a 'common good' of man. This does not signify a simple label nor a mere compromise but a "basic and existential reality."[8]

106

Now it may be, as Roy insists, that the reality intended by the term nature or natural law has lost nothing of its forcefulness. However, the soundness of the "reality intended" has been seriously questioned. Indeed, one of the *periti* at the Council, while commenting on the natural law basis of the papal position on birth control, commented that "while I affirm the reality called 'natural law' it seems to me that it is neither natural nor law."[9]

It is quite clear that the papal condemnation on artificial birth control, principally on natural law grounds, has been one of the chief reasons for the resistance to the teleological underpinnings of natural law theory. An unfortunate outcome, however, has been that, instead of approaching the birth control issue as just one example of the dilemmas which will continually arise when dealing with secondary precepts of the natural law, there has been the tendency to approach all natural law concepts as excessively abstract and out of touch with the needs of the human person as a whole. Included in this deemphasis of natural law theory has been a neglect of Thomistic formulations of Christian social and political theory.

The judgment that St. Thomas' moral theory is "static" and "essentialist" would seem to imply that man's moral life is reduced to a passive, legalistic submission to a number of prefabricated rules. This interpretation places most of its emphasis on law and obligation, seeing these as elements external to man and having a compelling force that pays little attention to man's moral autonomy.

But if this is the authentic teaching of Aquinas with regard to man's moral life, there seems to be something surprising about the way St. Thomas opens the Second Part of the *Summa Theologiae* (the moral part as he calls it). He writes:

> Now that we have treated of the exemplar,
> i.e., God, and of those things which come
> forth from the power of God in accordance
> with His will, it remains for us to treat of
> His image, i.e., man, in as much as he too
> is the principle of his actions, as having free
> choice and the authority to govern himself [10]

107

It has been noted that Aquinas does not refer in this text to our freedom under God, but rather he prefers to speak of man as like God, like God's image. And we are "in God's image" because we too are originators of our own acts.[11] Aquinas holds that everyone has a natural inclination to do what he/she understands to be morally good. For example, once one understands that taking steps to cooperate with others is morally good, one will be inclined to prescribe it to oneself (e.g., let me seek to cooperate with others in community).[12]

The core of St. Thomas' theory of natural law is to be found in the use he makes of the Aristotelian belief in immanent purpose in nature. Unlike Aristotle, however, Thomistic natural law recognizes a provident God who creates purposefully. In doing so, God not only causes creatures to be. He causes them to be in the specific ways in which they exist and orders them to their specific goals. Providence is described in this context as a *rational* governance of created things, and rational creatures are said to share in divine reason "whereby it has a natural inclination to its proper act and end."[13] He considers: first, the goals or needs which he has in common with all substances to strive to preserve their being; second, the goals in common with animals, i.e., sex and protection and development of the family; and third, the goals or needs which are distinctive of rational creatures alone, *viz.* to know the truth and to cooperate with others in society. Each person by nature, then, inclines toward certain completive acts of his/her human nature; e.g., preserving his/her life, sexual union, and development of certain social abilities.

Practical reason, on understanding these objects to be the kind of things to which all human beings incline prescribes the pursuit of these completive, and hence morally good acts; for in our analysis of the meaning of a "morally good act" we are led to an understanding of these acts as conducive to the development of human nature. How do we know what kinds of acts are conducive to the development of human nature? We look at what kinds of things all human beings incline to. If all human beings incline, for example, toward social integration, then development of social capacities is completive of human nature. Practical reason, on understanding these objects to be perfective of our nature articulates "primary precepts of the natural law; e.g., we are able to arrive at judgments such as: "let me seek to preserve my life, or, "furthering the development of everyone's social capacities is a morally good act." As with the case of the absolutely first principle of practical reason (seek what is good, avoid what is evil), man can assent to the primary precepts of the natural law without having recourse to elaborate investigation. All men with the use of reason do assent to the precepts upon understanding the precepts' terms.[14]

> And so it is clear that moral precepts pertain to good morals; good morals are such as are in harmony with reason; and every judgment of human reason flows in some way from natural reason. Hence, it follows that all moral precepts belong to the law of nature, but in different ways. For there are some that are immediately judged to be done or not to be done by the natural reason of every man.... Others need a more subtle consideration of reason.[15]

Aquinas does not elaborate on the differences between the types of conclusions that can be drawn immediately, and those which demand further analysis; but some examples can be developed from his reasoning regarding the distinction between self-evident general principles "which need no further promulgation after being once imprinted on the natural reason" and "those which the careful reflection of wise men shows to be in accord with reason."[16] According to the principles of practical reason, human evil is to be avoided, and humans should act reasonably toward the others with whom they are naturally inclined to live. From these principles, one can conclude with little reflection to the general norm, not to steal. But it takes considerably more reflection to decide when a particular situation justifies stealing. For example, in his treatment of the right use of property, St. Thomas argues that in cases of "urgent and blatant necessity," the right of private ownership reverts to common possession. The condemnation of theft presupposes the legitimacy of private property. However, the issue of when precisely private property is no longer legitimate, and who is in a situation of desperate need, demands considerable reflection, as well as, perhaps, character formation, before a decision can be reached.[17]

> When a person is in some imminent danger,
> and there is no other possible remedy, then
> it is lawful for a man to succor his own
> need by means of another's property, by
> taking it either openly or secretly; nor is this
> properly speaking theft or robbery.[18]

A second example comes to mind from a consideration of the primary precept that "one must seek to preserve all human life." Little reflection is needed to draw the conclusion that it is wrong to take innocent human life without cause. But to define "innocent human life" requires considerable analysis and deliberation on contingencies, as anyone can testify who has struggled over the dilemmas surrounding abortion and euthanasia. A concluding example can be drawn from a consideration of St. Thomas' primary precept that "humans ought to take reasonable means to cooperate with others in the community." From this principle, reason can conclude to a general judgment that one must treat equals equally. Yet considerable determination is required as to how the principle of justice that demands equal treatment for equals is to be applied in a particular social context. In 1896, for example, the Supreme Court, in Plessy v. Ferguson, held that equal but separate facilities—segregated black and white restrooms in railroad stations—conformed perfectly to the Fourteenth Amendment's mandate that all citizens of the United States be accorded the equal protection of the law. It took considerable development of the conscience of the American people before the Warren Court finally annulled laws requiring segregated facilities.

In St. Thomas' view of moral reasoning, then, we must distinguish between the first principles of the practical order, the judgments arrived at by a simple application of these same principles to human actions, and the judgments made in dependence upon a full consideration of diverse and changeable circumstances. None of these judgments is arrived at by purely deductive processes.[19] It is true that the nature of man can be found by a reflective inspection and analysis of his activities, culminating in an intellectual insight that man is a rational animal, a being composed of body and soul. And by an examination of man's nature and activities, the essential ends of that activity can be found. From them, the primary precepts of the natural law might be said to be deduced. But the secondary principles, with their wide range and varying degrees of remoteness from the primary precepts, are not reached by a purely deductive process. They depend largely upon observational or experiential procedures. The process of derivation is not a strictly logical or deductive one, but involves the use of *synderesis* or direct moral intuition to arrive at basic principles. *Synderesis* entails also the exercise of practical reason to apply those principles to varying and contingent circumstances.

> Wherefore the first practical principles, bestowed on us by nature, do not belong to a special power, but to a special natural habit, which we call *synderesis*. Whence *synderesis* is said to incite to good, and to murmur at evil, in as much as through first principles we proceed to discover, and judge of what we have discovered.[20]

For example, in the field of social and economic activities, the social thinker must therefore take account of his own limitations as a man, the concrete situation, and social determinations. He must develop his ethical insight by his own mature and balanced appraisal of the ever varying social setting. [21]

St. Thomas' approach to natural law is, then, not the "deductivist-static" theory suggested by many critics. For Aquinas, there are two ways of deriving something from the natural law—one way, like conclusions from principles, the other, like certain determinations of common principles.

> Every human law has just so much of the nature of law, as it is derived from the law of nature. But if in any point it deflects from the law of nature, it is no longer a law but

111

> a perversion of law. But it must be noted
> that something may be derived from the
> natural law in two ways: first, as
> conclusions from premises, secondly by way
> of determination of certain generalities.[22]

It is precisely through this second mode of derivation that modern popes, such as Leo XIII and Pius XI, have applied the natural law doctrine to the content of the right of private property. The right to private property is a relative right, relative to man's historical condition. Except for the fall, private ownership would not be necessary. It is not an institution of natural law in the strict sense. Yet it is not opposed to natural law, but added to it through the discovery of human reason. The basis for the right of propriety ownership is found in human convention, *jus gentium*, and in positive law.[23]

> Community of goods is ascribed to the
> natural law, not that the natural law dictates
> that all things should be possessed in
> common and that nothing should be
> possessed as one's own, but because the
> division of possession is not according to the
> natural law, but rather arose from human
> agreement which belongs to positive law....
> Hence the ownership of possessions is not
> contrary to the natural law, but an addition
> thereto devised by human reason.[24]

In the secunda secundae, articles 1, 2, and 7, Aquinas argues that man has natural dominion over things "because by his reason and will, he is able to use them for his own profit, as they were made on his account."[25] Property is considered an "indispensable external field" giving scope to man's creativity. He reinforces his argument by adding that man becomes an image of God through his stewardship over the earth's resources.[26]

In question 66, article 2, Aquinas emphasizes that man has indeed two rights in regard to the possession of exterior things. The one right, the right of ownership is confined to questions of production and exchange. In this respect man is permitted to possess things as his own.

> Two things are competent to man in respect of exterior things. One is the power to procure and dispense them (procurandi et dispensandi)[27]

The second right concerns the use of possessions; and in this context we ought not to hold things privately but as common property in order to share them freely with others in their need.[28] This sharing of our holdings with the needy is not a matter of choice. It is an obligation deriving from natural law, and resting upon those who have a superabundance of the world's goods (res,quas aliquid superabunter habent, ex naturali jure, debenter pauperum sustentationi). The reason for this is that according to natural law, this use by man of the earth and its resources results from the subordination of the less perfect to the more perfect. And private ownership, an institution of human law cannot go counter to the natural law. Hence, in necessity, all things must exist as shared.[29]

It has been noted that this use of the earth's resources by man is indeed a use rather than enjoyment strictly so called, it is a uti rather than a frui, it is the order of means and not of ends, since the cultivation or development of the earth's resources is a means to man's fulfillment as a whole.[30] Aquinas' central focus regarding the relative advantage of private ownership, therefore, is not dominion over things, or the right to ownership, but rather the proper use of things, namely virtue, i.e., human development. Private ownership is necessary because it serves the end of human development better than common ownership. Whether it is the question of the universal right to use, or the restricted right to proprietary possession, what is uppermost in Aquinas' thought is the human end of property.

In his *Commentary on the Politics*, Aquinas will emphasize that the details of such a system for the common use of property would have to be worked out by the "good legislator."[31] It is the responsibility of the good legislator to craft laws which will provide the means for its citizens to live virtuously and happily.[32] It is precisely for this reason that Aristotle and

113

St. Thomas have referred to the state as a "perfect society." Unity and peace will be achieved when society is organized around man, his ends and the vital tasks of his self fulfillment. Each individual must be provided the scope to participate in building up this social order. This social order begins to deteriorate when the citizen's social participation in the life of the community is restricted to a merely passive and subservient role and he/she is deprived of any active and constructive part in shaping the life of the community, political as well as industrial. Pope John—Paul II would appear to be echoing the concerns of Aquinas in *Centesimus annus* when he writes:

> The individual today is often suffocated between two poles represented by the state and the market place. At times it seems as though he exists only as a producer and consumer of goods, or as an object of state administration. People lose sight of the fact that life in society has neither the market nor the state as its final purpose, since life itself has a unique value which the state and the market must serve.[33]

Catholic views on the right ordering of society, then, tend to focus on a commitment to certain fundamental values—the right to human dignity, the need for human freedom and participation, as well as the importance of community and the nature of the common good.[34]

According to many Catholics who wrote on the social question in the nineteenth century, these fundamental values were being undermined by the *laissez-faire* varieties of capitalism which obscured the reality of labor and capital's mutual dependence and thereby left the industrial worker isolated in an environment that offered them marginal subsistence and periodic unemployment. To many Catholic social thinkers who were writing at this time, there were two great enemies of the true, Christian social order: 1) They claimed that the liberal, secular and individualistic spirit of the French Revolution had undermined the political and spiritual foundations of the old Christian order. Society no longer was conceived

114

as a living organic entity, much like the human body with a head and diverse members, but rather as simply an aggregate of individuals, each going his/her own way. 2) In addition, the commercial and industrial revolutions had swept away the independent, self-sufficient artisan class of the Middle Ages and had destroyed the guilds which had protected its status and privileges. With the autonomy enjoyed by the guilds, there developed provision for direct worker representation in the control and operation of the economy, with limited supervision by the state. A contemporary analogy would be "some kind of tripartite entente of government, business, and labor unions" with a view to reducing class conflict.[35]

It is important to grasp the character of this social concern. It was not a simple interest in the poor. That had been a characteristic of the church in every epoch. What was needed under industrialism was not only a concern for poverty, but a program to deal with its causes. The concept of justice, as well as charity, would have to be incorporated into any political theory that would meet effectively the social problems in the industrial world.

There were a variety of suggestions as to how the essentially social and communal aspects of the economic system might be restored. Some Catholic thinkers continued to be supportive of classical economic liberalism. Charles Périn, for example, argued that all that was needed to assure a responsible capitalist social structure was the moral reform of the individual.[36] He accepted the principle of association, but saw no reason for a return to the medieval craft guilds:

> The guilds had their day of greatness and prosperity in the Middle Ages; and to attempt to revive them now, with privileges and powers of constraint such as they enjoyed then, would be to engage in an impossible struggle against the deepest convictions of the society of our own day.[37]

115

The type of association favored by Périn was the religious confraternity, which would serve to provide the religious training and encouragement needed to more actively participate in the political and economic system.

Other Catholics maintained that moral reform of the individual, though necessary, was not sufficient. They argued that the economic system itself should be changed in favor of the social and economic structures of the Middle Ages, when a mass of autonomous groups flourished and when functional self-government was held to be essential for a truly free society. This movement toward a return to the medieval guilds developed into an ideology called "corporatism." But its advocates were by no means in agreement as to how precisely the medieval guild structure should be applied to the contemporary political and economic scene.

Emile Keller, for example, suggested that it would be necessary to go beyond simply the formation of worker's associations, and of promoting among employers a spirit of justice and charity. If the workers were to be really free, "they would have to possess some property, whether as individuals or in a corporative way."[38] Some type of joint control in the economy might be shared, for example, between unions of workers and employers.

Influenced by such ideas, Albert de Mun launched a corporative program to encourage groups of employers and of workers to study how to advance the interests of the trade. He argued for unions of employers and workers who would be joined in a single body for the defense of moral and material interests under the guidance of the church. Initiative would come largely from the employers. These would enjoy a privileged status in public law and would be closely associated with the state. Along with these "mixed unions" would be larger groupings in religious associations in which all the members of the worker's families would participate and which would provide a wide variety of social, educational, and moral services. Funds for the associations would be provided by dues from the workers and contributions of the wealthy, since their possessions obligate them to charity. The driving spirit of "this new corporation" is captured in remarks made by Père Marquigny, chaplain to the associations formed by de Mun, when he offered his judgment of the work being done by the corporative groups:

116

This arrangement is in accordance with Catholic thought in coordinating management with association. The dependence of each upon his fellow which is here established, embraces the whole man, morally and materially. When the corporation is so ordered and unites a body of workers belonging to the same craft, where the employer who must take the lead in the world of labor, finds that position which is naturally his, the present will have nothing whatsoever to learn from the past.[39]

Implied here was the belief that, with the formation of these associations, men spontaneously would grasp the objective need for rules of social cooperation, and that they would more or less automatically come to embrace the ideals of human solidarity.

Other corporatists advocated a more radical social and political transformation. They did not restrict the movement to particular crafts or an industry. Influential corporatists such as René de la Tour du Pin advocated implementing the "corporative" plan for the reorganization of society as a whole."[40] La Tour du Pin's ideas came closest perhaps to state corporatism. In his vision of a corporative system, the associations of workers and employers in the separate trades or industries would enjoy semi-autonomous political and judicial rights, powers, and privileges.

In coordination with the state the corporative groups would have the responsibility of regulating prices as well as wages for their own protection. The employers were to be in control and were to paternalistically guide their workers for their own good. These institutions were to replace both the liberal, democratic parliaments which were developing in Europe at that time as well as the capitalist system. The corporation rather than individuals would own all property. They would regulate political and social relationships between members and would meet in a larger corporate parliament to decide issues concerning the whole nation. Short of this radical social and political transformation, many Catholics held that no social reform was possible.

It would appear that La Tour du Pin stood alone in insisting that true reform could come only by a radical alteration of the status quo. Albert de Mun, for example proposed that "corporative groups" be given official recognition in order to be able to more effectively act as intermediaries between individuals and society. But he did not expect that his "corporative regime" should have responsibility for every facet of the socio-economic structure. He was confident that social legislation could play a decisive role in social reform, provided that laws were enacted in keeping with "the spirit of association" of the old craft guilds. He writes:

> A start for justice for the people will be given by those who are able to enact laws which will respect the divine law, protect the weak, curb competition, prevent excessive demands on labor, and give back to workers, in their Sunday rest, the means of safeguarding their souls and their bodies. There, gentlemen, in this threefold concord of managerial responsibility, guild organization and social legislation, we have a social system which will bring peace to the world of labor and open up for our country a destiny far different from that of the revolutionary disorder into which we are now sinking.[41]

Although the various advocates of corporatism differed significantly with regard to the exact blueprint for social reform, there could be found common patterns of agreement. The movement encouraged a spirit of solidarity through formal association of the parties who worked in and benefitted from the economy. It would be a free association, but one which the state recognized. One of its major functions would be to bring together employers and workers to overcome the mistrusts of class conflict. The tendency toward mistrust would be overcome, it was thought, because the corporative associations provided for a pluralism of social actors. Higher levels would not usurp the authority of lower levels except when necessary.

> They will reestablish a family bond between employers and workers and teach them in the contracts by which they are bound together there are more duties and obligations than the exchange of a wage against an agreed work task.... Such an association will work against and defeat mistrust, strengthen the spirit of solidarity, give protection against the willfulness of malcontents and threats of disaffection and open the way to comfort and future security.[42]

It was within this context of intellectual debate and efforts at setting up reformed social institutions that Leo XIII made public his opinions on the corporatist movements. Leo was greatly impressed by the writings of Bishop Wilhelm Emmanuel von Ketteler of the German diocese of Mainz. Ketteler began as an extreme corporatist, but came to support a reform of the existing system. Reform would entail a respect for the spirit of the medieval guilds. He pointed back to the Middle Ages when the autonomy of spontaneously formed social groups, such as towns, guilds, and religious associations, were not mere creatures of the state, but were real entities anterior to the state. Bishop Ketteler taught 19th century clerics and laymen that "the state had the duty of furnishing by means of legislation the necessary assistance to the working class in organizing a corporative structure in which the new corporations would enjoy autonomy within their respective spheres."[43]

In *Humanum genus*, Leo recommended the establishment of worker guilds to better the condition of the working classes. He saw the need for associations of this kind to restore organic links between workers, management, and the different levels of government. Leo writes:

If our ancestors, by long use and experience, felt the benefit of these guilds, our age perhaps will feel it the more by reason of the opportunity which they will give by crushing the power of the sects.[44]

As to the specific form that the new associations might take, Leo remained neutral.

...Some opportune remedy must be found quickly for the misery and wretchedness pressing so unjustly on the majority of the working class: for the ancient working man's guilds were abolished in the last century and no protective organization took their place.[45]

Leo was unwilling to lay down a specific form that the association might take. It has been noted that the Pope had apparently given support to the "mixed unions" of employers and employees advocated by the corporatists. Yet he always added qualifications, such as, "at least in regard to their substance...and under such forms as the new conditions of the time permit." But by the time of the writing of *Rerum novarum* there can be found an appreciation of the need also for strictly voluntary professional working-class organization with a limited role of the state in directing them. What was uppermost in the pope's mind was that such private associations could be an excellent means to "re-knit the connecting tissues of a society which individuals had reduced to isolated units."[46] On this point, Leo will write that:

It is gratifying to know that there are actually in existence not a few associations of this nature, consisting either of workmen alone, or of workman and employers together, but it were greatly to be desired

120

that they should become more numerous and more efficient.[47]

It was Leo's conviction that associations should be organized and governed so as to furnish the most suitable means for enhancing the material and spiritual condition of all members of society.[48] Further still, in pursuing this goal, Leo argued that special concern must be given to the economy's impact on the poor and powerless; for they are particularly vulnerable:

> The richer classes have many ways of shielding themselves, and stand less in need of help from the State, whereas the mass of the poor have no resources of their own to fall back upon and must chiefly depend upon the assistance of the State. And it is for this reason that wage-earners, since they mostly belong in the mass of the needy, should be specially cared for and protected by the government.[49]

Pius XI was thoroughly in accord with Leo XIII in rejecting the extreme type of corporatism advocated by La Tour du Pin. Yet he was a realist in recognizing social reform would not be accomplished without the objective assistance of some type of institutional restructuring.[50]
The pope writes:

> When we speak of the reform of institutions, the State comes chiefly to mind, not as if universal well-being were to be expected from its activity, but because things have come to such a pass through the evil of what we have termed "individualism," that, following upon the overthrow and near extinction of that rich social life which was once highly developed through associations

121

of various kinds, there remains virtually only individuals and the State.[51]

Pius XI was in agreement with his predecessor that capitalism, though perhaps here to stay, must be looked upon, not as an end in itself, but as a means for the full development of all members of the greater community. The economic system, whichever form it takes, must remain loyal to a double responsibility, in that man's personal as well as social needs must be met. It should be noted, however, that Leo XIII was working against the background of the nineteenth century, where problems tended to be less complex. His remedies were fairly uncomplicated. These included a defense of private property against socialism as well as the promotion of labor unions and social legislation to better the condition of workers.[52] Primary emphasis was directed toward the legitimate claims and aspirations of individuals. Pius XI, on the other hand, was working out of the economic and social problems flowing from the depression. He was concerned, too, with the mounting tide of political totalitarianism and the success of communism. This crisis made the pope aware of the great changes which had come over the economic system since the turn of the century. Liberal capitalism, which in the past was made up of relatively small firms, had been succeeded by monopolistic concentrations of capital resulting not simply in economic liberalism but a true "capitalist regime" which, if it is proven beneficial to mankind, "needs to be strongly curbed and wisely ruled."[53] It was not possible, therefore, for the pope to remain content with reiterating the principles initiated and pursued by his predecessor. It was necessary for Pius XI to examine more minutely the social principles of Leo XIII and attempt to make further application of them to changed conditions.[54]

In the hands of Pius XI this "further application" took the form and shape of what might be termed a "modified corporatism," very much in the spirit of Bishop Ketteler. Pius XI called for the reestablishment of "orders" or corporate groups.[55]

The pope's development of the principle of corporatism, often called the heart of the Encyclical (76-98), draws upon, but modifies considerably, the corporative schools of the nineteenth century. Although quite open and flexible in implementation, it refers to an organization, private in nature, but possessing legally enforceable powers in governing the profession or groups concerned. Such a group would be the exclusive representative of the occupation in question. The main purpose of such a type of social organization would be: 1) to build a framework which would facilitate the practice of social justice; 2) to restore pluralism in society, thus achieving a structural barrier against either individualism or statism; and 3) to replace class-struggle and an overly competitive mentality with a cooperative approach to common problems.[56]

The pope considers this form of organization just as natural to man as the formation of cities or towns to meet man's social and political needs.

> For under nature's guidance it comes to pass that just as those who are joined together by nearness or habitation establish towns, so those who follow the same industry or profession—whether in the economic or other field—form guilds or associations (collegia seu corpora), so that many are wont to consider these self-governing organizations, if not essential, at least natural (*naturalia*) to civil society.[57]

It should be noted that Pius XI is not recommending a return to the guilds of former times. The guilds of the Middle Ages were, after all, thoroughly immersed in the concrete circumstances of a particular age in history and could not be easily transplanted to the modern scene. They were oriented toward a particular type of economy which today is obsolete.[58] Nevertheless, the medieval guilds were grounded in a spirit that is limited to no single period or economic system. The guild's philosophy implied that a person's occupation in life is not merely a personal, private affair. It has a definite bearing on the social body of which he/she is a member.

> For there was a social order once which, although indeed not perfect or in all respects ideal, nevertheless met in a certain measure

123

the requirements of right reason, considering the conditions and needs of the time. If that order has long since perished, that surely did not happen because the order could not have accommodated itself to changed conditions and needs...but rather because men, hardened by too much self love, refused to open the order to the increasing masses as they should have done.[59]

Pius XI is realistic enough to see the value of proper competition and the inevitability of some clash of interest between capital and labor, but he rejects an economic order that emphasizes exclusively the divisive elements in the economy to the detriment of cooperation and order.[60] Social order, rightly conceived calls for organized cooperation within industries and occupations, as well as cooperation among these groups. Such cooperation would be directed toward the common good of the country, thus freeing government from the excessive detail burdening it today and allowing the state to more properly exercise a subsidiary function.

The supreme authority of the state ought, therefore, to let subordinate groups handle matters and concerns of lesser importance... thereby the state will more freely, powerfully and effectively do all those things which belong to it alone because it alone can do them: directing, watching, urging, restraining, as occasion requires and necessity demands.[61]

The "orders" or corporate groups would not replace organizations such as labor unions or employers' association dedicated to the exclusive interest of a particular class, but would serve to assist the "lesser organizations" to expand their horizons to include the common good of the industry and of the community-at large.

And may these organizations, now flourishing and rejoicing in their salutary fruits, set before themselves the task of preparing the way, in conformity with the mind of Christian social teaching, for those larger and more important guilds, industries and professions....[62]

It is natural that men who have interests in common should come together in association. But that is not to say that they will or ought to cease to watch over their separate interests. By arguing for the establishment of vocational groups, Pius XI is arguing from the indisputable democratic principle that all who contribute to the economic and cultural welfare of the community should be entitled in equal measure to participate in the forming of decisions on matters directly affecting them. This contribution is not made by individuals as such but by social groups. Their members are bound together within the framework of social cooperation by their social function, and thus form a vocational group to meet the needs of the greater society.

Pius XI looked upon the vocational group as an important avenue for fostering what Aristotle and Aquinas referred to as "the noble types of friendship." Friendship implies communication in some common good mutually and reciprocally possessed. In each and all of them there is community of interests, common aims, mutual agreement, reciprocal advantage—in a word, communication in some common good, or friendship. And praiseworthy as friendships that arise from communion in useful or delectable goods may be when they pursue utility or pleasure in due moderation, the noblest friendships are those which are centered in the good which is desirable in itself, the common good of man as man. Of such are the natural societies or friendships of the domestic community— the family—and the political community—the state.[63] Friendship for Aristotle and Aquinas is indeed a noble virtue. And in its purity, it is the highest kind of love—the mutual benevolence (well-wishing) of man as man, the effective desire of good for one another entertained and reciprocated among human beings.[64]

125

The pope is seeking here to raise labor to the full status of a principle of order in society and economic life. Individualistic liberalism on the other hand had made property, indeed capital property, the decisive ordering principle in the economy and in society. It considered dependent labor merely as a commodity and as a means of production in the service of capital and profit interest.[65] What Pius XI has in mind, therefore, is the creation of institutions that will make it possible for the worker to engage his personality in every aspect of his occupational work.

> For man's productive effort cannot yield its fruits unless a truly social and juridical order watches over the exercise of work, unless the various occupations, being interdependent, cooperate with and mutually complete one another and, what is still more important, unless mind, material things and work combine and form, as it were a single whole.[66]

Pius XI was cautious as to the precise form "a truly social and juridical order" might take. And perhaps rightly so, in order that the principle might be applied to different contexts. Some interpreters approached this section of the document as a blueprint to be quite strictly applied.[67] Others have cautioned that the wording of this document itself suggests a more flexible interpretation.[68] For example, Pius XI was extremely careful to distinguish the idea of the "natural" as opposed to the "essential" character of the guilds, just as property possession is considered natural but not essential as a means to human development. The trade guilds "have no existence before the establishment of social ties through the mediation of the industry or profession." It is true that the guild, as with the establishment of a system of private enterprise, "does possess a foundation in nature, that its existence rests on a natural community of interests; they are, in a sense, institutions of natural law.[69] But these institutions must be "built up" through the creative efforts and moral commitment of the guild members.

> Therefore, it is most necessary that
> economic life be again subjected to and
> governed by a true directive principle...—
> social justice and social charity—must
> therefore be sought whereby this dictatorship
> may be governed firmly and fairly.[70]

It should be noted that in treating of the relation of social organization to the virtue of "social justice," Pius XI's employment of this virtue has a meaning somewhat more technical that in contemporary usage. The pope has in mind the virtue of "legal" or "general" justice as developed in the political writings of Aristotle and St. Thomas. In the moral and political philosophy of Aristotle and St. Thomas there is a place for the general condition of righteous living which results from the cultivation of all the virtues. Aristotle sees in it a disposition arising from the due observance of all moral laws and the cultivation of all good habits. Because of its reference to the conforming of life and conduct to the laws of morality, Aristotle gives the technical name of "legal" justice to this universal or common virtue which embraces all virtues and makes for the proper exercise of all of one's faculties and powers toward the living of the good life;[71] for until individuals are so properly disposed, there will be little inclination to rectify specific inequalities among members of society through the so-called "particular virtues" of justice (commutative and distributive):

> Legal justice does indeed direct man
> sufficiently in his relations toward others.
> As regards to the common good it does so
> immediately, but as to the good of the
> individual, it does so mediately. Wherefore

there is need for particular justice to direct a man immediately to the good of another individual.[72]

For Aquinas the proper order of society will not be achieved until there is a right ordering in the interior disposition of its citizens: It is to legal or social justice as the "directing principle" that Aquinas appeals to for the proper reconstruction of the social order.

> Every virtue strictly speaking directs its act to that virtue's proper end: that is should happen to be directed to a further end either always or sometimes, does not belong to that virtue considered strictly, for it needs some higher virtue to direct it to that end. Consequently there must be one supreme virtue essentially distinct from every other virtue, which directs all the virtues to the common good; and that virtue is legal justice.[73]

Pius XI's indebtedness to St. Thomas regarding the relevance of the virtue of social justice is well illustrated in *Quadragesimo anno* when he says that:

> The institutions themselves of peoples and particularly those of all social life ought to be penetrated with this justice, and it is most necessary that it be truly effective, that is, establish a juridical and social order which

will, as it were, give form and shape to all
economic life.[74]

In *Quadragesimo anno* 73, there is a paragraph that provides
insight as to how precisely social justice might serve the particular virtues
of justice. In paragraph seventy-three the pope suggests that, where
existing conditions in industry do not permit the payment of a family
living wage, it will fall to the virtue of social justice to provide the
incentive for new institutional patterns of mutual action that will make
such a wage possible:

> Let, then, both workers and employers
> strive with united strength and counsel to
> overcome the difficulties and obstacles and
> let a wise provision on the part of the public
> authority aid them in so salutary a work.[75]

It should be noted that more is involved here than a simple case of
commutative justice. Employers and contractors who find themselves
individually in this position of being unable to pay a living wage are, as
a group, bound in strict duty to organize, support and promote institutions
which will reorganize the whole industry with the prime aim of removing
the causes which keep it from practicing commutative justice and
distributive justice. In *Quadragesimo anno*, Pius XI attempted to restore
to professional organizations and occupational groups the task of
administering private property for the common benefit of all. In the
contract by which they are bound together, there are more duties and
obligations than simply the exchange of a wage against an agreed upon
work task. Involved here is a much broader sense of accountability. In
Pius XI's view, this broader sense of accountability will not be achieved

until a family-like bond is reestablished (as in the ideal of the guilds of an earlier epoch) between employer and employees.

One might speculate regarding the spheres of self-government that could occur in a developed vocational organization of society. Indeed, the twenty-sixth session of the International Labor Conference held in Philadelphia in 1944 set the tone as to the kind of cooperation and collaboration required. The council recommended the advancement of industry through the setting up of functional bodies for cooperation of management and labor in the continuous improvement of productive efficiency and its application to the wider interest of the social sphere.[76]

Other recommendations (many of which have been established since Pius XI's encyclical) would be: 1) the securing of social peace by collective agreements; 2) the regulation of wages and other conditions of work in each occupation as well as by conciliation and arbitration in labor disputes; 3) the carrying out of tasks of social policy within the framework of the State's social legislation with respect to the conditions of the particular industry; 4) in the sphere of economic policy, the control of the economy by securing the fulfillment of the social function of competition, which would be one of the chief objects of self government in an economy organized on a vocational basis; 5) cultivation of a sense of professional responsibility and honor among the members of the industry or profession; 6) the exercise of limited "juridical powers" in matters of professional conduct; 7) vocational education; 8) the institution of a charter by each occupational group as a legal basis for the performance of all these functions of self government within the framework of the coordinating measures taken by the state.[77]

Underlying this cooperative spirit is also the attempt to check the "abuse of anonymity" so often prevalent in our current large multi-national corporations. Overtures toward profit sharing and co-partnership are recommendations very much in keeping with Pius XI's policy recommendations. This theme was pursued enthusiastically by his successor:

> Where large scale enterprise appeared today to be more productive, it ought to be made possible to improve the wage contract by assimilating it somewhat to a contract of partnership.[78]

The pope suggests that efforts to arrive at vocational groupings, no matter what form they eventually take, will themselves serve, to some extent, as a means to bring class conflict to an end. Indeed, the very act of taking into account the common interest of the vocational group will prepare those involved to recognize the rights which belong to each and every member of the group. Hopefully, this recognition will be transformed into institutional patterns of mutual action and interdependence necessary to bring about the realization of the particular manifestations of justice (commutative and distributive).

> It is the function of social justice to require of each individual that which is necessary for the common good. Consider a living organism: the good of the whole is not being properly secured unless arrangements are made for each single member to receive all that it needs to fulfill its own function. Exactly the same is true of the constitution and government of a community: the common good of a society cannot be provided for unless each individual member,

131

a human being endowed with the dignity of
personality, receives all that he needs to
discharge his social function.[79]

ENDNOTES

1. Maurice Cardinal Roy, *Reflections on the Occasion of the Tenth
   Anniversary of the Encyclical Pacem in terris of Pope John XXIII*
   (April 11,1973), #128.

2. Paul Sigmund, "Natural Law and Social Theory," *Calgary Aquinas
   Studies*, ed. A. Pareil (Toronto: Pontifical Institute of Medieval
   Studies, 1978), p.74.

3. *VI Ethic.*, lect. 1131. English translation cited is *Commentary on
   the Nicomachean Ethics*, 2 vols, C.I. Litzinger, O.P., ed.
   (Chicago: Henry Regnery, 1964), Vol. II, p.547. The Litzinger
   translation will be cited throughout.

4. *I Ethic.*, lect. 32-35, vol. 1, P.16. "It is desirable therefore when
   treating of these variable subjects and when arguing from them as
   premises, to bring out roughly the outlines of the truth, and to
   conclude about these things which occur in the majority of cases."

5. *I Ethic.*, lect. 52, vol. 1, P.25. "Now if the better known
   absolutely are the same as the better known to us, the reason
   proceeds from principles as in mathematics. If, however, the better
   known absolutely are different from the better known to us, then

we must use the effect-to-cause procedure as in the natural and moral sciences."

6. Joseph Gremillion, *The Gospel of Peace and Justice: Catholic Social Teaching Since Pope John* (Maryknoll, New York: Orbis Books, 1984), p.8.

7. Maurice Roy, *op.cit.*, #129.

8. *Ibid*, #129.

9. Gregory Baum, "Remarks on Natural Law," in *Natural Law in Political Thought*, ed. Paul Sigmund (Cambridge Mass: Winthrop Publishers, 1971), p.203.

10. ST, I-II, Prologue. English translation cited in English Dominican Fathers' three volume American Edition, St. Thomas Aquinas, *Summa Theologica* (New York: Benziger Brothers, 1947).

11. Ignatius T. Eschmann, O.P., "St. Thomas' Approach to Moral Philosophy," *Proceedings of the American Catholic Philosophical Association*, 31(1957), 25. See also R.J. McLaughlin, "Christianity, Humanism and St. Thomas Aquinas," in, *The Question of Humanism: Challenges and Possibilities*, edited by David Goicoechea (Buffalo, NY: Prometheus Books, 1991), 70-82.

12. See how this point is examined in St. Thomas' *Tract on Law*, ST I-II, especially Q. 90-101. See also ST, II-II, q.Sl, a.2.

13. ST, I-II, q.91, a.2; ST, I, q.44, a.l.

14. ST, I-II, q.94, a.2.

15. ST, I-II, q.100, a.1.

16. ST, I-II, q.100, a.3.

17. For example, witness the heated debate regarding the "positive right" of our citizens to a decent minimum of health care, and further still, what should be considered a "decent minimum"?

18. ST, II-II, q.66, a.7.

19. ST, I-II, q.94, a. 5 and 6; ST, I-II, q.100. a.1 and 11.

20. ST, I, q.79, a.12.

21. *II politic.*, lect 1, "the situation in which men stand relatively to one another" is also the key idea in St. Thomas' political theory; for his awareness of the need for an experiential starting point leads him "to seek out what well-ruled people do and what men of practical wisdom propose." Commenting upon the interdependence of ethical insight and social facts, Luigi Sturzo has remarked that: "What we call moral law is a rational norm derived by experience from social phenomenon, from facts; and, in the same way the facts are the concretization of human rationality impregnated with ethical values, with moral law. Unfortunately man is not infallible; he makes mistakes both of aim and of action; and hence the eternal reality and the ethical norms never coincide perfectly with what is rational, and are always in need of adjustment to bring them into line with rational, moral law."

Luigi Sturzo, "The Influence of Social Facts on Ethical Conceptions", *Thought*, vol. 20, (1945), p.III.

22. ST, I-II, q.95, a.2.

23. ST, II-II, q.66, a.2.

24 ST, II-II, q.66. a.2, ad 1.

25. ST, II-II, q.66, a.1.

26. ST, II-II, q.66, a.1. See also Jean-Yves Calvez, S J. and Jacques Perrin, S J., *The Church and Social Justice: The Social Teachings of the Popes from Leo XIII to Pius XII* (London: Burns and Oats, 1961), 194. "The end of property will always be to give external expression to human liberty. Property is the indispensable external field for the liberty of a person who is indissolubly body-soul.... By reason of this link between property and liberty, of which it is the means of expression necessary for a corporeal being who is involved in nature, but involved as a reasoning being, the church sees in property a basic element which dominates the whole of economic life. It is, therefore, always in defense of personal human liberty and never for the protection of the acquired rights of security holders that the church, though often badly misunderstood in the matter, insists both on the right of property and on its institutions."

27. ST, II-II, q.66, a.2.

28. *Ibid.*

29. ST, II-II, q.66, a.7. See also ST, I-II, q.105, a.2.

30. Marcus Le Febure, O.P., "Private Property' According to St. Thomas and Recent Papal Encyclicals," in St. Thomas Aquinas, *Summa Theologia* vol. 38 "Injustice" (II-II, q.63-67) (New York: McGraw Hill, 1974), 275-283.

31. *Politic*. II, 4 ("Quomodo autem usus rerum propriarum possit fieri communis hoc pertinet ad providentiarum boni legislatoris.")

32. *X Ethic*, V, 6; ST, II-II, q.90-100 for an understanding of the notion of law as the ruling force in society we must turn to the Thomistic theory of law. According to St. Thomas positive or human law renders explicit the demands of natural law which, in turn, is based on the eternal law of God as embodied in the nature of things. Further still, for St. Thomas the ruler receives his right to rule through the consent of the people. The so called "divine right of kings" must be confirmed by the people at large or their representatives.

33. John-Paul II, *Centesimus annus*, 49.

34. Charles K. Wilbur, "Argument That Pope Baptized Capitalism Holds No Water," *National Catholic Reporter*, June 7,1991., p. 8.

35. Howard Dickman, *Industrial Democracy in America* (LaSalle, Ill.: Open Court, 1987), pp. 187-188. J.B. Duroselle, *Les Débuts du catholicisme* social en France: 1822-1870 (Paris: Presses universitaires de France, 1951), p. 24. Richard L. Camp, *The Papal Ideology of Social Reform* (Leiden: EJ. Brill, 1969), p. 26.

36. Georges Jarlot, S.J., *Le régime corporatif et les catholiques sociaux* (Paris: Flammarion, 1938), pp. 17-29.

37. Charles Périn, *De la richesse dans les sociétés chréstiennes* (Paris: 1861), vol. II, p. 306; cited in Calvez and Perrin, *op.cit.*, p. 462.

38. George Jarlot, *op.cit.*, p. 35.

39. Cited by G. Jarlot, p. 47.

40. Henri Rollet, *L'action sociale des catholiques en France*: 1871-1901 (Paris: Boivin et Cie., n.d.), pp. 56 ff; Jarlot, op.cit., pp. 89-94; Matthew H. Elbow, *French Corporative Theory*, 1789-1948 (New York: Columbia University Press, 1953), pp. 55-80.

41. Albert de Mun, *Speech at Nantes,* cited in Calvez and Perrin, *op.cit.*, p. 405.

42. *Ibid*, p. 405.

43. William E. Hogan, *The Development of William Emmanuel von Ketteler's Interpretation of the Social Problem* (Washington, D.C.: Catholic University of America Press, 1946), pp. 80 ff.

44. *Humanum genus*, 35, (On Freemasonry), April 20,1884 in E. Gilson (editor,) *The Church Speaks to the Modern World: The Social Teachings of Leo XIII* (Garden City , NY: Doubleday,1954) p.135.

45. *Rerum novarum*, 3, Gilson, p.206.

46.　　Calvez and Perrin, *op.cit.*, p. 406.

47.　　*R.N.*, 49, Gilson, p. 232. It has been argued that Leo's decision to put the strictly worker's unions on the same basis as the mixed unions may have resulted from the advice of the American Cardinal Gibbons, that in his conversations with Gibbons the pope realized that he must compose his text in a sense that would be acceptable to the entire world, and he knew that many of the terms, so dear to European social catholics, would be meaningless, or worse, in America. As a realist, once he had grasped the distinctive character of the American scene, he could be presumed to make a place for it in the encyclical. See, for example the encyclical addressed to the American bishops, *Longinqua oceani* of 1895 where Leo takes into account the special conditions in American trade unions.

48.　　*R.N.*, 57, Gilson, p. 236.

49.　　*R.N.*, 37, Gilson, pp. 225-226.

50.　　In a slightly different context, in commenting upon the relationship of the ethical inspiration of socialism to the ethical inspiration of Christianity, Josef Tischner states that "socialism suggests that one should begin by ordering the relationship of human beings to the riches of this earth since objective reality precedes what is subjective. To be concrete, one must first abolish private property and introduce a just division of material goods. This end is achieved by conflict and struggle against the owners of the riches. Christianity proclaims that one should begin differently; one must start by putting in order the relationship of one human being to another, by introducing the harmony of love." Josef Tischner, *The Spirit of Solidarity* trans. Mark B. Zaleski and Benjamin Fiore, S J. (San Francisco: Harper & Row, 1982), p. 49.

51.   Pius XI, *Quadragesimo anno*, 78.

52.   It should be emphasized, however, that Leo was concerned with more than an *ad hoc* response to current social inequities. Terrence McLaughlin reminds us that the encyclical *Rerum novarum* was titled *De Conditione Optificum*, on the condition of the workers; but it was not concerned exclusively with the workers. McLaughlin writes: "A better description would be: on the rights and duties of capital and labor. Even this does not cover the subject matter because, as Pius XI points out, Leo had in mind the reconstruction of the social order, which is the title which he gives to his own encyclical on the same subject." Terence P. McLaughlin, C.S.B., ed., *The Church and the Reconstruction of the Modern World: The Social Encyclicals of Pius XI* (Garden City, N.Y., Doubleday, Image Book, 1957), p.218.

53.   *Q.A.*, 88.

54.   T. McLaughlin, *op. cit.*, p.218. See also R.N., 37 and Q.A., 38.

55.   The word *ordo* (plural ordines) is used by the pope throughout *Quadragesimo anno* to indicate the new organizations which he had in mind. It has been variously rendered into English by the terms "occupational group," "vocational group," "functional group," and sometimes by the term, "guild" or "corporate group." In his anthology of the encyclicals of Pius XI, Joseph Husslein

writes: "The essential idea conveyed by the word *ordo*... is that of the complete organization of a trade, or industry, or profession, in such a way that all the fully organized employees and all the equally fully organized employers, in any one given occupational or functional field, are united into one general *ordo* (order)."
Joseph Husslein, S.J., ed., Social Wellsprings, vol. II, *Eighteen Encyclicals of Social Reconstruction by Pope Pius XI* (Milwaukee: Bruce Publishing Co., 1943), p.208.

56. *Q.A.*, 81., "First and foremost, the state and every good citizen ought to look to and strive toward this end: that the conflict between the hostile classes be abolished, and harmonious cooperation of the industries and professions (*ordinum*) be encouraged and promoted."

57. *Q.A.*, 83.

58. *Q.A.*, 78.

59. *Q.A.*, 97.

60. *Q.A.*, 88. "Just as the unity of human society cannot be built upon class warfare, so the ordering principle of economic affairs cannot be left to free competition alone.... Free competition, however, though within certain limits just and productive of good results, cannot be the ruling principle of the economic world."

61. *Q.A.* 80

62. *Q.A.*, 87. The pope was well aware that his advocacy of "vocational groups" would not, and probably should not, completely absorb associations such as labor unions. But "vocational groups" might go a long way toward checking the tendency toward self-interest and the formation of pressure groups by labor and management alike. The common interests of these organized professions could warn us against putting too much emphasis on whatever divides class from class. See also *Q.A.*, 82; 83; 84. In *Q.A.*, 84, the pope notes that "this unifying force is present not only in the producing of goods or the rendering of services—in which the employers and employees of an identical Industry or Profession collaborate jointly—but also in that common good*, to achieve which all Industries and Professions ought, each to the best of its ability, to cooperate amicably."
*The Latin text adds *civitatis*, that is, of the body politic.

63. Aristotle, N. *Ethics* VIII.

64. St. Thomas, VIII *Ethics*, 1,7, n. 1632.

65. *Q.A.*, 83. "Labor, as our predecessor explained well in his encyclical, is not a mere commodity (*vilis merx*). On the contrary, the worker's human dignity in it must be recognized. It therefore cannot be bought and sold like a commodity."

66. *Q.A.*, 69. See also *Q.A.*, 53.

67. "It is our ambition to be the first country to give a practical response in political life to the appeal, of this noble encyclical (*Quadragesimo anno*)." See *Address of Chancellor Dollfuss in Vienna, September 9, 1933*, cited in Husslein, p.175. Husslein comments that Dollfuss took for the foundation of Austria's constitutional life "the corporative principle" of Pius XI.

68. *Q.A.*, 85. "Concerning matters, however, in which particular points, involving advantage or detriment to employers or workers, may require special care and protection, the two parties, when these cases arise can determine separately or, as the situation requires, reach a decision separately."

69. Jean-Yves Calvez, S.J. and Jacques Perrin, S.J., *op. cit*, p.423. See also, *Q.A.*, 83. "many are wont to consider these self-governing organizations, if not essential, at least natural to civil society."

70. *Q.A.*, 88; see also 90.

71. Aristotle, *Nich. Ethics*, V, 1129b-1130a; See also S.T., II-II, q.61, a.2, ad.4 when Aquinas writes: "Movement takes its species from the term "whereunto." Hence it belongs to legal justice to direct to the common good those matters which concern private individuals: whereas on the contrary it belongs to particular justice to direct the common good to particular individuals by way of distribution."

72. S.T., II-II, q.58, a.7, ad.1. See also q.58, a.5.

73.   S.T., II-II, q.58, a.6 ad.4. See also S.T. I-II, q.113, a.1: "Since justice, by its very nature, signifies a certain rectitude of order, it may be taken in two ways: First, inasmuch as it signifies a right order in man's act; and thus justice is placed among the virtues— either as particular justice, which directs a man's acts by regulating them in relation to his fellow man, or as legal justice, which directs a man's acts by regulating them in their relation to the common good of society. Second, justice is so-called inasmuch as it signifies a certain rectitude of order in the interior disposition of a man...insofar as...the inferior powers of the soul are subject to the superior...and this disposition the Philosopher calls justice metaphorically speaking. See also Aristotle, *Politics* II, 7,1267B 6-9; "The beginning of reform is not so much to equalize property as to train the nobler sort of natures not to desire more, and to prevent the lower from getting more."

74.   *Q.A.*, 84.

75.   *Q.A.*, 73.

76.   See *Official Bulletin*, International Labor Office, vol. XXVI, 1., June, 1944, p. 3.

77.   Johannes Messner, *Natural Law In the Western World*, trans. J. J. Doherty (St. Louis B. Herder, 1964), pp.441-442.

78.   Pius XII, Message of I Sept. 1944; *AAS* 36, p.254.

79.   *Divini Redemptoris*, 71.

"Rerum novarum" and the
Politics of Liberty

Christopher Knight

During the nineteen eighties, it seemed to many that the thinking of the so-called "new right" was likely be the dominant political philosophy of the next generation. For not only had the short term economic success associated with the adoption of more laissez-faire economic policies in several countries led to a general optimism about the future, it had also, for many, underlined the perceived lack of success of the sort of social democratic consensus which had dominated their politics since the second world war. In addition, the growing recognition of the failure of Marxism-Leninism in the east, leading to its collapse at the end of the decade, left many with the impression that any sort of socialist vision of society had been effectively abandoned except as a sentimental hankering after lost and impossible ideals.

Central to this success of new right thinking in the west was the rhetoric of freedom employed by its proponents, which seemed to strike a deep chord among those dissatisfied with the post-war consensus. Freedom from state interference in economic activity was, in fact, only a part of this successful libertarian rhetoric. For the appeal of the rhetoric was due, it would seem, as much to its stress on individual responsibility, as something good in itself, as to its recipe for escape from the economic inefficiency of state-dominated institutions and policies. It was, in fact, an appeal which seems genuinely to have tapped what was an already existing if previously inarticulate criticism of the state-oriented solutions to social problems which had dominated the western European political consensus since the second world war. For these solutions, it seems to have been widely believed, had produced a "dependency culture" which had inhibited the development of individual dignity through responsibility, as well as an economy which had inhibited the creation of both individual and corporate wealth.

The gap between rhetoric and reality which often emerged under new right governments was not, however, widely noted except among libertarian "extremists" of the right and campaigners for civil liberties usually associated with the left. When they pointed out the markedly authoritarian and centralising tendencies of some new right governments beyond the purely economic sphere, the response of those governments and of many of their supporters was, essentially, that people could only be trusted to use their freedom for the public good when that good was an accidental secondary effect, as in economics. Freedom, for such purveyors of libertarian rhetoric, was something to be limited to the freedom to make money without the shackles of state interference in the processes of the market. Thus, even on the right, there grew a gap between those for whom libertarianism was simply another term for laissez-faire economics, and those for whom, though it included such economic libertarianism, it had a deeper meaning related to human responsibility and dignity.

The dominance of new right thinking of both varieties, characteristic of the nineteen eighties, has, however, more recently given way to a new uncertainty among conservatives. The recognition, not only of the fragility of the economic successes associated with new right policies, but also of the consenques of those policies, both for the most disadvantaged members of society and for widely valued social services, has, it would seem, led to a new openness in political thought. The resulting search for a political philosophy which combines mechanisms which would guarantee greater economic stability and social welfare with the genuine insights of the new right about the efficiency of market mechanisms has, however, led to few new insights. Even among commentators of a moderately left-wing persuasion, it has often involved little more than an attempt to modify the insights of the new right with some appropriate fine tuning based on an older social democratic consensus.

In Britain, interestingly, this has been exemplified by the entry of catholic social thought into secular political consciousness. This was brought to wide public attention by comments in the press on an article in the April 1991 edition of "Marxism Today." In that article, Will Hutton noted the distinction between the new right thinking associated with the Thatcherism of the eighties, and the "social market" aspect of much

145

continental European conservatism of the "Christian Democrat" variety, towards which, he suggested, British conservatism in the post-Thatcher era seemed to be moving. Central to the article was the idea that one of the most important influences on mainland European conservatism's belief in the social market was catholic social thought.

"It is," he said, "this credo, with its marriage of belief in markets and a strong system of social provision, that characterises christian democracy —and it seems to represent the kind of acceptable softening of the edges of Thatcherism that the Conservative Party must now accomplish."[1]

This article was commented on in two journals influential in conservative circles in Britain, *The Spectator* and *The Times*. In the former, catholic social thought was largely dismissed as the economic equivalent of a pious belief in motherhood and apple pie.[2] In the latter, however, Clifford Longley, under the heading "Rome finds a ready ear in high places," noted both the actual influence which such thought appeared to be having among some highly placed conservatives, and noted the increased interest that might be expected because of the 1991 conferences to be held to mark the centenary of the papal encyclical *Rerum novarum*. Recognising that encyclical as the beginning of the modern phase of catholic social teaching, he suggested that future evolution of British conservative thought might well look to the concepts of subsidiarity and solidarity, both hitherto unfamiliar in British political debate, and both characteristic of twentieth century catholic social teaching.

His comments on these concepts in relation to current British political life were perceptive. Explaining subsidiarity (perhaps over-simplistically) as the need to pass "power as far as possible downwards," he noted the way in which "Mrs. Thatcher's government, for all its rhetoric to the contrary, concentrated power at the centre." Solidarity, he then went on to suggest, presents to conservatives "an even more radical challenge, as it meets the free market imperative to treat individuals as mere economic units with an equal insistence that man is a social animal existing in relationship with others.... Subsidiarity and solidarity supply a theory of the role of the state which is dangerously overlooked in British political philosophy."[3]

If up to that time overlooked as concepts, at least one of these words quickly entered the British political vocabulary, proving at least half- wrong Longley's belief that any British conservative wishing to use them as concepts would have to use different terms. Within a few weeks of that article in *The Times* and of one the previous week in "The Spectator," both of which highlighted the concept in catholic social thought, the word "subsidiarity"—previously almost entirely absent from British public political debate—had been used, as *The Independent* reported, by the Prime Minister himself in the House of Commons.[4] The context was the debate about national sovereignty in the European Community, and in the same context, and only a few days later, that newspaper commented on the concept in a leading article. The Community, it said, "must not only reform its institutions but also take a new look at the old problem of subsidiarity, which goes back many decades. Europe's Christian Democrats like to point out that one of the first definitions of subsidiarity is to be found in Pope Pius XI's encyclical *Quadragesimo anno* of 1931, which says that 'it is an injustice, a grave evil and a disturbance of right order for a larger and higher association to arrogate to itself functions which can be performed efficiently by smaller and lower societies.' In other words, the debate is a broad historical one about the proper ordering of human society and the control of power." [5]

In practice, as these uses of the concept of subsidiarity demonstrate, many of the heirs of the new right have yet to take seriously its content at scales smaller than that of the nation state. Nevertheless, its adoption by those of this persuasion, even at this smaller scale, would be natural enough. For the rhetoric, if not the reality, of subsidiarity, is part of the new right inheritance of the newer, more searching conservatism. *Rerum Novarum*'s insistence on the limitations of the role of the state in relation to the individual household, for example,[6] and the main part of its list of duties of government within these limitations,[7] could be carried almost word for word over into a conservative election manifesto.

If people of this persuasion believe that they can find a new justification for their instincts in Catholic social thought, however, even a cursory reading of *Rerum novarum* and its successors will give them pause for thought and consternation. For they will find in those encyclicals not only much to support their own particular brand of the appeal to

147

liberty. They will find also a much wider conception of liberty—one which sees poverty, exploitation and powerlessness as much a matter of bondage as any undue interference by the state. As Longley's article pointed out, what has come to be called solidarity is an equally integral part of that thought as is subsidiarity, and provides an immense challenge to the unthinking reliance on laissez-faire economics which is often a marked characteristic of those who are now taking up subsidiarity as a clarion call. For the development of what Longley calls "*Rerum Novarum*-style Christian democracy in Britain" would require an attentiveness to aspects of *Rerum novarum* which sit uneasily with that remnant of new right libertarian rhetoric which is still powerful in British conservative thinking.

Thus, for example, the conservative looking for Catholic support will find, in the encyclical of 1891, claims for a role for the state in protection of the poor—and not only in, if including, situations in which "employers laid burdens upon workmen which were unjust, or degraded them with conditions which were repugnant to their dignity as human beings."[8] There is also a strong sense, in the encyclical, of the wider rights of working people. "The first concern of all," it says, "is to save the poor workers from the cruelty of grasping speculators, who use human beings as mere instruments for making money."[9]

On the question of wages, for example, it explicitly rejects the concept of their being set by market forces alone. "Let it be granted," it says, "that as a rule, workman and employer should make free agreements, and in particular should freely agree as to wages; nevertheless, there is a dictate of Nature more imperious and more ancient than any bargain between man and man, that the remuneration must be enough to support the wage-earner in reasonable and frugal comfort. If through necessity or fear of a worse evil, the workman accepts harder conditions because an employer or contractor will give him no better, he is the victim of force and injustice."[10]

In relation to this question of wages, it is noteworthy that the encyclical makes suggestions which relate directly to the modern British debate. For the encyclical envisages not direct state interference in working agreements, but rather "that recourse should be had to Societies or Boards... or to some other method of safe-guarding the interests of the wage-earners; the State to be asked for approval and protection."[11] For it was, interestingly, precisely the modern working out of this idea in the social market aspect of Christian democratic thought to which the recent articles in the British press drew attention. Longley, for example, noted that, "What Mrs.Thatcher objected to as 'socialism' in the draft European Charter, such as a role for trade unions on company boards, is orthodox Catholic social teaching, and taken for granted by Christian Democrat governments."[12] And as Hutton noted, in a wider context, "British ideas of the social market are still a long way from those in mainland Europe." He went on to suggest that "This is where the role of Catholicism—or at the very least an active notion of Christianity—is important. The European idea of social means a much more comprehensive notion of inclusive societal obligation than the British Right dares recognise but suspects. Christian democrats do not see it as quasi-socialism; it is a philosophy which expresses Christian solidarity—for the Christian in their title is not idle. Christians do not pass by on the other side of cardboard city or excuse it as both an incentive and warning to the hoi polloi; it is a phenomenon which requires redress and attention.... "[13]

This attempt to modify New Right thinking through aspects of catholic social teaching may turn out to be of considerable importance for the future of the political thought. In the way in which it has thus far manifested itself, however, it suffers from the way in which it takes for granted that subsidiarity and solidarity are necessarily in a particular sort of tension. For the chief manifestation of solidarity is seen, in almost all these comments in the secular press, as being through state mechanisms. As a result, there is a strong tendency to see subsidiarity either as merely a matter of "markets" and economic efficiency, with solidarity as the chief thing to be considered, or else as itself the chief good, with solidarity as a mere safety net. The former emphasis is to be found implicitly throughout Hutton's article, for example, manifested in a number of assumptions, and not least in the claim that a particular phenomenon not only "requires redress and attention," but , as he goes on to suggest, requires them "necessarily by the state and with public money." For him, catholic social teaching seems to mean little more than that "you can still consent to massive social welfare while believing that competition brings better results." [14]

These sorts of assumption point to the heart of the dilemma of any sort of politics of liberty. Freedom from state interference and freedom from poverty for those "at the bottom of the heap" are widely seen as incompatible ideals, and the art of political judgement is, as a result, seen as that of judging how much to compromise the one for the sake of the other. It is this aspect of most people's response to the various forms of libertarian rhetoric which is challenged, however, by a deeper look at the sort of catholic social doctrine which developed from *Rerum novarum*. For the possibility of a "third way" sketched out in that and in subsequent encyclicals cuts across the widespread belief that a critique of state-oriented political and economic life is the sole property of the proponents of laissez-faire economics. For the encyclical and its successors combine a trenchant critique of capitalist theory with a profound sense of individual responsibility and the danger of improper collective control. Such a combination either has to be taken seriously, therefore, as a genuine contribution to a "third way" debate, or, as is more often the case in the secular world, dismissed as incoherent wishful thinking.

The idea that it is possible to be both anti-capitalist and also against state socialism in its various manifestations is suggested not only by catholic social teaching, however. The person who wishes to dismiss its combination of solidarity and subsidiarity, as incoherent by definition, has to deal also to deal with the existence of a number of long standing "socialist" libertarian traditions. These, while dominated in twentieth century socialism by state-oriented versions of that creed, and therefore not widely known, have, even in recent years, not been without influence. Many, however, while intrigued by or even supporting those aspects of the "counter culture" of the late 'sixties, or of the modern "green" movement, influenced by such traditions,[15] tend to be ignorant of the libertarian socialism from which these ideas have grown.

This ignorance, not only of the details but even of the existence of such traditions, leads, as we have noted, to a widespread belief that the political spectrum extends simply from a "laissez-faire" libertarianism of the right to a semi-totalitarian state-socialism of the left, and that political judgement is therefore the art of holding the genuine insights of the two extremes in some sort of creative tension at an appropriate intermediate point. This assumption is, moreover, adopted uncritically by the majority of Christians who seek a critique of social and economic policies in the light of their faith. Surprisingly few, even of those in communion with Rome, seem aware of that social teaching emanating from Rome which, in some respects at least, provides a "third way" perspective not unlike that provided by a libertarian socialism.

Thus, while many Christians have rightly condemned both the practical outcome of new right policies and much of the "doctrinal" belief about human beings that constitutes their justification[16], much of their subsequent argument about Christian political judgement has been about where on that spectrum a balanced theological view would lead. Beyond and even within Roman Catholicism, many such judgements have been, as a result, little more than a restatement of the sort of position frequently articulated before the second world war, and crystallised in William Temple's widely-influential "Christianity and the Social Order" (whose recent re-issue contained a foreward, appropriately enough, by Edward Heath[17]. Such judgements have, more often than not, except perhaps in terms of acknowledging the efficiency of market mechanisms, effectively denied the validity of that libertarian instinct intrinsic to some forms of socialism and explicit in the rhetoric which has made the new right so powerful.

The two approaches which question the simple spectrum model of political options—those of catholic social teaching and of the "anarchist" left—are often held to have little in common. Certainly there has, historically, been little interraction between them. This is hardly surprising, perhaps, given the reactionary role assigned (and not without reason) to conventional religion in most nineteenth and early twentieth century socialist thought. This meant that, until recently, little attention was paid to papal pronouncements by socialists of any variety.

Even when such attention was given, as in Henry George's "The Condition of Labour", explicitly written as a response to *Rerum novarum*, there was little fruitful interraction—despite, in that particular case, the religious as well as economic basis of its critique of the papal teaching. This seems to have been due largely to the way in which catholics of the late nineteenth and early twentieth centuries, following the lead of Leo XIII, tended to make little differentiation between different varieties of socialism. They tended to react strongly against all of them, not least for their perceived attack on religion. Thus, for example, as de Lubac noted in his study of the thought of Proudhon, one of the earliest and most influential exponents of a libertarian socialism, while the general neglect of that thought in the mid-twentieth century was surprising, the fact that by then "he should not be known by Catholics... or that they should see him as a bugaboo, is less surprising. There are great reasons for such ignorance ... In the last century Proudhon was one of the strong opponents of our faith, and that in a manner most violent and very provoking."[18]

The days of catholic reaction against secular frameworks of thought are now, however, well and truly over, and it might well be that a fruitful interraction which should have begun a century ago can now begin. For the very fact, that there exist these two main alternatives to the simple spectrum model of political options—both in some sense providing anti-capitalist and non state-oriented analyses of economic and political life—inevitably makes one wonder what a genuine encounter between the two might allow to emerge.

Such a dialogue would, in its fulness, have many facets of course, and here we shall outline only two of them. We shall do so in terms of the sort of criticism which at least some libertarian socialists would make of two aspects of the broad sweep of catholic social teaching since *Rerum novarum*, and also of how these criticisms might be explored by Christians in explicitly theological terms. The first aspect of catholic social thought at which we shall look is that underlined by such socialists in their opposition to the state. The second is that aspect of freedom from poverty and exploitation which is underlined in libertarian socialist thought by its insistence on access to and control of the means of production by individuals or small groups in voluntary cooperation.

Before looking at the first of these—the question of the role of the state in recent catholic social thought—it is perhaps worth reminding ourselves that the question of a proper theological attitude to the state is a far older one than is sometimes realised. For example, it is clear from a number of passages that feeling against the principle of external government belongs to one of the oldest strands of Old Testament belief. Those opposing the foundation of the monarchy (e.g., Judges, 8: 22f; 1 Samuel 8:1 ff) are particularly eloquent of this strand of thought, and they have been taken up by liberation theologians such as Jose Porfirio Miranda in their analysis of what he calls the "radical anarchism" in the Old Testament, which insists that "God and human beings cannot reign at the same time." [19]

There appears to be some considerable truth in this analysis, though whether the New Testament can also, as Miranda insists, bear the same sort of interpretation, is problematic. Passages such as the Magnificat and the teachings of Paul about Law are, indeed, highly evocative, but their application beyond their immediate context is, as always in such cases, difficult. To claim, as Miranda does, that there is an explicit libertarian strand of social teaching running through both testaments is, surely, to go beyond what sober exegesis allows. At the most, one can perhaps say that there is a strong biblical concept of liberty which, while it does not lead directly to the sort of political libertarianism for which Miranda pleads, is certainly consonant with it.

If there is no explicit consistent biblical teaching about freedom and the state, however, the Christians of the early centuries were not slow to draw out a concept of liberty which they believed was certainly implicit in scripture, and to analyse the state in terms of it. Elaine Pagel's book, "Adam, Eve, and the Serpent", for example, while primarily about the development of Christian teaching on sexuality in the early centuries of the church's life, stresses the extent to which, up to the time of Augustine (and well beyond that in the Christian east), the gospel message was seen to be summarised in the word "freedom." The Christian life, she rightly says, was seen in those early centuries primarily in terms of the recovery of the human capacity for self- government. This applied not only to attitudes to sexuality, but also to those dealing with life in society. She cites in particular St. John Chrysostom, who could, for example, contrast the empire with the church by saying that "There, everything is done through fear and restraint; here, through free choice and liberty."[20]

Pagel sees in the patristic tradition up to the time of Augustine a highly ambiguous attitude towards the state, and only with the development of an Augustinian attitude to fallen human nature, with its pessimistic denial of any human capacity for self-government, do we find anything like the modern attitude to the state. For, she says, "Augustine draws so drastic a picture of the effects of Adam's sin that he embraces human government, even when tyrannical, as the indispensable defense against the forces sin has unleashed in human nature."[21]

It is now well-known, of course, that this picture of original sin— so often called upon by conservatives in their defence of their unwillingness to extend their libertarianism beyond the economic sphere—was an innovation. The earlier picture, typified by the teaching of Irenaeus, was one in which the image of God in humanity is distorted in the "fall", but not completely destroyed. In this earlier model, sin restricts the scope of free will rather than destroys it, and though only the grace of God can turn humanity from its self-centredness back to the proper use of its freedom, there is still within human nature, by virtue of the grace inherent in creation, a possibility of creative as well as of destructive behaviour.

It was, however, the Augustinian picture of "original sin," (one which Pagel perhaps attributes too much to Augustine and not enough to later "Augustinians") which passed into the common currency of western theology, and ultimately into secular political thought. As a result, it is still the case that a fear of disorder is so instinctive that even many of those inherently predisposed to a libertarian framework of political thought, such as those on the new right, will behave in a remarkably authoritarian manner over what they see as potential "anarchy" (which literally, of course, means not disorder but simply the state of being without government). In this, many Christians, with their still quasi-Augustinian concept of original sin, seem to agree. As William Temple put it, "Freedom is a finer thing than order, but order is more indispensable than freedom. If freedom is so developed as to turn into anarchy and chaos, men will always accept the alternative of tyranny in hope that order may be restored."[22]

This Augustinian view of the state clearly had its influence on modern catholic social thought, particularly in its earlier phases. Leo XIII, for example, in the year after *Rerum novarum*, was to refer to "all public order being impossible without a government."[23] This was only six years after his major encyclical, "On the Christian Constitution of States," which had attacked democracy itself on precisely these grounds. Dismissing "the deceptive wishes and judgements of the multitude"[24] as a proper basis for government, he stressed, in earlier encyclical, that "the doctrine that popular sovereignty, irrespective of God, resides in the masses, is indeed a doctrine exceedingly well calculated to flatter, and to inflame many passions; but it lacks all rational proof, and has not the power of insuring public safety, and the maintenance of order."[25] That some degree of participation in government by the people might, "at certain times, and under certain laws... not only be of benefit to the citizens, but even their duty"[26] was as far as he was prepared to move from the doctrine that "the authority of rulers is vested with a sacredness more than human."[27]

Reaction against the secular political version of the Augustinian concept of original sin was to be found then, and is to be found now, primarily among those libertarian socialists happy to use the term "anarchist" to describe themselves. This term is, of course, a problematic one for many people because of the violence that was characteristic of one aspect of its historical manifestation. In practice, however, this tradition of political thought, stemming from the writings of nineteenth century figures such as Bakunin, Proudhon and Kropotkin, has many facets, including, for example, a strongly pacifist one, of the sort associated with Tolstoy. As Kropotkin pointed out in his article on anarchism in the famous eleventh edition of the *Encyclopaedia Britannica* of 1910, the public impression that violence was of the essence of anarchism was completely false. (This did not, however, prevent the editor of the Encyclopaedia from feeling it appropriate that a footnote should be added giving a lengthy account of "Anarchist outrages.")

The sort of anarchism to which I should like to draw attention here is, needless to say, that philosophical sort which, like Kropotkin's or Tolstoy's, at the very least eschews violence whenever possible. In a modern form, it is perhaps best illustrated by the writing of the British anarchist, Colin Ward, who seeks to "win over our fellow citizens to anarchist ideas, precisely through drawing upon the common experience of the informal, transient, self-organising networks of relationships that in fact make the human community possible, rather than through the rejection of existing society as a whole in favour of some different kind of society where some different kind of humanity will live in perfect harmony."[28] He quotes approvingly, for example, one of the leading American anarchists of the twentieth century, Paul Goodman, for whom "A free society cannot be the substitution of a 'new order' for the old order; it is the extension of spheres of free action until they make up most of social life."[29]

Such thinkers see the right ordering of society in terms of the extension of "spontaneous order"—free associations of various sorts—in place of hierarchically imposed order, and they thus implicitly reject the Augustinian assumption that creative cooperation can only be maintained by coercion or pure self-interest. They adopt, rather, an attitude to human self-centredness which is consonant with Irenaeus' view of it, stressing the tendency in human nature to mutual aid as well as to self-centredness. They typically cite historical examples of such spontaneous order in situations in which ordinary civil government has broken down, but Ward sees the spontaneous tendency for people to associate together for mutual benefit also in more mundane cooperation of the sort which the new right also tends to find laudable: the housing association, for example, or the workers' cooperative. (Ward occasionally, for example, comes in for praise in the idiosyncratically right wing *Spectator* for his writing on such themes.)

If this sort of anarchy is far from that feared so much by Leo XIII, moreover, it finds parallels in more recent papal social teaching, particularly that of John XXIII. For, as Donal Dorr has noted of the latter, "The whole presupposition of his two great social encyclicals was that people needed only to be encouraged and animated to cooperate more fruitfully. He presumes not merely the ability to cooperate but the fundamental willingness of people and nations to cooperate even at the cost of personal, sectional, or national sacrifice."[30]

Whether, historically, this change is due simply to the absence of the non-theological factors of the sort which so affected Leo's judgement, or whether there has indeed been at work here a change of attitude towards original sin of the sort implicit in much Christian thought in recent years, is difficult to determine. If the latter, then, in the judgement of some, such an approach might be seen as a manifestation of a nineteen sixties optimism which fails to do justice to the depth of original sin, even in an Irenaean picture of it. Whatever one's theological judgement on this issue, however, what is important is that the attitude to free cooperative effort it manifests has clear implications for the older attitude towards the state as an indispensible safeguard against chaos. It implicitly opens up the

156

possibility of analysing human cooperation and its limits in a way which would not have been possible a hundred years ago, and does so in a way which imposes a specifically theological task, or at any rate an anthropological judgement.

This recognition of a relatively recent stress on free cooperation does not imply, of course, that such a stress is unrelated to what had gone before. For there are certain parallels with the thinking behind *Rerum novarum* itself. First of all, though the role of the state in the encyclical and its predecessors is an important one, it is limited. The prime unit of society is, in Leo's thinking, not the state but the "domestic household" which, since it "is anterior both in idea and in fact to the gathering of men into a commonwealth... must necessarily have rights and duties which are prior to those of the latter, and which rest more immediately on Nature."[31] Societies for mutual help of one sort or another are encouraged, especially workmen's associations based to some extent on "the Artificers' Guilds of a former day... adapted to the requirements of the age in which we live—an age of greater instruction, of different customs, and of more numerous requirements in daily life."[32]

In matters such as these, there is much with which the proponent of the new right and of the libertarian left might feel entirely comfortable. Where the latter would part company entirely with the new right and partially with catholic social teaching, however, is in rejection of permanent hierarchies and of a capitalist economy. For if they believe it proper for human beings to be "self-employed" and responsible for their work, they reject utterly the sort of accumulation of capital and power in a few hands which any capitalist system will allow. Property, in such an analysis, is not simply a matter of possession. There is, certainly in the anarchist tradition that goes back to Proudhon, a strong defence of the sort of property that provides freedom—one's dwelling place, one's place and tools of work, the immediate products of one's labour. But there is also the property which, as Proudhon claimed "is theft," and must be abolished, so that every "owner" in the new system will be "responsible for the thing entrusted to him; he must use it in conformity with general utility, with a view to its preservation and development; he has no power to transform it, to diminish it, or to change its nature; he cannot so divide

157

the usufruct that another shall perform the labour while he receives the product."[33]

The consonance of this sort of vision with both the stewardship concept of creation in the opening chapters of Genesis and of the spirit of the Jubilee laws of property in Leviticus is striking. For those who take seriously these Old Testament passages as a foundation stone for thinking about the relationship of people to the earth on which, and the society within which, they live, there is much in Proudhonian anarchism's approach which will seem very familiar. What is equally striking, however, is the consonance of this outlook with aspects of the spirit of *Rerum novarum* and its successors, albeit coupled with a fundamental disagreement with the form of the defence of private property to be found in *Rerum novarum* itself.

The encyclical's defence of private property begins with an attack on "socialism"—which, as we have already noted, was a political philosophy whose variations and nuances had no part in Leo XIII's thought. It was a word which simply conjured up for him a vision of inevitable civil disorder and, as Dorr has noted, acted for him simply as "a kind of short-hand word whose meaning included all kinds of political extremism."[34] The resulting fear of any sort of socialism was such, as Dorr further notes, that it "led him to modify an earlier draft of *Rerum novarum* in which the right to private property had been subordinated to the wider principle that the goods of the earth are for the common good. So he gave ... a quite different emphasis from that of traditional scholastic teaching."[35]

This new emphasis was defended in terms of the natural desire of people for property. In a way which can have had little truth for the mass of people in late nineteenth century industrial society, the encyclical talks of property as the equivalent of wages, sentimentally suggesting that a working man might build up " a ... little estate" if "he lives sparingly, saves money, and invests his savings, for greater security, in land"[36] Such possession was, the encyclical went on, a "natural right"[37] which was associated with that human nature which made provision not only for the present but for the future.[38]

The logical flaw of this sort of defence, which ignored the nature of the property held, was pointed out clearly in Henry George's response to the encyclical, "The Condition of Labour." Using an argument also adopted by Bishop Nulty of Meath some years earlier, in addressing the land question in Ireland,[39] he pointed out what the pope's defence of property in land would mean if for the word "land" one substituted the word "slave." The encyclical's sixth paragraph would, he pointed out, then conclude with the words:

> Thus, if he lives sparingly, saves money, and invests his money for greater security in a slave, the slave, in such a case, is only his wages in another form; and consequently a working man's slave thus purchased should be as completely at his own disposal as the wages he receives for his labour.[40]

"Nor," George went on to argue, "by turning your argument for private property in land into an argument for private property in men am I doing a new thing. In my own country [the United States], in my own time, this very argument, that purchase gave ownership, was the common defence of slavery. It was made by statesmen, by jurists, by clergymen, by bishops; it was accepted over the whole country by the great mass of the people. By it was justified the separation of wives from husbands, of children from parents, the compelling of labour, the appropriation of its fruits, the buying and selling of Christians by Christians. In language almost identical with yours it was asked, 'Here is a poor man who has worked hard, lived sparingly, and invested his savings in a few slaves. Would you rob him of his earnings by liberating those slaves?' Or it was said: 'Here is a poor widow; all her husband had been able to leave her is a few negroes, the earnings of his hard toil. Would you rob the widow and the orphan by freeing these negroes?' And because of this perversion of reason, this confounding of unjust property rights with just property rights, this acceptance of Man's law as though it were God's law, there came on our nation a judgement of fire and blood."[41]

George's faith in the benefits of a competitive economy and his denial of any role for the state in the organisation or control of production have a surprisingly modern ring for the late twentieth century reader, whatever that reader may feel about his solution to the problem of property, in terms of a tax on land value through the socialisation of rent. What is important in the present context, however, is not the viability of a modern form of such proposals (interesting as such a discussion might be, especially in a third world context,) but the basic insight about property contained in his criticism of *Rerum novarum*. For it is an insight which has something in common with that of Proudhonian anarchism, and which manifests a vision of human nature and responsibility—if not of the consequences of that vision—very similar to those outlined in the encyclical.

It rests, for George, on the distinction between ownership and possession. There are certain things—the products of their labour—which rightly belong to people to use or dispose of as they will, and certain things (for George the God-given land of the earth) on which there is a proper common claim. There arises, he claims, "anterior to human law, and deriving its validity from the law of God, a right of private ownership in things produced by labour—a right that the possessor may transfer, but of which to deprive him, without his will, is theft. This right of property, originating in the right of the individual himself, is the only full and complete right of property. It attaches to things produced by labour, but cannot attach to things created by God."[42]

For the Proudhonian anarchist, this would be insufficient as an analysis, and not least because no distinction is made by George between capital and labour; it is as much a theological argument about the God-givenness of the land as it is an economic argument. The important thing about both in relation to catholic social thought, however, is that a distinction is made, in a way which *Rerum novarum* and its successors fail to make, between different sorts of property. That such distinctions have often been made over-simplistically is not in doubt,[43] but this in itself does not negate the insight that different sorts of property do have different ramifications for society as a whole. In analyses of the sort we have noted, there is, together with an encouragement of the sort of property for which *Rerum novarum* sees a positive role in fostering human dignity and responsibility, the important recognition that certain capitalist property rights inevitably have the opposite effect, and that to treat the two as indistinguishable is to commit a far-reaching category mistake.

160

In practice, however, such a failure of distinction has not been entirely unrecognised in more recent papal teaching. Pius XII, in particular, put back onto the catholic agenda the scolastic idea that the right and value of private ownership must be seen in the context of a more general and fundamental right. Despite his own sympathy for democratic capitalist states—a contrast with the approach of his predecessor, (whose interest in fascist corporatism demonstrates an aspect of catholic social thinking which is nowadays often conveniently forgotten)—he was far from blind to some of their tendencies. "Undoubtedly," he taught, "the natural order, deriving from God, demands ... private property ... But all this remains subordinated to the natural scope of material goods and cannot emancipate itself from the first and fundamental right which concedes their use to all men; but it should rather serve to make possible the actuation of this right in conformity with its scope."[44]

Similarly, in the first half of the twentieth century, there were a number of groups, led largely by catholic laypeople, which began to attempt a working out of the teachings of *Rerum novarum* which implicitly went beyond that encyclical's limitations. The "personalist" thought common in England, discussed particularly in Dominican circles, and bellowed at the public by G.K.Chesterton and Eric Gill, was often associated with the economic doctrine of "distributism," and had parallels in the teachings of Peter Maurin in the United States, popularised by his *Easy Essays* and by the journalism of the saintly Dorothy Day and others of his "Catholic Worker" movement. It found a theoretical base in the Thomist personalism of Jacques Maritain and, to a lesser extent, in the Orthodox personalism of Nicolas Berdyaev. Whether through these theologians or through their popularisers, it constituted what was, for some fifty years, a theological form of anti-capitalist libertarianism which was profoundly influential in parts of the Roman Catholic world, finding echoes, too, in the Anglican circles influenced by people like Conrad Noel and the Christendom Group.

Moreover, if that sort of critique became muted in the face of the state-oriented solutions to social problems which constituted the secular post-war consensus in western Europe (and even, to some extent, in North America,) the particular problems of large parts of Latin America continue to evoke a "Liberation Theology," whose connection with these streams of libertarian thought is an important one, all too easily overlooked by those who see its secular political affiliations as simply Marxist.

It is here, in fact, as much as anywhere else, that the sort of dialogue between libertarian socialist traditions and official catholic social teaching—for which we have made an implicit plea in what we have said so far—finds a particular relevance. For that theology of liberation which has arisen from Latin America has emerged not from a particular attentiveness either to the Vatican social teaching of the last hundred years or, despite its frequent use of Marxist categories, to any particular secular political creed. It has emerged first and foremost directly from the situation of oppression of many of the people of Latin America, interpreted through reflection on the biblical theme of liberation, and through the imperative seen in that interpretation to bring about that liberation at every level of existence.

This does not mean, however, that liberation theology has nothing to learn from either Vatican social teaching or secular political creeds. Though it has emerged from neither, it clearly reflects the concerns and analyses of both. Many liberation theologians, in particular, have clearly been deeply affected by their reading of Marx. When their writings are looked at carefully, however, the political themes which they adopt from Marx seem to be rather selective. The impression is, in fact, often of a closeness not so much to state-oriented Marxism as much as to precisely those libertarian socialist traditions which we have noted, with their reflection of certain of the underlying ideas of Vatican teaching.

It may well be that this arises from the Christian and intrinsically grass-roots spectacles through which the theologians of liberation have read Marx. As Linda Damico has suggested in a recent study, what they seem to do is to, "downplay, if not discard, those Marxist components which are antianarchist ... The Marx of liberation theology is, in part, an anarchist Marx."[45] Thus, she suggests, what emerges in the literature of such theologians is an aspect of liberation theology which may properly be termed an "Anarchist Dimension."

There seems to be much truth in this analysis, and it leads to the likelihood that those many commentators who have insisted on reading the theologians of liberation simply through Marxist spectacles have missed something of considerable importance. This may well, of course, have been due to the uncritical use of the simple spectrum model of political options which we have questioned here, for it seems that much of such commentary—both from the right and the left of the political spectrum—has rested on the assumption that to be anti-capitalist is to be at least quasi-marxist. Damico has, therefore, made an important point in her (perhaps too emphatic) assertion that "The economic, political, social, moral, and, to some degree, the religious vision of the future is the same for both the leading anarchists ... and for many liberation theologians."[46]

Even allowing for the modifications to this analysis which might be necessary, this genuine similarity, once recognised, leads to the possibility of interesting new perspectives within liberation theology itself. One such new perspective might be in terms of a modification of certain views common in the theology of liberation. For much of what Damico sees rightly as parallels between classical anarchism and liberation theology relates directly to aspects of historical anarchism which many libertarian socialists of the present day would see as extremist positions. These positions, while understandable in terms of the conditions which evoked them, they would see as being in need of considerable modification in the light of more recent experience and reflection. By enabling liberation theology to tap this experience and reflection, the recognition of parallels between that theology and classical anarchism might lead to an interesting new openness of that theology to the evolution of socialist thinking in the developed west.

If a modern libertarian socialism simultaneously illuminates and challenges the liberation theology which has emerged from the situation of Latin America, however, it might have no less an effect on official catholic social teaching as it has emerged from the concerns of the industrialised west. For while there may now be much to be said for viewing those concerns in terms of the possible modifications to new right thinking which could come about through dialogue with catholic social teaching, such modifications, in themselves, will fail, as we have noted, to address important issues of the sort which liberation theology has highlighted.

The chief of these, we have suggested, is that of a proper understanding of property rights—an issue which links the situations to be found at all stages of economic development. Thus, although the manifestations of, and proper response to, corporate sin in the Latin American context will be very different to those in the industrialised west, the underlying problem of developing a proper understanding of property is, it would seem, not dissimilar in the two areas. Thus at a deeper level than that of manifestation and response, the situations which have evoked both official catholic social teaching and liberation theology are linked in a significant way, and the two cannot be treated as essentially unrelated. They will, if they are examined at this deeper level, be mutually illuminating in a potentially fruitful way.

In an article published in 1990, I asked, of official catholic social teaching and libertarian socialism, whether it might be that "Together ... those traditions can enable Christians to enter a dialogue with the theoreticians of the new right which is not simply one based on incoherent antagonism, as so often seems to be the case at present." [47] At the time that article was written, in the late nineteen eighties, it still seemed that dialogue with the new right was the perspective from which to draw together a number of libertarian traditions which seemed in danger of remaining virtually unknown to one another. I pointed out that there was often a confusion of terms, so that, for example, the word "capitalism" itself was often used in different ways.

I used, to illustrate this confusion, an article in *The Spectator* by Auberon Waugh, in which he praised the traditional conservatism of France for its recognition that there are two threats to what he labelled "conservative civilization—call it capitalism, a free society or what you will". For as well as state-oriented socialism, he suggested, there is the threat from the activities of "financiers." There are, he said, with clear distaste, "two currencies—the ordinary pounds and dollars accumulated by the industry and thrift of the working population and the junk pounds or dollars which exist on video screens as the accumulation of gambling and asset-stripping operations by financiers."[48]

The echoes here, I suggested, were more of G.K.Chesterton or Peter Maurin than of a coherent defender of laissez-faire capitalism, reminding one of one of the latter's *Easy Essays*:

The capitalist system / is a racketeering system / because it is / a profit system. / And nobody / has found a way / to keep the profit system / from becoming / a profiteering system ...."[49] For Waugh, I noted, as for many upholders of an old-fashioned pre-new right conservatism, the word capitalism seems to imply property as a guarantee of freedom, including that of enjoying the fruits of one's own labour—precisely the sort of property defended in the sort of catholic social teaching of the pre-war years which we have noted and in Proudhonian anarchism. Such conservatives fail to see, I suggested, that this conception of property can be maintained in any other system than laissez-faire capitalism, which clearly has aspects which they deplore. For to talk of a non-capitalist economy is, for such defenders, to attack all for which they believe their "conservative civilization" stands, and necessarily to support a Marxist vision of the alternative.

"This is not," I then said, "to say that the instincts which underlie the new right are simply those of the theological personalist or the political anarchist disguised by a confusion of vocabulary. There are profound differences of understanding of the human condition between the three streams of thought. Nevertheless, a failure to recognise common ground can only inhibit true dialogue, and it is the conviction of this essay that a more profound understanding of the theology of freedom than has hitherto been apparent, together with a fuller understanding of all political traditions with a strong libertarian component, including non-capitalist ones, will alone make possible a creative as well as critical dialogue with what is undoubtedly the most powerful political philosophy of the late twentieth century."[50]

The observations about a new interest in catholic social thought among conservatives, with which we began, both underline that point and slightly change its emphasis. For it would seem that the need is no longer one of finding an opening for dialogue with proponents of new right policies who are disdainful of any other perspective. Both on the right and on the left of the political spectrum, there is now a widespread agreement with the new right's emphasis on market mechanisms as efficient providers of many goods and services, coupled with a new openness to exploring what the concept of solidarity might be about. The complementary concept of subsidiarity, while part of the rhetoric inherited by a post new-right conservatism is, however, still to be fully understood on both sides of the political spectrum, except perhaps by a few who had previously taken a full-blown libertarianism to heart.

This new exploration of both solidarity and subsidiarity is, at heart I believe, an exploration of what it is to be a human being. It is, implicitly, a groping towards what a theologian might call a theological anthropology. For most people active in this political debate, of course, that quest will never be more than implicitly theological, and anything which smacks too much of explicit theology will be likely to be counter-productive. This, however, is precisely where catholic theology's traditional use of "natural law" can be most effective. No matter how much such a concept may have been misused in the past, a revived and revised picture of human nature, which is consonant both with what God has revealed in Christ, and with what is observable in human beings as they are, could, when it is the latter which is stressed in dialogue, be of immense importance in helping people of all faiths and of none to build a theoretical picture of human society which can, in the different ways appropriate to different cultures, enable a new consensus about the basis for a right ordering of that society to emerge.

The theological task which this requires is an immense one in itself. As we have suggested, it requires perhaps above all a realistic understanding of what it is to be a "fallen" human being in a "fallen" society, called to manifest (and yet continually failing to fully manifest) that redemption and liberation to which all are called in Christ.

If we adopt too optimistic a picture, we shall be in danger of falling into a dangerous utopianism. If, on the other hand, we adopt an Augustinian pessimism, we shall perhaps fall on the other side of the reality of what it is to be human, and fail to allow the development of human dignity through genuine responsibility.

If we adopt too collectivist a picture of solidarity, we shall, for a different reason, equally fail to recognise the responsibility which belongs to each human person. If, on the other hand, we fail to recognise that to be a "person" is, in a theological sense, to be far more than simply being an individual, here too we shall err grievously, in failing to recognise the intrinsic social dimension of human existence.

If we ignore the empirical truth of Arthur Young's dictum that "Property is the magic that turns sand to gold," we shall be guilty of an unrooted theoreticism, an inability to recognise what a revived and revised natural law might teach us. If we fail to recognise the structural injustice inherent in too general a definition of property, however, we shall be guilty of withholding from many that modicum of such a magic which is their right.

If we fail to recognise the importance of market mechanisms in efficient distribution of goods and services, we shall have failed to learn the lesson of recent history. If we were to rely on nothing else, on the other hand, we would not only be guilty of the continuing deprivation and exploitation of the poor. We would be guilty also of nothing less than that idolatry of the market against which Christian social teaching has consistently cried out.

Whatever our theological judgement on these questions, the importance of them is immense. For only if we answer them adequately can we get to the true heart of the political questions which we have asked, those questions of how, in a fallen world, all people can have the freedom to develop in dignity and in responsibility, free from degrading poverty and structural injustice, free also in their cooperation with others, as a sign and manifestation of that solidarity of all humankind which the church proclaims to the ends of the earth.

I should like to end with a sort of extended footnote, whose validity or otherwise is quite independent of what has preceded it. I have, at least implicitly, made a plea for the continuing development of a theological anthropology, for its use both in evolving a Christian social perspective and in fostering dialogue with and between different secular political traditions. This plea rests on the conviction that such dialogue is essential to the future well-being of humankind, and the need for a footnote to that plea arises from my conviction that such a development cannot simply be an intellectual task, important as hard and clear thinking will be to its success. It is also, I believe, a spiritual task. It is not merely a matter of thinking about what we are as human beings, for such thought must be based, I believe, on a recognition of what we are at that far deeper level which precedes thought.

The reasons for this belief I have outlined elsewhere,[51] not the least of them being a number of insights from the sociology of knowledge which convince me that there are always pre-theoretical assumptions behind any argument, and that unless these are undistorted, any subsequent argument will always have, at the very least, distorting blind spots. In that discussion I have suggested that right social thought and action must be based on a deeper theological experience of what it is to be human than that provided even by the deepest reflection on scripture and tradition. For me, such experience will be essentially ecclesial and eucharistic. It is what we experience of our humanity in our foretaste of the banquet of the Kingdom—the eucharist—which gives meaning to our life in the world.

At one level we might approach this as a psychological experience. In my article I suggested that this might be understood in terms of the interraction of theology with psychology in the thought of Mircea Eliade. For, in his analysis, (with its links to the work of Jung for those who would prefer a purely secular framework), all human beings, irrespective of religious belief, indulge in mythological behaviour which is related to that "Great Time" to be found in one guise or another in all mythological systems. In this view, the human being encounters the numinous whenever he leaves the secular time in which history unfolds, and enters the sacred time which gives it meaning. In its Christian manifestation this is, for Eliade, during that "liturgical time in which the Christian lives during the divine service ... the time in which the Word is made flesh, the illud tempus of the gospels."[52]

The average Christian may not find this an easy way of expressing an experienced reality, but it does relate directly, it seems, to one which is much more familiar, and which provides a theological way of looking at the question—one which can be taken as independent of any particular psychological insight. For the catholic tradition's concept of the eucharistic anamnesis, in which the saving acts of God are not merely "remembered" but actually "re-called" in the sense of being made present to those who "Look for the coming of His Kingdom," is very close to this concept of liturgical time as analysed in the light of universal mythological thought. Indeed, in the eastern Christian tradition especially, the eucharist can be seen primarily in these terms, the past and future both being being made present in the eucharistic action, so that the function of the liturgy can be seen as precisely that of constituting the church as the presence and communication of the Kingdom that is to come.

This eschatalogical emphasis may at first seem antithetical to the concern for the world of present day reality which evoked these thoughts, but we should perhaps not forget that even in liberation theology, which is often accused of an undue emphasis on the present at the expense of the eschaton, there is often a clear recognition that a proper eschatalogical emphasis is, in the words of Gutierrez, "not an escape from history, but ... has clear and strong implications for the political sphere, for social praxis."[53] He speaks movingly of the way in which "Every prophetic proclamation of total liberation is accompanied by an invitation to participate in eschatalogical joy,"[54] and of how this is focussed in the eucharist, "a feast, a celebration of the joy that the Church desires and seeks to share."[55]

In the sort of psychological-cum-theological perspective I have mentioned, it is, in fact, precisely the numinous experience of liturgical time in worship, and especially in the eucharist, which makes the concerns of our "profane duration" psychologically meaningful, and which provides a direct experience of, and insight into, that reality of human unity in diversity to which all are ultimately called—and to which our present life in society should approximate as closely as fallen human nature allows. The deeper and pre-theoretical understanding we need to develop a theological anthropology is, therefore, to be found precisely through that experience of the eschatalogical fulness of our humanity, in relation to others and to God, which is ours unconsciously in the Eucharist.

That pre-theoretical basis for our thinking which we need, then, is one which is not intellectual but spiritual in the deepest sense. Right thinking and action, in this perspective, can only be based on right worship. For, such an analysis would suggest, it is precisely that eschatalogical dimension of true relationship with God in Christ, which we experience most fully in worship, which makes the "return to the world" from the liturgy meaningful and fruitful both for belief and praxis. For

169

that return, as one of the chief theologians of the eastern Christian tradition puts it,

> ...neither destroys nor alters the eschatalogical fulness of the liturgical experience. It is the dynamic affirmation of it, the way the eucharist is personally put into action; it is the struggle of freedom to be transfigured into love, to transfigure every corner of life into eucharist. The realization and revelation of the body of Christ at every eucharistic synaxis is God's continuing entry into the world; it is the dynamic start of the transfiguration of the world and of history.[56]

For the theologian, the recognition that right theological thought and action require a deeper spiritual dimension is both a humbling one and one which simultaneously justifies his or her whole enterprise. To be reminded that the true love of our neighbour, as manifested in social and political action, requires true experience of our own deepest nature, as manifested and experienced in worship, is, in fact, not to devalue the former, but to recognise more fully and deeply than before both its source and its goal.

REFERENCES

1. W. Hutton, "A Rosier Shade of Grey," *Marxism Today* (London) April 1991, p. 15.

2. N. Malcolm, "The road which starts at Tory Central Office and leads to Rome," *The Spectator* (London) 13 April 1991, p. 6.

3. C. Longley, "Rome finds a ready ear in high places," *The Times* (London) 20 April 1991, p. 8.

4. *The Independent* (London) 20 June 1991 p. 1.

5.   Anon.,"Enlarging the EC debate," *The Independent* (London) 29 June 1991 p. 14.

6.   *Rerum novarum....* (henceforward RN), para. 16.

7.   *RN* para. 39.

8.   *RN* para. 39.

9.   *RN* para. 45.

10.   *RN* para. 49.

11.   *RN* para. 49.

12.   Longley *op. cit.*

13.   Hutton *op. cit.*

14.   *Ibid.*

15.   See e.g., M. Bookchin, *Toward an Ecological Society* (Montreal 1980).

16.   See e.g., R. Preston. *Religion and the Persistence of Capitalism* (London 1979); also *The New Right and Christian Values.* Edinburgh University Centre for Theology and Public Issues: Occasional Paper No.5 (1987).

17.   E. Heath, Foreword to W.Temple, *Christianity and the Social Order*, (new edn. London 1976).

18.   H. de Lubac, *The Un-Marxian Socialist.* (London 1948) p.vii.

19.   J. P. Miranda, *Communism in the Bible*. (Maryknoll, NY, 1982) p.72.

20.   Quoted by E. Pagels, *Adam, Eve, and the Serpent*. (London 1988) p. 103.

21.   *Ibid*. p. 113.

22.   Temple *op. cit*. p. 83f.

23.   Leo XIII, "Au milieu des Solicitudes" qu. by D. Dorr, *Option For The Poor*. (Dublin 1983) p. 38.

24.   Leo XIII, "On the Christian Constitution of States" (London 1886) p. 32.

25.   *Ibid*. p. 37.

26.   *Ibid*. p. 40.

27.   *Ibid*. p. 32.

28.   C. Ward, *Anarchy in Action*. (2nd. edn. London 1982) p. 5.

29.   *Ibid*. p. 14.

30.   Dorr *op. cit*. p.90.

31.   *RN* para. 13.

32.   *RN* para. 53.

33.   P-J. Proudhon, *What is Property*, tr. B. J. Tucker, (New York 1966) p. 42.

34.   Dorr *op. cit.* p. 46.

35.   *Ibid.* p. 47f.

36.   *RN* para. 6.

37.   *RN* para. 7.

38.   *RN* para. 8.

39.   T. Nulty, *An Essay on the Land Question.* (1881) abr. version in H. George, *The Condition of Labour.* (new. ed. London 1934) pp. 201ff.

40.   George *op. cit.* p.36.

41.   *Ibid.* p. 36f.

42.   *Ibid.* p. 3f.

43.   See e.g., A. M. C. Waterman, "Private Property, Inequality, Theft" in P. Jefferson (ed.) *Voice from the Mountain: New Life for Old Law.* (Toronto 1982).

44.   Quoted by Dorr *op. cit.* p. 290 n. 34.

45.   L. H. Damico, *The Anarchist Dimension of Liberation Theology* (New York 1987) p. 10.

46.   *Ibid.* p. 193.

47.   C. Knight, "Christians and the Politics of Liberty," *Theology,* XCIII (1990) p. 195.

48. A. Waugh, "Can the ghost of Marshall Petain yet save us from Thatcher?" in *The Spectator* (London) 26 Aug. 1989 p. 7.

49. P. Maurin, *Easy Essays.* (Chicago 1977).

50. Knight *op. cit.* p. 196f.

51. C. Knight, "'Send Us Out Into the World': Liturgy as Edification", in *Modern Churchman.* (forthcoming).

52. M. Eliade, "Myths, Dreams and Realities" in F. W. Dillistone (ed.) *Myth and Symbol.* (London 1966) p. 42.

53. G. Gutierrez, *A Theology of Liberation.* (Rev. Edn. London 1988) p. 122

54. *Ibid.* p. 120.

55. *Ibid.* p. 148.

56. C. Yannaras, *The Freedom of Morality.* (Crestwood, NY, 1984) p. 90.

Subsidiarity and Sphere Sovereignty: Catholic and Reformed Conceptions of the Role of the State

Jonathan Chaplin

A noteworthy characteristic of recent political thought is an emerging awareness of the inadequacy of a fundamental premise of the classical liberal tradition, namely that the central problems confronting political philosophy can be reduced to a singular relationship, that between the individual and the state. Philosophical reflection has for too long been preoccupied with a cluster of dilemmas arising from this relationship: how to derive the authority of the state from the individual, how to render the state accountable to individuals, or how to protect the individual against the state. It is being realised that these problems cannot adequately be answered so long as the vast terrain of social relationships and communities existing alongside the individual and the state is taken into political account. The realisation is dawning that we cannot grasp the nature of the political association unless we also understand the nature of the numerous non-political associations which frame the larger part of the social life of the individual; that human beings are social creatures not just in that they live in 'society,' but in that they live in multiple and diverse societies; and that if these diverse expressions of our sociality are not fostered and protected against deformations arising from an exaggeration either of state power or individual liberty, we shall be impoverished as citizens as well as in our other social roles.

This theme, on which little that is original has been said by political philosophers since before the second world war, is attracting renewed interest across the ideological spectrum. Neo-conservatives in the USA, attacking bureaucratic 'megastructures' like the state and the large corporate institutions, urge a recovery of these 'mediating structures' (Berger and Neuhaus's term) which buffer the individual against them. Neo-liberals, exposing the inefficiency and illiberality of the public sector, seek to shift the responsibility for economic coordination and welfare provision onto private organizations. Neo-socialists, disillusioned by the failed promise of state-administered socialism, join with Greens and feminists in urging a new variety of decentralized, pluralistic socialism ('associationalist socialism,' as Paul Hirst characterises it) which meets human needs by means of, rather than at the cost of, democratic participation.

We may therefore be witnessing a rebirth of 'pluralism' (strictly, of 'normative' pluralism, as distinct from the supposedly purely 'descriptive' variety of pluralism developed by American political scientists in the nineteen-fifties and -sixties and still influential today). While profound divergences remain between these various strands of thought, there is at least a consensus that the modern state has overreached and thereby incapacitated itself, and needs to be refashioned in a way that respects the independent contributions of a plurality of associations, communities and institutions which have for too long either atrophied through neglect or collapsed under direct assault.

We have, of course, been here before. Among the many works voicing similar concerns in the early decades of this century was *Quadragesimo anno* (1931):

> Things have come to such a pass through the evil of what we have termed 'individualism' that, following upon the overthrow and near extinction of that rich social life which was once highly developed through associations of various kinds, there remain virtually only individuals and the State. This is to the great harm of the State itself; for with a structure of social governance lost, and with the taking over of all the burdens which the wrecked associations once bore, the State has been overwhelmed and crushed by almost infinite tasks and duties (78).

176

Today the role of this 'structure of social governance' is being rediscovered once again. The specific form of the structure recommended by Pius XI—a kind of liberal corporatism—may not be our guide today, but the broad contours of the social vision underlying it do indeed merit critical reappropriation and elaboration.

The purpose of this paper is to highlight the importance of this task by bringing the Catholic vision expressed in *QA*, and specifically the ideas of subsidiarity and associational autonomy which are central to it, into critical interaction with a parallel vision and principle from the Reformed tradition. I focus on the most highly developed version of this Reformed vision, one which emerged in the late nineteenth-century from a revived Dutch neo-Calvinism, and in which a different idea of associational autonomy—'sphere sovereignty'—is fundamental. This pluralistic Reformed conception, although not widely known outside the Netherlands, is arguably the most substantial example of a Protestant social and political theory in the twentieth century. It decisively influenced the course of Dutch political history, fashioned the structure of some primary Dutch social and political institutions, and left its imprint upon the character of Dutch Christian Democracy. Although rooted in quite different theological and philosophical foundations, it shares a great deal with the Catholic conception (more than it has often been willing to admit). I shall suggest that key elements of both of these political philosophies need to be incorporated into a contemporary Christian theory of the state.

In the first section of the paper I review the origins and meaning of the principle of subsidiarity, drawing both on papal statements and on interpretations of the principle by Catholic philosophers, especially those associated with Solidarism, such as Heinrich Rommen, Johannes Messner, Oswald Von Nell-Breuning (author of the first draft of *QA*). The Reformed conception of sphere sovereignty is introduced in the second section. Special attention is given to the two most articulate advocates of the idea, the nineteenth century theologian and statesman Abraham Kuyper and the twentieth century legal philosopher Herman Dooyeweerd. The final section makes preliminary suggestions regarding a critical interaction with the other varieties of pluralism referred to above.

PART I: SUBSIDIARITY

The term 'subsidiarity' has recently made its appearance within British political discussion because of its relation to the idea of federalism. European Christian Democrats have apparently been employing the term to persuade the reluctant British that federal European institutions will only take over functions currently performed by national governments when it become evident that the latter are incapable of discharging them efficiently. Some British commentators appear to think that the term is just another example of technocratic Eurospeak. Others believe they have scored a point by noting that, since the principle of subsidiarity does not indicate precisely which powers ought to be transferred to the European level—it doesn't tell us whether seat belts should be regulated from Brussels or London, for example—the term must be just another example of woolly Continental thinking. (If subsidiarity did indicate this kind of thing, it would not, of course, be a principle at all but a policy, but leave that aside.) Clearly a great deal of clarification will be necessary if the term, but more importantly the concept, is to be employed constructively in the debate about the future shape of Europe.

Federalism is, however, but one specific application of the principle, one addressed to the question of the division of powers between different levels of government. The principle operates much more widely, as a basic guideline for the distribution of functions as between the state and all other bodies. It holds that the state ought not to assume tasks which other communities can perform for themselves, and counsels that what Pius XI termed the 'structure of social governance' should not be needlessly overridden by political governance from above. Traditionally these other communities are known in Catholic thought as 'lesser' or 'subordinate.' The term in fact includes both subordinate political bodies such as municipalities or provinces, and non-political bodies such as families, unions, or schools.

This political application of the principle will be primary concern, but it is essential to note that subsidiarity also applies to fundamental relationships between the individual and any community (or 'the community' in general). Subsidiarity has always been understood to apply comprehensively to all social relationships and thus lies at the heart of Catholic social philosophy.

178

Before briefly recapitulating the relevant themes of this philosophy, an outline of the history of the principle is necessary. The term 'subsidiarity' does not appear in *Rerum novarum* but the idea is operative in it nonetheless. Although *RN* cannot be said to have actually 'taught' the principle, as the *New Catholic Encyclopedia* claims, the principle is undoubtedly implied at several points in the document. It draws a careful distinction between lesser or 'private societies' and the larger society, and affirms that the state has a duty to give legal effect to the natural right of individuals to join such 'private societies' (51). In particular, it endorses at length and enthusiastically the virtues of workingmen's associations (RN.48-51). As Calvez and Perrin put it, for Leo associations like these could 'help re-knit the connecting tissues of a society which individualism had reduced to isolated units' (p.408). Consistent with this *RN* also affirms the independent rights of both the family and religious orders against the state and urges that they must be vigilantly protected against unwarranted state intervention (RM 14;53). Further, where such intervention proves necessary, 'the law must not be asked to do more nor to proceed further than is necessary to put right the wrong' (29).

The principle of subsidiarity can therefore be said to be founded in *RN*. However, as is well known, it receives its first explicit papal formulation in Pius XI's *Quadragesimo anno*:

> Just as it is gravely wrong to take from individuals what they can accomplish by their own initiative and industry and give it to the community, so also it is an injustice and at the same time a grave evil and disturbance of right order to assign to a greater and higher association what lesser and subordinate organizations can do. For every social activity ought of its very nature to furnish help to the members of the body social, and never destroy or absorb them (79).

On a number of occasions Pius XI's successors have reaffirmed the principle explicitly. Pius XII did so on several occasions, (e.g., in a speech to the new cardinals, 1946, cited in Calvez and Perrin, p.122 n). John XXIII reaffirms it and employs it at several points in *Mater et magistra* (53,117,152), which also contains a lengthy section acknowledging the importance of the growth of 'associations' (59-76). He also applies it to the international sphere in *Pacem in terris* (140). Paul VI employs it, though without mentioning the term, in *Populorum progressio* (33). Happily, subsidiarity also received mention in *Centesimus annus* (15, 48), together with the complementary principle of solidarity. *QA* remains the classic explicit formulation, though other themes in subsequent social encyclicals, especially elaborations of the meaning of the common good, clearly bear upon its interpretation and application.

So much for the history of the idea, what of its detailed meaning? Let us take its general sense first, and then consider at greater length its political application. The term 'subsidiarity' derives from the Latin word *subsidium*, meaning help or aid. It is in fact already implied in the conception of the relationship between the individual and society which is at the base of Catholic social philosophy. Humans are social creatures unable to realise their ends in isolation from others. They need the *subsidium*, the help, of society in order to be human. Society itself thus performs a 'subsidiary function' in relation to persons; 'all social activity is of its nature subsidiary,' as Pius XII put it. A 'subsidiary' function is not a 'secondary' one but rather an indispensable auxiliary one. Society performs a subsidiary function not simply when the individual meets a crisis, but as a matter of course.

The same point emerges from a consideration of the concept of the common good. The good of the individual cannot be realised apart from the good of the whole. The common good takes priority over all individual goods, but only in the sense that the individual needs what is contained in the common good in order to attain his individual good. The good of individuals is embraced within it, fulfilling it by offering those conditions resources, opportunities, and securities without which the individual cannot realise his own ends. Whatever limitations are imposed by the common good upon the exercise of individual rights are imposed in order to guarantee conditions in which such rights may be effectively realised. In a radical sense, the meaning of personhood" 'the right of society, the common good, is necessarily within the rights of the person

180

which it guarantees. It transcends the person only because it is also indwelling in him.' (Calvez and Perrin, p.118)

Now the help (*subsidium*) offered by society as such to the individual is nothing other than that which is contained in the common good. Hence, as Messner puts it: 'the law of subsidiary function and the law of the common good are, in substance, identical.' The principle of the common good both legitimates collective action but at the same time limits such action to that which is necessary to help individuals in the realisation of their own ends in responsible freedom. The common good authorises the community no further than to the point at which individuals require its aid. (Messner, p.196) Subsidiarity is thus an inherent feature of the common good, not a qualification of it.

Let us turn now to the application of subsidiarity to the relationship between the state and lesser communities. A preliminary question is what falls under the heading of 'lesser communities.' Thomas Aquinas only discusses in any detail the family and the household, but modern Catholic philosophers, such as Rommen and Messner, take cognisance of a much wider range of communities typical of a differentiated industrial society. Following the lead given by Leo XIII, who specifically acknowledged workingmen's associations as having a natural foundation, they have extended Thomas' Aristotelian argument for the organic evolution of state from household, to include not only lesser territorial groupings, but also professional and vocational organizations, religious, national, cultural and educational bodies. (Rommen, p.301) Sometimes a distinction is drawn between communities directly ordained by nature (family, locality, occupational group, state, international society), and associations based on freely chosen ends (unions, employers' associations, charitable groups and so on). (Messner, p.138)

Human society is envisaged as a divinely ordered hierarchy of qualitatively different communities each ordered to distinctive, non-transferrable ends rooted in man's rational nature and governed by natural and divine law. The ranking of the communities is determined by the hierarchical arrangement of ends. Particular communities come into existence in the social process as expressions of particular aspects of human social nature. While man's supernatural end is his highest, he can only move towards it through this plurality of natural associations, each directed to fulfilling one partial end and possessing a unique character and range of rights and duties determined objectively by natural law. As John Paul II puts it in *CA*:

> The social nature of man is not completely fulfilled in the State, but is realized in various intermediary groups, beginning with the family and including economic, social, political and cultural groups which stem from human nature itself and have their own autonomy, always with a view to the common good. This is what I have called [in Sollicitudo rei socialis] the "subjectivity" of society...(14).

The subordination of lesser communities to those above them in the social hierarchy does not compromise their separate identity nor diminish their independent (relative) value. As Rommen puts it: 'All organizational forms have their intrinsic values and their objective ends, the upper form does not make the lower form superfluous; it must never abolish it, nor may it take over its functions and purposes.' (p.301) In the strict sense, every higher community performs a subsidiary function with respect to those below it, (but this point tends not to be pursued, for reasons we explore later).

It is the essential subsidiary function of the state with respect to the lesser communities which attracts the greatest interest. The general principle is that the state has a duty to offer lesser communities such help as is needed in order for the latter to realize their distinctive ends. All that was said above about the subsidiary function of society with respect to individuals also applies to the state's subsidiary function with respect to lesser communities.

The state is the supreme guardian of the common good of the whole society. As such it is empowered to act in a variety of ways in order to secure that overriding moral end. The state's authority is in principle as wide in scope as the attainment of the common good requires. But it is no wider. Just as the common good includes within itself the

182

good of individuals, so it also includes the particular goods of the lesser communities. It is necessarily pluralistic in character. Hence the state cannot thrive at the expense of the rights of its citizens, nor of the rights of the lesser bodies within its jurisdiction. The state must enable lesser communities to be themselves. In practice this will mean that the acknowledgement of a substantial measure of autonomy on the part of lesser communities will be an essential ingredient of the common good.

The protection of the autonomy of lesser communities will safeguard individuals from the likely encroachments of a burgeoning centralized state. Individual freedom is extended by safeguarding associational freedom. Protecting this autonomy is, moreover, crucial to the proper functioning of the state itself, a point expressed in *QA*:

> The supreme authority of the State ought, therefore, to let subordinate groups handle matters and concerns of lesser importance, which would otherwise dissipate its efforts greatly. Thereby the State will more freely, powerfully, and effectively do all those things that belong to it alone because it alone can do them: directing, watching, urging, restraining, as occasion requires and necessity demands. Therefore, those in power should be sure that the more perfectly a graduated order is kept among the various associations, in observance of the principle of "subsidiary function," the stronger social authority and effectiveness will be [and] the happier and more prosperous the condition of the State. (80)

The autonomy of the lesser communities comes to legal expression in their possession of special rights. Messner is especially emphatic in asserting the principle of juridical pluralism (and on this he acknowledges the contribution of late nineteenth-and early twentieth-century legal pluralists such as Gierke, Duguit, Hauriou, and Gurvitch). Corresponding

183

to the plurality of communities there is, he holds, a 'plurality of categories of equally original fundamental rights, none of which can be derived from another' (p.177). These rights move in different orbits and are qualitatively different from, and irreducible to, each other. Although the state is responsible for establishing a legal framework within which lesser communities can securely exercise these particular rights, it is not itself the source of these rights. Such rights are essentially natural rights, rights which the state merely codifies and balances in positive law. The state affords lesser bodies the necessary legal recognition, but 'it is their essence, their ends, that control the legal forms, not vice versa.' (Rommen, p.143) Such associations should therefore in general be left free by the state to adopt their own internal rules. On the other hand these must be conducive to realising their natural moral purposes. The freedom of association is more than the individual's right to join an association. It also carries with it the duty to see that the association fulfils its morally legitimate purpose. If this duty is not fulfilled, it may be necessary for the state to intervene to ensure that it is. This would not be a violation but a restoration of the natural rights of the association.

The special rights of lesser communities constitute a major limit to the exercise of the sovereignty of the state. The possession of sovereignty is indeed an essential concomitant of the state's duty to the common good of the whole society . Since only the state has this duty, only it has this right. Although the state's rights and those of lesser communities are 'equally original,' they are not 'equal' (i.e., identical in content). But political sovereignty must be carefully defined. It emphatically does not mean legal omnicompetence, but only legal universality and finality. The state's writ certainly runs throughout its entire territory and takes precedence over the lesser authorities of other bodies, acting as final adjudicator in cases of conflict. But since the spheres of authority of the lesser communities are also original and rooted in nature, they may never be conceived as mere delegations of political authority.

We must now explore further what the state may do as it acts subsidiarily towards the lesser communities. A very wide range of activities have been proposed as warranted by the principle, but three particular kinds of activity may conveniently be distinguished: enabling, intervening, and substituting:

1. ENABLING activities will involve the creation of the necessary general legal, economic, social and moral conditions in which lesser communities can flourish. Legally, a just and stable order must be established in which the special rights of lesser communities are upheld. Economically, as *Centesimus annus* puts it, the state acts by 'creating favourable conditions for the free exercise of economic activity, which will lead to abundant opportunities for employment and sources of wealth' (15). Socially and morally, it is the task of the state to foster harmonious relations between individuals and between communities and to encourage those public virtues which foster healthy community activity.

2. INTERVENING activities, i.e., interventions in the internal affairs of a lesser community, are justified when there is some obvious deficiency or distortion within them which may affect the common good. These might include either negative interventions (restrictions) such as tightening the election procedures of a large, undemocratically run trades union or limiting the rights of corporate shareholders, or positive interventions (provision) such as supplementing low income with welfare payments. Such intervention must always aim at restoring the ability of lesser communities to fulfil their own responsibilities to the wider community. That is, the intervention is justified not in terms of the benefits accruing to the particular communities themselves, but to those accruing to the common good.

Not surprisingly, different authors, and different popes, interpret the scope of legitimate intervention differently, but let us take Rommen as an illustration. He envisages a programme of social legislation protecting the worker, recognising the rights of trade unions, abolishing child labour, defending agricultural holdings, imposing progressive taxation, curbing monopolies, granting privileges to farmers cooperative, ensuring honesty in financial institutions, protecting the small saver, or imposing tariffs (pp.321-4, 351-2). Such intervention must however be no more than a 'reconstitution of the order of self-initiative' (p.304).

3. SUBSTITUTING activities, in which the state directly assumes tasks specifically belonging to lesser communities, are in general ruled out. Direct responsibility for the partial common goods of lesser communities fall outside the political order. Hence comprehensive nationalization and a centrally planned economy are in principle excluded.

But in exceptional circumstances when a particular community is chronically deficient and incapable of performing basic functions, such substitution is justified, temporarily if possible. Substitution is thus an 'accidental mode of subsidiarity,' as Calvez and Perrin put it (p.336). However, in addition, it is sometimes acknowledged that the state may need to take over certain essential activities performed by lesser bodies where these grow to the point at which they become indispensable to the common good, perhaps by bringing certain natural monopolies into public ownership (*QA*, 179, *CA*, 48).

These, then, are the broad contours of the conception of the role of the state generated by the principle of subisidiarity. As a preparation for discussing the Reformed idea of sphere sovereignty, it is worth pausing to explore just one of the important questions that arise from the above account, namely the idea that the various communities are hierarchically arranged. The notion of hierarchical ordering is fundamental to Thomist metaphysics. Whatever is made of its general merits, it creates a problem when applied to the social world, (one which here can only be briefly characterised). It is plausible to acknowledge that human beings function within a diversity of communities, but it is problematic to view these as ranked within a hierarchy. In what sense does the state rank 'above' the lesser communities, or the local community 'above' the family? Is the corporation above the union, or vice versa? Where are political parties or schools positioned in the hierarchy? And, perhaps most awkwardly, in what sense does the church as the supernatural community crown the entire hierarchy? It appears difficult to find a satisfactory single criterion according to which a complete ranking could be achieved—which suggests that the very idea of a ranking may be misplaced.

The problem with the idea of hierarchy can also be seen by exploring the question of why, as Calvez and Perrin point out, 'subsidiarity only looks one way,'(p.332) It is not difficult to see the initial plausibility of this with respect of the state (central or local). While the state fulfils a subsidiary function towards the lesser communities, they do not fulfil a similar function towards it. In a wider sense, the lesser communities do assist the state in its task insofar as they effectively fulfil their own functions and thus make state aid unnecessary. Yet it is not

186

part of their primary purpose to be responsible for the state in the way that the state is essentially responsible for them. However, it is more difficult to see why subsidiarity is only a one-way function with respect to the relationships between the various lesser communities themselves. It has already been noted that few interpreters of subsidiarity have much to say about how higher communities other than the state are supposed to aid those below it in the hierarchy. This may be because it is in any case difficult to determine whether some communities are above or below others. It is also, crucially, because aid evidently goes in both directions. Does the corporation aid the trade union or vice versa? Does a professional association aid a university, or vice versa? It would appear that a much more complex account of the possible linkages between the numerous communities that make up a modern differentiated society is required. On this, the Reformed conception may have something to offer, though, as we shall see, it has its own limitations too. To this conception we now turn.

PART II: SPHERE SOVEREIGNTY

'Sphere sovereignty' is the central concept in the main tradition of social and political thought emerging from nineteenth-century Dutch neo-Calvinism. (For accounts of the content and context of Dutch Calvinist social and political thought see Wintle and Woldring.) The Dutch phrase *souvereiniteit in eigen kring* is literally translated as 'sovereignty in one's own sphere.' It was noted initially by Guillaume Groen Van Prinsterer, historian and critic of the French Revolution and leader of a group of Protestant members of parliament, though the term received its classic formulation in the numerous writings and speeches of Abraham Kuyper (1837-1920), theologian, Reformed church leader, political party leader and Prime Minister from 1901-5. (For accounts of Kuyper's life and thought see Vanden Berg, Van Til, Langley, Skillen 1974 and Skillen 1991.) Kuyper developed it into the organising category of a distinctive Calvinistic social theory. This theory was subsequently developed systematically to a high pitch of philosophical sophistication by Herman Dooyeweerd (1894-1975), a professor of law at the Free University of Amsterdam (founded by Kuyper).

Some of the many parallels between this Calvinist conception and Catholic social thought can be briefly outlined. Each begins by repudiating both the individualistic social theories characteristic of Enlightenment liberalism, and the universalistic theories developed in reaction, whether Romantic, Hegelian, or Socialist. The individual is acknowledged as an essentially social being, created by God to live within a variety of different communities, yet never to be subsumed within them. Both develop emphatically pluralistic conceptions of society, viewing it as consisting of a wide variety of qualitatively different communities, destined to co-exist in harmonious balance. Each conceives of the state as having a special responsibility for acknowledging and protecting these communities, and warns against the danger both of state domination of such communities and of state negligence in failing to prevent the domination of one community by another or the domination of individuals by the more powerful communities.

The differences will emerge as we proceed, but the similarities are striking, not only of substance but also of context. The two theories were formulated at roughly the same time. Kuyper's first major statement of 'Souvereiniteit in eigen kring' ('sphere sovereignty') appeared in 1880 (Kuyper: 1956, pp.39-73). A second major contribution came in 1891 in a speech to an ecumenical congress of social thought entitled 'Het sociale vraagstuk ende christelijke religie ("The Social Question and the Christian Religion'), which cites *RN* approvingly (Kuyper: 1956, pp.74-113, now translated as *The Problem of Poverty*, Skillen: 199). These two documents were possibly as influential in shaping the course of Dutch neo-Calvinist social action as *RN* was in shaping subsequent Catholic social action. Kuyper's vision was developed philosophically by Dooyeweerd between the 1920s and 1950s, roughly the same period during which Solidarist philosophers did much of their most productive work. And each produced dense and extensive works of systematic social philosophy (neither of which are read very much today!).

What then was Kuyper's Calvinist vision of society? Kuyper's corpus is enormous, but the essential contours of this vision can be found in the two documents just cited and in his best known English work, *Lectures on Calvinism* (Kuyper: 1931), delivered at Princeton University in 1898. Kuyper regards Calvinism not primarily as a theological but a cosmological framework. It generates a distinctive worldview which has implications for every area of life and thought. His aim is to articulate these implications, urging the construction of a comprehensive vision as broad as that of both catholicism and 'Modernism.' He rejects (though not consistently) the Catholic distinction between natural and supernatural ends. Grace does not perfect nature, it radically restores it to its originally perfect created purposes. Nor is the mediation of the institutional church necessary in order to allow grace to redeem the world. For example, Kuyper always opposed clerical control of non-ecclesiastical institutions such as unions, parties, etc. Grace operates directly within every sector of human life.

A Calvinist cosmology grounds Kuyper's social and political thought. Over against idealistic and monistic theories of the state current in Europe at the end of the nineteenth century, which held that the state's sovereignty was in principle unlimited, Kuyper posited the notion that every community or 'sphere' within society possessed its own distinctive 'sovereignty' over its own affairs. Absolute sovereignty belongs only to God, but he delegates particular sovereignties to various social spheres, not mediately via the state or the church, but immediately, directly. Each sphere—family, locality, church school, union, business, academy, state, and so on—receives a divine mandate direct from God. Society is an 'infinitely complex organism'(Kuyper: 1956, p.44) comprising a multiplicity of social spheres, each equipped with its own rights and duties, each required to fulfil its own distinctive tasks, and all enjoined to respect the rights and duties of all the others. These spheres are not simply juxtaposed alongside each other but organically linked, and this organic bonding is itself part of God's creational design. Here Kuyper clearly shows the influence of various streams of organicist thought emerging especially from the Romantic movement and the Historical school of law. Indeed he proposes a Christianized version of the idea of a *volksgeest*, which animates the larger organism of the nation, which in turn is a member of the organic community of mankind (see Dengerink, pp. 140ff).

Kuyper's theory differs from Romantic organicism fundamentally, however, because he conceives of the entire social organism, and its parts, as standing under a universally valid divine law for the cosmos.

189

Romanticism and Historicism exalt individuality at the expense of universality, while Kuyper posits a universal order of law within which individuality finds its proper place. This universal law is differentiated into a series of particular 'laws of life' (*levenswetten*) or 'ordinances' (Kuyper: 1931, p.70) holding for each dimension of the world. Each social sphere stands under such a law, which determines its nature and purpose by a kind of inner necessity. This is an internally generated force, implanted by the Creator, which inclines human beings to group themselves in certain specific configurations for the purpose of pursuing a specific activity. Clearly, this brings Kuyper very close indeed to a concept of social teleology. Indeed Frederick Carney has identified such a concept as characteristic of several early Calvinist writers. However, it differs from the specifically Thomist version in that it lacks the idea of a social evolution of one type of community from another.

Kuyper's conception of the state differs from that in Thomism, however. (Kuyper: 1931, ch.3) Standing above the organic unity of the nation is the state. The state is a post-fall divine ordinance, instituted as a response to the disintegrating effects of the fall on the organic unity of society. It is not a 'natural head' growing organically from the nation but a 'mechanical' one, imposed from without, not necessarily founded on a single nation, yet charged with the task of re-establishing unity wherever possible. And a major part of this task will involve justly balancing and protecting the other social spheres.

The state is sovereign, but only within its own sphere. It is the uniquely public authority, yet it stands alongside other spheres as one divinely ordained institution among many. The sovereignty of the state meets its limit in the sovereignty of the other spheres: 'within each of the different social spheres, it has no authority; in these spheres other authorities rule which derive their power not from the state but from God. The state can only recognise or acknowledge the authorities in these spheres. (Kuyper: 1956, p.45) The spheres are co-ordinately, not hierarchically related to the state and to each other. One of its principal tasks is to protect the sovereignty of other spheres from either internal decay or external encroachment.

What then may the state legitimately do? In an early work, he distinguishes between the state's 'normal task' and its 'subsidiary' task,

190

which he defines in terms very close to those found in Catholic writers, as aiding those communities which are in some degree unable to fulfil their function. (Ons program: Amsterdam, 1879, cf pp.199-200, 300-1) Later, however, he related his notion of state intervention more closely to the idea of sphere sovereignty. In the *Lectures on Calvinism*, he proposes a three-fold task. First, the state must adjudicate in cases of conflict between spheres, compelling by law mutual regard for each other's boundaries. Second, it must defend individuals from the abuse of power by other members of the sphere. Third, it must 'coerce all citizens to bear personal and financial burdens for the maintenance of the natural unity of the state.'(Kuyper: 1931, p.97) It is noteworthy that while the first two aspects of the state's task are defined in terms of sphere sovereignty, Kuyper finds it necessary to add, in the third, what amounts to an acknowledgement of the 'common good.' Dooyeweerd faces precisely the same issue, as we shall now see.

Herman Dooyeweerd adopted a far more rigorous theoretical approach to social theory than Kuyper. Not only was he seeking to construct a philosophy to rival that of Thomism, he was at pains to point out the fundamental differences between his Calvinist philosophy and the Catholic alternative. Nonetheless, significant similarities remain. All the points noted above on which Catholicism and neo-Calvinism agreed apply to Dooyeweerd. It is impossible here to do justice to the complexity and sophistication of his thought. (For introductions to Dooyeweerd's thought, see Skillen: 1974, Kalsbeek and McIntire. The most accessible of Dooyeweerd's English works are Dooyeweerd: 1979 and Dooyeweerd: 1986. His magnum opus is Dooyeweerd: 1953-8.) We shall only highlight a few significant points on which Dooyeweerd advanced Kuyper's theory.

Dooyeweerd grounds his social and political thought on a systematic ontological framework rooted in the notion of divine sovereignty. God orders creation through law in two dimensions, the 'modal' and the 'individual.' Creation is structured according to a series of modal aspects all of which condition every discrete entity (e.g., spatial, biotic, logical, social, ethical), or 'individuality structure.' There are three basic categories of such structures: things, events, and social relationships. Each 'functions in,' either as object or subject, all the modal aspects: a tree, for example, displays physical and biological aspects subjectively, and psychic, social, economic, juridical, and faith aspects objectively (i.e., as an object to human psychic, social, economic functioning). Social relationships—a category including every kind of community, institution, association or inter-personal relationships—also function in all these aspects, and exist as individuality structures, each with their own 'structural principle' which determines their distinctive nature.

The significant point about an individuality structure is that its distinctive identity is determined in particular by its 'qualifying function,' which is the key to its structural principle. This notion of individuality structures each with their own qualifying function is a development of Kuyper's notion of 'laws of life' each governing a particular sector of reality. All social relationships have qualifying functions. A family, for instance, is 'qualified' by the ethical aspect, while a church is 'qualified' by the faith aspect. Dooyeweerd tries to insist that this notion is fundamentally different from the Thomistic idea of social teleology. Social relationships may have many purposes, but purpose is not the same as internal structure. Rather, structure determines purpose. But 'structure' turns out to be understood in terms very close to the Thomist idea of 'end'. The structure is determined by the qualifying function, that which essentially characterises a social relationship. This, however, is just what an 'end' does. Indeed he himself applies the term 'destination' (*bestemming*) to the essential nature of a social relationship.

However, Dooyeweerd does not conceive of either the modal aspect or the individuality structures as arranged hierarchically. No social relationship, for example, stands above another in the divine order: like Kuyper, he regards them as equivalent, though irreducibly distinctive. Over against the Catholic idea of a hierarchical subordination of one community to another, Dooyeweerd posits that of a horizontal coordination of communities. No spatial metaphor can fully do justice to the complex interrelationships among human communities, but Dooyeweerd holds that a horizontal one is preferable to a vertical one. On this, I suggest, he is right. The idea of subordination implies that a lesser community is somehow incomplete, lacks self-sufficiency. But if it is true, as we suggested earlier, that all communities perform subsidiary functions towards all others—that the family needs the corporation and the school as much as they need the family and each others—then all communities are equally lacking in self-sufficiency. In that case, it becomes redundant to speak of any of them being arranged according to a hierarchical subordination. Now it is true, of course, that Thomism posits degrees of self-sufficiency. All lesser communities lack self-sufficiency, but some lack it more than others. I suggest that it is exceedingly difficult to operationalize this essentially quantitative notion of self-sufficiency. Different communities, precisely because they are qualitatively distinguished from each other, just provide different kinds of help to one another. The corporation offers job opportunities to families, while the family offers mature adults capable of work to the corporation (at least when each functions properly). In other words, we need to distinguish between different kinds of subsidiary relationship. The general concept of subsidiarity needs specifying with respect to particular kinds of relationship between communities.

Can the same also be said of the state, however? It may be that lesser communities stand in horizontal relationships to each other, but can the same be said of the state's relationship to such communities? Earlier it was suggested that the idea that 'subsidiarity only looks one way' does at least seem appropriate regarding the relationship between the state and the lesser communities. However, in view of the foregoing, there seems after all to be no inconsistency in saying that subsidiarity here is also a two-way process. Just as the family provides mature workers to the corporation, so it provides mature citizens to the state (of course it does many other things too). If we acknowledge that the family is in some sense the 'basic' unit of society whose demise would imperil the future of society as a whole, there is no reason why we should not term the help it offers, a 'subsidiary function'. Similarly, without the taxes provided by corporations, the state's revenue would be considerably reduced.

What then is distinctive about the state? To answer this we need to specify precisely its unique subsidiary function. Earlier it was acknowledged that the state has a primary responsibility for other communities whereas they do not have such a primary responsibility for it (or for each other). The state uniquely is charged with directly promoting the common good of the whole society. We might therefore say that the subsidiary character of the state is a primary aspect of its nature, whereas the subsidiary character of other communities is a secondary aspect of theirs. Dooyeweerd expresses this by pointing to the state's uniquely public character. His use of the term 'public' is close in meaning to the term 'common good.'

Is this to re-import the notion of hierarchy? Not necessarily. The concept of subsidiarity, thus reformulated, can stand alone without implying that of hierarchy. But we do need clearly to distinguish between the different kinds of authority that attach to each different community. The nature of the authority is determined by the 'end' or 'qualifying function' of a community. This function determines not only the internal nature of the community but also, and as a consequence, the kind of 'help' it can offer to other communities. The authority of the state is not essentially a spiritual, moral, social or psychological kind of authority but a legal kind. It performs its subsidiary function towards other communities by means of law, by establishing a just legal framework within which other communities can operate. As Dooyeweerd puts it, the state is qualified as a 'public-legal community.' It is important to note here that he also fully shares the legal pluralism that was seen to be favoured by Catholic writers such as Rommen and Messner. Each social relationship possesses original rights deriving from its 'juridical sphere sovereignty' which may not be overridden by the state. Nonetheless, with respect to public law, the state does indeed stand above all other communities in a hierarchical relationship. Its sphere sovereignty is a public legal sovereignty. This is not a general hierarchical priority, only a functional legal, and hence a limited, one. I suggest that this way of conceiving the relationship between communities helps to overcome some of the problems associated with the concept of a social hierarchy. The principle of subsidiarity need not be abandoned, but it does need to be specified more closely by applying the notion of equivalent, differently qualified, social relationships.

A problem does, however, remain with Dooyeweerd's conception of the state. The state is qualified as a 'public legal community.' Its 'end' is public law. He derives from this the notion that the central task of the state is the promotion of 'public justice' (*publiek gerechtigheid*). When this concept is expounded in detail, however, it turns out to mean

194

essentially a just interrelating of the rights of other social spheres. Public justice consists in a harmonious balancing of multiple juridical sphere sovereignties. This notion has obvious affinities with, though is not identical to, the Catholic understanding of distributive justice, in which the idea of a proportionate distribution of benefits and burdens is central. But neither distributive justice nor any other concept of justice, has ever been seen in Catholic thought as the primary principle governing the state's activities. This principle is of course that of the common good.

I suggest that Dooyeweerd's notion of public justice is too narrowly juridical to capture all that we, and indeed he, wish to see the state do. In fact his detailed policy prescriptions are not too dissimilar to those found n the Catholic tradition (though he is critical of the Catholic acceptance of publicly authorized corporations, preferring them to remain essentially private in character). Strictly, he does not seek to deduce everything the state may legitimately do from the notion of public justice. The 'task' of the state—what it actually does—is distinguished from the 'internal structure' of the state—what it essentially is. The notion of public justice is given by the internal structure of the state (it is given in its qualifying function), and it is not possible simply to derive what its task is from the notion of public justice.

The problem, however, is that he fails to offer a clear principle for determining what the task of the state actually is. He acknowledges that its precise content will vary historically (more, or different kinds of, intervention may be appropriate in one period than another), but fails to supply a criterion by which it could be recognised. He does come quite close, employing two ideas that appear to meet what is required. One is that of the 'atypical' task of the state, distinguished from the 'typical' task which is determined by the state's structural principle. This is however, an isolated reference and is not integrated into his broader theory. The second is the idea of the 'public interest' (*publiek belang*, derived from the Latin, *salus publica*). But his repeated claim is that this notion is empty and easily abused unless its content is determined by the idea of juridical sphere sovereignty. It cannot, I think, satisfactorily be defined by juridical sphere sovereignty alone. The scope of the term 'public' cannot be reduced merely to respecting and balancing the various rights of particular communities. Essential activities like building roads or determining a common currency cannot be derived from such particular rights. Certainly these rights should be respected when roads are built or currencies adopted, but these activities do not flow from such rights. Performing them is not to satisfy rights but to enhance what might be termed 'welfare.' A notion like the public interest or the common good or the general welfare is, I suggest, essential to an adequate conception of the state. The fact that it has always been notoriously difficult to define has led many political theorists to abandon the term entirely, but somehow it proves impossible to exclude it permanently from actual political discourse.

Part III: POINTERS   TOWARDS   A   CONTEMPORARY RESTATEMENT

It has been suggested that the Catholic and Reformed conceptions of the state discussed here both contain valuable elements which could contribute towards the development of a contemporary Christian conception of the role of the state. In this final section, a few preliminary suggestions are ventured as to what might be required if this project were to be undertaken.

It is worthwhile, first of all, to reflect on the overall conception of the state which might emerge from a critical synthesis of these two theories.   It is clear that both classical liberal and state socialist conceptions are excluded from the start. But does this mean that we are left merely with a general conception which is compatible with anything from moderate socialism to social liberalism to paternalist Toryism? It may indeed be the case that the concrete outworking of the principles of subsidiarity and sphere sovereignty would closely resemble in many particulars the specific recommendations of either of these other conceptions. (The same could also be said about each of them with respect to the other two.) But none of these other views is as thoroughly committed to the distinctive kind of pluralism—we might call it 'communitarian pluralism'—which is the heart of the Christian theories outlined here. We can summarise the core ideas of this communitarian pluralism thus: first, there exists a diversity of essential, divinely created, human purposes each of which needs to be concretely pursued within a corresponding community with a distinctive character appropriate to that

196

purpose; second, each of these communities must be enabled by the state (and indeed by everyone) to pursue its particular purposes in responsible freedom and security. What we have, therefore, are at least some of the foundations of a genuinely distinctive conception of the state.

One outstanding problem, potentially very worrying, must at least be noted here. This is the viability of the idea, underlying both the Catholic and the Calvinist conceptions, that certain communities have a universal foundation in the order of creation. Any theory which posits the existence of universal social structures faces the seemingly insurmountable difficulty of distinguishing between what is universal and what is individual in such structures. The obvious temptation, frequently succumbed to by Christian thinkers and others, is to identify what is universal with what is simply prevalent in one historical epoch (as, for example, our century has done with the Victorian patriarchal nuclear family). Conclusions cannot be reached without extensive cross-cultural research. But the very idea of universal social structures is itself quite intelligible. After a detailed study of the place of the guild in western history, Anthony Black comes to a conclusion which has obvious general relevance to the project of Christian social and political theory here being recommended:

> We need to recognise that the community of labour—the idea of the guild—has a moral dimension. It is essential to man, as is family or friendship; it is deeply, perhaps genetically, imprinted upon the human psyche.... It is implanted in our experience as a species.... The configurations of man's social instincts cannot, any more than his physical or emotional make-up, be radically altered.... Community of labour and groups that go with it cannot be reduced to any or all of the specific functions they may fulfil; they are social units with human meaning, like families.... This does not mean that the work group is an absolute, any more than

197

the nation-state; it can go wrong. But, as a
category of social life, it has its own unique
and irreplaceable place in human affairs.
(Black, p.241).

A pluralist theory of the kind proposed here would need to be
founded in a series of such case studies, as well as in wide-ranging
macro-sociological studies of the complex interactions between the various
communities.

What might such a theory have to offer to the broader discussion
now emerging about the role of the state with respect to other
communities? Three contributors to this discussion were noted at the
beginning of this paper. I shall comment on just two of them here. The
neo-conservative interest in pluralism ought to be ungrudgingly welcomed.
Central to its contribution is the idea that certain kinds of community
ought to be protected and nurtured because they 'mediate' between the
individual and the 'megastructures' of society. The precise nature of this
'mediation' needs careful spelling out, however. At times it appears as
if its principal object is 'legitimation,' the maintenance of those values
necessary to sustain a stable democratic society. The risk here is that the
instrumental value of these intermediate structures may be emphasised at
the expense of their intrinsic value (their 'independent end' or 'qualifying
function'). Families, neighbourhoods, churches and voluntary associations
do not exist primarily to stand 'between' anything, but for their own sake.
Viewing mediating structures instrumentally also risks blunting their direct
or indirect responsibility to challenge and disturb the political order.
Certainly families should produce 'active citizens,' but citizenship often
requires confronting or even obstructing the smooth operation of an unjust
political process (even if it is a democratic one, for democracy is no
guarantee of just outcomes). A third problem is that a narrow focus just
on 'people-sized institutions' appears to let the 'megastructures' off the
hook. Megastructures can be contained or even broken up. The
corporation and the union too need to become 'people-sized institutions.'

Neo-socialist interest in pluralism is equally welcome. The central
aim of a decentralist socialism is the maximization of democratic
participation. This is to be applied to the polity, to the economy, and to

civil society in general. Power is to be distributed widely in the political system—through local units of decision-making and deliberation, devolution, enhancement of individual rights and so on—and in the economic system—principally through industrial democracy. Various criticisms might be made of each of these two elements, but in general an emphasis on decentralization and participation comports well with the kind of communitarian pluralism outlined above. However, a question that needs to be posed is whether the third arena of participation—'civil society' beyond the economy—is accorded sufficient importance. There has always been within socialism an exaggerated emphasis on the importance of the state and the economy, to the detriment of all the other 'spheres' of social life, each of which possesses its own intrinsic value. There has often been a tendency to regard these other spheres as peripheral, distant from the real action. There has thus also been a temptation to make communities like the interests of the family, the church, the school, the cultural association, the local community and so on, subordinate to the supposed demands of ideological conformity, political change or economic growth. Whether this tendency will be fully repudiated remains to be seen (though Paul Hirst's *Law, Socialism and Democracy* gives some ground for encouragement).

This conclusion has done no more than sketch a series of projects which are necessary in the articulation of a conception of the state consonant with Christian premises. Only the barest outlines of the 'communitarian pluralism' proposed here have been drawn. While such a pluralistic conception would not make up anything like the whole of a genuine theory of the state, it ought, I suggest, to be a central element within it. Part of the 'fourth revolution' being envisaged in this volume must therefore be, not a radical socialism, nor a radical liberalism, but a radical communitarian pluralism.

BIBLIOGRAPHY

Berger, P.L. and R.J. Neuhaus (1977) *To Empower People: The Role of Mediating Structures in Public Policy* (Washington, DC: AEI)

Black, A. (1984) *Guilds and Civil Society* (London: Methuen)

Calvez, J-Y. and J. Perrin (1961) *The Church and Social Justice* trans. J.R. Kirwan (Chicago: Henry Regnery)

Carney, F.S. (1966) 'Associational Thought in Early Calvinism' in D.B. Robertson (ed.) *Voluntary Assocations* (Richmond, Va.: John Knox)

De Gaay Fortman, W.F. (1956) *Architechtonische critiek. Fragmenten uit de sociaal-politiek geschriften van Dr. A. Kuyper* (Amsterdam: H.J. Paris)

Dengerink, J.D. (1948) *Critisch-historisch onderzoek naar de sociologische ontwikkeling van het beginsel der "souvereiniteit in eigen kring" in de 19e en 20e eeuw* (Kampen: Kok)

Dooyeweerd, H.J. (1953-8) *A New Critique of Theoretical Thought* 4 Vols. (Amsterdam: H.J. Paris)

Dooyeweerd, H. (1979) *Roots of Western Culture* trans. J. Kraay, eds. M. Vander Vennen and B. Zylstra (Toronto: Wedge)

Dooyeweerd H. (1986) *A Christian Theory of Social Institutions* trans. M. Verbrugge, ed. with intro J. Witte (La Jolla, Ca.: Herman Dooyeweerd Foundation/Jordan Station, Ont.: Paideia Press)

Hirst, P.Q. (1986) *Law, Socialism and Democracy* (London: Allen and Unwin)

Hodgson, G. (1984) *The Democratic Economy* (Harmondsworth: Penguin)

Kalsbeek, L. (1975) *Contours of a Christian Philosophy* (Toronto:Wedge)

Kuyper, A. (1931) *Lectures on Calvinism* (Grand Rapids: Eerdmans)

Kuyper A. (1956) 'Souvereiniteit in eigen kring' in De Gaay Fortman

Kuyper, A. (1956) 'Het sociale vraagstuk en de christelijke religie' in De Gaay Fortman

Langley, M.R. (1984) *The Practice of Political Spirituality: Episodes from the Public Career of Abraham Kuyper 1879-1918* (Jordan Station, Ont.: Paideia Press)

McIntire, C.T. ed. (1985) *The Legacy of Herman Dooyeweerd* (Lanham and London: University Press of America)

Messner, J. (1949) *Social Ethics* trans. J.J. Doherty (St. Louis, Mo: B. Herder)

Nell-Breuning, O. von (1937) *The Reorganization of the Social Economy* (New York: Bruce Pub. Co.)

Rommen, H. (1945) *The State in Catholic Thought* (St. Louis, Mo. and London: B. Herder)

Rustin, M. (1985) *For a Pluralist Socialism* (London: Verso)

Skillen, J.W. (1974) *The Development of Calvinistic Political Theory in the Netherlands* (Unpublished Ph.D. dissertation, Duke University)

Skillen, J.W. ed. (1991) *The Problem of Poverty* by A. Kuyper (Grand Rapids: Baker Book House)

Van Til, H.R. (1959) *The Calvinistic Concept of Culture* (Philadelphia: Presbyterian and Reformed Publishing Co.)

Vanden Berg, F. (1960) *Abraham Kuyper* (Grand Rapids: Eerdmans)

Wintle, M. (1987) *Pillars of Piety: Religion in the Netherlands in the Nineteenth Century* (Occasional Papers in Modern Dutch Studies No.2) (Hull: Hull University Press)

Woldring, H.E.S. and D. Th. Kuiper (1980) *Reformatorische maatschappijkritiek* (Kampen: Kok)

The Scope for Solidarity in an Advanced Mixed Economy - Towards a New Model

Johnathan Boswell

1. The term 'solidarity' featured in *Mater et magistra* and *Gaudium et spes* and has loomed large under John Paul II, notably in *Redemptor hominis, Sollicitudo rei socialis* and *Centesimus annus.* It is used broadly as a variant on communion, charity, brotherhood, the gift of self, regarding others as persons and neighbours[1], also on earlier terminologies of 'friendship', 'social charity' and 'a civilisation of love'.[2] It denotes a concern for 'the common good' in the pure sense of that concept: to make available the means of true fulfilment for both persons and communal groups.[3] This makes for a difference with typical secular usage. Solidarity is partly subjective, an attitude or disposition 'in the heart', which tends to go well beyond time and human measurement: another contrast with conventional social science. It is also objective, a matter of conduct, praxis or behaviour. It is to apply at all levels (individual, family, organisation, nationally and internationally) and in every sphere (including the economy). It is seen as the proper response to significant socio-political and economic trends towards increasing interdependence.[4] And it is to be dynamic, expressed through 'ever-widening circles' and 'a progressively expanding chain.'[5]

2. How far recent official documents clarify the meaning of solidarity —and whether the term may have been a shade over-stretched—it is, perhaps, too early to say. As clear as ever, though, are solidarity's intimate relationships with, first, freedom, power-sharing or, as recently stressed, 'democratic participation, and second, with distributive justice and the option for the poor.[6] This triad of values is distinctive, with a multi-faceted solidarity

at the peak, inspiring and modulating both democracy and justice. To have it so vigorously restated contrasts strikingly with more dominant philosophies which put solidarity lower down or leave it out altogether, particularly the New Right. But the Catholic 'communitarian' viewpoint[7] also stands out from its neighbours. Protestant sources, whatever their inspiration in other ways, have been less firmly and coherently communitarian. In secular thought, reviving interests in community, civil society and citizenship, although significant and a welcome opportunity for dialogue, tend to be muted or fragmented.[8]

3.   However, solidarity plus participation and social justice is notoriously hard to relate to an advanced economy. Middle-level thinking is badly needed on the complex territory between values, principles, social ethics, and praxis or policy. This is primarily a task for scholars and practitioners inspired by Catholic social values, in dialogue with sympathetic secular tendencies. It is a task which I believe has been seriously neglected, particularly in recent decades.[9] In this paper I argue, contrary to dominant stereotypes, that solidarity already finds limited representation in advanced mixed economies through phenomena of 'public co-operation', whose varying strengths between sectors and whole systems are influenced to some degree by measurable and partially reformable structures.

4.   Let me say at once that I'm not a whole-hogging 'structuralist'. Other influences are important. One is national emergency. A still more significant factor is culture, ideology, beliefs. I explore all this in a recent study of community values and priorities and the modern mixed economy.[10] But certain sorts of structures play a neglected, substantial role, and should be of concern to Christians. These structures affect relationships both between economic interests, and between economic interests and society. They create certain specific barriers: excessive volatility, disproportionality, opacity, and social distance. They reduce the chances for reasonable degrees of constancy, participation and

accountability in economic affairs, and for social contact between persons and sectors. And to reform these bad structures at certain critical points is an important condition, though not the only one, for solidarity in the economy to improve.

5.   I believe that as our distinctive Catholic social thinking gets further clarified and developed, radical implications follow. A clearer differentiation emerges not only from libertarianism, egalitarianism and utilitarianism, but also from those doctrines' counterparts in political economy, particularly the cults of competitive individualism and centralised direction. Soggy, eclectic 'middle ways', which short-change the distinctiveness or even disguise it, are surpassed. Positive, alternative poles of attraction emerge, linked to solidarity. Part of such a model is explored, in outline, in what follows.

Equipping ourselves for the search
6.   Two powerful images cloud our view as to an advanced mixed economy's openness to solidarity. One pictures a stony, unyielding recalcitrance, the other an easy adaptability, even an already accomplished accommodation. Both images are mistaken.

7.   A first step is to recognise two disturbing imbalances: disturbing, that is, until we begin to see how they can be redressed. At the economy's grass roots strong doses of solidarity are attainable but ambivalent; whereas across a whole modern economy solidarity is imperative, partly for the very reason just mentioned, but diluted. Take first the grass roots imbalance. It is a familiar point that camaraderie, mutual aid, team spirit may well flourish within particular workplaces, trade unions, boardrooms or professional groupings, but certain dangers for wider or national or international interests.

8.   The second imbalance is more complex. That forms of solidarity are imperative across a whole modern economy and beyond cannot be emphasised too much. This is partly because of increasing

socio-political and economic interdependences; partly because, without some economy-wide community, there are acute dangers either from selfish sectionalism, or from too much central state direction, or from perverse interactions between sectionalism and direction. Catholic social teaching's thrust is clear. Wide economic solidarity is ethically vital, whether in household decisions about earning, consumption and investment, or in relationships between sectional interests and government. It is a further essential for people's growth in virtue, their development as persons through community in 'ever-widening circles' and a 'progressively expanding chain' (see above). Yet across a whole system solidarity is highly problematic.

9. Both markets and bureaucracies easily breed a numbing reductionism to impersonality, anonymity, mere technique. 'The person' becomes the 'organisation', and solidarity may get lost inside the organisation long before it can begin to be shown to those outside. The 'outside' interests calling for solidarity increasingly diversify. Customers, suppliers, competitors, local citizens, third parties represent a horizontal form of diversity; the local authority, the state, the transnational agency a vertical one. Future generations add an intertemporal twist. Choices between alternative forms of solidarity become inescapable. An organisation may bend to social pressures by spending a lot on anti-pollution but ignore official appeals for pay or price restraint. Should it respond to both precepts, if necessary on smaller scales? Some of the values calling for solidarity may not be represented by concrete groupings or pressures. Should a company or other sectional entity be concerned about such non-embodied values? Can it afford to be? On top of all this are major structural problems to do with contact and communication, to be discussed later.

10. One might conclude that if wide solidarity still emerges, it is bound to be much less than heroic or saintly; more like the practice of virtue in politics; a process of balancing contributions; perhaps a matter of 'a few percent' at best.

206

11. Its investigation is far from easy. Dominant economic and political stereotypes must be overcome. An empirical fishing expedition will not suffice, nor some rapid leap from values to supposedly unambiguous facts. A theory or theories are essential if only to suggest where and what to look for, or at least knowing what theories one is using, to avoid unconscious dependences. Earlier Catholic thinkers did not hesitate to make a robustly (small 'c') catholic use of existing secular theories. Of course, Max Scheler, Luigi Sturzo and Francois Perroux, for example, themselves produced formidable relevant theories. But the external currents of thought such theorists drew on included early institutionalist economics, economic history and sociology, theories of under-consumption, redistribution and full employment, models of solidarism, guild socialism, the New Deal, industrial democracy. Today the need is no less for theories from 'outside the camp' if we are to observe community phenomena properly.

Fragmented pointers

12. Fortunately, help comes from several quarters. A few leading economists act as whistle blowers on economics. They demonstrate how inadequate the core economic paradigm of utilitarian individualism is even just for purposes of economic prosperity and a satisfactory market economy. They call for extensive deviations from narrow self-interest; for, in jargon terms, 'sub-maximising'—as if economics itself needed systematic anti-bodies.[11]

13. Then, both economic and political theory help to measure something which those of us with direct corporate experience already know from the inside: that economic institutions typically have a lot of social discretion. Market power measures off part of that discretion, the limitations of government controls and laws another. Indeed, some studies go on to show how modern corporations have actually used their social discretion towards public opinion and government: to avoid or defy, to conform

207

responsively, or occasionally to set higher standards. Comparable findings emerge for trade unions.

14. More significant, I think, is the extensive work of political scientists and others on 'corporatism' and 'corporatist' systems: work neglected by Catholic observers, in my view unfortunately (though the historical reasons are understandable). Over long periods, some West European economies have sustained advanced levels of 'corporatism' or system-wide representation of economic interests. In those countries, both public powers and public responsibilities have been widely shared with business, labour and other economic organisations. Industrial relations peace and voluntary incomes restraint have been important features. Balanced economic success has been achieved, also over long periods: that is, steady growth and high employment, and in some cases a mildly improving income distribution, as well as moderate inflation and steady prices.[12] (There are some ethical gains, too, see later).

15. But these indications are fragmented and come from over-specialised disciplines. Can they be combined? Can we unite the scattered terminologies of 'sub-maximising', 'business social responsibility', 'private performance of public duties', 'democratic corporatism', *sozialpartnerschaft, freiwillige dizciplin* and the rest? Furthermore, can we add indicators from the much less researched area of personal economic responsibility. Issues of comprehensiveness arise, even of reforming effectiveness. Without a unifying concept, we cannot be sure of investigating all the relevant phenomena, nor their possible explanations, nor the implications for policy. The required concept, I suggest, has to be mainly descriptive, a bridge between Catholicism and secular thinking, and at arm's length from 'solidarity'. 'Solidarity' itself is not ideal for this purpose. Its unmeasurable subjective component and linkage with a special concept of the common good (see above) should also keep it distinct.

16.   Solidarity as ethical ideal surely merits its own real-life intermediate concept in political economy. The ideal of economic liberty has long possessed such a concept, namely competition. The ideal of economic equality has relied on a model of perfect central control. Why should not the ideal of solidarity on community also develop its own mediating concept in economic affairs?

Public co-operation' as bridgehead

17.   I believe that a concept which fits these criteria well is 'public co-operation'. What this means is that economic decision units freely collaborate with each other, external groups or government in the cause of public interests. They thereby engage in forethought about public interests and often, too, external discussion. They adjust their activities with public interests in mind, and as a result of all these processes they incur immediate costs. This concept of a collaborative, resource-contributive economic responsibility is concrete, and comprehensive. It embraces the phenomena of an individual citizen giving time to the needy, pursuing a simpler lifestyle or caring for the environment, as well as a company, a trade union or a profession practising economic restraint and contributing to public policy.

18.   But in practice, public co-operation varies a good deal in strength. At the grass roots, to repeat, the question is how far a person or organisation considers public interests, consults with others about them, alters economic behaviour with social factors in view, and incurs related sacrifices in the shape of time, money or financial advantages foregone. All these processes are a lot more measurable than might be thought, and no less measurable in principle than, say, degrees of competition, although their measurement is still in its infancy. Thus, some well-researched companies or trade unions emerge fairly clearly as more publicly co-operative, overall, than others.[13]

19.   At economy level, I have already mentioned three indicators: 'corporatism' (or extensive public participation by economic interests; 'social partnership' (or peaceful and collaborative industrial relations); and voluntary incomes restraint. On these tests, it is clear that some Western economic systems have broadly been more publicly co-operative over long periods (Austria, West Germany, the Netherlands, Sweden, Norway), but others less so (Italy, France, U.S.A., U.K.).[14] This is not to deny that individual sectors within the respective countries can sometimes buck the trends. Nor to dispute the continued importance, in all these systems, of both competition and state direction. Mixed economies are always mixtures of competition and direction but, and this is the nub, complemented by varying degrees of public co-operation.[15] The habit of stereotyping modern systems exclusively in terms of competition and direction has long been anachronistic, a legacy of tired, polarising doctrines in political economy. We badly need the concept of public co-operation as well. Without this, or something like it, we cannot fully understand the present operation of these systems, let alone any scope they offer for solidarity.

20.   As to the latter, the shortfalls are clear. Local or sectoral fragments of intensive 'social responsibility' have practical limits, however great the subjective idealism that lies behind them. To be fully effective, public co-operation has to be multilateral, the work of many hands. Even where high-level public co-operation persists over long periods system-wide, as in parts of central and northern Europe, the ideals of Catholic model solidarity are short-changed. There are failures in the representation and participation of less privileged interests like the unemployed, and in redistributive justice, sometimes in subsidiarity. A further proviso brings us back to the important distinction between 'public interests' and 'the common good'. The 'public interests' co-operated with reflect a country's existing social norms, public opinions and governmental precepts. But these may be loaded with a materialism at odds with the common good as the pursuit of those values which, in Paul

VI's words, fulfil 'all men and the whole man.'[16] Furthermore, solidarity involves a subjective or reflexive aspect, through personal dispositions (see above). The measurement of public co-operation's operational processes (public interests reckoned with, external groups considered, immediate costs sustained and the rest) cannot capture this inner core; for its evaluation, where present, lies beyond time and human agency.

21.   Nonetheless, if competition and direction each merit one-and-a-half cheers from a Catholic social viewpoint, public co-operation deserves two, perhaps even two-and-a-half. It is close to the perennial Catholic vision of pluriformity, confederalism, a consensus amongst decentralised units, a free union of diverse parts. It is near to the collaboration and co-responsibility among economic interests, social classes and the state consistently exhorted since 1891. And it is central to the project of moderating both sectional selfishness and central *diktat* as a condition for subsidiarity, democratic participation and social justice.

22.   Thus, it is reasonable to see public co-operation at least as a bridgehead, a mediating phenomenon, something a fair way up the mountain, if still quite far from the peaks. I hope this point will become clearer as we go along.

Anti-co-operative structures
23.   At the start of this paper, I promised more than a brief discussion of solidarity's existing, limited manifestations, as just completed. I raised a more daunting interpretative or explanatory issue. How do these manifestations appear to come about? What forces appear to obstruct or encourage them? I gave notice of a 'structuralist focus here, while emphasising my belief in the importance of other factors: emergency and, more particularly, beliefs and ideology.

24.   I am using the term 'structure' not in the sense of any measurable 'system'; not as typically used by economists, e.g., structures of markets, production, prices etc.; not the industrial sociologist's

211

structures of power or status in the firm. My concern is with fairly persistent configurations surrounding economic institutions and decisions, which relate specifically to dimensions of time, size, perception and contact. A 'bad structure' is one that stymies relationships between economic interests, those they affect, and the organs of civil society and government. It impedes communication, hence public co-operation, and hence, crucially, the scope for solidarity. For example, a bad structure may set up barriers to trust or contact, even bare recognition, between economic units. It may conceal from those units the social consequences of what they do, even the existence of social groups they impact on. It may prevent economic interests from being appraised and influenced by public opinion, social agencies or elected public authorities. One sort of bad structure involves 'prisoners' dilemmas': where decision makers are so mutually cut off that their catch-as-catch-can behaviour actually makes everyone worse off in the end just on a narrow definition of 'worse-offness', even before reckoning with the sub-ethicality of the original cut-offness itself.

25.   These structures have not, in general, featured in Catholic social thinking any more than elsewhere. They are not as divisive and unjust as the ones discussed by liberation theology. They have analogies with some earlier currents in 'Christian sociology', and with the mainstream Catholic corporatists (although the latter were more interested in formal institutions than in the more radical concept of structures in my sense).

26.   To get a rough sense of rather better structures, we need look no further than the world of *dives* in the Gospel parables. The rich men in the Gospels are tied into local habitats where transactions, even consumption habits, tend to be visible. They are likely to be aware of the human effects of their actions and are physically close to the people they affect. Thus, some rudimentary social disciplines apply. It is difficult to exploit, cheat or bully without being watched or condemned. Such conditions are not untypical

of many pre-industrial systems up to the Industrial Revolution. They are still recognisable in the medieval city state of the Merchant of Prato.[17] They did not distribute property equitably, still less ensure good economic behaviour, whether from *dives* or a Marco Datini. But such structures had certain rough-and-ready moral advantages. They could at least bring social consequences to bear, identify good and bad behaviour more clearly, enable public opinion to be focussed, and reinforce the idea that economic activity always carries ethical implications.

27.   Let us now glance at the bad structures generally to be found in advanced mixed economies—excess volatility, disproportional size, opacity and social distance—and the issue of their reformability.

Volatility and disproportionality
28.   Some volatilities carry a clear ethical stigma: witness terms like 'fly-by-night' salesman or 'commercial cowboy'. Others, while suspect, are inevitable in a growing economy: thus, the new industry operating on the margins of social propriety as well as technological novelty.   Some bad volatilities tend to reflect economic conditions which ought to be improved generally, as with extreme rates of bankruptcy or juvenile unemployment. Others could be amenable to changes in management cultures in the longer-term, for example, a multinational's practice of constantly moving its executives around between jobs and places. It is necessary to make these distinctions because a critique of volatility should not undermine economic dynamism, let alone personal freedom.   Nor does it imply a simple, proportional relationship between co-operativeness and sheer continuity. But some volatilities of persons, institutions or property holdings are at once hurtful to public co-operation, threatening to solidarity and relatively reformable. Some of these lie outside the scope of this paper: for example, an excessive turnover of house ownership, fuelled by 'deregulation', over-borrowing and dubious tax concessions, one which undermines rather than encourages the responsibilities of private property.

213

29.   One bad volatility which does lie within my scope arises in a country's public sector. This is an extreme discontinuity in the public institutions and officials dealing with economic affairs and relationships with business. The to'ings and fro'ings of public officials can well exceed those of their sectional opposite numbers. The turnover of the relevant public institutions is often more rapid than that of the business, labour or professional units they are dealing with. Hence, the public bodies lose out in credibility and consistency, the learning curve, and influence. But, of course, not every country has the extreme public sector volatilities characteristic of, say, Britain or the U.S.A. Another bad but reducible category arises within the financial private sector, in capital markets, particularly in the 'market for corporate control.' I refer to the phenomena of 'churning' of financial assets and of take-over mania. Here again there is damage to society's ability to keep tabs, as also to trust and mutuality between economic interests, and to the notion of private property as an area for social duty and personal virtue.

30.   The second category of bad structure, a controversial one, relates to organisational size. It is easy for fashion to exaggerate the influence of size factors generally; still more to swing from one sort of size *angst* to another. 'Big is best' was long the conventional cry; 'small is beautiful' followed. Both are suspect. The principle of subsidiarity, often misinterpreted as a mandate for unqualified decentralisation, at least counsels caution. Subsidiarity's presumptions favour greater power sharing and participation across the board; often, but not always, outright smaller units; also the supplemental resources of larger social agencies, government and transnational entities where appropriate. And such 'appropriateness' should reflect considerations of wide solidarity. Indeed, the greater status of solidarity, as stressed by Catholic social teaching, has to be taken into account in discussions of a 'subsidiarity' all too often torn from its original communitarian moorings.[18] And if this is done, a key test becomes, what is the best size distribution of economic units for

214

decentralised diversity to accord with public co-operation or free collaboration?

31.   To answer this, I suggest something near to an ancient Greek precept, one swayed by social theory but mainly teased out from modern economic history. The formula is 'village-type numbers at national levels.' The idea is that public co-operation is best served by a reasonable compactness in the principal economic interests. A favourable size distribution is one where some responsibility for most economic activity is held by hundreds of units rather than thousands, let alone tens of thousands. Such compactness appears to be a moderate facilitator (as I say, the 'size effect' must not be exaggerated) of public oversight and social accountability. It clears the way for a sharing of public duties, and the emergence and sustenance of national consensuses, for example on incomes restraint.

32.   The attainability of village-type numbers depends to a major degree on a political economy's size. A tiny country overshadowed by a single multinational defies the formula. Austria or Sweden, being smallish, find village numbers easier. In large-ish systems like Britain, France or Germany, again the difficulties increase. But country size is not the only factor. Representative patterns also have an influence. Sometimes this influence is adverse, as with the unduly fragmented trade union, professional and employer organisations in Britain.

Opacity and social distance

33.   It is a regrettable fact that most economic sectors tend to lie outside the social disciplines of visibility, either to each other, or their markets and publics, or the state. Opaqueness is the general rule. This is set in relief by the few sectors which offer quite high social visibility, notably retailing. Retailing activities tend by their nature to be relatively visible to customers, local communities and public opinion. But in the main, social transparency can be achieved only by laws enforcing disclosure, and by social

monitoring agencies which open things up further. For there is a strong presumption as to their potentially benign effect on public co-operation. When firms are observed by significant others, and conscious of this, there is a greater likelihood of their being socially sensitive. When the 'others' include third parties, organs of civil society, public opinion and public authorities, the sensitivity takes on more civic and public overtones.

34.   But the conditions for organisational transparency to apply both comprehensively and fairly are rigorous. Legal disclosure requirements would extend to many institutions now largely or completely exempt. Social monitoring, or the evaluation of economic organisations by pressure groups, media and public bodies, would be improved. There are gaps in monitoring. There are also distortions. Not only familiar biases, for example by the press, but also pressures on economic units which can become too adversarial or competitive and, in the aggregate, extravagant. In effect, a multiplicity of social monitors tell economic organisations to do often contradictory things, each making strong demands, oblivious of the others and of alternative pressures. In one way, this is unfair to the economic organisations, faced as they are by genuinely conflicting social precepts; in another way, it lets them off too lightly. The fragmentation and confrontation may even have doubtful effects on public co-operation overall.

35.   From all this further priorities arise for reform thinking. On the one hand, the processes of social monitoring appear to stand in need of some monitoring themselves. *Quis custodiet custodies?* On the other hand, thought is needed about how to make public opinion more informed and active about the social responsibilities of economic organisations, perhaps through general education, perhaps through a new form of civic-economic education. Transparency and a better educated society are indivisible.

36.   The final set of bad structures is particularly extensive but also amenable to ramshackle experiment. If the structural obstacles to

public co-operation form a rough, sometimes hazardous terrain, we now come to a *massif central* split up by innumerable gaps and gulfs, rivers and rapids, lumps, ravines and fissures. I refer to the socio-spatial gulfs which exist between decision makers in different sectors and types of organisation. To some extent, these relate to gaps between social classes, though not necessarily in the ways usually discussed. Part of the trouble is that the very glaringness of these gaps often leads to makeshift, partial, *ad hoc* expedients without a coherent strategy or even a clear conceptualisation: a failing from which, historically, Catholic inspired reformers have been far from exempt.

37. It is easy to produce abstract formulas for bridging the gulfs. Emphasise wider social institutions which bring divided classes together. Find new ways of bringing home to economic units the social consequences of their actions. Regularise and make more open and accountable, through revised forms of corporatism, the relationships that are bound to exist (except in the panaceas of Austrian and Chicago economists) between sectional interests and government. Set up forums, perhaps particularly set up forums, for collaboration. The specifics are more complex and tough, and the priorities.

38. Take first the background social institutions. Neither schooling nor residential patterns nor training systems can be ignored. In a few countries, like Sweden and Norway, these sectors appear to do more for diffused inter-class contact and hence, indirectly, for public co-operation in the economy.[19] Then there is the question of forums within or around the economic system itself. A forum is a representative body where envoys or decision makers from different sections of the economy and society discuss and work together on public interests. It is very much a place for external colloquy (see above). Forums can offer a lot of scope for democratic participation, mutual learning and economic citizenship. In some contexts, though, not least in Britain, they have often been mis-specified, mal-located and misunderstood,

217

while too much, or rather the wrong things, have been expected of them, leading to may disappointments.

39.   Forums cannot be promoted in isolation from strategies against the other bad structures already discussed: volatility, disproportionality and opacity.   They cannot work well if the people and organisations involved are subject to extreme discontinuity, fragmentation or secrecy. Reverting to the point about background social contacts, forums cannot work well either if they alone are expected to bridge deeply entrenched social divisions: if the people involved are just 'thrown together' with no previous experience of each others' backgrounds, roles or problems. There is a wider cultural point, too, though it leads to issues largely outside this paper's scope. Forums have to be regarded not just as pieces of economic machinery but, more importantly, as further means towards power sharing, democratic participation and, yes, solidarity.

40.   In a more communitarian economy, each substantial organisation would have a forum attached to it: similarly, each locality or region. A national forum would bring together all the familiar sectional interests plus representatives of consumers, public agencies, marginalised groups like the unemployed. The national forum would be the hub of a network whose aims would be, first, to promote public co-operation in terms of national economic policies and issues like income restraint; second, to symbolise and to further a reintegration of economic life within civic-democratic processes;   and not least, third, to provide further direct opportunities for persons to exercise solidarity.

Summary
41.   Solidarity or pure community, with both democratic-participative and redistributive implications, forms the highest value in Catholic social teaching. But solidarity cannot be thought through to an advanced mixed economy without a mediating social science-type

concept, one also needed to unify the related phenomena and to counterweigh over-mighty competitive and *dirigiste* models. The concept suggested here, public co-operation, identifies processes of forethought, colloquy, adjustment and cost-bearing by economic decision units, and a number of equally measurable features economy-wide. The practice of public co-operation roughly approximates to solidarity, in varying degrees. But it is obstructed by, *inter alia*, structures making for volatility, disproportional size, opacity and social distance, which should be of concern to Christian social thinking. Along with public co-operation itself, these bad structures vary between sectors and, still more, countries. Reform implications arise in connection with 1. greater continuities, eg., in public sector institutions and capital markets, 2. national approaches to village-type numbers, 3. wider legal disclosure and improved social monitoring in the interests of transparency, and 4. background social institutions and a strategic network of forums to reduce social divisions and economic gulfs.

Final Comments

42. How far does this take us towards 'a new empirical and normative model'? Only part of the way, I guess, and sketchily. Clearly, the concepts I have suggested require much further work: public co-operation itself, and the measurement, still more the prescriptive contours, of continuity, proportionality, transparency and proximity. 'Part of the way' because, I repeat yet again, public co-operation as testing-ground for solidarity in the economy appears to rely on far more than structures. Regrettably, an element of emergency may well be needed, at least initially. Emphatically needed is a major shift in culture, attitudes and beliefs towards greater co-operativism and communitarianism. That shift would be required not just in public philosophy but throughout the economic culture: in economic models and studies, vocational education, organisational objects, management ideology, business norms and exemplars, cultural symbols and celebrations.

43. It should be clear that public co-operation, thus structurally, conjucturally and culturally underpinned, is not intended to eliminate market competition or state direction. Both these familiar forces will continue to be necessary and, in qualified ways, desirable. Rather, public co-operation's role is to correct, qualify and complement competition and direction, to harmonise and synthesise them. If competition and direction are the two pillars of a democratic mixed economy, public co-operation is to be its surmounting arch.

44. This model does not totally reject existing systems. It partly sympathises with calls to decentralise them, but not with blanket desires to miniaturise, localise or domesticate economic community, for these surely defy moral imperatives towards a wide, indeed widening, solidarity. The model differs from unduly accommodative and insufficiently communitarian 'middle ways,' as often discussed in relation to 'democratic capitalism' or a 'social market economy.'[20] 'Social market' notions still look overwhelmingly to the abrasive mechanics of competition and regulation to run the economy, while seeking to pick up the pieces through redistribution; but to some extent these aims are inconsistent. To limit solidarity-seeking to social welfare measures and the individual enterprise, as these notions imply, seriously short-changes the principle of personal development through community, participation and free associativeness. Solidarity's pursuit has to go well beyond the system's sub-units and care for its casualties, in order to embrace both its interconnections and the whole.

45. The inadequacy of concepts and methods rooted in narrow individualism becomes ever more clear. The 'profit maximising' norm; the cults of free markets, privatisation and commercialisation; the mutual exacerbation between sectional selfishness and heavy-handed central controls: all these are overdue for abandonment. So are pursuits of sovereignty for the entrepreneur, the worker, the consumer, the public service user,

the state, when in economic affairs as elsewhere, to adapt Maritain, the very concept of 'sovereignty' is 'intrinsically wrong.'[21]

46.   We need to recognise that even now a loose-strung social influence on resource allocation exists, one with its own pattern, which can be developed and built on. That development can be inspired, for Catholics and others, by a revived personalist communitarianism. Solidarity in the economy can be unpacked so as to reveal a hierarchy of community potentials [22], with elements of civility and urbanity, indeed conviviality, as well as co-responsibility and mutual aid.   The economy can be seen as a complex of inter-connecting cells whose reciprocities and common affiliations represent a vital force; an ensemble of communities not just interdependent but ethically complementary.[23]   The conventional rhetoric of 'rights', despite some merit, is inadequate for these tasks. Obsessions with 'rights' tend to ignore solidarity. To cite Simone Weil, they get stuck with 'ideas of sharing out, measured quantity... legal claims and arguments', even a certain 'mediocrity.'[24]   The search, rather, is for a loose economic confederalism; for elastic bands; for a social fabric not only to disperse power and resources widely but also to interweave and consociate the diverse units, working through education and example, social surveillance, and a removal of structural impediments.

Endnotes

1.   *Mater et magistra* 23, 157; *Gaudium et spes* 32; *Populorum progressio* 17, 67; *Sollicitudo rei socialis* 39, 40, 46; *Centesimus annus* 41.

2.   *Centesimus annus* 10.

3.   *Gaudium et spes* 26; *Centesimus annus* 51.

4.   *Sollicitudo rei socialis* 38, 39, 45; *Populorum progressio* 48; *Redemptor hominis* p.33; *Centesimus annus* 49, 51.

5.   *Gaudium et spes* 32; *Populorum progressio* 43, 44; *Centesimus annus* 43, 51.

6.   *Centesimus annus* 22, 46.

7.   *Gaudium et spes* 24, 32.

8.   This can fairly be said, I think, of M. Sandel, *Liberalism and the Limits of Justice*, 1983; M. Walzer, *Spheres of Justice*, 1983; and B. Barber, *Strong Democracy*, 1984.   For recent, firmer statements, see D. Marquand, *The Unprincipled Society*, 1988, and A. Oldfield, *Citizenship and Community*, 1990.

9.   J. Boswell 'Catholic communitarianism and advanced economic systems: problems of middle-level thinking since 1891', paper to conference on Social Catholicism and the Development of Catholic Social Doctrine, University of Hull, 12-14 April 1991.

10.   Jonathan Boswell, *Community and the Economy, the Theory of Public Co-operation*, 1990.

11.   T. Scitovsky, *The Joyless Economy*, 1976;   A.O. Hirschman, *Shifting Involvements*, 1982; A. Sen, *On Ethics and Economics*, 1987; A. Etzioni, *The Moral Dimension: towards a new economics*, 1988.

12.   For 'corporatist' studies, see (14) below.

13.   Boswell, *Community and the Economy*, op cit. 61-65.

14. P.C. Schmitter and G. Lehmbruch (eds.), *Trends towards Corporate Intermediation*, 1979, and *Patterns of Corporatist Policy Making*, 1982; European Industrial Relations Group, *Industrial Relations in Europe*, 1981; A. Cawson (ed.), *Organized Interests and the State*, 1985; C. Crouch and R. Dore (eds.), *Corporatism and Accountability*, 1990.

15. This idea owes much to J.M. Clark, *Economic Institutions and Human Welfare*, 1957; K. Boulding, *Beyond Economics*, 1948, and *Human Betterment*, 1985; and F. Perroux, *Economie et Societé*, 1960, and *Industrie et Création Collective*, 1964.

16. *Populorum progressio* 42.

17. Iris Origo, *The Merchant of Prato*, rev. edn. 1979.

18. See C. Millon-Delsol, 'Quelques Réflexions sur l'origine et sur l'actualité du principe de subsidiarité,' in A. Kalaydjian and H. Portelli (eds.), *Les Démocrates-Chrétiens et l'économie sociale de marché*, 1988.

19. M.D. Hancock, *Sweden, the Politics of Postindustrial Change*, 1972; H. Eckstein, *Division and Coherence in Democracy, a study of Norway*, 1966.

20. See M. Novak, *The Spirit of Democratic Capitalism*, 1987, and Les *Démocrates-Chrétiens et l'économie sociale de marché*, op cit. (But there are some significant differences between these models.)

21. J. Maritain, *Man and the State*, 1951, 29.

22. M. Scheler, *The Nature of Sympathy*, trans. P. Heath, 1954, and *On the Eternal in Man*, trans. B. Noble, 1960.

23. F. Perroux, *Economie et Société*, 1960.

24. Simone Well, *Selected Essays* 1934-43 (ed. and trans. R. Rees), 1962, 18-21.

"Radical" Economic Concepts from Leo XIII to the Present

Joseph W. Ford

Looking at the impact of Leo XIII's *Rerum novarum* over the long term means setting a viewing angle which may be insightful, but also may be highly personal and subject to the charge of "shoehorning" the material to fit. It is worth the risk, however, after analyzing recent papal and American episcopal pronouncements to suggest important linkages that extend further back in time, for there seems to be an unbroken thread, albeit hesitant and thin at times, that really is a century old. Catholic social doctrine, while perhaps not literally beginning with the 1891 encyclical, was given a major charge and refocusing by it which has not faltered to this day.

The angle of vision seems to have two facets to it. First, the encyclical and the encyclicals and episcopal statements that follow it propose economic concepts that are quite advanced (read "radical" from the title) for the times in which they were written. This has frequently meant that they were less than enthusiastically received by their listeners and had to await future ages for vindication. Somehow the authors had a genius and a vision of things whose time would come. Secondly—and this seems somehow more ordinary, but no less important—the fathers have placed much more emphasis on the economist's concept of distribution than on production. From Leo's emphasis on a just wage and the workers' right to join associations to achieve that to the American bishops' 1986 Pastoral Letter, *Economic Justice For All*, with its proposals for economic rights and a new American partnership, the thrust of Catholic social teaching has been on distribution. It has been legitimately criticized for this. An example: James E. Burke, former CEO of the Johnson and Johnson Corporation faults the American bishops for not understanding the importance of the private sector in generating jobs (27 million in the United States between 1970 and 1985).

In addressing this issue (unemployment rates), however, the bishops fail to give proper recognition to what has been accomplished in creating jobs in the United States...and although full employment is still the elusive goal of any just society, it cannot be mandated by government without threatening the very freedoms that made it possible to generate new jobs in the first place ("Reactions from Management" in *The Catholic Challenge to the American Economy* pp. 219-221).

It is the intention of this paper to trace and analyze these two characteristics over some selected terrain of the past century. We will examine the Bishops' *Program for Social Reconstruction* (1920), *Quadragesimo anno* (1931), *The Church and the Social Order* (1940), *Mater and Magistra* (1961), *Populorum progressio* (1967) and *Economic Justice for All* (1986) and *Sollicitudo rei socialis* (1987).

There are many fine papal quotes that can be chosen to start us off. Here is a particularly apt specimen:

> The social concern of the Church, directed towards an authentic development of man and society which would respect and promote all the dimensions of the human person, has always expressed itself in the most varied ways...the Magisterium of the Roman Pontiffs which, beginning with the Encyclical *Rerum novarum* of Leo XIII as a point of reference, has frequently dealt with the question and has sometimes made the dates of publication of the various social documents coincide with the anniversaries of that first document.

The popes have not failed to throw fresh light by means of those messages upon new aspects of the social doctrine of the church (*Sollicitudo rei socialis*, 1987, #1).

This quote, taken from a document published near the end of the century under review, truly stands astride the period by noting the effective commencement of Catholic social teaching and the unfolding nature of its expansion and growth.

So we begin with Leo XIII; a outline of *Rerum novarum* is unnecessary for our purposes, but an understanding of the times and the "conventional wisdom" in economic theory and social thought is. It was the apex of the social and ideological influence of the classical school of economics, even though the theory base of the school had begun to change. The distinction is important. The early Classical school of Smith, Malthus and Ricardo as major figures and Nassau Senior and John Elliot Cairnes in disciple roles had brandished the "natural laws of political economy" as being immutable and universal, akin to the laws of physics, chemistry and biology so that policy interventions were not only useless but destructive. Later writers, however, edged away from this rigidity indeed arrogance. John F. Bell expresses both positions well. Speaking of Cairnes (whom he calls "the last significant defender of the faith of the English classical tradition") he says:

> He believed that these laws expressed the phenomena of wealth as certainly as chemistry does for the phenomena of the functions of organic life. (J. F. Bell, *A History of Economic Thought*. 1967, p. 272)

Then there was John Stuart Mill:

> The liberal social views of Mill were often at variance with the economic fundamentals in which he believed....He lived at a time when the present was breaking radically with the past, yet he could not make a complete transition in his own thought. (Bell, pp, 270-1)

Even though the belief in the natural laws of the marketplace was losing theoretical legitimacy, it still commanded formidable, almost unquestioned authority in the worlds of business, ideology and law. This was the explicitly delineated atmosphere that Leo XIII confronted. Unions were variously denounced as socialistic, contrary to "scientific" laws or utopian. Wages were set by these supreme forces, a solemn consummation of contract by buyer and seller of labor that could not be interfered with without imperiling the foundations of civilized life. This

226

was a world of *caveat emptor* in which it was the individual's fault for buying a product which was dangerous to society, a world where unions were viewed as combinations in restraint of trade under the Sherman Antitrust Act (Loewe v. Lawlor, 1907).

How quaint, therefore, that Pope Leo should write an Encyclical entitled *Rerum novarum* ("On the Condition of the Working Classes"). How interesting that the document strongly supported the idea of a just wage whereby the worker could support himself and family in decent comfort and could prudently save "a little wealth."

If a worker receives a wage sufficiently large to enable him to provide comfortably for himself, his wife and his children, he will, if prudent, gladly strive to practice thrift; and the result will be, as nature itself seems to counsel, that after expenditures are deducted there will remain something over and above through which he can come into the possession of a little wealth. (*Rerum novarum* #65.)

How human Leo was, we can suppose, when he comes out in support of workers" associations without ever calling them unions. Papal doctrine on trade unions begins with *Rerum novarum*, although "nowhere in the text...do we find some Latin approximation to the word 'union'...To find in *Rerum novarum* a justification and recognition of trade unions calls for most careful reading and exposition." (J. Calvez and J. Perrin, *The Church and Social Justice.* 1961, p. 381.) Nevertheless, it is agreed that the Pope clearly had in mind devices which would ensure justice for the worker. Listing a number of institutions for the poor, mutual and groups agencies, foundations for boys and girls and the aged. But associations of workers occupy first place, and they include within their circle nearly all the rest...it is most clearly necessary that workers' associations be adapted to meet the present need. (*Rerum novarum* #68, 69.)

And again he writes more bluntly, "man is permitted by a right of nature to form private societies" (*Ibid.* #72.) Such statements, even though they lack the word "unions" are clear in their radical nature for the late nineteenth century and its orthodoxy. Commentators agree, Thomas Bokenkotter called Leo a sensitive scholar who helped break the church out of its state of siege mentality and place it on a new footing with regard to modern secular culture. He noted that the encyclical has rightly been called the *Magna Carta* of social Catholicism.

In opposition to the orthodox liberal capitalism of the age, it justified the need of some state intervention to protect workers' interests. It championed the worker's right to a living wage, denying the supremacy of the economic laws of the market and, as noted above, defended the worker's right to organize (*A Concise History of the Catholic Church* pp. 341, 348.) Jay Dolan portrays Leo as a progressive church leader who in *Rerum novarum* analyzed the conditions of labor and offered a program of reform based on social justice. (*The American Catholic Experience*, p. 334.)

Historians also agree that the impact of this socially progressive encyclical was less than overwhelming. "Of course, the encyclical went unheeded by many Catholics. It did not stop the spread of Marxian socialism among the workers, but it did meet with considerable response." (Bokenkotter, p. 348.) Pope Pius XI, in his commemorative encyclical *Quadragesimo anno*, noted this explicitly:

Some minds were not a little disturbed, with the result that the noble and exalted teaching of Leo XIII quite novel to worldly ears, was looked upon with suspicion by some, even amongst Catholics, and gave offense to others. For it boldly attacked and overthrew the idols of Liberalism... and was so far and so unexpectedly in advance of its time....(Introduction)

Dolan suggests reasons for the lack of a deep American Catholic response. American church leaders were concerned with a number of internal disputes; conservatism was on the rise in the church and thus suspicious of social reform; this conservatism emphasized charity, not justice. Devotional Catholicism nurtured a private, rather than a social religion.

On a national level, it is difficult to find any further recognition of the Pope's social encyclical. Initially it was welcomed with enthusiasm, but within a few years it was put on the shelf to gather dust....A crusade for justice would have to wait for another time. (Dolan, p. 335.)

It becomes clear that Leo XIII had enunciated a theme (the condition of the working class) that began a profound shift in the role of the Church, but it is also clear that most people were not ready to hear him. This radical economic formulation is the first example of our theme and is acknowledged as the jumping off point of modern Catholic social teaching. It also focuses much of that teaching, although not all, on the distribution aspect of economic systems. It is useful to recall that classical economics of the nineteenth century had convinced itself of the laws governing distribution of wealth into wages, rent, interest and profit. These had, by Leo's time a practical finality to them and social teaching attacked them on the basis of justice. With the laws surrounding production thought to be set, economics was beginning to explore the distribution loophole suggested by J. S. Mill and others. Social doctrine could play off this.

On a more theological aside, it can be noted that perhaps Catholic social doctrine leaps forward when it gets in touch with the truly radical implications of Christianity. Church support of labor now had an intellectual support principle, rooted in the tradition of natural law, courtesy of *Rerum novarum*, rather than based merely on the pragmatism of an immigrant church. Labor organizations were a natural human right of workers. (Dolan, pp. 338-9)

Msgr. John A. Ryan

Although Leo's encyclical initially was not widely noticed in the United States it did inspire a young priest in Minnesota, John A. Ryan, to devote his life to the pursuit of justice....He translated Leo's principle into concrete American terms and concluded that the right could be implemented only by minimum-wage legislation. (David O'Brien, "The Economic Thought of the American Hierarchy" in *The Catholic Challenge to the Economy*, 1987, pp. 31.)

Ryan's name was perhaps the most well-known among a number of committed individuals in the American social justice movement in the early part of the century. He was a moral theologian who taught that subject at St. Paul's Seminary in Minnesota; his doctoral dissertation at Catholic University (in moral theology) was "A Living Wage" It was published in 1906 with an affirming preface by the most famous American economist of the time Richard Ely, and is a brilliant synthesis of economics-self-taught and morality. It was well-received. (Dolan, p. 342-3)

Ryan was influenced by the social gospel movement and by the under-consumption theory of John Hobson, and his analysis of the wage issue from moral and economic perspectives focused on the unequal distribution of income and wealth. This was not only morally unacceptable but economically disastrous as the American economy evolved to a more consumer-driven system. (O'Brien, p. 31.) Wages should be high enough to allow the worker to live with the dignity of a human being which is the worker's right. Thus the living wage is a right derived from the worker's personal dignity not from custom, bargaining power or remnants of the old Classical subsistence theory. Ryan said:

> The laborer's right to a living wage stands out in clearest light once we lay firm hold of....the fact that the laborer is by nature—prior, consequently, to any contact—a person, a being endowed with certain indestructible rights. "Indestructible" by other men, be it always understood... The subject of the labor force must be dealt with, not as a thing, but as a person. As a person he has an indestructible right to a decent livelihood. (John Ryan "The Laborer's Right to a Living Wage" (1902) in Aaron Abell (ed.) *American Catholic Thought on Social Questions.* 1968, p. 240)

He takes the argument a step farther in order to ensure that a living wage means compensation sufficient for decent living for the worker's family as well. This reasoning too is based on the provocative idea of a right derived strictly from natural law and justice. It is not based on general justice or equity or vague notions of social justice. Rather it derives from the worker's right to full self-development "Abstracting from a supernatural vocation, the average man cannot properly develop his personality outside of conjugal life." (Ryan, *op. cit.*, p. 248.) And again. "The right to marry, not the duty of maintaining a family, is therefore the true *cause* of the moral claim to a family wage." (p. 250.)

Early on in his dual career Ryan sharply altered the focus in the debate on wages in an industrializing society by placing it on the plane of natural law. Three things are of particular interest to us here. First, wages viewed as a natural right of the person undercut the argument of wages derived from the unanswerable economic laws of the market and hastened its demise. Second, his use of the natural right argument is taken directly from the encyclical, and indicates its slowly gathering importance. As noted above, arguing for workers' groups and for a living wage from the root of natural law enveloped the discussions with a legitimate intellectual tradition that propelled Catholic social thinking for decades. Third, our particular conceit in this paper is that radical/unorthodox economic ideas have been an ongoing feature of these ecclesiastical positions.

Not only was the natural law concept provocative and unsettling in this age but in Ryan's hands, it led to the demand and agitation for minimum-wage legislation to achieve it. He became a major name advocating such changes, and he helped write such a law in Minnesota. He was convinced, as others were at the beginning of the century, of the need for government intervention to bring about change in the social order.

Ryan's insistence on natural human rights and the dignity of the human person...placed him in the mainstream of American reform thought, though all the time, he insisted-and rightly so-that he was following the thrust of *Rerum novarum*. (Dolan, p. 343.)

In the aftermath of World War I, broad concerns of social and economic reform received a more sympathetic hearing. The American bishops set up the National Catholic Welfare Council in 1919 (renamed the National Catholic Welfare Conference in 1922.) Ryan was named head of its Social Action Department and the Administrative Committee published a famous document in 1920 written by him. This was the "Bishops Program of Social Reconstruction" and it was a wide-ranging call for social reform. It called for social insurance for sickness, accident, unemployment and old age, for producer and consumer cooperatives, stock and profit-sharing programs, co-partnerships and public agencies for employment and decent housing. (O'Brien, p. 32.) In addition, it proposed minimum-wage and minimum age legislation, regulation of public utility rates and guarantees of the workers' right to organize. (Dolan, p. 344.)

On the surface, the document seems to be easily interpreted for its historical place: it is a shopping list of unorthodox, indeed, radical ideas for the time; and it should be viewed as a precursor of the New Deal reforms of the 1930's. And yet historians find this a troublesome interpretation. O'Brien says that while the *Bishops' Program* highlighted main defects of the market system (economic waste and inefficiency in production and distribution of goods, and a great maldistribution of income), a bishops' pastoral letter that year warned against radical remedies (p. 32). Abell says that the Program "was more reminiscent of prewar Progressivism than anticipatory of the New Deal. Nevertheless it was rightly viewed as a forward-looking document." (Abell, p. 326)

It may be best, therefore, to view these 1920 proposals as "radical" only in the sense of being too forward-looking for their time. All these were hardly original with the bishops; they had been suggested before and were usually perceived as socialistic or worse. But the church eventually recognized that these were principles derived from justice. From the Forward of the document:

Its practical applications are of course subject to discussion, but all its essential declarations are based upon the principles of charity and justice that have always been held and taught by the Catholic Church. (in Abell, p. 327.)

Ryan was under no delusions that these proposals would be accepted, even though they were popular and widely discussed. "It is not to be expected that as many or as great social changes will take place in the United States as in Europe. Neither our habits of thinking nor our ordinary ways of life have undergone a profound disturbance." (Abell, p. 333.) Ryan was right; the consumer-driven, materialistic, "return-to-normalcy" 1920's derailed any broad-based support of the proposals and they languished. Nevertheless something important had happened. The concern of the American church for the worker had shifted from one based on charity and paternalism to something which now had an intellectual principle at its core: rights to which the worker was entitled because of his or her dignity.

"In the Fortieth Year"

The end of the fourth anniversary decade of *Rerum novarum* was unusual indeed. By 1931 the end of the world seemed to have come, with economic and financial collapse worldwide. Whereas Leo wrote at a high point of the capitalist system's performance and talked about reforms within the economic system, Pius XI, forty years later, was forced to question, along with many others it must be noted, the appropriateness of the economic system itself. He could title the encyclical "On Social Reconstruction" because most scholars acknowledged the demise of Economic Liberalism and were debating great systems change.

"The capitalistic system is not evil in itself, but it is evil to the extent that it scorns the dignity of workers, in that it concentrates wealth and economic power in the hands of a few.... Free competition has destroyed itself. Economic dictatorship has supplanted the free market." (Harte, 1956, p. 79.)

In America leading economists were debating and propounding the Stagnation Thesis and the Mature Economy theory, all foretelling the end of growth and the reality of coming to grips with the cessation of economic growth. This focused attention on the distributive questions in society; Pius XI extended Leo's idea of a just wage into the "living wage" (John Ryan's influence) so that a man could support his family in comfort and save as well. The new order to be reconstructed was to be one based on the principles of justice and charity—on "social justice—a term he introduced into the Catholic vocabulary and made a key term of social Catholicism" (Bokenkotter, p. 354.)

The central focus of *Quadragesimo anno*, then, was not a limited and concrete set of issues, but the problem of economic systems themselves; catastrophic world collapses in the economic and financial markets forced many societies to face this basic issue in the early 1930's. Just as some economic structures (e.g., the United States) were profoundly and permanently altered at this time, so too:

The pope's principal proposal was not an alternate organization of the economy, but the articulation of   principles according to which a new system could be built...Catholic social teaching moved in the direction of designing a fundamentally new type of economic organization. (Calvez, 1987, p. 17.)

233

These principles included social justice, as noted above, and that of subsidiarity which states that for things necessary for justice government should do only those which cannot be done by private groups or local public authorities. The emphasis continued to be on aspects of distribution rather than on production principles, and Pius XI continued in a more explicit way the papal tradition of refraining from aligning with particular systems and emphasizing underlying principles. The latter were to bear fruit much later on.

Pius asked for a reconstruction of the social order—but based on social charity and social justice, one that avoided the excesses and failures of the schools of economic individualism and economic supremacy. Social charity and social justice are the "true and effective guiding principles." (*Quadragesimo anno* Part II, Section 5) Pius was interested in doing a "structural analysis" of society to focus on the inadequacies and inherent injustices of the system (Donal Dorr, *Option For the Poor*. 1983, p. 58). A key factor in the analysis is his recognition that wealth gives power, that a relatively small group of people and organizations control vastly disproportionate amounts of wealth. Remember that it was at this same approximate time that Adolph Berle and Gardiner Means published (1932) their classic and seminal work, *The Modern Corporation and Private Property* in which they estimated that the 200 largest nonfinancial corporations (less than .07 percent of the total) controlled almost 50 percent of all U. S. corporate wealth in 1929.

The pope recognized that a State largely controlled by such groups becomes a slave to their interests. At this point Pius makes his most radical criticism of the capitalist system as it has developed since the time of Leo XIII...It begins as free enterprise; and this includes free competition. But a natural result of the competition is that only the toughest survive. Before long the free competition is only a myth and an ideology. Public authorities must ensure that free competition is kept within just and definite limits and that economic power is kept under control. This amounts to a radical change in the structures that had shaped the Western world. (Dorr, p. 61. *emphasis added*.)

Pius's call for a new social order to reconstruct society is both subtle and complex. He seems to have been ambivalent about the capitalist system of his time but then in 1931 so were a lot of other people. Rather than select a specific economic system as correct, he properly sidesteps that by articulating general principles that all systems are to be judged against and by assessing the systems by them. This is exactly what the American bishops did in their 1986 Economics Pastoral Letter "Economic Justice For All." But in 1931 the talk was more about broad economic systems and less on narrow mechanical problems, so his call for controls over the markets fell on some sympathetic ears. Keynes was already edging towards his *General Theory*, Roosevelt's governmental initiatives were two years away.

Pius is viewed as a radical because he went far beyond Leo XIII in his criticism of capitalism. Three major factors are cited to bolster this: a) the collapse of the financial and economic markets was so profound as to question the viability of the market system itself; b) the market systems had ceased to be free but were bastions of concentrated wealth and power; and c) a reasonable alternative, the corporatist/fascist model *seemed* to be available. (Dorr, p. 67-8) The shortcomings of the capitalist model—manifested in its total destruction in a depression that was eons worse than any other collapse—robbed the model of its last vestiges of legitimacy.

With Pius, therefore, we are talking about "radical" thought in a way that is an extension of, but very distinct from the thought of Leo. The former's concern was not just with workers, but with the whole socio-economic order of society with the basic causes of injustice and poverty. The church, therefore, begins its formal analysis of economic systems as such with Pius; it searches for some kind of "middle way" between capitalism and socialism. This culminates in the 1986 Economic Pastoral Letter's rather rigorous analysis of what's right and what's wrong with the market economy and with the present pope's carefully nuanced hymn to the market's successes and shortcomings.

Papal questioning of the functional validity of the capitalist system led to a number of episcopal spinoff reactions. The most important of these was "The Church and the Social Order" published by the Administrative Committee of the American bishops' National Catholic Welfare in 1940. This was a curious blend of economic proposals and moral exhortations in an organic concept of society. The problems noted by the bishops were by this time distressingly familiar: concentration control of capital, maldistribution of wealth and income, insecurity of the workers and inferior wages. (O'Brien, p. 35.)

The proposals of the bishops to alleviate these were perplexing. On the one hand, they were unorthodox, calling for more state action to make private property serve the common good, to curb confrontations between labor and management and to expand the ownership of property. They supported unionization, collective bargaining, and wage increases derived from profits not higher prices. (O'Brien, pp. 35) On the other hand, however, the bishops spoke vaguely about the creation of guilds or vocational groups to bring people together for moral unity. It was an era in which one could speak of alternative economic structures, but it was also nearing the end (1940) of that era when the bishops spoke. Thus it had less impact than the 1931 statement

"The Church and the Social Order" like the "Bishops' Program of Social Reconstruction," did not stimulate renowned activism, but instead marked the end of such a period. (O'Brien, p.37.)

A Trial Balance?

It seems appropriate to pause here for a moment and evaluate what has been covered. If we stretch the meaning of "radical economic concepts" to something more flexible and less literal in tone, there is much to note. Bokenkotter puts it broadly and aptly. Leo XIII knew the importance of breaking the Church out of its siege mentality and placing it in a new relationship with the modern secular culture, particularly the Industrial Revolution (*op. cit.*, p. 341.)

Social Catholicism was the response of the church to new conditions of society caused by the Industrial Revolution and the advent of the mass society....

The most crucial problem...was the problem of the exploited and oppressed factory worker (*op. cit.*, p. 342-4.) The encyclical of 1891 directly challenged the economic liberalism of its day at its zenith of acceptance and initiated Catholic social teaching. It began a long papal tradition—carried down to this day—of abhorring socialism and of accepting guardedly private property. That free economic systems do not always have optimal results, that exploitation could be inherent in a system, that workers have rights—all these ideas were unorthodox and

236

unpopular and qualify as "radical." Their articulation by Leo reflects his genuine shock at the poverty and defenselessness of the working class. (Dorr, p.44.) This heightens the paradox of the pope: his espousal of truly unacceptable views to the mainstream apologists, on the one hand, and his total unwillingness to support anything viewed as "revolutionary." As Dorr notes (p. 45-6), the church was shocked by two major events, the French Revolution and the wave of revolutionary tumult in the nineteenth century, and the loss of temporal power by the papacy after 1848.

A century of reflection on Leo's achievement suggests that it was a major, courageous and yet cautious first step, the opening of the windows, the lifting of the siege viewpoint, the commitment of the church to social consciousness—in a phrase, the turning point beyond which there is no turning back. Sixty years of perspective on Pius XI and *Quadragesimo anno* also makes it very clear that it is more than just a commemorative essay and certainly more than a transitory piece mired in the 1930's depression. As noted earlier, this is a shift to a structural type of analysis, free of allegiance to any economic system and free of the obsessive concern for stability.

More Recent Developments

Most of us view World War II as a watershed period, a great turning point. In the West capitalist systems made a surprising return and an unexpectedly triumphant one as well! Optimism and economic growth characterized the 1950's in the advanced countries, but pessimism and slower growth were prominent in Third World systems. This dichotomy is reflected in two encyclicals, *Mater et Magistra* (John XXIII in 1961) and *Populorum progressio* (Paul VI in 1966). The tone and thrust of these two encyclicals separated by only five years is remarkably different, but tumultuous change and a new pope help to explain the contrasts. In *Mater et Magistra* John XXIII mirrors the uncomplicated optimism of many: aware of gaps between have and have-not nations, sensitive to the maldistribution of income and wealth in societies, John believed that sustained growth could alleviate all this.

There are indications that Pope John took a rather optimistic view of what might be expected from capitalist society in the future...John accepted the common assumption that rapid economic growth offers the

237

easiest way to overcome the problem of the unequal distribution of wealth. (Dorr, pp. 92-3.)

Where is the "radical" in all of this? It is hard to find because John was a believer in the ability of a system experiencing success to evolve gradual change within it without disruptive confrontation. John was one who changed the tone of the church (even before Vatican II) to a more confident and optimistic one that was compatible with the age. But some unorthodox stuff can be teased out of *Mater et Magistra*. In the section entitled "Balancing Economic Development and Social Progress" John refers to the very rapid evolution of various countries since World War II and notes a strict demand of social justice, which explicitly requires that, with the growth of the economy, there occur a corresponding social development" (#73). Then follows the key passage:

From this it follows that the economic prosperity of any people is to be assessed not so much from the sum total of goods and wealth possessed as from the distribution of goods according to norms of Justice, so that everyone in the community can develop and perfect himself (#74).

In this statement can be found both links with the past and anticipations of the future. The reference to the development and perfection of the individual reflects Leo's concern (See #9, 15 and 42, among others) and Pius's reiteration of it (especially Section II part I.); there is an unbroken line through all this time. Anticipations of the U.S. bishops' 1986 Pastoral Letter on the economy stressing that the economic system is to be judged on what it does for people, rather than to people are evident in the statement. (Economic Justice For All, #1.)

The grim realities of the Third World countries were not lost on Pope Paul VI and he issued a major document on economic developed in *Populorum progressio* (1967). Here was a significant change, along with the documents of the Second Vatican Council, in Catholic social thought. An explicit recognition of the problems of the developing countries and of the international economic order permeates this encyclical.

This encyclical...rests on the conviction that the most pressing issue of the day was the plight of the many poor nations that lagged dramatically behind modern standards of development—a plight similar, on a world scale, to what confronted workers in Europe at the time of Leo XIII's *Rerum novarum*. (J. Calvez, 1987, p. 20)

Paul clearly (and early on) recognized the problem of underdeveloped nations in a global context as a "North-South" issue at a time when the world was preoccupied with East-West tensions. "The poor nations remain ever poor while the rich ones become still richer." (*Populorum progressio*, #33, 57) The existing international order, he said, was the major culprit because the free trade system could no longer guide international relations Bold transformations, innovations that go deep must reform the system" (#32).

This does not mean demolishing the competitive system, but it does mean the free trade must be linked to the demands of social justice, "What was true of the just wage for the individual is also true of international contracts" (#59). Leo's seminal work was now being extended to the international sphere. Dorr says it flat out:

"It can be said that it does at the global level what Leo XIII's *Rerum novarum* did at the level of the nation. Its concern is primarily with the relationship between rich and poor nations rather than rich and poor individuals or classes." (Dorr, p. 139.)

Paul VI says at the beginning of the encyclical (Paragraph #3, in fact) that, "today the principal fact we must all recognize is that the social question has become worldwide."

Twenty years later Pope John Paul II issued *Sollicitudo rei socialis* ("On Social Concern") to commemorate *Progressio populorum*. He lavished great praise on the earlier document and, in fact, dwelled on it at some length, allocating two sections out of seven; much of the rest of it was spent extending it and applying it to the contemporary world (J. Ford, *Economic Development and Values: Life Beyond Gross National Product*. 1990, p. 172.)

John Paul's vision of economic development is a radical one indeed. "The aim of the present reflection," he says, "is to emphasize, through a theological investigation of the present world, the need for a fuller and more nuanced concept of development." (*Sollicitudo rei socialis* #4.) The two decade interval between the two encyclicals showed distressingly modest progress in the underdeveloped world; John Paul saw this as underdevelopment not only in the economic sense, but in the cultural, political and human dimensions as well. He asks if it is because of a too narrow idea of development, that is, a mainly economic one. (#15.) His term is rather "authentic human development," something to be measured and oriented according to the totality of the person. Material goods are to be seen as a gift from God and to be enjoyed as the fruits of human effort, but as people subject to the will of God, this also means subordinating the possession and use of these goods to a greater social good.

The obligation to commit oneself to the development of peoples is not just an individual duty...it is an imperative which obliges each and every man and woman as well as societies and nations (#32).

Those who share in the developmental process must be fully aware of the individual's *total* claim to rights. This includes—and this is explicitly stated (#33)—economic rights and this suggests a final connective link in our story. This is the one between *Sollicitudo rei socialis* (dated December 1987, although actually completed in February 1988!) and *Economic Justice For All*, the Pastoral Letter on the Economy by the National Conference of Catholic Bishops in 1986. The bishops maintained that people have a right to employment, to decent food and housing, and that these economic rights are to have the same "pride of place" in American culture as political and civil rights. (*Economic Justice For All*. 1986, #80-84.) Given the controversy that the bishops ignited with this and other bombshells, this "radical" idea is one that many of us are not ready to deal with yet.

We have travelled almost a full century over selected terrain. The focus has been on what we've termed "radical" complete with the quotation marks. The latter are significant because "radical" has in all of the documents sampled usually meant premature or anticipatory. This seems to flow from the church's moral vision of the economic scene, and it is this moral perspective, so embarrassing, awkward or even repugnant to some, that propels the church to radical heights at times.

From Leo's prudent yet fearless foray into the rights of workers ("new things" to be sure in 1891) to the U.S. bishops' Economic Pastoral's advocacy of economic rights, the conventional wisdom (Galbraith's wonderful phrase) of the era has been confronted and thrown off balance. When the church is in touch with this moral perspective and articulates it, it fulfills its mission of comforting the afflicted and afflicting the comfortable. A wonderful image by Eugene Kennedy in his analysis of *Sollicitudo rei socialis* may be a fitting end.

John Paul II has bravely refused to allow the church to be present in world affairs somewhat like a clergyman at a political dinner, a symbol of domesticated religion invited to ease the consciences and the digestive tracks of the powerful with vague but affable prayers. These diners, looking up from their endless courses are troubled by the pope's insistence that religion is tested and proven in daily living and that we share the burden and opportunity to make the world a more hospitable community for all people. (E. Kennedy, 1988, p. 11)

REFERENCES

Aaron Abell (ed.), *American Catholic Thought on Social Questions*. Bobbs-Merrill Co., 1968.

JF Bell, *A History of Economic Thought*. 2nd Ronald Press Co., 1967.

Thomas Bokenkotter, *A Concise History of the Catholic Church*. Doubleday Image Books, 1979.

J.Y. Calvez, "Economic Policy Issues in Roman Catholic Social Teaching" in Thomas Gannon (ed.) *The Catholic Challenge to the American Economy*. Macmillan Co., 1987.

J.Y. Calvez & J. Perrin, *The Church and Social Justice*. Henry Regnery Co., 1961.

Jay Dolan, *The American Catholic Experience*. Doubleday & Co., 1985.

Donald Dorr, *Option For the Poor*. Orbis Books, 1983.

Joseph Ford "Economic Development and Values: Life Beyond Gross National Product" in S. Natale & J. Wilson (ed.), *The Ethical Context for Business Conflicts*. University Press of America. Oxford Philosophy Trust, 1990.

Thomas J. Harte, *Papal Social Encyclicals: A Guide and Digest*. Bruce Publishing, 1956.

Eugene Kennedy, "Pope Thoroughly Moved, Arms to Disturb Us." *National Catholic Reporter*, May 27, 1988.

David O'Brien, "The Economic Thought of the American Hierachy" in *The Catholic Challenge to the American Economy*. 1987. pp.31.

The Social Encyclicals and Social Security

Charles F. O'Donnell

INTRODUCTION AND BACKGROUND

When Pope Leo XIII's encyclical *Rerum novarum* was published on May 15, 1891, the world of the end of the 19th century was greatly different from today's society. As one considers the then prevalent attitude on social justice, the words of Pope Leo XIII are even more remarkable and prophetic. Yet while there has been tremendous improvements in the condition of labor today, the agenda and challenge put forth by Pope Leo XIII represents an unfinished agenda.

As the pope proclaimed his support for the rights of the workingman to own property, to form worker associations and be entitled to a just wage, this was in sharp contrast to the economic philosophy of the day. The prevalent wage theories were the classical theories of the wages-fund articulated by John Stuart Mill, the Ricardian-Malthusian subsistence theory of wages or the infamous "Iron Law of Wages." The Marxian interpretation of wages argued that the workers were exploited by the capitalists who achieved their profits by forcing the workers to create surplus value. In *Das Kapital*, Marx wrote that the capitalist made his money by sucking the blood of living labor.

Pope Leo XIII's call for social justice was another example of the Pope's foresight and vision. In 1891, Germany was the only country to have established a program of social insurance. The German Parliament passed a sickness and maternity law (1883), workman's compensation (1884), old age, invalidity and death benefits (1889) at the request of the Kaiser and Chancellor Bismarck. The latter, a political realist, saw the popular support for the German Socialist groups who advocated social legislation. To shift support from these organizations, Bismarck, through the Kaiser, enacted social reforms to undermine the Socialist's platform.

In the United States, the labor movement was extremely weak in the 1890's. The Haymarket Affair had discredited the Knights of Labor and the American Federation of Labor, a basically conservative craft-oriented union, was in its infancy. Management was aggressively anti-union and effectively used the courts to block labor efforts to organize the labor force. For example, in the 1890's, the provisions of the Sherman Antitrust Law was used to break the Pullman Strike. In 1900 the total union members is estimated at being from 791,000 to 868,000, which represented only 3 to 4 percent of the civilian force. The labor movement in America did not achieve full rights until the Wagner Act or the National Labor Relations Act was passed in 1935. This *Magna Carta* of labor granted unions the right of collective bargaining almost half a century after *Rerum novarum*.

The ethical and moral aspects of social security must be viewed in the context of the traditional teachings of the church on social justice with particular emphasis on the just wage. I will argue later that the social security program is merely an extension of the just wage. Throughout the social encyclicals, there have been constant references to the rights of the worker to earn a just wage.

THE JUST WAGE
Pope Leo XIII wrote that:

> ...it may be truly said that it is only by the labor of the working man that States grow rich. Justice, therefore, demands that the interests of the poorer population be carefully watched over by the administration so that they who contribute so largely to the advantage of the community may themselves share in the benefits they create—that being housed, clothed, and enabled to support life, they may find their existence less hard and more endurable. (*Rerum novarum*, Paragraph 27)

> ...to labor is to exert one's self for the sake of procuring what is necessary for the

244

purposes of life, and most of all for self-preservation. "In the sweat of thy brow thou shalt eat bread". (*Ibid.*, Paragraph 34)

In discussing how wages are determined, Pope Leo XIII stated:

...There is always underlying such agreements an element of natural justice and one greater and more ancient than the free consent of contract parties, namely, that the wage shall not be less than enough to support a worker who is thrifty and upright. If compelled by necessity or moved by fear of a worse evil, a worker accepts a harder condition, which although against his will he must accept because the employer or contractor imposes it. He certainly submits to force, against which justice cries out in protest. (*Ibid.*, Paragraph 34)

In *Quadragesimo anno.* Pope Pius XI reaffirmed Pope Leo XIII's statement on the just wage when he wrote:

...in the first place, the wage paid to the workingman must be sufficient for himself and of his family.... Every effort must therefore be made that fathers of families receive a wage sufficient to meet adequately ordinary domestic needs. If in the present state of society this is not always feasible, social justice demands that reforms be introduced without delay which will guarantee every adult workingman just such a wage. In this connection we might utter a word of praise for various systems devised and attempted in practice, by which an increased wage is paid in view of increased family burdens, and a special provision is made for special needs. (Paragraph 71)

In his encyclical on *Atheistic Communism*, Pope Pius XI repeated his support for the just wage but expanded the principle of the just wage to include social insurance programs when he wrote:

> But social justice cannot be said to have been satisfied as long as workingmen are denied a salary that will enable them to secure proper sustenance for themselves and their families; as long as they are denied the opportunity of acquiring a modest fortune and forestalling the plague of universal pauperism; as long as they cannot make suitable provision through public or private insurance for old age, for periods of illness and unemployment. (Paragraph 52)

SOCIAL SECURITY AS AN EXTENSION OF THE JUST WAGE

In all of the subsequent social encyclicals, from Pope John XXIII's *Pacem in terris* to John Paul II's recent encyclical, there is reaffirmation of the just wage. What I would like to discuss now is the issue of social security and the encyclicals. In today's society, when one considers the compensation of employees, this is a much broader concept than merely wages and salaries. In 1990, the total compensation of employees in the U.S. was \$3,244 billions, of which \$539 billion was in the form of what the national income accounts calls supplements to wages and salaries. Supplements, or what is normally called fringe benefits, represent almost 17 percent of total compensation. As the costs of fringe benefits have increased, especially in the health insurance area, fringe benefits are a very significant factor and have become a major issue in collective bargaining as corporations are trying to reduce their costs by requiring workers to pay more of the health costs.

Social security or social insurance can be considered to be an extension of the *just wage*. Father John Cronin wrote that social insurance is an integral part of the wage level that a family needs. He realized that workers, if they had a truly adequate wage, could theoretically provide for all their needs. However, the realities of modern life make it difficult for workers to save enough money for their retirement or to provide for the loss of jobs or disability. (Cronin, p. 245.) Most workers do not have enough insurance to protect them if they die with dependent children, or they are disabled. Workers cannot protect themselves from the ravages of unemployment which creates economic, social and psychological hardships to workers. There is a need for social insurance to protect the workers and their families.

Social insurance may be defined as the method by which society provides protection for the individual against forces over which he or she has no control. For example, unemployment insurance compensation replaces part of the income lost by unemployment. Old age benefits replaces earnings lost when a worker retires.

In Pope John XXIII's encyclical *Mater and Magistra*, he refers positively to the development of social security programs especially in the most developed nations. (Paragraph 48)

Pope John makes special reference to the needs of agricultural workers:

> In agriculture the creation of two forms of insurance seems essential: one covering agriculture produce, the other covering the farm labor force and their families.
>
> Because, as is considered certain, the return per capita is generally less in agriculture than in the industry and service sectors, it is scarcely in keeping with the standards of social justice and equity to set up systems of social insurance or of social security in which the allowances granted to farmers are substantially lower than those allotted to persons engaged in other sectors of the economy. For social policy should aim at

guaranteeing that, whatever the economic sector they work in, and whatever the source of their income, the insurance allowances offered to citizens should not vary materially.

Systems of social insurance and social security can contribute effectively to the redistribution of national income according to standards of justice and equity. These systems can therefore be looked on as instruments for restoring balance between standards of living among different categories of the population.
(Paragraph 135,136)

In *Pacem in terris*, Pope John XXIII wrote that:

...every man has the right to life, to bodily integrity, and to the means which are necessary and suitable for the proper development of life. These means are primarily food, clothing, shelter, rest, medical care, and finally the necessary social services. Therefore, a human being also has the right to security in cases of sickness, inability to work, widowhood, old age, unemployment, or in any other case in which he is deprived of the means of subsistence through no fault of his own.
(Paragraph 11)

...It is necessary also that governments make efforts to see that insurance systems are made available to the citizens, so that, in case of misfortune or increased family responsibilities, no person will be without the necessary means to maintain a decent standard of living. (Paragraph 64)

John Paul II, in his encyclical *On Human Work,* stated:

> ...a just wage is the concrete means of *verifying the justice* of the whole socioeconomic system. Just remuneration for the work of an adult who is responsible for a family means remuneration which will suffice for establishing and properly maintaining a family and for providing security for its future. such remuneration can be given either through what is called a *family wage*—that is, a single salary given to the head of the family for his work, sufficient for the needs of the family without the other spouse having to take up gainful employment outside the home—or through *other social measures* such as family allowances or grants to mothers devoting themselves to their families (p.46).

The pope wrote that workers and their families should have health and disability insurance and that the insurance programs should be "...easily available for workers and that as far as possible it should be cheap or even free of charge" (page 47). Pope John Paul II stated that workers should have "...a right to a pension and to insurance for old age and in case of accident at work" (p.48).

The pope's statement that the family wage "...that is, a single salary given to the head of the family for *his work,* sufficient for the needs of the family without the other spouse having to take up gainful employment outside the home," has been very controversial. The pope may be presenting this as an ideal but the reality of contemporary society raises questions about its reality. In the U.S., the role of women has changed in the postwar period. In the late forties the labor force

249

participation rate of women was only about 25 percent while today women constitute over 40% of the labor force.

Women want to combine the roles of wife, mother and professional and not be only the *homemaker*. This is for a variety of reasons. Many women consider themselves professionals. Twenty or thirty years ago, women went primarily into the professions of teaching, nursing and social work. Today women are going into business areas. Almost fifty percent of the MBA students at Iona are women.

There is also the economic reality. Most young married couples need two incomes to meet their expenses. The average home in Westchester County is approximately $285,000.

In the United States, the Social Security law used to be interpreted in a way that the dependent spouse was considered to be a woman. In the late sixties a man, whose wife died and there were surviving children, sued and won the right to receive a father's benefits. Today the U.S. law is sexually neutral in its definition.

ADVANCES IN SOCIAL SECURITY

Since the time of Pope Leo, there has been significant improvements in the development of social insurance throughout the world. In 1987, over 141 countries had some program of social security. There are 130 countries with old-age, invalidity and survivors programs, 136 countries with workmen compensation laws, 84 countries have sickness and maternity programs, 63 nations supplement family income with family allowances, and forty nations have unemployment insurance plans. (Haanes—Olsen, p. 20) Therefore, social security has expanded from Germany as the only country with social security to world-wide coverage of individuals by social insurance.

A strong social security program is consistent with the church's teachings on social justice. Social security represents a continuation of the age-old custom of one generation providing for the needs of another and in turn being provided for the next generation. The OASDI program is basically an inter-generational transfer, i.e., it represents a transfer of funds from the working population to its beneficiaries. Although the form of providing for the aged, survivors and disabled has changed from a family-centered system to the institutionalized social insurance system, there remains a link between the two. Both are inter-generational transfers and relationships. In the extended family, the relationship was direct and personal while in social security it is impersonal and indirect but, nonetheless, real.

Social security is probably the best way of protecting the individual from loss of income suffered because of unemployment, disability or old age. As social insurance provides benefits on the basis of *earned rights* without the demeaning *means testing* of welfare, it promotes the maintenance of the individual's dignity and self-respect.

This is in keeping with Pope John XXIII's statement in *Pacem in terris* that the state should "...work to expand (the individual's) freedom as much as possible by the effective protection of the essential personal rights of each and every individual." (paragraph 65)

SOCIAL SECURITY IN AMERICA

In the United States, the Social Security Act was signed into law on August 14, 1935, over 44 years after *Rerum novarum*. There were a number of reasons why the United States was one of the last western nations to develop a program of social insurance. There was the philosophy of "rugged individualism" and self-help. It was generally assumed that the elderly should be provided for by their family and that the social insurance programs that developed in Europe in the late 19th and 20th centuries were "...detrimental to American ideals and traditions, destructive of individual character and personality, ruinous to family traditions and subversive of the basic principles of our government." (Epstein, p.63). The prevalent view that the family could provide for the aged was shattered in the Great Depression. Unemployment rose to incredible levels—especially among elderly workers—and workers lost their ability to earn an income, the basis of their security. With the wave of bank failures and the virtual collapse of the financial markets, the life savings of individuals were wiped out. Private pensions were also adversely affected. Forced to turn to private charity, millions found that these agencies had neither the resources nor the staff to handle their problems. The public then turned to state and local welfare agencies which were incapable of providing the massive amount of assistance needed. In desperation, people turned to the federal government and public pressure led to the establishment of a comprehensive program of economic security, especially Social Security. The original law had several parts—unemployment insurance, old age insurance (OAI) and federal grants to state and local government to establish welfare programs.

The original provision for old-age insurance was very restrictive, covering only about half of the labor force. Unfortunately, the law excluded for administration and constitutional reasons casual workers, domestic servants, agricultural workers, employees of not-for-profit firms as well as state and government employees. Many of these workers were among the poorest individuals and the most in the need of a program for retirement. Currently, the social security system covers almost the entire labor force.

The original OAI law provided benefits for only the retired workers. In 1939, the law was amended to include family protection both during retirement and upon the death of the worker. This represented a shift in the emphasis of the OAI program from individual protection to family protection or from a program of individual equity to social adequacy. It reflected a recognition of the need to provide protection to the worker's families. This is in keeping with Pope Pius XI support for social insurance to "...provide sustenance for themselves and their families" (*Quadragesimo anno*, Paragraph 52.)

Over the years, the social security system has been broadened to include disabled workers and health care for the elderly. Currently, almost 40 million Americans receive a social security check each month, about a sixth of the population receive OASI benefits. Recent emprovements in Social Security benefits have significantly reduced poverty levels among the elderly. In 1959, 35 percent of the elderly lived in poverty with the poverty levels of unrelated individuals being approximately 60 percent. In 1987 the poverty level for the elderly had declined to 12 percent over and 24 percent for individuals. (SSB, Annual Statistical Supplement, 1989, p. 124) Without social security, it is estimated that 1 out of every 2 senior citizens would be living in poverty.

UNFINISHED AGENDA

While there have been significant improvements in the lives of individuals over the 100 years since the *Rerum novarum,* there are many areas where Pope Leo XIII call for social justice has not been fulfilled.

As Pope John Paul II stated in his recent encyclical:

> Today more than ever, the church is aware that her social message will gain credibility more immediately from the witness of actions than as a result of its internal logic and consistency. This awareness is also a source of her preferential option for the poor, which is never exclusive or discriminatory toward other groups. This option is not limited to material poverty, since it is well known that there are many other forms of poverty, especially in modern society—not only economic, but cultural and spiritual poverty as well. The church's love for the poor, which is essential for her and a part of her constant tradition, impels her to give attention to a world in which poverty is threatening to assume massive proportions in spite of technological and economic progress, in the countries of the West, different forms of poverty are being experienced by groups which live on the margins of society, by the elderly and the sick, by the victims of consumerism and even more immediately by so many refugees and migrants. (*Centesimus annus,* Paragraph 57)

In the U.S. there are many populations where the general improvement in economic conditions has not been realized. The preferential option for the poor is not a reality for these individuals.

The recently released report by the National Commission on children found that one out of every five children in America live in poverty and that "...today, children are the poorest Americans." (*New York Times*, 6/26/91 p. A22) If one studies the poverty statistics more closely, the level of poverty among families headed by a female householder was 54.7 percent in 1987!

In May of 1990, the rate of unemployment was 5.3 percent with 6.7 million people unemployed. In June 1991, the rate of unemployment had risen to 7.0 percent and the level of unemployment to 8.745 million, an increase of almost two million over the period. In a recession, it is normally expected that the unemployment insurance will work as an *automatic stabilizer* with the program replacing part of the earnings lost by unemployment. A *New York Times* article reported that

> ...the program is so starved for administrative funds that it cannot be run properly; less than half of those out of work are receiving benefits compared to 75 percent of those unemployed in the mid-1970's; few of those unemployed longer than six months get any benefits and severe cuts have been taken in programs that have shown some success in removing from the unemployment rolls those people who remained jobless for long periods. (Holmes, p. E5)

Because of low level of benefits, many workers do not even apply for them. In Massachusetts where enefits can be as high as $423 a week, two-thirds of those out of work apply. In Virginia, where the maximum is $198 a week, only 17 percent of the jobless apply. (Holmes, p. E7)

When workers were unemployed, they lost not only their jobs but in many cases their fringe benefits, especially their health insurance. "It is estimated that 37 million people have no insurance—and that even the middle class is suddenly vulnerable to huge increases in premiums and out of pocket charges or to denial of insurance because of a preexisting condition if they change jobs. The system also leads to collosal administration waste." (Kuttner, p.16)

In the U.S., public policy has long differentiated between what one might call the worthy poor and the poor. The welfare program is a classic example of this differentiation. There are two forms of welfare—a program called Supplement Security Income (SSI) and a program of Aid to Families with Dependent Children. The SSI is a federal program for the elderly and the disabled while the AFDC is predominately a state and local program with federal grants to the state and local governments. In December 1990 the average SSI benefits per recipient was $277.65 per month, while the AFDC paid a monthly benefit of $374.00 per family of three or $124.67 per individual. (SSB, ASS, 1990, p.4)

The level of payments to AFDC clearly violates Pope John XXIII's statement that social justice and equity requires that the benefits of social insurance programs should "...not vary materially." (*Mater et Magistra*, p.136)

The OASDI program has been designed to be a tripartite system of income maintenance with social security benefits being the base or floor to be supplemented by private pensions and personal savings. For many Americans, this is a myth. In 1990, a study of private pension systems found that only 53 percent of the full-time private wage and salary labor force were covered by a pension, leaving about half of the private labor force uncovered. Many of those covered by plans might not receive benefits if they change jobs because they lack vested rights to the pension. Studies of OASI beneficiaries constantly show that less than half of the beneficiaries receive either a private or public pension to supplement the social security check. (Pension Trends, p.2)

Workers, who always worked at the minimum wage, received a social benefit in December 1989 of $5,700, while the poverty level for an elderly individual was $5,947. The problem is not with the Social Security benefit itself. A minimum wage earner has a replacement ratio of almost 60%, that is his SS benefits represented 60% of the premiums covered earnings. During his/her work life, a wage earner has little ability to save and is generally not covered by a private pension.

CONCLUSION

Unfortunately, there seems to be no desire or inclination in America to address the unfinished agenda. President Johnson's War on Poverty is a fading memory. The budget crisis and the Gramm-Rudman Act limit the ability to respond to these challenges. In the 18th century, the French school called the Physiocrats believed that the State should adapt its expenditures to meet its revenues, and not its revenues to its expenditures. (Gide and Rist, p. 61) This was basically the policy adapted by the Reagan administration when it proposed significant cuts in taxes in 1981. Over time, the reduction in government revenues lead to the current situation where the federal government's ability to undertake new programs is severely limited by the fiscal crisis.

Moreover, there seems to be little hope that any significant legislation will be enacted in the near future to address the problem of poverty among children and the elderly, to remedy the deficiencies of the unemployment insurance programs, or to address the welfare programs. In 1971 when President Nixon proposed a major reform of welfare, he called it a program that served no one well—not the taxpayers or its recipients. Most experts believe that the current welfare system contributes to the breakup of families. This is against the consistent Catholic social thought that government programs should promote the stability of the family. As Pope John Paul II said, "...the family is the heart of the culture of life." (*Centesimus annus*, Paragraph 39)

There seems to be little probability that there will be new programs to address the issue of health care for those not covered by health insurance at work or those who lost this coverage because they are unemployed.

Thus, the agenda for social justice through social insurance is still unfulfilled. Pope John XXIII's call that "...a human being...has the right to security in cases, inability to work, widowhood, old age, unemployment, or in any case in which he is deprived of the means of subsistence through no fault of his own" (*Pacem in terris*, Paragraph 11) is still a goal and challenge.

Over 200 years ago, Samuel Johnson wrote that "...a decent provision for the poor is the true test of civilization." (Levitan, p.111)

This is still a test and challenge for all of us and part of our unfinished agenda represented by Pope Leo XIII's plea for social justice for the workers and the poor.

REFERENCES

Cronin, John F. *Social Principles and Economic Life*. Milwaukee: The Bruce Publishing Company, 1959.

Epstein, Abraham. *Insecurity: A Challenge to America*. New York: Harrison Smith and Robert Haas, 1933.

Gide, Charles, and Rist, Charles. *A History of Economic Doctrines*. 7th ed. Boston: D.C. Heath and Company, 1949.

Haanes-Olsen, Lief. "World Wide Trends and Developments in Social Security, 1985-1987." *Social Security Bulletin*, February 1989: 14-26.

Holmes, Steven A. "Fallback for the Jobless Has Little to Fall Back on." *New York Times*, 17 February, 1991: E5.

Pope John XXIII. *Mater et Magistra*: Edited by Donald R. Campion, S.J. and Eugene K. Culhane, S.J., New York: The American Press, 1961.

Pope John XXIII. *Pacem in terris*. New York: The American Press, 1963.

Pope John Paul II. *Centesimus annus origins*. 16 May 1991. Vol. 21: No. 1.

Pope John Paul II. *On Human Work*. Boston: St. Paul Editions, 1981.

Kuttner Robert. "A Second Opinion on the Democratic Health Plan." *Business Week*, 1 July 1991: 16.

Levitan, Sam A. *Programs in Aid of the Poor for the 1970's*. Baltimore: The Johns Hopkins Press, 1969.

"Pension Trends." *Monthly Labor Review*, Feb. 1990: 2.

"The Poorest Americans: A Bold-Flawed-Remedy for Children." *New York Times* 26 June 1991: A22.

U.S. Department of Health and Human Services, Social Security Administration. *Social Security Bulletin, Annual Statistical Supplement 1989*. Washington: U.S. Government Printing Office, 1989.

Rerum novarum and the Modern Corporation

Bernard Brady, Kenneth Goodpaster,
and Robert Kennedy.

This paper argues that *Rerum novarum* is a classic text. The relevance of Pope Leo's famous encyclical is particularly evident as it relates to contemporary business ethics. The paper is in three sections. The first section examines *Rerum novarum* and considers the elements of the document that give the text the character of a classic. The second section examines the relation between contemporary business ethics and Leo's conceptual frameworks and normative discourse. The final section illustrates successes and failures of corporations "doing the right thing" along lines indicated by *Rerum novarum*.

Part I

Rerum novarum as a Classic Text

The promulgation of *Rerum novarum* on May 15, 1891 marks the birth of modern Catholic social thought. Leo's now famous encyclical was the first official papal pronouncement containing normative ethical discussion on a particular social issue, namely, the revolutionary changes that industrialism brought to economic relations in Europe.[1] For one hundred years now, Leo's encyclical has continued to direct Catholic social ethics both in form and in substance. The many social encyclicals and episcopal documents following *Rerum novarum*, as well as the vast array of commentaries and critiques, bear witness to its continuing relevance. This section of the paper will argue that not only is *Rerum novarum* relevant to contemporary discourse in social ethics, but that the the text is a classic in the discipline of Christian social ethics.

A classic text, according to David Tracy, "articulates a question worth asking and a response worth considering."[2] Moreover, unlike a period piece, a text that once bore fruit but whose meaning is now spent, a classic has a "permanence and an excess of meaning."[3] The "possibilities of meaning and truth"[4] communicated in a classic have a certain timelessness inviting continual discussion, appropriation and interpretation. Tracy writes:

> Classics endure as provocations awaiting the
> risk of reading: to challenge our compla-
> cency, to break our conventions, to compel
> and concentrate our attention, to lure us out
> of a privacy masked as autonomy into a
> public realm where what is important and
> essential is no longer denied.[5]

To suggest *Rerum novarum* is a candidate for consideration as a classic is not to say that a simple repetition of Leo's thinking is sufficient to address the social problems and economic issues facing the contemporary world. Nor is it to say that everything in *Rerum novarum* contains permanent and essential moral truths. Like any other text, *Rerum novarum* is deeply rooted in its particular historical context. It addresses a very specific economic condition and, to a certain extent, expresses an antiquated social vision.[6] Despite these contextual realities and historical limitations, *Rerum novarum* continues to have a disclosive power for social ethics. Significant elements of the text, especially Leo's description of social issues and his normative response, transcend the particularities of nineteenth-century industrial Europe and invite contemporary consideration. Two significant questions *Rerum novarum* asks and addresses are: what are the characteristics of a moral workplace? and, what are the characteristics of a moral economic order?

The Moral Workplace

According to Leo, a moral workplace is characterized by employer-employee relations based on natural justice (RN 63). Such relations are marked by mutual responsibility, cooperation and harmony. The burden of Leo's discussion is to explore the practical implications of justice between the two groups, i.e., each giving to the other what is due.

Responsibilities and Rights

Rerum novarum is remembered most for its strong defense of the worker. Leo goes to great length to promote the dignity of the worker and subsequently the well-being and stability of the worker's family. In service of this goal, Leo proclaims three basic rights: (1) the right of workers to a living wage (9, 32, 61-63); (2) the right of persons to own property (10-12, 65); and (3) the right of persons to participate in voluntary groups and associations (72-73,76). Leo's social thought, while highlighted by a strong use of rights language, is not to be understood, however, as simply a worker's bill of rights. The first word in social morality for Leo is responsibility. Leo understands persons to have fundamental anthropological orientations, namely, to God, to family, and to society. Morality, moral norms, values and judgments, are defined in relation to the demands of these orientations. The pope addresses the question of justice in the workplace by reminding the participants of their specific moral responsibilities. He speaks both to employers and employees in terms of their "being," their moral dispositions and attitudes, as well as their "doing," their actual behaviors or practices in the workplace. He instructs workers to be industrious (81) and to perform their work conscientiously (30). Aware of the inhuman working conditions and the reality of strong insurrectionary movements, he cautions them to pursue their demands with reason (81) and to avoid violence or causing injury to their employer or their employer's property (30). Since it is the workers' cause at stake (82), and it is they who live in "miserable and wretched conditions" (5) and work under the "yoke almost of slavery" (6), Leo spends proportionately much less time discussing the moral responsibility of workers in comparison to his discussion on the responsibility of the owners.

On the first reading of *Rerum novarum*, it is surprising to hear Leo's adamant criticism of the rich, the owners of the factories. In his words, they are greedy, avaricious, and grasping (6, 59). They are prone to what he refers to as, "the twin vices: of excessive desire for money and thirst for pleasure" (42). He warns them against treating workers as slaves or using workers only as means for personal gain. In a moral workplace, the employer recognizes two realities: (a) the basic dignity of the worker as a person and, (b) the fact that the fundamental source of wealth is provided by the worker's labor. According to Leo, the worker uses mental energy and bodily strength and "impresses a kind of image of his person" (15) on goods of the earth. Through labor, the worker "so thoroughly intermingles" with these goods that the product becomes "for the most part quite inseparable" from the labor (16). Moving from this labor intensive theory of property[7] Leo asks, "Would justice permit anyone to own and enjoy that upon which another has toiled? As effects follow the cause producing them, so it is just that the fruit of labor belongs precisely to those who have performed the labor" (16). "It is incontestable," says Leo, "that the wealth of nations originates from no other source than from the labor of workers" (51). Leo thus exhorts employers to respect the dignity of the human personality of their employees by paying them a just wage (32, 63-65). A just wage is nothing more than compensation given to the worker for product that the worker, in a sense, "owns." Leo describes such a wage to be large enough to enable the worker "to provide comfortably for himself, his wife and his children" (65).

A moral workplace protects the religious and spiritual well-being of workers. Employers must respect the obligation of workers to care for their families (31), and thus they ought not expose workers to sinful situations (mixing the sexes in the workplace[8] was one of the "pernicious incitements to sin" according to the pope, 53). Respecting the dignity of human personality, moreover, includes assigning appropriate work based on strength, age and sex (31, 60); allowing workers adequate rest intervals; limiting work hours (59); and providing safe working conditions (64). Finally, Leo warns employers against harming the savings of workers "by fraud, usury or coercion" (32).

Creating Justice in the Workplace

Leo's primary focus on the employers and the rich has not gone unnoticed by commentators. Donal Dorr, for example, suggests that Leo "gives very little encouragement to activism on the part of the workers in the struggle for rights."[9] He describes Leo's approach to be "top down" rather than "bottom up" as it encourages *conversion* of those in power rather than active *confrontation* by the poor.[10] By Dorr's reading, Leo does not encourage the workers to be the primary agents of social change. This is a crucial point to consider in the continuing relevance of the document. We argue that while there are strong elements in *Rerum novarum* favoring social harmony and critical of violence, Dorr's critique is overstated. The text does not simply encourage workers to wait for the coming of a better day. The "top down/ bottom up" distinction does not capture the nuances of Leo's model for pursuing institutional reform. The pope's model of working for justice in the workplace places responsibility on the three main actors in industrial relations: the workers, the government and the owners.

The Role of Workers

Leo's moral counsel to workers is strikingly different from the propositions of other social reformers or social revolutionaries. The pope avoids two extremes. He does not merely call workers to live the virtues of charity and patience nor, on the other hand, does he encourage "the forcible overthrow of all existing social conditions,"[11] as did Karl Marx forty years before. Instead, he encourages workers with a sense of the dignity of their work (37) and empowers them to organize and form associations (68-80). These groups, modeled on medieval guilds, would mediate the concerns of workers with the owners and help workers develop their condition.[12] Associations give workers a position of strength from which to press their demands and advocate institutional reform. What this says, using Dorr's categories, is that while the actual responsibility for implementing reform in the workplace comes from the "top down," such change may surely be initiated from the "bottom up."

The Role of Government

Leo believes that government has a responsibility to promote the common good and to defend the dignity of persons, particularly the workers (48, 54). In contrast to his understanding of socialism of his day, Leo argues for a real but limited moral authority of the state. Throughout *Rerum novarum*, the pope upholds the integrity of interpersonal relations

263

and social groups. None of the parts of society, for example, the family, private associations or the workplace, ought to be absorbed by the state. Two dangers which would justify state involvement are: (a) serious injury or harm to individuals within these relations and, (b) if the activity of a part threatens the peace and order of society. Unfair wages and dangerous working conditions fit these criteria. As a workers' strike disrupts the order of society, Leo suggests the state ought to intervene to stop this "evil" (53, 56). State intervention in the workplace may be appropriate, but this external force is not sufficient to create a moral workplace. The owners must ultimately shoulder this burden.

The Role of Owners

When injustice occurs within a specific social setting, such as a workplace, to whom do we make our primary and indeed our strongest moral claim? Leo tells us that we are to call upon those who are most directly responsible for such conditions. His appeal is to the moral conscience of those who have set up and run the system, those who can most directly alter the existing situation. Leo understands the causes of social problems to be complex, but wonders, if the employers would just fulfill their basic responsibilities, would not that "remove the bitterness and the causes of the conflict?" (32).[13]

Leo's discussion of the determination of wages, which he labels "a matter of very great importance" (61), illustrates the responsibility he places on the owners. The pope asks, whether an employer's obligation to the worker is fulfilled by merely paying the agreed upon wage. His answer is no. Justice demands that the employer protect the stability of the worker, and thus the worker's family, by providing a living wage and safe working conditions. Although this might take the employer beyond the level of responsibility dictated by the market, it is not to be understood as an act of supererogation. It is rather an act of justice; the owners must give the workers their due (29).[14]

Rerum novarum displays a confidence in reason and an optimism that persons are open to change through rational discourse. But the question remains from the proponents of "bottom up" solutions to social reform. Why should the owners be moral? What is in it for them? Leo's answer, though not without a religious warning of the dangers of wealth

(32-33), is grounded on exploring common understandings of moral responsibility for persons. It is simply the right thing to do. The marketplace cannot be our moral guide, nor can the state. Justice must find its place in the action and character of those who are responsible for life in the workplace. Leo is indeed quite happy to cite many who have already "rightly perceived what the times require" and are presently "experimenting and striving to discover how...[to] raise the non-owning working class to higher living levels" (75).

The Moral Economic Order

The pope's vision of a just economic system mirrors his teachings on a moral workplace. In a sense, his discussion of the moral economic order is an expansion of his teachings on the moral workplace. In *Rerum novarum* Leo likens society to a human body wherein "the different members harmonize with one another" (28). As in the body, each part has both a fundamental integrity of being and function as well as a fundamental orientation to the whole, so too in society. He writes, each "class needs the other completely: neither capital can do without labor, nor labor without capital. Concord begets beauty and order in things" (28). A just economic system is peaceful and orderly (53), characterized by: (a) the virtuous collaboration and participation of all economic actors and, (b) the promotion of the material and spiritual/moral well-being of all participants. The fulfillment of these conditions necessitates a special concern for the poor.

In *Rerum novarum*, Leo explicitly condemns the socialism of his day and implicitly condemns the capitalism of his day. His criticism of socialism is multifaceted. Socialism, says Leo, promotes a false equality among persons, suggests the classes are necessarily hostile to one another, denies the validity of private property, and promotes a vision of an unjustly intrusive state (7-28). Leo's criticism of capitalism focuses on its practices of usury, its *de facto* limitation of private property (in contrast to the *de jure* elimination of private property of socialism), its excessive competition, its laissez-faire attitudes, and the fact that it has left workers defenseless in the face of these practices.

While Leo condemns these two dominant and competing economic structures,[15] he does not reject the validity of a market system of economic production and distribution.[16]   His strong agrarian images suggest he is quite comfortable with the validity of buying and selling goods and services.   Although he makes the moral distinction between "just ownership of money" and "just use of money" (34),   he has no general aversion to the accumulation of wealth through just means. Indeed his plea on behalf of the workers is that they may "come into possession of a little wealth" (65).   A just economic order and economic prosperity for all members of society is an element of the common good. He writes:

> States are made prosperous especially by wholesome morality, properly ordered family life, protection of religion and justice, moderate imposition and equitable distribution of public burdens, progressive development of industry and trade, thriving agriculture, and by all other things of this nature, which the more actively they are promoted, the better and happier the life of the citizens is destined to be (48).

Perhaps the most outstanding issue in Leo's vision of the just economic system is his advocacy of private property.   Leo argues that the right to own private property is conferred on persons by nature (10) and ought to be considered "sacred" (65). He then proclaims, "the law ought to favor this right, and, so far as it can, see that the largest possible number among the masses of the population prefer to own property" (65). The recognition of the right to own property and the concerted effort to broaden ownership are essential elements of a just economic system.   Leo argues, moreover, for a number of pragmatic reasons, that broadened participation of property ownership will solve many of the the ills plaguing society.   Property ownership will give the formerly poor a degree of personal satisfaction and security.   It will ultimately ease the tensions between the rich and the poor and solve the problem of emigration (66).

Rerum novarum is a classic text in Christian social ethics as it provokes readers to address concerns that have significant contemporary ramifications. Leo's questions of the moral workplace and the moral economic order demand to be continually re-asked. A moral workplace, he believes, requires the free and active participation of the workers and owners. The burden of responsibility for creating a moral workplace falls on the owners, the employers. A just economic order is characterized by free and active participation of all in the progressive production and just distribution of goods. It demands the government have a limited but very real moral charge. The most important and practical way of attaining a just economic order is to defend the right of private property, promote the moral responsibilities of property ownership, and pursue programs that allow the masses to own property. This will establish the conditions for stability and security of the worker, the worker's family, and the society as a whole.

Part II

Rerum novarum and Contemporary Business Ethics

Much has changed in the economic order and in the world of work since *Rerum novarum* was written. The foundations of the largest economies have shifted from agriculture to manufacturing, and from manufacturing to information-based services. Labor unions have ascended and, to some extent, descended in power and influence. Management has largely been separated from ownership in the modern corporation. Communism has come and, if we are to believe the most natural interpretation of recent events, gone. Capitalism has embarrassed itself on numerous fronts, from multi-national exploitation of Third World populations to environmental degradation of land, air, and water. U.S. corporate scandals during the '70s and '80s have been commonplace: Wall Street insider trading, defense contractor fraud, savings and loan mismanagement.

Change and a New Field

During the last 25 years, we have seen the rise of new and intense interest in business ethics. Philosophers and theologians have sought to apply their understanding of basic moral concepts and principles to the operations of the modern corporation. This activity has given rise to new interdisciplinary efforts and to dual career competencies (in the humanities and in business administration). The revitalized field of business ethics displays a dynamic, multi-leveled approach to economic and moral reflection: the individual person in the workplace interacting with the corporation as a moral context or culture, and the corporation as a moral agent interacting with the wider social system (e.g., socialism, democratic capitalism, etc.).

What is striking about this new field and confirming of our thesis that *Rerum novarum* is a classic text, is that contemporary business ethics displays both conceptual and normative contours that map directly onto those of Leo's encyclical.[17] Furthermore, many of the topics that are of concern today in business ethics have their ancestry in issues discussed in *Rerum novarum* a century ago: topics like employee rights, just wages and working conditions, limits on both state power and market forces, and the importance of respectful dialogue in the process of conflict resolution.

Thus while much has changed during the twentieth century, and the ethical issues today are in many ways "new," there is a perennial relevance to the ethical outlook of *Rerum novarum* and there is even a topical linkage that is undeniable. Let us take a closer look.

Micro and Macro Arenas

As we pointed out in *Part I*, *Rerum novarum* moves naturally between two arenas of social thought, what we might call the *micro* arena and the *macro* arena. The former has to do with the relationships and responsibilities in the workplace between employees and corporate managers, who were influenced directly then, but only indirectly today by owner/investors. The *macro* arena has to do with relationships and responsibilities in society at large between corporations and other groups, including customers, suppliers, government, education, and host or local

268

communities. At the macro level, we refer to relationships between economic, political, and cultural influences in a "social order."

Contemporary business ethics looks at challenges in the micro arena in terms of the rights and responsibilities of employees and managers: the workplace (or corporation) as a moral environment.[18] Whole journals are devoted to the exploration of these challenges.[19]

We may see less today in Europe and America some of the 19th century evils of child labor, inhuman working conditions, arbitrary dismissal, and substandard wages, though in Third World countries such evils are still common. Even in Europe and America we continue to be concerned about the treatment of women and minorities, occupational health and safety, employee rights to privacy, free speech, and due process.[20] These are clearly concerns that are continuous with themes in *Rerum novarum*.

As to challenges in the macro arena, the degree of government interference in free market dynamics is a central business ethics theme as it relates to consumer safety, environmental protection, and corporate community involvement. And while organized labor has in some ways become less of a "macro factor" in advanced economies, unions can be expected to play significant roles as manufacturing finds new geographical concentrations. Again, there is continuity with themes in *Rerum novarum*.

Patterns of Ethical Thinking in Management

Whether the arenas are those mentioned in Leo's encyclical or their contemporary counterparts, the *outlook and approach* to them in business ethics today demonstrates a deeper sense in which *Rerum novarum* has the character of a classic. Consider the following widely-used inventory of approaches to corporate responsibility:

(Type 1)   The Logic of Self-Interest
(Type 2)   The Logic of External Constraint
                (a) The Invisible Hand Version
                (b) The Visible Hand Version
(Type 3)   The Logic of Conscience.[21]

Each of these "logics" represents a different, though not exclusive, approach to justifying and institutionalizing ethical values in business. Let us first describe each category and then relate the contemporary use of this *set* of categories to Leo's approach in *Rerum novarum*. Our conclusion will be that the encyclical anticipated many of the central features of the modern debate in business ethics, both in the micro arena and in the macro arena.

Type 1. The logic of self-interest. While this approach may seem like a limiting case, on the borderline of genuinely ethical reasoning, it is often appealed to either as psychologically or organizationally more realistic than the alternatives considered below. Current discussions of phrases like "honesty pays," "good ethics is good business," and "you do well by doing good" indicate either a naive faith in the convergence of self-interest and morality or a weak allegiance to morality when it involves a cost.

Type 1 thinking is present wherever worker rights, product safety, or community well-being are pursued solely with an eye to self-interest as the overarching value. It is important to emphasize, however, that this need not mean *ignoring* concern for others. Some interpretations of "public relations," for example, seem to fit the *Type 1* pattern.

Type 2. The logic of external constraint. *Type 2* thinking incorporates respect for workers and others not merely in terms of the "value to self" of such respect, but as a constraint on the pursuit of self-interest in the first place. There are two distinct versions of this logic. The first looks primarily to market forces as surrogates for morality; the second to political and legal forces.

The invisible hand version. Some accord importance to ethical values in business decision making, but insist that they enter through the competitive system. Thus management attention to ethics, beyond attention to competitiveness, is unnecessary. Remembering Adam Smith, we can refer to this as the "invisible hand" logic, since the market becomes a substitute for conscience. Nobel laureate Milton Friedman is the most well-known contemporary exponent of this view.

The visible hand version. Those who hold an external constraint view of business ethics, but do not trust the invisible hand of the market to moralize corporate behavior will often turn to the visible hand or "hand of government" approach. Here the state (through laws or the regulatory process) is relied upon to protect workers, consumers, and communities from both the self-interest of corporations and the forces of market competition. Exponents of this view tend to see themselves as liberals rather than conservatives on economic issues, but they nevertheless share with their conservative opponents an "external constraint" orientation: Ethics does not enter management decisions directly, but indirectly through outside influences on the decision-making process, the "rules of the game."

Type 3. The logic of conscience. This last approach to business ethics introduces moral reasoning directly into management thinking. It goes beyond external constraints on the belief that such constraints may be necessary but are not sufficient to protect the rights and interests of employees, customers, and communities. Each stakeholder group, not just stockholders (or investors or owners), is taken as deserving moral consideration by management. Conscience is understood to follow imperatives that go beyond the laws of economics as well as the civil law.[22] In the words of one business leader, James Bere of Borg-Warner Corporation:

> Any business is a member of a social system, entitled to the rights and bound by the responsibilities of that membership. Its freedom to pursue economic goals is constrained by law and channeled by the forces of a free market. But these demands are minimal, requiring only that a business provide wanted goods and services, complete fairly, and cause no obvious harm. For some companies that is enough. It is not enough for Borg-Warner. We impose upon ourselves an obligation to reach beyond the minimal.

271

Contemporary Patterns in Leo's Thought

There are numerous places in *Rerum novarum* which can be said to anticipate this contemporary typology. In his discussion of the features of the moral workplace, Leo criticizes *Type 1* logic both on the part of employers (greed, excessive desire for money, thirst for pleasure, using workers as means for personal gain) and on the part of workers themselves (avoiding violence, injury, and unreasonable demands).

Type 2 logic also comes under criticism in *both* of its versions. As we have seen, Leo's critique of socialism includes a strong rejection of the unjustly intrusive state and of threats to private property. The moral credentials of civil law and political power are real, but limited.

At the same time, the invisible hand of the market is also rejected as a moral surrogate, not only in Leo's criticism of excessive competition, but especially in his discussion of a just, living wage. Free market forces are not enough, he argues, if they do not take into account the stability of the worker, the worker's family, and the safety of the work environment. These are not market "negotiables."

Finally, the appeal that Leo makes in *Rerum novarum* to the *consciences* of the manager/owners, to their sense of what is right, and to conversion rather than confrontation indicates a clear prescription in favor of *Type 3* logic. This is the logic of the conscientious manager in the micro arena who takes seriously the fact that employees have rights and interests beyond those supported by market forces and legal statutes. And it is the logic of the conscientious corporation in the macro arena that guides its conduct mindful of markets and laws but also mindful that these constraints do not always represent the true needs of all stakeholders, especially the powerless and the poor.

A century ago, when the contours of the "new things" were only barely perceptible, the author of *Rerum novarum* anticipated the anatomy of several business logics, and chose to appeal not to self-interest, nor to free markets or state control, but to corporate and managerial conscience. It was as if even then, an appeal to impersonal forces was thought to be far less likely to succeed than a heartfelt appeal to personal ones, even if the persons involved were (and are) weak, vulnerable to greed, and often encumbered by fiduciary obligations.

In a recent article in the *Harvard Business Review* entitled "Why Be Honest if Honesty Doesn't Pay?" (September-October 1990) authors Stevenson and Abide conclude in secular categories what Leo concluded with the eyes of faith a century before:

> The importance of moral and social motives in business cannot be overemphasized. A selective memory, a careful screening of the facts may help sustain the fiction of profitable virtue, but the fundamental basis of trust is moral. We keep promises because we believe it is right to do so, not because it is good business... [But] since our trust isn't grounded in self-interest, it is fragile. And, indeed, we all know of organizations, industries, and even whole societies in which trust has given way either to a destructive free-for-all or to inflexible rules and bureaucracy.

These authors remind us that *Type 3* thinking on the part of the owners and managers of capital is both superior and fragile to *Types 1* and 2. This conviction, on its most natural reading, is the guiding spirit in *Rerum novarum*, and the source of its plea for a conversion of conscience instead of confrontation. Topically, conceptually, and in the end normatively, the encyclical anticipates and reinforces the thrust of much contemporary work in business ethics.

Part III

Rerum novarum and Modern Corporate Behavior

In the second part of our paper we suggested that some of the themes of *Rerum novarum* converge with, but have not necessarily conditioned, important elements of contemporary thinking about business ethics. Now we wish to ask whether this convergence of theoretical frameworks and visions of possibilities for the marketplace is reflected in the conduct and aspirations of modern corporations. In other words, do we have any reason to believe that the message of *Rerum novarum* would be recognizable and acceptable to modern business? With some important qualifications, our answer is yes. Though many corporations — perhaps even most — do not yet instantiate the ideals of *Rerum novarum* and Type 3 thinking, we believe that some do.

We illustrate this with respect to the question of a moral economic order by looking at three incidents involving successful companies. In our view, the behavior of these companies was a result of deeply held convictions about the nature of the organization and its responsibilities to the community. We do not suggest that the decision-makers in these companies were directly influenced by *Rerum novarum*. In all likelihood, they were entirely unfamiliar with the document. Rather, we contend that, as a classic text, *Rerum novarum* articulates some foundational truths about human persons in organizations, and about the relationship of these organizations to the larger communities in which they function. Reasoning independently, contemporary business ethics affirms many of these themes. It should come as no surprise, then, that some decisions of successful modern companies might be consistent with the insights of Leo XIII.

Dayton Hudson Corporation:
Management and Government as Partners

The first incident we wish to consider involves a very successful American retailer in a characteristic management challenge of the '80s: a hostile takeover attempt.

In early June, 1987, the top management of the Dayton Hudson Corporation (DHC) learned that the company was probably the target of a hostile takeover attempt. DHC was a $9 billion public corporation, chartered in Minnesota, that operated some 475 large retail stores in 34 states. The company was distinguished for its community involvement. Since 1946 it had annually donated an amount equal to 5% of its taxable income to social action and arts organizations.

At the time DHC first learned that it was a takeover target, no public declarations of intent had been made. However, there was unusual activity in DHC's stock and rumors were floating around Wall Street. The firm identified as the raider had recently made several unsuccessful attempts to acquire other large corporations in the retail industry.

After carefully considering its options, management decided to approach the governor of Minnesota to ask him to call a special session of the legislature for the specific purpose of tightening Minnesota's takeover laws. Within ten days the legislature met and passed legislation that had the effect of temporarily discouraging the takeover attempt.

The bill passed by the Minnesota legislature aimed to protect companies by addressing the problem of tender offers. It required approval of the majority of disinterested shareholders before a bidder could gain voting rights for a controlling share of the stock. It also required the approval of a majority of the disinterested members of the board of directors (i.e., those who were neither managers nor representatives of bidders) before the bidder could enter any business combination with the target. Furthermore, and perhaps most importantly, it prohibited the sale of a target company's assets to pay debts incurred in financing a hostile takeover for a period of five years.

One of the most controversial provisions of the Minnesota bill, however, was the stipulation that the board of directors of a target company could legitimately take into consideration the interests of a wide range of groups in exercising their "business judgment." In discharging their duties, directors were authorized to consider "the interests of the corporation's employees, customers, suppliers, and creditors, the economy of the state and nation, community and societal considerations, and the long-term as well as short-term interests of the corporation and its shareholders including the possibility that these interests may be best served by the continued independence of the corporation."

The action of the legislature is significant for several reasons. First of all, the bill that the legislature enacted was essentially identical to the proposal made by DHC. It represents a coalition between the board of directors and the management of a major corporation and the legislative branch of government. This coalition was set in opposition to corporate

275

raiders who intended to "bust up" companies in order to recover their assets for other purposes.

And some would add that the coalition placed management over against shareholders as well, since the changes that management proposed in the existing legislation would impose limits on the ability of shareholders to sell their shares by making those shares less desirable to potential raiders. In effect, the board of directors and management of the company proposed on this occasion that the legislature make it more difficult for shareholders to dispose of their property (i.e., their shares) in any way they wished. DHC argued that the benefits to the community of the continued independence of the company required that the community set protections in place, even when those protections threatened the rights of the owners of capital.

The restriction on the sale of assets is another way in which the legislature sought, at the request of management, to protect the independence of the company. Many raiders were motivated by the desire to control the assets of target firms, assets that could be sold for considerable profits. However, the sale of these assets would usually mean the dismemberment of the firm. The legislature, supported by the majority of the citizens of Minnesota, considered the continued independence and integrity of DHC to be an asset to the community whose value exceeded the tax revenues and employment it provided. Dismembering this asset, even if the jobs and tax revenues could somehow be preserved, would nevertheless destroy the institution.

A third significant aspect of this incident has to do with the legislature's expansion of the "business judgment" rule. In general, the business judgment rule protects managers and members of a board of directors from liability for decisions made within the scope of their authority when it is reasonable to believe that such decisions were made in good faith. Commonly, it has been held that managers and boards of directors had a principal, and perhaps even an overriding, obligation to maximize the wealth of shareholders. *Rerum novarum* clearly envisions a set of responsibilities for managers that looks beyond profits to the common good. In an important way this legislation, which stipulates that the impact upon other "stakeholders" may legitimately be considered in business decisions, reflects this concern for the common good.

Merck & Co.:
A Corporation Acts for the Common Good

This view of business corporations as participating in a larger system, with obligations to and dependencies upon, that system, is gaining greater currency in the corporate world. While this view may not dominate board rooms and management suites, it is frequently instantiated in corporate mission statements and policies. This is true, for example, for Dayton Hudson and for Borg-Warner, whose chairman, James Bere, we quote above. It is also true for Japan's Canon Inc., whose chairman, Ryuzaburo Kaku, has spoken recently of the imperative for business corporations to move beyond a narrow view of their own interests. On Kaku's view, to which he insists Canon is committed for the future, a corporation must recognize that its good is unavoidably linked not only with the good of its immediate community, but with the common good of humankind. The recognition of such a linkage is illustrated by an incident involving Merck & Co., the largest pharmaceutical manufacturer in the world.

Over a period of years Merck invested millions of dollars to develop a treatment for river blindness, a disease that affects nearly 20 million people in less developed countries. The treatment was remarkably effective, but the governments of countries afflicted with the disease were unable to afford to purchase and administer the drug. Failing to secure support from wealthier nations, Merck eventually decided to make the drug available without charge forever. But this did not solve the problem entirely. No organization existed to distribute and administer the drug effectively. In the end, Merck formed a committee at its own expense to ensure the distribution of the drug.

Once again, we can hardly maintain that such decisions characterize the modern corporation. We do, however, suggest that such choices are thoroughly consistent with the vision of *Rerum novarum*, where those who manage resources are encouraged to use them for the benefit of all. In this case, Merck controlled not only the drug but also sufficient financial resources to enable it to act upon a recognized moral obligation to help those in serious need. While it may be argued that the company has probably benefited in some way from its generous actions —

277

it *has* gathered favorable publicity and won an important award — anticipation of these benefits may indeed not be adequate to explain its actions. Truly ethical decision making may result in benefits to the decision maker, whether it be an individual or a business corporation.

Such decision making, however, often takes place in circumstances in which the best intentions are restrained by practical limitations. In the macro-economic sphere Leo hoped for, and encouraged, associations and coalitions between the major participants: management and owners of capital, government, and labor. The Dayton Hudson Corporation was able to form such a coalition. Merck was not able to do so, but had the will and sufficient resources to move forward on its own. Our third illustration concerns an incident in which a company with good intentions was unsuccessful in forming the needed coalition.

Velsicol Chemical Corporation:
The Need for Collaboration

Agriculture in less developed countries is often primitive, but the need for agricultural products, whether for food or for cash, is great. Yields can be dramatically improved through the use of modern methods and technologies, but sometimes these carry substantial risks. One such risk attends the use of pesticides. Farmers in these countries are often illiterate and untrained in the use of such toxic chemicals. Frequently they are unaware of or misinformed about the danger these chemicals pose to humans. In many cases they buy their pesticides from local dealers who also know little about them and who repackage them in small, unlabeled containers such as soda bottles. The World Health Organization has estimated that 750,000 cases of poisoning occur each year, resulting in 14,000 deaths.

Velsicol Chemical Corporation, a major manufacturer and exporter of pesticides, became concerned about the issue and invested about $100,000 toward the development of a pictographic labeling system intended to communicate the dangers of pesticide misuse. However, the U.S. government and the governments of nations to which the pesticides were exported were unwilling or unable to enact and enforce labeling requirements, nor were other manufacturers willing to help develop and adopt a standard labeling system. Despite a strenuous effort, the company was unable to persuade other pesticide manufacturers to join voluntarily in the development of an adequate labeling system. It realized that if it were to do so on its own, the costs involved would make its products prohibitively expensive. Discouraged by the lack of government support and by the failure of other manufacturers to join its project, Velsicol abandoned its labeling plan.

Whether Velsicol should have continued regardless of the lack of support, or whether it should have ceased manufacturing pesticides after it became aware of the dangers of uncontrolled use, may be debated. What seems clear is that without an alliance of some sort, the practical difficulties attendant upon following through on its good intentions overwhelmed the company. Other firms, in a variety of other fields, have argued that their obligation to act for the common good is severely limited when such action places them at a serious competitive disadvantage. While Leo might well not have agreed with this line of argument, he surely saw the importance of cooperation between key participants in the economy. Modern managers concur, at least insofar as they look to government to provide incentives to act well by establishing a "level playing field" through legislation and other forms of regulation.

Is *Rerum novarum* Compatible with the Modern Corporation?

Would Leo's vision of a moral economic order find recognition and acceptance in the modern corporation? We believe that at least some elements would be familiar to and endorsed by modern managers. These elements include the recognition that modern business corporations are part of a larger economic whole and that they have obligations to the well-being of this whole. Furthermore, it is appropriate for key participants in the economy to collaborate in efforts to secure the common good where the efforts of a few are insufficient for success. While few modern managers are likely to have read *Rerum novarum* carefully, we feel sure that many would find there ideas that would resonate with contemporary business ethics and with their own convictions about the nature of competent management.

Conclusion

This paper has shown that *Rerum novarum* is a classic text. *Rerum novarum* asks two fundamental questions: what are the charac-teristics of a moral workplace? and, what are the characteristics of a moral economic order? These questions need to be continually grappled with in specific contexts. Moreover, *Rerum novarum* provides certain conceptual frameworks and articulates basic moral norms that are still informative, particularly for business ethics, a century later. In *Rerum novarum*, Leo anticipates some significant elements of contemporary business ethics. His calls for a just and living wage, safe working conditions, and a broad range of property ownership, need to be repeated with fervor today, especially in developing countries. His "Type 3" thinking, addressing the conscience and moral responsibility of managers, is absolutely necessary in the contemporary business world. Finally, as our cases indicate, Leo's insight into the interrelatedness and interconnectedness of all members of society, with the consequent need to form coalitions and social consensus in favor of justice and the well-being of all, is a truth that cannot go unheard. *Rerum novarum*, though a century old and the product of a previous time, is indeed a classic text.

REFERENCES

1.   This is not to suggest popes before Leo did not engage in social teaching. Michael Schuck describes the content of pre-Leonine papal encyclicals (1740-1877) and argues that the teaching of this period "plays a vital role in understanding the content and coherence of encyclical social teaching as a whole," *That They be One: The Social Teaching of the Papal Encyclicals. 1740-1989*, Georgetown University Press, 1991), p.33.

2.   David Tracy, *The Analogical Imagination: Christian Theology and the Culture of Pluralism*, Crossroad, 1981), p.102

3.   *Ibid.*, p. 154.

4.   *Ibid.*, p. 68.

5.   *Ibid.*, p. 115.

6.   Tracy notes that classics are "radically particular in origin and expression" p. 132.   He also suggests each classic inevitably produces a dialectic that is "at once liberating and manipulative" p. 351.   Two themes in *Rerum novarum* that are particular to Leo's context and less than liberating in the last decade of the twentieth century are a) Leo's understanding of the necessity of the Church in remedying social ills, and b) his normative anthropology.   On the first issue, Leo believed that "only a return to Christian life and institutions will heal" society, 41, *Rerum novarum* National Catholic Welfare Conference, 1942).   Only the Church had the ability to correct the social problem.   See also 6, 28, 29, 41, 45.   This theme had not been repeated in Catholic social thought since at least John XXIII until John Paul II's encylical *Centesimus annus*, Liberia Editrice Vaticana, 1991), 5.   Second, Leo's anthropology suggests a static view of rich and poor, see 26 and 28, as well as a strong commitment to a division of the sexes.   His normative description of the relation between the sexes would be described as "complementary but hierarchical."   Contemporary discourse on the relation between the sexes speaks of two other descriptions "equal but differentiated" or "identical and interchangeable."   These categories are found in Lisa Sowle Cahill, *Between the Sexes: Foundations for a Christian Ethics of Sexuality*, Paulist Press, 1985).   See Leo, 53,60.

7.   Compare *Rerum novarum* 14-15 with John Locke, *The Second Treatise of Government*, introduction and notes by Peter Laslett (New American Library, 1965) for a very similar labor-intensive theory of property.

8.   See footnote 6.

9.   Donal Dorr, *Option for the Poor: A Hundred Years of Vatican Social Teaching*, Orbis Books, 1983), p. 21.

10.   *Ibid.*, p. 20.

11.   Karl Marx, "Communist Manifesto,"*The Marx-Engels Reader*, Robert Tucker, ed., W.W. Norton & Co., 1972), p. 362.

12.   Leo cautions Christians to be aware of some contemporary associations which undermine society and the church (74). Workers' associations ought themselves be governed by the standards of justice and ought to be oriented to the common good (76).

13.   Leo notes that, "Labor which is too long and too hard and the belief that pay is inadequate not infrequently gives workers cause to strike" (56).

14.   In *Rerum novarum* there is a distinction between the requirements of justice (29, 49) and the duties of charity (36, 43-45, 83). The rights of persons: to a living wage, to own property, to form associations, and to social participation, clearly fall under the directives of justice. The giving of alms, except in the case of extreme need, is not a part of justice but rather a necessary part of charity, the law of Christ. Leo writes, "When the demands of necessity and propriety have been sufficiently met, it is a duty to give to the poor out of that which remains" (36). In contrast to the demands of justice, the demands of charity are legally unenforceable (36).

15.   Leo believed the errors of capitalism and socialism developed from the more fundamental error of liberalism. See for example *Rerum novarum*, 1.

16.   For the most extensive discussion of morality and the market

system in official Catholic social teaching see John Paul II, *Centesimus annus*.

17. This fact is dramatically emphasized in John Paul II, *Centesimus annus*. We shall leave this connection for another occasion.

18. See Goodpaster, K., "Notes on the Corporation as a Moral Environment," HBS Case Services 9-386-012, Revised 4/86. Reprinted in Andrews, *Ethics in Practice*, (Harvard Business School Press, 1989).

19. E.g., *Employee Responsibilities and Rights Journal* (Chimezie Osigweh, Norfolk State Univ., VA, Editor-in-Chief), *International Journal of Value-Based Management* (Samuel M. Natale, Iona College, NY, Editor-in-Chief).

20. See Matthews, Goodpaster and Nash, *Policies and Persons: A Casebook in Business Ethics* (McGraw-Hill, 2nd Ed., 1991).

21. See Goodpaster, "Ethical Imperatives and Corporate Leadership," in Andrews, *Ethics in Practice*, Harvard Business School Press, 1989. Also see Christopher Stone, *Where the Law Ends: The Social Control of Corporate Behavior* (Harper & Row, 1975) and Thomas Donaldson, *Corporations and Morality*, (Prentice-Hall, 1982).

22. For a fuller development of the role of conscience in decision making, especially its degree of objectivity and universality, see Goodpaster and Matthews "Can a Corporation Have a Conscience?" *Harvard Business Review*, Jan-Feb. 1982. On the transcultural dimension, see Goodpaster, "Note on Relativism in Ethics," HBS Case Services #9-381-097.

The Information Age
and Rerum novarum

Sebastian A. Sora
Samuel M. Natale

I. INTRODUCTION

In exploring the Information Age from the perspective of *Rerum novarum*, one is amazed how easily the document lends itself to the current age. To explore this concept, we have tried to characterize the current age, overview the church's social teaching, identify key principles of the encyclicals that derive their strength from *Rerum novarum* and then tried to understand these principles in light of specific areas of development within the information age.

Sociologists do not agree on whether the age you and we find ourselves in is rightly called the 'Information Age.' Perhaps this is because ages tend to get named only after there is a sense that things will never be as they were, or because the perspective of history must be viewed from afar. Be that as it may, today's age is popularly called the 'Age of the Computer' or the 'Information Age.' In 1957, Daniel Bell, a Harvard sociologist described the approaching society as Post-industrial. This term is non-descriptive. The Post Industrial society was characterized as one based on services. It is important to understand what these services are.

In the U.S., the distribution of jobs within the service sector has remained constant at 11%, if we remove the rapid growth of workers in the information sector. In fact the growth of workers who deal with information, has increased 6 fold in the last 30 years. With this growth comes the realization that power is not money in the hands of a few, but information in the hands of the many (Naisbitt, 1984).

Peter Drucker has argued the importance of knowledge as the key to productivity and competitive strength. And it is the computer that is permitting us to manufacture information as factories manufactured goods in the early 20th century. The lives of people have changed, and the thesis that the age has changed is consistent with the facts.

These are some dates of historical significance. In the U.S., in 1956, the number of white collar workers began to outnumber blue collar workers, while in 1956, the Atlantic Cable Telephone Service was established. Finally in 1957, the Soviets launched Sputnik. These events set the stage for moving information and data around the world rapidly. In fact such movements can only be understood from the perspective of information and its wide availability.

The revolutionary and technological events of the last 35 years, demonstrate the characteristics of this Information age. The underlying motivator of the age is our ability to get data and create information so as to speed up the rate of change. So great has the rate of change been advanced, that we find today that the knowledge rate doubles every 4 years and that more information has been produced in the last 30 years than in the previous 5,000 (Linowes, 1987).

The stage has been set, but we cannot forget what John Dewey stated in *Democracy and Education*, that "history deals with the past, but this past is the history of the present," and this becomes an important corrective in our analysis.

The Information Age

Walter Wriston in *The State of American Management* equated the machines of the Industrial Revolution with muscle and the computer of the current age with one's mind and memory. This simile is a powerful one because it encapsulates what is occurring in first world countries today, and can be the impetus for third world nations to leap frog into the 21st century.

In the early 1970's, around the time that *Octogesima Adveniens* was issued, a new technology was developing in the computer laboratories. It is finding wide applicability today in business and its application set will grow widely over the next 10 years. Its generic name is 'Artificial Intelligence.'

During the 70's AI remained a research item and applications were limited. Around the same time, and in a separate context, the concept of databases was evolving and getting wide acceptance. During the 80's the database philosophy permeated industry and research in the U.S., Europe and Japan.

A data base is a collection of facts which can be accessed by individuals and other computers to be used in computation or to be cross-related with other data to form information quanta.

Today, we can say with conviction that AI gives us the promise of 'creativity,' while data bases are the drivers to creativity in that they contain data. It is only a matter of a short time until development will make commercially available links between the two. In fact such links are available today for specific application sets.

What is AI? We should think of it as a combination of hardware and software that employs knowledge in the form of rules to solve problems in specific areas of expertise that ordinarily require human intelligence. Let's look at a simple example.

The field of finance seems to be the most aggressive in commercially available AI packages. Let us suppose that an individual would like to buy a vehicle, but is unsure if he can afford it, and maintain his current life style.

The computer will ask: 1. Do you want to buy a car? 2. What is the price of the car you want to buy? 3. What is your yearly income? 4. What are your total monthly expenses? 5. What percent of your salary do you save or want to continue to save?

Based on a rules set, as follows:

1. If income is > 0, then monthly income = income / 12
2. If monthly income < monthly expenses, then print DO NOT BUY CAR and stop.
3. If price > 0 and (monthly income - monthly expense) - (monthly income * 10%) is < price/24 *1.10, then print BUY CAR, else print THE MAX YOU SHOULD SPEND ON THE CAR IS (monthly income - monthly expense) - (monthly income * 10%) * 24 WHICH INCLUDES INTEREST CHARGES.

The computer will advise the user how much he should spend. The rules base could be further augmented with information of the maximum and minimum prices that cars are being sold for and supply information on the most competitive insurance brokers.

Artificial intelligence systems of this type have special code sets that are known as "inference engines." These programs effectively execute the rules to arrive at a decision. They are sophisticated enough to do both forward and backward chaining, and to derive answers based on fuzzy expectations. Fuzzy logic can be thought of as "not determined logic" as when one needs to ask the question "how much." Thus a fuzzy query is, "Is she guilty of neglect?" Here the definition of 'neglect' and 'guilt' is questionable and its definition is a function of time, place, and context.

To work forward from a statement of need or backwards from a defined goal yields different solution domains. To ask a question as in "how much is recommended to spend based on these assumptions?" or "is this good?" requires different rules and different processes. These systems now have the potential to correct text, not only as to spelling but as to sense, they can advise on legal matters, and perform navigation duties in ships and planes, and finally they can teach and preserve skills. However, questions of goodness or quality of life or fairness have answers driven from documents like the encyclicals. How can we be assured that the systems can answer in the best possible moral manner?

The real explosion in the use of AI will occur over the coming decade, with the advent of the intelligent data base. Recently, capability has been made available that enables users to accomplish things such as discovering hidden knowledge or answering vague questions within fuzzy probability domains.

The term 'hidden knowledge' is an interesting term because for the first time we don't focus on the data but on the relationship between the datum. If I can relate datum to datum, rules can be created to discover relationships, patterns and correlations. Statistics could be used to characterize data occurrences and rules developed to provide new data insight. Hypotheses can be tested about the data, and questions asked of the data which are statistically approximated from a certainty perspective.

A complete revolution is at hand. Up until this time, computers have been used for computation. The 1990's are the dawn of decision

287

making systems. The research going on today will enable computers to read written language, understand natural speech, translate documents. The revolutionary change was the focus on relationships among data. Once relationships can be characterized, all of these things will be possible.

One must not lose sight, however, that the underlying mechanism for these systems is a deterministic view of causality and control. Bureaucracies can grow because this mechanistic view coupled with large data availability, enforces their existence. Government and international organizations will be able to absorb large amounts of data and create information; all of this will lead to enhanced analytical capabilities. Clearly this will improve decision making and planning capabilities of such agencies, but the dangers are real. Bureaucracies can control vast quantities of personal information—personal privacy can become endangered. People are made into number sets which correlate to a whole life of activities. Differences can be deleted or changed and then rejustified. The rights of the individuals can be abridged subtly, as reference by John XXIII in *Mater et Magistra.*

Incomplete research will be difficult to identify, video images will be alterable, the age can become Orwellian, if we lose sight of the sanctity of the individual, the value of the worker beyond his or her being a consumer. A case can be made that the current advances will ensure that large institutions will become larger because they have resources today to ensure their growth and dominance.

We don't wish to point out only the dark side of what technology is yielding. Global communication has clearly created the reality of the global village, and with the power of artificial intelligence we could magnify the rate of learning for 3rd world nations and speed the world into a period of specialization and contribution. This would be in total keeping with Paul VI in his encyclical *Populorum progressio.*

The growth of knowledge should eradicate fear of difference and also act to maximize the best in nations. However, the bases of these changes for good, will depend on how well we focus on the sanctity of the individual, the specialness of the worker and his or contributions to society. To focus on them as a consumer only will demean them from the perspective of a creator of goods and services

In the book, *Knowledge and Computer-Mediated Work*, it is pointed out that the clerk or knowledge worker goes in and out of tasks without an understanding of how the tasks relate to each other, or the meaning of the overall job. As we have more and more of this black box processing, fewer and fewer people will have an understanding of how things are accomplished. A black box is a simile for seeing result without cause. Thus it is imperative as we move into the current age, that people be educated and that overall awareness levels of the individual be increased. Without this education, people will not understand their value, and this issue of value is a key point of the church's social teaching.

II. Church's Social Teachings

The social documents of the church have in fact moved in an opposite direction from that suggested by the Information Age and, as such, provide a strong corrective.

Although the church has always had a social dimension, its formulation has been the result of social change, accident, political pressure and genuine discernment which has impelled the church over the past hundred years to respond to a number of ad hoc issues which now comprise its social teaching. The goal of the documents is to respond to a contemporary context which included, under the pontificate of Leo XIII, the problems of millions of industrial workers in North America and the newly industrialized portions of Europe...issues of urgency such as child labor, sub-human working conditions, etc. were in the foreground.

The church was slow to react to government destabilization in Europe during the 19th century, and only begrudgingly tolerated democracy as a valid form of government. These contextual reactions formulated the theoretical underpinnings of the church's social teachings. These documents reflect ambivalence characterized by conflicts between strong social conservatism and, at the same time, a critique of the capitalist model (and its anthropological error), as well as its lack of concern for the poor.

It was the fall of the capitalist system, as evidenced by the 1929 stock exchange crash, which gave impetus to the growing concern of social injustices wrought by such a system. This, in part, resulted in

Pius XI's social document, *Quadragesimo anno*, in which he recommended a corporatist system.

With the spread of communism and world war II, Pius XII focused on the need for the west to protect itself against Communism. It was to be one year before the Second Vatican Council, when John XXIII issued *Mater et magistra* (the first social encyclical in thirty years) that a clear line was drawn and a new direction demanded.

John XIII made two important points in this encyclical. Namely that something had become stultifying in the church's social position: concern for stability had taken precedence over concern for equity and justice; and concern over the rights of property owners had taken precedence over concern for the marginalized. He argued that the right to private property had been too extremely formulated. He exhorted that we must set out "to determine clearly the mind of the church on the new and important problems of the day"(para 50).

The essential emphasis was on his strong affirmation that the right to private property was subordinate to the more fundamental principle that the things of the earth were intended for the use and benefit of all. John's thinking was reemphasized in 1965 with *Gaudium et spes*, but now he linked his thinking with a just international economic order.

The fundamental concepts of "use and benefit of all" was extended by Paul VI in the encyclical *Populorum progressio*. In 1967, Paul VI detailed the church's enhanced understanding of humankind and the rights appertaining. The document was criticized and time has shown that it was overly optimistic. The concept of human development formed a strong social corrective that it was not merely superfluous goods, the left-overs, that were to be given to the needy (GS 69.1); rather, the poor have a right to an adequate share of the earth's reserves. This would result in the expropriation of under-utilized large estates (GS 76.6) or, in our current context, empowerment of the people with technological skill.

In the year 1971, on the 80th anniversary of Leo XIII's encyclical, we have the beginning of a series of encyclicals which concern themselves with the themes of changing world order through the people. Paul VI's *Octgesima adveniens* called for political action for world peace and justice. In 1975, Paul VI shifted to emphasize the application of the gospels to the present world and acknowledged a contextual approach to social problems in an explicit way. John Paul II, in 1979, explored the state of contemporary life in the modern world, in the encyclical *Redemptor hominis*. With the centenary celebration of *Rerum novarum*, John Paul II issued his encyclical *Centesimus annus* that turns the world's attention not only to the changing order but, equally to the cause of that change, the entrance of the world into the Information Age. John Paul II emphasizes that, "In our time, in particular, there exists another form of ownership which is becoming no less important than land: the possession of know-how, technology and skill. The wealth of industrialized nations is based much more on this kind of ownership than on natural resources." This, he speaks of later in the document, is causing marginalization of people by denying them access to training and development-a new ecclesial theme. In fact, the pontiff argues, this technological illiteracy creates a new form of poverty.

III. Principles that Underlie the Encyclicals

Fulfilling its prophetic role, the Church (historical contexts notwithstanding) continues the dual role of denunciation and proclamation. This has been reflected in the social documents' underpinnings in the following areas: 1. economics, 2. labor relations, 3. global relations, 4. militarism.

Our concerns would address the first three areas. In economics, the church deplores concentrated wealth because it promotes greed(RN); this concentration enables dictators to control investment and credit (QA) and profit becomes the chief incentive to economic development (PP), not human welfare. The church proclaims that the world must review the allocation of resources and monitor policies of multinational corporations (PT), who act as agents that transfer wealth among nations. It urges the state to distribute wealth in a more equitable manner, especially when the factors of production are not effectively employed. The church supports expropriation for the common good (PP) and supports economic structures that enable the equalization of wealth.

In labor relations, the church believes that the workers should participate in the ownership of the means of production and receive just wages (QA). Here the Information Age seems to be enabling this ownership of means, but technology is also depriving many workers of their previous employment (HW). To support just wages, the church believes that trade associations will balance management power (RN), with equitable relations especially between capital and labor (RN). Worker and management should be partners to achieve high productivity and worth (QA), with labor getting priority over capital (LE).

In international relations, the church laments the fact that the gulf between the 3rd World and 1st World nations is increasing(MM). When nations pursue their own development, with little concern for their effect, other states become oppressed (PT), political refugees abound (PT), and power and wealth become concentrated in the hands of a few (JW). This all leads to economic imperialism with the potential for violence, torture, terrorism and discrimination (RH).

The essence of the church's social teachings is that we must seek a global and just distribution of created goods (QA). The creation of goods implies that less developed countries must be aided (MM) and that public policies must support the settlement of refugees (PT). The right to development is composed both of economic growth and participation by the people a justice in the world (1971); training of people is required to bring the marginalized into the Information Age and make information technology tools available to everyone. The above discussion forms the underpinnings of the church's social teaching.

IV. Areas of social activity that the Information Age directly effects

Lets us now review those areas that we feel are most vulnerable to conflict with the church's social teaching during this information age.

1. Privacy

The issue of personal privacy has gained enormous significance in the Information Age. Specifically, with the issue of debit cards to purchase items as well as the rise of scanners when purchasing items, it is now possible that one's "tendencies" are assessed and sold to entrepreneurs and other agencies. Today, one can electronically retrieve information on the food products one purchases, phone calls one makes (and to whom); whether one purchases birth control items and the kinds of literature or magazines one might receive which could reveal both political interests, sexual orientation and a host of other personal variables.

With the advent of the computer, one's medical records are now accessible and often a manager can have access to one's personal health (eg., cancer, AIDS, etc.). This information can be used to assess (inappropriately) one's hireability, promotability, tenure, etc. This information has a direct effect on the issues that *Rerum novarum* addressed, i.e., worker dignity. The availability of this data, sold to the highest bidder and tied to universal identification numbers, e.g., drivers license or social security, can form a trace on any person's total life.

Today, there are no controls on this information. Further companies have already begun selling information crosslinked to any characteristic a user would want.

2. Medicine and health

Although we have discussed parts of this issue (see privacy), it now becomes an issue of justice to explore who gets what kind of medical treatment. Is medical treatment available generally. What objective criteria are used to treat individuals with scarce medical resources? Certainly, based on the generic argument of human dignity and human rights, current criteria of "economic power and social importance" will not be acceptable.

The Information Age now permits decisions to be made without the distinctly human/spiritual dimension, necessary for such decision. Decisions become based on the numbers, not the unique needs of each person.

3. Social fabric

The entire social fabric has undergone expansion as has the nature of the family. The role of women appears a significant issue here where equity is demanded on the basis of basic principles, if not spiritual law.

Growing cultural pluralism regarding issues of gender equality and sexual variety has also changed our whole understanding of the experience of humankind in the search for intimacy. How are these varieties of experience to be assessed, judged, tolerated, or celebrated.

Again the Information Age has shifted our focus. The magisterium no longer has control on information. In fact, the information flows through multiple perspectives and prisms into the world such that people are empowered to make their own decisions based on data and personal integrity. One can question seriously the necessity of being "told what to do" both on grounds of cultural/individual maturity as well as the principal of subsidiarity which would claim quite clearly that what can be done by a "lower" order ought not be appropriated to a "higher" order.

Further, in view of the information now available and cultural disparity now operative, one might even expect an apology or regret for errors committed in the name of a demand for orthodoxis. In fact, the Information Age would demand a shift from orthopraxis to orthodoxy—but this time based on data, information, knowledge and wisdom which, in principle at least, can be modelled and executed objectively.

4. Rise of multinationals/new order

The rise of multinationals is an economic consequence of the availability of information. Multinational corporations are a way of transferring wealth and product throughout the world. As such, these organisms need timely information with regard to price, politics, peoples, customs and resources. The resultant new order, which is based not on national boundaries but on product availability and production, leads to an homogenization of the world people. Customs become blended, foods become standardized, and the peoples of the world are brought into a consumer mentality. This is absolutely required for profitability.

On the positive side, the new order can lead to equalization of wealth, if countries enact controls on their consumerism. The new order can lead to peace, if resultant trade is based on equity. Finally, the new order can lead to an understanding of innate human needs, if the multinationals are not allowed to compete unfairly.

5. Technology/education

The first world has a dominance in developing technology. This is because of the cost of developing these technologies and the historical stabilities that are required. However, Third World countries can now leap frog in the 21st century through education. This education can increase the availability of the natural resource which is the fuel of the information age, and that is possession of know-how. No longer must countries have other natural resource to compete. That key resource can be its people.

With knowledge doubling every 4 years, schooling must not be denied to anyone. Governments must supply the best of teachers to create a citizenry of contributing men and women. Failure to keep pace will create a growing gulf between the First and Third Worlds. The result will be technological illiteracy and starvation.

Finally, in an age of instant communication, education in the Information Age will be virtually free. Satellite beaming to centralized systems is a reality today. What is required is to make education meaningful to the populace so that they want to know. Without this focus on education, rampant consumerism and a growing disparity between the haves and have nots will become a reality.

V. Conclusions

What has been accomplished by this paper is a focus on what the Information Age is, and why it is different from all the ages before. Seen through the encyclicals, we can see how this age can both support the Church's social teachings or act directly opposite to them. Clearly, the key attributes of the age are the information technologies, the collection of data that can be available, and the importance that empowerment will have. Unfortunately, empowerment will only come to those who are skilled and trained. Thus, education for the first time becomes the democratic tool for all peoples. Without this education, the gulf between the rich and the poor will increase. The rise of the multinational has the potential of creating unbridled consumerism and transfer of wealth. Education is the only tool left to bring to people the sense of liberty and empowerment that is required. The real wealth of the age will be information and the wealthy will be those who 'know.'

The impact of the Information Age and the Intelligent Machine will also challenge the magesterium in new and difficult ways.

If people are sufficiently empowered (at least in principle) then they do not need to be told what to do and when. In fact, one can argue that traditional fall-back positions such as natural law, etc. can be submitted to new and corrective analyses.

This would show itself most powerfully in a new understanding of the whole range of theologies of work, the role of profit-making in the world and other issues such as gender equality, sexual variety, the place of children and the role of the family.

An AI model would force the users to claim certain principles at the same level each time and/or force them to indicate why they have changed their position. Term such as "it is not unreasonable to say that" would be (thankfully) vacated of meaning and authorities as well as individuals would be pushed to acknowledge that the positions they demand as themselves or others subject to them, might be an interpretation of information but not an "eternal" truth emanating from some vague idea with no definable or accountable parameters.

Europe: A new theme for Catholic Social Doctrine

Peter Hebblethwaite

Pope Leo XIII was a European who never left Europe. He was born and brought up in the Campania to the south of Rome. The main industry: banditry. As Nuncio to Belgium 1843-46 he had his only experience of "abroad," and made quick trips to London, Paris and Cologne. He must have had some knowledge of the harshness and squalor of life in the early phase of the industrial revolution. He was Bishop of Perugia in central Italy 1846-78. Chief industry: chocolate-making (especially *baci*, kisses). Elected pope in 1897, he became "the prisoner of the Vatican" and kept the papal court in being so that it would be ready to resume its old ways once sovereignty over the Papal States was restored.

Leo was the author of *Rerum novarum*. It sees the whole world through European spectacles. For Leo and his advisors social problems were European problems—though they had some inkling about labor problems in the US. Yet the debate about trades unions was a European debate: it made little sense to talk of freedom of association in Hong Kong or the right to strike in the Belgian Congo. Leo's vision is of a semi-feudal world in which "the simple workman, surrounded by his numerous family, settles down to his frugal but sufficient meal, the just reward of his labour."

St. Pius X has no social doctrine, so we'll skip him. Benedict XV became Pope at the outbreak of World War I which destroyed for ever the Europe Leo XIII had known. On its first anniversary, July 28, 1915, Benedict spoke of this "horrible slaughter (*carneficia*) which dishonours Europe," and a letter of Cardinal Pompilj, his Vicar for the diocese of Rome talked about "the suicide of Europe."

But for the belligerents—especially France, Germany and Austro-Hungary, this defeatist talk sapped the morale of the troops. In Paris

Leon Bloy compared Benedict to Pontius Pilate, while from the pulpit of the Madeleine Dominican Pére Sertillanges exhorted the French to shed their blood for France, remarking that, at least for the time being, the Pope's appeals for peace did not apply.

Benedict stood alone, though like his patron, St. Benedict of Nursia, the spiritual father of Europe, he claimed that "no one can stop a father crying out to his sons, *pace, pace, pace.*" So he cried out. No one listened. Apparently. But perhaps his words struck home on a deeper level. The conclusion to a 1923 survey by M. Vaussard, *Enquete sur le nationalisme*, led some Catholics to say that "the next heresy to be condemned by the Church will be nationalism."

In the 1920s, nationalism seemed more menacing than Communism which was then young, feeble and undergoing many struggles. It had a long way to go before becoming a world-power. Vaussard's *Enquete* showed that nationalism and Europe are opposite poles. Where nationalism prevails, Europe is torn apart. Conversely, European unity will require the death of nationalism, something ex-Prime Minister Margaret Thatcher is loath to admit.

But that truth required the horrors of World War II to become self-evident to many Europeans. In 1946, Marshall Aid was offered to all European countries devastated by war including those of Eastern Europe: Stalin ordered them to reject the offer, describing it as a tainted U.S. bribe and "dollar imperialism." That set up the frontier between plenty and poverty in Europe that is still there today.

Although the trio of committed Christian politicians Robert Schuman, Konrad Adenauer and Alcide De Gasperi grasped what had to be done, two unbelievers set them on their way.

Jean Monnet was a French businessman who worked on the post-war plan that revitalised France. He was a great believer in creating institutions that possessed their own dynamism—like the Iron and Steel Community which so tied in the industries of France and Germany that they could never again go to war. In Monnet's institutional scheme, you get led on from *crise* to *crise*, stopping the clock where necessary to beat the deadline. Altiero Spinelli, a Communist in his youth, was a European federalist who while spending sixteen years in Mussolini's prisons dreamed of a Europe in which tyrannies like those of Hitler and Mussolini

298

would be impossible because the main strength of Europe would lie in the smaller regions, while the European federal government would be controlled by a federal parliament. Neither Monnet nor Spinelli ever said much about religion.

I mention this "secular" origin of the European Community as a reminder that, whatever the bigoted Irish Protestant Dr. Ian Paisley might think, the Treaty of Rome did not imply Rome-rule; and that whatever the Polish Pope John Paul II might think, it is not and never has been an expression of late-Christendom, still less the *nuova cristianita* (the new christendom) of which Jacques Maritain is deemed to have spoken.

However, the idea of Europe was taken up by the Christian Democrats and by none more eagerly than Giovanni Battista Montini, archbishop of Milan from 1955. From Milan Montini had proposed a meeting of secretaries of European bishops' conferences which might have developed into a Euro-equivalent of CELAM. The plan came to nothing at the time. The difficulty with any European Conference of Bishops is that the Bishop of Rome has to be part of it. But he is not an equal.

Montini did not repine. Instead he blessed a statue of "Our Lady of Europe" at Alpe Motta near Campodolcino (Sondrio) in the Italian Alps on September 8, 1958, as Pius XII, who pointedly had not made him a cardinal, lay dying.

He surveyed Europe's recent tragic past:

> It seemed that the entire soil of Europe was blood- soaked, and that fire and hatred raged between peoples. Military war, civil war, social war, ideological war, cold war, hot war—these were the actors in the last act of the drama. Then we looked at each in astonishment and stupor, and understood that it was all great madness, useless slaughter, as the pope said.
>
> Why should we fight when we are all sons and daughters of the same land. We look back at past history, at the drama which brought us here, with a feeling of horror and dread. And then just one words wells up from our heart, *Pace! Pace!*

That's exactly what Benedict had tried to say in 1917 when the conditions were not so propitious. But Montini, in September 1958, captures well the Italo-Franco-German reconciliation that was at the heart of the European Economic Community (as it was then known) created by the Treaty of Rome in 1957.

His vision did not include, in 1958, Britain and Ireland;and when he searched for a "wider Europe" beyond the confines of the EEC, he turned to the East and looked at the Poles and the Czechs and the Slovaks and so on. It was the Europe of the Madonna, and that was the point of the statue, Our Lady of Europe.

When he became pope and took the name Paul VI Montini developed these ideas. He made St. Benedict patron of Europe in 1964, during the darkest moment of the third session of the Council: hardly anyone noticed. All his life long he had seen the Benedictines as the builders of Europe, Christianising, civilising, as the Barbarians at the gates mounted attack upon attack.

But though European, Paul VI was not Euro-Centred. *Populorum progressio* marked a further step towards universalising Catholic social doctrine already begun by Pope John XXIII. *Mater et magistra* envisaged with calm the welfare state, free health care and education, nationalisation of basic industries—all of which had been anathema to Pius XII who saw in them, or said he saw in them, manifestations of the *Leviathan* of Thomas Hobbes.

With *Pacem in terris*, Pope John had spoken for the first time in an encyclical "to all men [and women] of good will." Not only that, but he saw three signs of the times, precursors of the Holy Spirit, in the growing empowerment of the workers, the end of colonial regimes, and the promotion of women in society.

In *Populorum progressio*, Paul VI recognized the north-south divide as more important for the future than the east-west (communist-capitalist) divide. The problem was how to to share the world's limited resources between the developed world and the world *en voie de development*. The Europe of *Populorum progressio* was only one example of the developed world, and though it might lose out to the rapidly developing countries of the Pacific rim, Europe would still be stirred by ancestral memories of Christendom.

Paul VI yields to no one in his work for Europe. He was a "good European," but with eyes and ears open for the rest of the world. Superficially, Pope John Paul II has been more obviously European of popes. He has spoken from all the *haut-lieux* of Europe: Compostela, Vienna, Trier, Canterbury, Assisi, not to mention Rome itself. He has made 55 Euro-speeches and there are more to come. He has restored to the map Velherad in Moravia and Gniezno in Poland.

Mieszko I was baptized at Gniezno in 966, thus establishing the Polish Church and the Polish nation. From there in 1979 John Paul began his campaign to transform the map of Europe: the method was bold in conception, and simple in execution. He simply proclaimed the "spiritual unity" of Europe in Gniezno as though somehow it could be brought into existence by papal *fiat*.

The Europe of John Paul II does not appear on any map. In the last article written before he became pope, he enquired where the easternmost frontier of Europe was to be found. It was not on the ground, but in the mind: it was where the spirit of liberty born in Christian Europe encountered and overcame the spirit of tyranny coming from the east.

If Marx stood Hegel on his head, here was Pope John Paul standing Marx on his head, and getting away with it because in Poland, even in 1979, it was evident that Marxism as a coherent intellectual force, capable of expressing ideals and shaping culture, rang hollow. Of course it still had institutional power, it had the *apparat* and the *nomenklatura*, but these were dwindling assets, with a very short shelf-life.

The election of a Polish pope and the event of Gniezno changed the Vatican's *Ostpolitik*, changed Poland and changed Europe.

But the Vatican's *Ostpolitik* had been in the hands of Cardinal Agostino Casaroli since 1967. It was based on the assumption that there were three stages to be gone through: the *esse*, the *bene esse*, and the *plene esse*. First the Church had to struggle from its *esse*, its bare survival; then it might hope to journey towards its bene *esse*, where a measure of freedom was achieved in organization and education, but where the *plene esse*, the fulness of the rights of the church, lay far ahead beyond some distant, shimmering horizon.

Seen from 1975, the year of Helsinki, the regimes of "real socialism" had not conceded much and still had a very permanent feel. They were kept in place by geo-politics more than consent. Andrei Sakharov theory of convergence was sometimes used. These regimes would be modified from within. We were all growing together: our bourgeois aspirations would eventually coincide. The Polish pope shattered all such timidities.

The election of Polish pope made an immediate and dramatic difference to the Vatican's *Ostpolitik*. John Paul II made it clear that he saw his pontificate as correcting an historic imbalance that was also an historic injustice: the disparity between Eastern and Western Europe in the life of the Church. In practice this meant tilting the balance in the other, neglected direction, and trying to break the dominance of Western Europe in the Church's life. More immediately and more practically, Vatican Radio stepped up its broadcasts in Polish, *l'Osservatore Romano* came out with a Polish-language edition for the first time, and a Polish desk was opened in the Secretariat of State. The result was a further decline in the use of Latin. So by the time of the first visit to Poland in June 1979, John Paul has used his power within the church. But in terms of international relations in he had only spiritual power; yet this "spiritual power" should not be thought of as ineffectual. The Polish government certainly had the *physical* means to keep the pope out of his homeland: but in practice it could not stop him going home, still less censor him once he was there. That gives some indication of the force of "spiritual power."

The effects of this "spiritual power" during this first visit to Poland in 1979 were soon felt. It boosted the self- confidence of Poles so that they could imagine the formation of Solidarity the following year. The visit was a kind of informal plebiscite which revealed the gulf between *le pays légal* and *le pays réel*. It also taught them about the use of non-violent methods. They should not reply to violence with violence; they should not rise to the bait of "provocation;" they should not sink to the level of their discredited opponents.

John Paul acted as a tribune of the people. He articulated their aspirations. Reviving the theme of the millenium celebrations of 1966, he claimed that the church embodied the soul and the culture of the Polish nation in a way the party could never aspire to. Quoting the Jesuit poet of the renaissance, Piotr Skarga, he compared the faith of Poland to an oak tree with deep roots that could be shaken but never overthrown. "Come Holy Spirit," he cried, "renew the face of this earth, of this land (*ziemen*)!"

This became a prayer said daily in all churches in Poland. So as a result of this one visit, the Communist government was delegitimated. The banners of the Polish revolts in the 19th century bore the legend: "For our Freedom and Yours!" Now as then Poland's freedom was to be the prototype of the freedom that would come to Eastern Europe in "the time of the Spirit." Don't ask when that is: it is not given to us to know the times and the seasons and we shouldn't ask. All one can say is that ten years later the earth shook. Yet back in 1979 it did seem very strange to be talking about the spiritual unity of Europe. Whatever else could be said about Europe in June 1979, it was still materially divided by the iron curtain, by military alliances and by ideology. So what did it mean to talk about spiritual unity? Did it belong to a fantasy cloud-cuckoo land?

In fact it was a claim, a very steely claim, that the divisions of Europe were man-made, artificial, anomalous, and must be brought down as soon as possible.

Poland in the first place, and then the other countries of what we choose to call Eastern Europe, were to rejoin the Europe from which they had been so cruelly and artificially excluded. So the transformation of the *Ostpolitik* was complete:it flowed into the *Europapolitik*. Moreover, the Eastern Europe envisaged by Pope John Paul was neither an inferior partner nor a suppliant begging for some crumbs from the success story of the European Community. It had its own specific contribution to make. Poor in material terms, it was spiritually rich and had something essential to offer.

This was signalled in the customary symbolic language of the Vatican. On December 31, 1980, in his apostolic letter *Egregiae virtutis,* John Paul II proclaimed Sts. Cyril and Methodius co-equal patrons of Europe. Europe already had a patron, St. Benedict, given the post by Paul VI in 1964. Did the new appointment mean that Benedict had failed or proved an incompetent patron?

No, but the trouble with Benedict and his monks was that he was too closely and too exclusively associated with the evangelization of *Western Europe*. Cyril and Methodius, two ninth century Greek monks from Salonika, represented "the wider Europe" before the divisions of East and West had set in. John Paul later wrote an encyclical, *Slavorum apostolorum*, the first to be devoted to Europe. Cyril and Methodius were models of ecumenism and models of evangelization today because they translated the Gospels into the language and hearts and customs of the Slav peoples.

Moreover, John Paul insisted that the church needs both traditions just as the body needs two lungs to breath—the "Latin" tradition which is rational, juridical and practical needs filling out by the "Eastern" tradition which is more mystical, intuitive and Spirit-led.

What was Moscow making of the Slav pope with such wholly unexpected initiatives? It was still the period of stagnation. The success of *Solidarnosc* in Poland meant that the pope was clearly seen as a formidable foe.

No sooner had John Paul convalesced after Mehemet Ali Agba's assassination attempt, May 13, 1981, than he counter-attacked. He believed that he had survived the assassination attempt "providentially," that is for some purpose, and he attributed his survival to Our Lady of Fatima where, in 1917, the Virgin Mary was believed to have appeared to a group of peasant children.

In the encyclical *Laborem exercens* (3 September, 1981), John Paul "stole the Marxist clothes" in asserting the priority of "labour" over "capital" (13) in the name of Christian humanism. He was interested in worker-participation in factories.

The death of Leonid Brezhnev on November 10, 1982, made little difference to the Vatican's *Ostpolitik*, merely emphasizing the pope's resolve compared with Soviet flabbiness. The Soviet leadership floundered during the 16 months of Yuri Andropov and the 3 months of Konstantin Cernenko.

In this period the pope was even more aggressive towards communism. There was no question of dialogue or even peaceful co-existence. A battle was raging for the future of the world. It stretched from Poland to China and to Latin America.   From now on there would be ruthless confrontation and competition.

The visit to Nicaragua in March, 1983, was another episode in the anti-communist campaign.   John Paul assumed that the Sandinistas were thorough-going unreconstructed Marxists, and that Christians like Fr. Ernesto Cardenal were naive dupes.   This ideological option, linking Nicaragua to the Soviet Union, was very close to that of President Ronald Reagan's "evil empire" speech.

The Vatican equivalent duly came in the Instruction "On Certain Aspects of Liberation Theology" (September 3, 1984).   It said:

> A key fact of our time ought to evoke the reflection of all those who would sincerely work for the true liberation of their brothers: millions of our own contemporaries legitimately yearn to recover those basic freedoms of which they were deprived by totalitarian and atheistic regimes.

So this theme went right to the top of the papal agenda. The text goes on even more fiercely:

> This shame of our time cannot be ignored: while claiming to bring them freedom, these regimes keep whole nations in conditions of servitude which are unworthy of mankind.

Those suspected of supporting Marxists, such as liberation theologians, are deluded like Lenin's "useful idiots."

The 1986 encyclical on the Holy Spirit, *Dominum et Vivificantem*, took the gloves off and denounced Marxism by name as "essentially and systematically atheist" (56). With this denial of God "we find ourselves he says," at the very centre of what could be called the 'anti-word', that is to say the 'anti-truth'" (37). In effect, this was to say Marxism was the "work of the devil."

The encyclical was dated May 18, 1986. It showed no awareness that a new first secretary, Mikhail Gorbachev, was in place in the Soviet Union and seemed to be talking a new language, and in particular a new language about Europe, describing it as our "common European home."

305

It all sounds very distant now, but this is what Gorbachev said in *Perestroika*:

> Having conditioned myself for a new political outlook, I could no longer accept in the old way the multi-coloured, patchwork-quilt-like political map of Europe. The continent has known more than its share of wars and tears. It has had enough. Scanning the panorama of this long-suffering land, and pondering on the common roots of such a multi but essentially common European civilization, I felt with growing acuteness the artificiality and temporariness of the bloc-to-bloc confrontation and the archaic nature of the iron curtain.

The echoes of the papal language—"common roots," archaic nature of iron curtain, irrelevance of frontiers—may have been accidental: there are only a finite number of things you can say about Europe. The essence of this quotation is, however, that Gorbachev was wanting to join Europe and would do, as far as in him lay, whatever was needed to that en—human rights, democracy, the market. When Gorbachev called his first conference on human rights, only veteran novelist Graham Greene took him seriously.

It took a long time for the Vatican to respond positively to Gorbachev's initiatives. On his 1987 visit to Poland John Paul spoke as though President Wojczek Jaruzelski's regime was already doomed. But after this final delegitimation of the Polish Communists and perhaps sensing victory in the air, the tone of Vatican diplomacy began to change.

Casaroli, if not the pope, came to believe in Gorbachev's sincerity. By now Gorbachev had visited every significant European capital except Rome; he could hardly go to Rome without seeking an audience with the pope; and he could not see the pope unless he had something to offer; and what that really meant was religious liberty and legalisation for the Ukrainian Catholic Church as well as freedom for the Catholics of Lithuania, Latvia and Byelorussia.

But the diplomatic coup of a Gorbachev visit, this historic first, had to be worked for on the Vatican side and earned by Gorbachev. Public abuse of Marxists dropped out of Vatican documents from 1987 onwards. The encyclical *Solicitudo rei socialis* even-handedly condemns both imperialisms, the one dominated by profit and the other by power. U.S. conservative Catholics were shocked and tried to explain this away.

Dialogue, once proscribed, was now presented as the the only way forwards. Casaroli enjoyed a late summer, a *Nachsommer*, while Ratzinger fell silent on political matters and devoted himself to castigating the German Greens as pagans.

The millenium celebration of Christianity in the land of Rus in 1988 provided a convenient and non-committal way through to Gorbachev. No attempt was made to put the Soviets in the wrong; on the contrary, everything was done to make it easy for them to accept the idea of a powerful Vatican delegation. In the end, no less than ten cardinals went to Moscow to celebrate one thousand years of Christianity in "Russia." Their presence was a reminder of history: when Prince Vladimir was baptized in 988, the schism between East and West, Constantinople and Rome, still lay ahead in the future, being conventionally dated 1054.

What was achieved by the visit of such a powerful delegation to Moscow in summer 1988? Nothing much except the prospect, at last, of a Gorbachev visit to the pope. Casaroli had a personal meeting with Gorbachev, handed him a letter from the pope, and concluded that "his position is solid."

The pope began to catch the new mood. Asked by a Soviet journalist what he thought about the "new climate" created by the 19th Party Congress, John Paul replied:

> It is too soon for me to give an evaluation, but certainly we follow the climate of *perestroika* with great interest. This democratisation, this greater participation of the citizens in social and political life, fulfills the expectations not only of the Eastern countries but also corresponds to the social teaching of the Church.

Guarded though this was, it was a long way from "the shame of our time."

So Gorbachev and Raisa were finally able to visit the pope on December 1, 1989, shortly before going off to meet President George

Bush on storm-tossed Malta. It was agreed that the Ukrainian Catholic Church should be legalized, and that there should be an exchange of diplomatic representatives. Archbishop Francesco Colasuonno took up his post in Moscow in March 1990, the first Vatican diplomat in Russia since the time of Catherine the Great.

Gorbachev's second visit to the pope, on Nov 18, 1990, also preceded a meeting with Bush, not to mention the other signatories of the Conference on Security and Co-operation in Europe (CSCE) agreement in Paris which completed the work of Helsinki(1975) and provided a new "Charter for Europe."

That sounds like a happy ending. All the objectives of the Vatican's *Ostpolitik* have been achieved, and it can now be dissolved into its *Europapolitik.* "Europe" now means the whole of Europe, east and west. The time of anomaly is no more. Religious freedom is now the norm, with local difficulties in the Ukraine and Romania where the Orthodox Church is reluctant to hand back the properties seized in 1946 and 1948, respectively. But elsewhere, even in Albania, there has been great progress where Mother Teresa has been welcomed back as the world's most famous Albanian. Not only the *bene esse* but the *plene esse* may be said to exist throughout most of the continent.

The institutional celebration of this new state of affairs is the Synod of European Bishops, meeting in Rome, scheduled from November 2—Thanksgiving Day in the U.S.—to December 14. For the first time ever, bishops from the Atlantic to the Urals will discuss the future of their common European home. The Synod theme combines Acts 1, 8 and Galatians 4, 31 "that we may be witnesses to Christ... who has set us free." Though the outcome of the Synod is uncertain as I write, it is unlikely to depart too far from the position-paper which bears the personal stamp of John Paul II and contains his verdict on the European events of 1989-90.

John Paul believes that what happened demands a providential interpretation. The Holy Spirit was at work refashioning Europe. But he is not the only actor on the stage of European history. The church has always regarded history as "a dialogue in which God's initiative and human response both play their part." That seems to mean that we should not be content to cry "miracle" at this "new crossing of the Red Sea" (as

Cardinal Jozef Glemp has called it) but should roll up our sleeves and join in. Or it may mean that Lech Walesa and Solidarity proposed and then God disposed.

Communism, defined as "an ideology which claimed to have replaced Christianity with a secular sort of religion, a synthesis of all the 'scientific' progress of the age," has collapsed. Christianity, he says, "has passed through perhaps the greatest crisis in its entire history since those first persecutions which sought to wipe out the infant church." So there are bouquets for the persecuted but brickbats for "liberation theologians."

The document says:

> In many western countries there is a widespread persuasion that to stand up in defence of the poor one must actively promote communism or at least accept the principles of Marxist analysis and submit to a communist regime. In the propaganda of many of the developing countries marxism, with its downgrading of faith and denial of religious freedom, is presented as the way to overcome poverty and achieve better living conditions.

This raises a question. Who is to speak for liberation theologians who would undoubtedly find this passage muddled and inaccurate?

So far the experience has been (in principle) objectively described; now we move on to analysis. There is much praise for the heroism of the East:

> Experience of resistance has provided the church with many martyrs and confessors of the faith; it has also led to greater solidarity between the faithful and the hierarchy, closer co-operation between clergy and laity, leading to the sharing of joint undertakings and the practice of common prayer.

There is much truth in these remarks; yet martyrdom is a diminishing capital and in Poland particularly a dangerous neo-clericalism could fritter away everything that has been gained.

309

The *itinerarium* also makes the bold claim that "events" have "put an end to the gulf which once existed between the church and the legitimate aspirations of the workers." This remark would need some geographical specification before it can be discussed. The text goes on to explain:

> The old ideological impediment, that alternative secularist pseudo-religion which used to restrict or exclude any Christian presence among the working classes, no longer exists. We see restored the innate inclination and natural convergence of the aspirations of the poor towards the Gospel.

Would that it were so, and that the sad heritage of the nineteenth century could be shrugged off just like that. Yet apart from Poland, it is difficult to think of country which illustrates these propositions.

After this praise for the East, some tough remarks are addressed to the West:

> Questions are being asked about the roots, values and history which contribute to the definition of 'European'. Can the unity of a whole continent depend solely on the convergence of material interests?

That is a loaded question, expecting the answer no for the text goes on to say that to use a material yardstick would surely divide rather than unite, setting some European groups and social classes against others, and aligning Europe as a whole and the other rich nations against the rest of a world dominated by disease, poverty and war. As during the Gulf War, the pope runs the danger of being applauded mainly by the left, by the former Communists now in the Italian Democratic Socialist Party for example. There are dangers in fortress Europe, but they will not be averted by stirring up envy and resentment.

Finally, there is a powerful indictment of the European Community. The peoples of Central and Eastern Europe long for freedom and "a fully human existence." But now the questions come thick and fast:

310

Is it possible to satisfy these aspirations merely by introducing western economic and political systems into these countries?... Western nations may have succeeded economically and politically, but are they really examples of progress as regards culture and morality?

Once again, num-questions, expecting the answer "no." Nowhere is the question asked: what is the price of freedom?

There seems to be no recognition that democracy requires the freedom to go wrong. We get the following rather shaky assertion on democracy:

> The restoration of democracy in central and eastern Europe, and recognition there of the church's unique role in civil society, will come about mainly by faithful adherence to the values of Christian culture in both its forms, western (Rome) and eastern (Byzantine)."

Does this mean that "Byzantine" culture, with its strong tradition of conformity to the czars, will naturally support autocratic regimes which legislate for virtue? And which tradition is Poland, Latin by religion, Slav by race, to follow?

Someone will surely try to redress the balance. I would expect Cardinal Basil Hume, Archbishop of Westminster, to repeat very firmly what he said at Ampleforth Abbey in August 1990:

> The three patron saints of Europe represent the undivided Church of the first centuries. They came from different cultures, East and West.... Neither East nor West has a monopoly of charism, courage or wisdom. This enterprise demands equal sacrifice and the commitment of both East and West. It will be a hazardous, complex and exhausting work. It will draw on all our spiritual energies. It is, however, a task that we cannot refuse to undertake.

Amen to that.

From Rerum novarum to John Paul II: International Economics as an Empirical Testing of Adequacies in Catholic Social Teaching

Prof. Stephen F. Frowen

I.   Introduction

The third social encyclical letter of Pope John Paul II *Centesimus annus*, dated 1 May 1991 (the Memorial of St Joseph the Worker) to commemorate the 100th anniversary of Pope Leo XIII's celebrated encyclical *Rerum novarum* of 15 May 1891, not only engages in a discussion of the characteristics of the latter but also in a dispute on socialism versus capitalism concluding with a conditional approval of capitalism. As is appropriate in doing justice to *Rerum novarum*, John Paul concentrates on socio-economic issues such as private property, profit and the universal destination of material goods, because of their intrinsic relationship with natural law and divine revelation.[1] Of course, in elaborating on these matters, it is not the intention of the pope to provide directives in the economic sphere or to spin out economic theories for solving specific problems. In para 7 of *Sollicitudo rei socialis*, the pope emphasises that the church speaks as an "expert in humanity" with the aim, firstly, of scrutinizing the signs of the times and of interpreting them in the light of the Gospel; and secondly of creating an awareness—
equally profound—of her mission of "service." This mission is distinct from the function of the State, even when the church *is* concerned with concrete human situations, as for example, in the economic sphere. Specific references in the Encyclical letters to the notorious economic inequalities, internationally and within individual countries, may serve as an example.[2]

II.   Capitalism Reviewed

John Paul's conditional approval of capitalism, based on his view of the reasons for the failure of the state-monopoly-type of socialism as practised in the USSR and other East European countries until recently, in essence agrees to a surprising extent with that of the world's most influential economist this century—John Maynard Keynes. In his Berlin lecture in 1926 entitled, "The End of *Laissez-faire*",[3] which is a discussion of social assumptions, Keynes expressed the view that:

> Capitalism, wisely managed, can probably be made more efficient for attaining economic ends than any alternative system yet in sight, but that in itself it is in may ways extremely objectionable.

Karl Marx, in his *Theses on Feuerbach* in 1845 stated, what subsequently became a much quoted passage and can also be seen on his London tombstone at Highgate Cemetery, that "philosophers have only interpreted the world in various ways. The point, however, is to change it." Keynes clearly surpassed this injunction to philosophers.   He attempted to revolutionise a world suffering from the outstanding faults of the capitalist system in its failure to provide for full employment, and its arbitrary and inequitable distribution of wealth and incomes.

In his *General Theory of Employment, Interest and Money*, published in 1936, Keynes says in his concluding chapter:

> It is certain that the world will not much longer tolerate the unemployment which ... is ... inevitably ... associated with present-day capitalistic individualism. (Keynes, 1936, p. 381)

Today, more than half a century later, we live in a world not only of high inflation rates and interest rates, but also of rising unemployment. The rather unrestrained capitalism we have experienced since the early 1970s throughout most of the industrial world may not be entirely unconnected with these developments. Long-term economic success requires public co-operation, which has been in evidence in various degrees in social market economies, the most prominent example being West Germany, but scarcely under a virtually uncontrolled free enterprise system with its concentration on the private sector of the economy. (see J. Boswell, 1990)

III.   CA and International Economic Issues

Centesimus annus raises vital issues in the field of international economics, the main subject of this paper. Not surprisingly, John Paul reserves pride of place for the economic problems of the poorer nations, seeking ways to improve their economic conditions by appealing to the richer countries and international economic agencies for a pursuit of adequate economic policies. In this context, too, Keynes's views spring to mind when he talks of the economic causes of war, namely, the pressure of population and the competitive struggle for markets. In the concluding chapter of his *General Theory* we find the following statement, which still is of considerable topical importance:

> ... if a rich, old country were to neglect the struggle for markets its prosperity would droop and fail. But if nations can learn to provide themselves with full employment by their domestic policy, ... there ... would still be room for the international division of labour and for international lending in appropriate conditions. But there would no longer be a pressing motive why one country need force its wares on another or repulse the offerings of its neighbour, not because this was necessary to enable it to pay for what it wished to purchase, but with the express object of upsetting the equilibrium of payments so as to develop a balance of trade in its own favour. International trade would cease to be what it

is, namely, a desperate expedient to maintain employment at home by forcing sales on foreign markets and restricting purchases, which, if successful, will merely shift the problem of unemployment to the neighbour which is worsted in the struggle .... (Keynes, 1936, pp.382 - 83)

Here, in this 1936 passage, we have indeed some of the crucial present-day problems which John Paul highlights in his latest encyclical. The successes of West Germany and Japan in exporting vastly more than they are importing and thereby maintaining full employment were achieved at the expense of other countries running balance of trade deficits and suffering rising unemployment.

The considerable external imbalances between the advanced economies of the Northern hemisphere and the non-oil-producing developing economies of the South (the North-South divide) is the obvious and justified focus of John Paul's attention. These imbalances were largely the result of the sharp increases in the price of oil (both nominal and real), which occurred in 1973 and 1979, except for 50 imbalances existing before but were hidden by foreign aid receipts. The recession following the oil price shocks of the 1970s and other adverse economic developments during the 1980s, affecting both the advanced western economies and the less developed non-oil producing countries, caused further damage resulting from rising interest rates and (for the latter countries) a deterioration in their terms of international trade. The 1970s themselves were (as it seemed then) not too bad for the developing world. Oil producing countries showed huge external surpluses, which because of a low absorption capacity they could not employ domestically. They therefore placed their earnings with international banks—to a large extent in London—and these banks (the euro-banks) then onlent the deposits received to a large extent to the medium-income non-oil producing developing countries, often in Latin America. When subsequently interest rates in international money and capital markets began to rise sharply in the early 1980s, the debtor countries in the developing world had increasing difficulties servicing their external debt. The international debt crisis finally broke out as a result of the Mexican default in 1982 and the Reagan policy in the U.S. As the crisis deepened, even frail attempts on the part of the developing world to pay what to them were exorbitantly high interest rates absorbing up to half their export earnings, caused unspeakable suffering to a large part of the population in the debtor countries.

While during the quarter of a century from 1950 to 1975 developing countries on average still achieved a 3.4 per cent growth rate in their gross national product, the growth rates of many developing countries after 1982, that is after the oil price shocks of 1973 and 1979 and after the Mexican default, ranged from negative to 3 per cent of gross domestic product. Although the top figure remained historically high, the general deterioration was aggravated further by most of the developing countries showing a decline of 8 per cent in physical investment.

However, some developing countries have been successful in maintaining satisfactory growth rates and the ability to service their external debt, which in turn ensured further inflows of foreign capital. These were countries, such as South Korea, following a prudent all embracing financial policy, which ensured the best possible use of the factors of production and prevented borrowed money being spent simply on consumption, as happened in so many of the developing countries. Thus, the poorer countries, too, have some responsibility for their own destiny.

The adequacy of Catholic social teaching, and for that matter of the social teaching of any church or religion, will ultimately depend upon *realistic* propositions being put forward. For example, it makes sense for John Paul to press for the huge resources being swallowed up by an insane arms race in the past to be put to better use, but the crucial question here is how to achieve this goal economically and politically.

John Paul is right, of course, in pointing out in *Centesimus annus* (CA) that the imbalances between the North and the South "have shifted the centre of the social question from the national to the international level." The advice given to the poorer countries is to take a more active part in the general interrelated economic activities at the international level, but it is recognised that the success of such a policy would depend on gaining a fairer access to international markets, "based not on the unilateral principle of the exploitation of the natural resources of these countries but on the proper use of human resources" (33). To find channels for realising this goal is a complex matter, but if it could be achieved it would certainly assist in meeting certain objectives stated in *Rerum novarum*, which still constitute a goal to be achieved in most of the developing countries, such as adequate wages, unemployment benefits, old age pensions and satisfactory working conditions with worker participation and protection, all things we tend to take for granted in many of the developed countries.

IV. The Transfer Problem and the Oil Price Shocks

The advice given by *Centesimus annus* to industrial countries is therefore to offer weaker nations better opportunities for taking their place in international economic life. The obligation of the latter would be "to use these opportunities by making the necessary efforts and sacrifices" (35). At the same time, the encyclical recognises the severity of the international debt problem. It accepts the legality and justice of the repayment of debts, but *not* at the price of "unbearable sacrifices" (35). Some definition of what should be regarded as "unbearable" would have been helpful. Another point to consider is that write-offs affect dividends and thus those who have invested in banks either directly or indirectly through institutional investors.

With regard to "legality," we should perhaps remind ourselves of Keynes's writings on reparations during the German debt crisis in the 1920s when he showed that pursuit of legality may not in fact be in the interests of the First World, that is the industrialised world (Keynes, 1919 and 1929). This problem is also high-lighted in Keynes's essay on French prices after 1918 in his *Essays in Persuasion* (Keynes, 1926).[4]

However, before discussing the transfer problem in greater detail, attention is drawn to John Paul's plea for providing the poor with realistic opportunities by means of a "concerted worldwide effort to promote development." He recognises that this involves sacrificing the positions of income and power at present being enjoyed by the more advanced economies. The decisive question then is how this can be achieved under a **decentralised** capitalist system which John Paul appears to favour. Capitalism, according to the *Oxford Dictionary*, means "the dominance of

317

private owners of capital and production for profit." Does this system make it likely that positions of income and power will be sacrificed voluntarily?

There are justifiable reasons for doubting whether a capitalist system can be sufficiently controlled by any juridical framework to achieve John Paul's aim of "placing the capitalist system at the service of human freedom in its totality...the core of which is ethical and religious." It seems to be the case that these conditions, on which John Paul's acceptance of capitalism depends, are in disparity with the whole idea of capitalism which in its essence is motivated by the pursuit of self-interest. This pursuit of self-interest is of course meant to benefit all, according to Adam Smith.

The plight of the poorer countries started with the oil price shocks of the 1970s, which virtually eliminated whatever small supply of private finance there was to the poorest countries in the 1960s, mainly located in sub-Saharan Africa. The so-called petrodollars earned in huge amounts by the oil-exporting countries found their way to the middle and high income developing countries, largely in Latin America and certain Asian countries. But this flow, too, slowed down as oil surpluses fell by 1976 and almost ceased after the Mexican default of 1982.

V. Essential Requisites for Developing Countries and the International Debt Problem

The main need for the non-oil developing countries now is the achievement of higher rates of investment and growth, but also a more active participation in foreign trade. This is clearly recognised in *Centesimus annus* when John Paul stresses the need for "fair access to international markets," but, alas, without defining what "fair" means. However, two further requisites are essential. Firstly, finance, by which is meant the supply of capital, particularly in the form of foreign capital inflows; and second a prudent financial policy. Of equal, if not greater, importance is a cut in population growth, as discussed below.

For a financial policy to be prudent, it would have to consist of an appropriate internal financial structure, a sound monetary and fiscal policy, controls of foreign exchange movements and of financial flows generally, and finally a close cooperation with external agencies. Without such an all-embracing financial policy to ensure the best possible use of factors of production, there would be a danger, as past experience has shown, that borrowed money is simply spent on consumption, and probably would be spent on consumption unless population growth is kept low.

Despite the lack of external finance throughout the 1980s, per capita consumption in some developing countries in the late 1980s was still the same as in the late 1970s. How did they manage? They allowed their investment in means of production to drop by one-third, with grave growth and financial consequences to follow. It is interesting to see how Chile and Mexico have nevertheless emerged more slowly.

The more prudent developing countries followed a sound financial policy of the type described and paid special attention to two decisive elements of such a policy: First, restraint in their fiscal policy, and second an encouragement of exports.

What we do find is that the developing countries which have emerged in external debt problems are precisely those showing increasing overall public deficits, which are themselves often a function of population pressure, combined with poor performances in the export field. Countries doing well—among them South Korea—are those showing a **decline** in their public deficit and an **increase** in exports. Of some importance to development, too, is a policy which ensures that savings are channelled into the type of industrial investment showing a high real return, preferably in hard currencies.

The crux of the major problem of some developing countries is a vicious circle they cannot escape from: Because of their heavy burden of external debt, they have difficulties furthering economic growth; but reducing their debt burden is hampered for lack of economic growth. The passage in **Centesimus annus** relating to the unsolved problem of the external debt of the developing countries is therefore highly relevant. However, all the devices suggested to reduce the debt burden of the poorer countries, (and to these we might also add the possibility for these countries to buy back debt obligations on the secondary market at substantial discounts), will do little to solve the longer-term problem of economic growth. Ultimately, it is the increase in total output, provided it is directed towards exports, that will go a long way towards attaining a more viable debt ratio. The only snag here is that if all developing countries successfully followed this policy, the export prices of their goods might fall, as supply exceeds demand—a consequence already seen in commodity markets.

Provided the developing countries persevere in their financial adjustment policies, raising new finance at more favourable interest rates and for longer periods from the commercial banks (ideally in collaboration with the International Monetary Fund and/or the World Bank) should get easier, although there is little ground to expect drastic improvements in the 1990s. In any case, much will depend on the financial need of the advanced economies themselves.

A helpful example to illustrate the international debt problem is Brazil. Outstanding foreign debt stood at $122 billion in the summer of 1991, which is second only to the foreign debt of the United States. (Total external liabilities of the developing countries amounted to $1.4 trillion in 1990 of which just over half came from private sources (see Frowen, 1991)). Because of its moratorium on debt repayments in mid-1989, Brazil is behind with interest payments to the amount of $8.5 billion on its outstanding foreign debt.

Meanwhile, a first disbursement of almost $1 billion has been paid to Brazil's 600 creditor banks. Altogether, $2 billion of outstanding interest payments are supposed to be paid this year and the balance converted into 10-year bonds with a three-year grace period. This will do nothing but lead to further indebtedness. Much depends now on further negotiations on rescheduling Brazil's commercial bank debt. With an annual gross domestic product of about $350 billion, Brazil is one of the 10 biggest economies in the world, but inflation last year was 1,800 per cent.

The problem for Brazil or any other developing country is that they cannot repay their foreign debt or the interest due on their external debt in **local** currency. The loans are denominated in hard foreign currencies of the leading industrial countries, with the U.S. dollar being the most prominent one. In other words, the payment of interest or repayment of the loan itself is only possible by utilising the proceeds from export surpluses arising from trade with hard currency countries. Yet these export surpluses are badly needed for development in the developing countries.

But there is a problem in this connection for the industrial countries of the First World too. Let us assume that all developing countries follow the example of South Korea, pursuing a prudent financial policy as a result of which they succeed in achieving export surpluses sufficient not only to pay the interest on their foreign debt, but also to repay the debt itself step by step. What effect would this have on markets in the industrial countries? Well, they would obviously be flooded with goods from the developing countries probably offering their products at highly competitive prices, so that many of the industrial countries' own factories would have to close down, as has happened at the British cotton industry. The end-result for the industrial countries would be mass unemployment, but they would have their outstanding debt properly serviced and eventually repaid. This surely cannot be to the overall advantage of the industrial countries, although we have to acknowledge the complexity that in the industrial countries lenders to developing countries differ from the industrial countries' workforce, both having different needs and aspirations.

Let us return to Keynes's view on the German reparation problem after World War One. Here we had in essence the same situation from which Brazil and many other developing countries currently suffer, except that it was official debt only. The reparation payments imposed upon Germany after World War One—no doubt perfectly justified in themselves—were nevertheless of a size Germany simply could not afford to pay. And if Germany had somehow managed to pay the required reparations, the German export surpluses required would surely have killed off the domestic markets of the creditor countries.

This is the situation viewed from a global aspect. It is different from the point of view of the individual lending bank, or maybe a group of banks having granted syndicated loans (the usual form of international lending). Here the crucial question is where to draw the line when deciding which, and to what extent, debts should be written off or rescheduled.

Even if we accept certain **moral** obligations on the part of the lending banks, we have to realise that financial institutions have also an obligation vis-à-vis their depositors who have a right to interest payments on their deposits, and a right to withdraw these deposits. If then the bank having onlent the deposits to a third world or any other borrower unable to repay the loan, the lending bank—if this happens on a large scale—may be unable to meet their own obligations vis-à-vis their depositors whose money it has accepted on trust.

In fact, the outstanding loans to Latin American countries alone granted by some of the largest international banks, especially in the US, amount to a multiple of their own capital. Writing off the loans in their entirety would therefore lead to bankruptcies among some of the most important international banks with disastrous consequences for the entire financial world.

Basically, a bank is quite happy to have an outstanding loan on a long-term basis, provided that the loan is serviced regularly by the borrower, in other words the interest is paid regularly. If a bank is repaid, it only has to find another borrower. Loans can simply be rolled over from period to period. Only if margins over LIBOR, i.e., the London interbank offered rate (both together making up the total interest on a loan) got too small to cover basic risks might a bank wish to be repaid. The main third world debt problem has in fact been the world-wide rise in interest rates since the late 1970s probably unexpected to the developing countries, but the unavoidable result of policies to fight inflation in the U.S., U.K. and other industrial countries, which made it impossible for many of the heavily indebted third world countries to meet their debt obligations. The *ad hoc* arrangements for Brazil I quoted do not constitute a long-term solution. A **real** help for the heavily indebted third world countries would be a **drastic** reduction in interest rates. How can this be achieved?

VI. The Problem of Interest Rates

The problem is that for a considerable period to come, interest rates in the world's money and capital markets are likely to remain high (see Frowen, 1991; for a discussion of the consequences of this trend and the moral issues involved in this connection, see Fonseca, 1988). We have the heavy borrowing requirements of the US to cover their continuous deficits, the borrowing requirements to rebuild the new East

German states of the Federal Republic and Kuwait, and finally and not least the huge borrowing requirements of the Soviet Union and other East European countries. And the third and fourth world countries themselves require substantial amounts of new capital to achieve higher rates of economic growth. Japan alone—even at a somewhat larger than its present substantial surplus—cannot finance the rest of the world; there are even signs that Japanese capital is now tending more to stay in Japan. Therefore, demand for capital will exceed supply in the world's money and capital markets, keeping interest rates at a level only the richest borrowers can afford to pay.

This I see as the real problem of third and fourth world countries today. There is only one solution, in my view, and that is **subsidised** interest rates for countries in **greatest** need. We already have this, of course, for fourth world countries, but on a very small scale through lending by one of the subsidiaries of the World Bank in Washington. Much more needs to be done on these lines by the governments of first world countries in collaboration with the major international economic agencies, such as the International Monetary Fund and the World Bank. The main aim here would be twofold: First, and most important, to reduce the interest burden on the **existing** foreign debt of developing countries. Second, to provide new loans on favourable terms. Commercial banks will always lend to a doubtful borrower, provided there is a government guarantee. Such a guarantee should only be granted to countries which do in fact follow a prudent financial policy, ideally to be supported by a structural adjustment programme adapted to the needs of individual countries to avoid the disastrous consequences of wrongly devised conditions the International Monetary Fund imposed in the past.

VII. Arms Race

Centesimus annus does not leave unmentioned the "insane arms race," which swallowed up huge resources so badly needed for the development of national economies and the financing of the less developed nations. With the conflict between East and West diminishing, enormous resources could, the pope indicates, be made available by disarming the huge military machines on both sides. However desirable this is, as well as arms control and an elimination of arms trade, we are nonetheless faced with the difficulties of converting factories from arms production to peaceful purposes. Also, if these factories start **adding** to the output of investment and consumer goods, not only must the demand be there but also the means to pay for these goods. If the latter problem remains unsolved because the industrial countries in recession will not reactivate their economies for fear of inflation, the closure of arms factories throughout the world will add huge numbers to those already unemployed. Rather than freeing resources for the poorer countries, the industrial countries would be faced with a potential additional burden for their social security services to pay the unemployed. This is a basic world-wide financial problem, which the monetarist policies pursued by the leading industrial countries are unlikely to solve. To achieve the desired goals, we would have to return to some of the basic thinking of John Maynard Keynes, thanks to whose policies we enjoyed, after the second world war, several decades of full employment and rising growth rates in many countries throughout the world.

VII. Exchange Rate Problems

A crucial issue neither *Centesimus annus* nor, to my knowledge, any of the previous encyclicals of John Paul touches on is that of exchange rate policies. And yet the choice between a fixed exchange rate system and a managed floating rate system can be of crucial importance to any country, not least to a developing country. There is of course no such thing in practice nowadays as a flexible or freely floating exchange rate system. The choice is simply between pegged or fixed exchange rates on the one hand, and a **managed** floating rate system on the other, with the monetary authorities in the latter case continuously intervening in the foreign exchange market, as they do also, of course, in a fixed rate system. The difference between the two systems is simply that under a fixed rate system, the value of the currency is fixed in terms of another currency with some band within which the currency is allowed to fluctuate, while under a managed floating rate system currencies float freely against each other—with the monetary authorities, usually the central bank, monitoring and affecting exchange rate movements through interventions in the foreign exchange market.

This factor, probably too technical to be considered in an encyclical letter, nevertheless affects economies deeply. Candidates for a pegged exchange rate are usually small open economies, including those in Eastern Europe, while floating exchange rates can be used successfully in a "currency area." The worst of all possibilities is a fixed and overvalued exchange rate which many of the developed countries have suffered from.

In this context credibility is a decisive criterion for the success of any economic policy and in particular any fundamental liberalisation in developing and socialist countries. Ultimately, the choice of the exchange rate regime depends on whether the exchange rate or the quantity of money has been selected as the nominal anchor of the monetary system. Currency reforms, which might favour economic developments in many of the developing and East European countries, are probably credible only when they are accompanied by a fixed exchange rate regime, combined with moves to make the currency freely convertible into other currencies.

In Eastern Europe, to which much of *Centesimus annus* is devoted, it is the **shortage** of goods which so far has been the main reason for inconvertibility. There is still (except in East Germany where on 1 July 1990 a currency reform was carried out and the Deutsche Mark of the Federal Republic of Germany introduced) a serious monetary overhang that gives rise to repressed inflation or to an open inflation during a currency reform. However, both inflationary situations could be cured by a properly designed and executed reform plan.

Recent evolution within the Third World towards more flexible exchange rate arrangements should be welcomed provided it is utilised for external adjustment needed to absorb external shocks. But if more flexible exchange rate arrangements are used to make up for internal mismanagement, then higher flexibility of exchange rates could mean the loss of a credible nominal anchor as a yardstick for monetary discipline.

IX. Population Explosion

Another topic highly relevant to the economic development of the poorer nations which John Paul fails to discuss in his latest encyclical is that of the population explosion, which is quite obviously closely linked to the problem of poverty in many of the developing countries. However,

Pope Paul VI refers to this vital issue in two of his encyclical letters, *Populorum progressio* (1969) and *Octagesimo adveniens* (1971). "It is certain", he repeats in the latter from *Populorum progressio*, "that public authorities can intervene, within the limits of their competence, by favouring the availability of appropriate information and by adopting suitable measures, provided that these be in conformity with the moral law."

We have to look at the relevant figures to understand the magnitude of the problem. The total world population was 5.3 billion in 1990, of which 4.1 billion, that is 77%, live in the underdeveloped regions of the South, 15% only in the developed market economies of the North, and 8% in the formerly centrally planned economies of Eastern Europe including the Soviet Union.

We know that in the developed countries, even among Catholics, families with few exceptions are small. I dare say that this is, again with few exceptions, **not** due to abstinence in sexual relations or infertility, but quite obviously to the use of some means of birth control. The knowledge about birth control is there, the facilities and means of using them are there, and the advice is there. And widespread use is being made of them —even among Catholics. The vast majority of people living in the underdeveloped world are still largely deprived of all this, and families are larger than can adequately be fed, clothed and housed.

With birth rates **decreasing** in the developed world and **increasing** (or in any case being considerably higher) in the underdeveloped world— especially in most of the African, Middle Eastern and Latin American countries—the world population in its composition will shift away from the developed to the underdeveloped world. How then can we solve the problem of poverty in underdeveloped countries? No country can sustain a 4 per cent per annum population growth as exists in certain parts of Africa. Even if the absolute level of total income in real terms would rise as a result of adequate assistance from the richer countries, income per head of the population may actually **decrease** if the population in the underdeveloped world grows too fast. Successful economies in, e.g., the Far East, such as South Korea, Singapore and Japan all have been low population growth countries.

Thus, with a decreasing percentage of the world population in the developed world and an ever increasing percentage in the underdeveloped world, we surely have an insoluble problem in attempting to improve economic conditions in the poorer countries. Should they not then try to help themselves by industrialising their economies in an attempt to become more self-sufficient? And if they succeeded, how would this affect the present industrial countries of the First World? We also have to ask ourselves how long this industrialisation of the Third World would take in the best case—probably long enough for millions to die of starvation in the meantime.

I do not want to sound overdramatic, but as an economist I cannot help agreeing with Bernice Hamilton when she refers to the population explosion in the poorer parts of the world and warns that, "The Church will continue to appear inhuman and foolish if it fails to tackle this problem soon with understanding and loving kindness."[5] Fortunately, the knowledge about birth control in some of the poorer developing countries is beginning to spread and the facilities and the means of using them is being made available. For example, the Planned Parenthood Federation of Nigeria, in close association with the Nigerian Family Health Service, has embarked on a widespread campaign in the media— TV, radio and newspapers—drawing attention to the need to control the number of children. With an annual per capita income as low as U.S. $200 (in 1989) and a 6.5% fertility rate, what prospects of survival would there be for Nigeria if this campaign failed to succeed?[6] Apart from excessive birth rates, there are other looming disasters in the Third World either caused or exacerbated by poverty, such as mass migration, stark famine and pollution, not to speak of AIDS—all of which form a sinister compound dwarfing the effect of the devastating droughts and plagues of the Middle Ages. Is the church tackling these problems as energetically as she should?

X. Information Explosion

Also in this volume there are references to the information explosion and its consequences—good or bad. And indeed, a button is pressed on the computer and we know exactly, for example, the trend of markets and prices of securities, commodities, foreign exchange etc. throughout the world.

In this situation what we would need, ideally, is a global social framework within which economics would be only one part and subservient to ethics. Too often nowadays policies are about economics, when they should really be in the first instance about a new social order to be achieved with the help of economics as an aid. (In many respects it would be a return to "political economy" in the true sense.) As G. Davidson and P. Davidson argued so persuasively in their joint volume *Economics for a Civilized Society* (1988), there are civic values such as love and justice and honesty and excellence as well as economic values of utility maximisation. It is in their view through intelligent economic policies that disparate values will be altered and only then will economic policies become more effective.

With regard to global solutions, there is no point in daydreaming about unrealistic and at least nowadays unattainable solutions. There is no global government and the existing international organisations are often largely controlled by a few of the richest countries of the world. Countries are breaking up, such as the Soviet Union and even smaller countries, such as Yugoslavia. The political union of Europe is difficult enough to achieve, as we all know from debates in this country.

Thus we are ultimately left with international organisations and in particular the international economic agencies (whatever their shortcomings) for global solutions. We may even have to add to them for specific purposes, such as achieving a greater degree of industrialisation and self-sufficiency in the underdeveloped world. But the attitude has to change among the richer countries. Only too often proposals are blocked by the rich countries because they are not prepared to add to their already existing commitments or fear the loss of markets. My outlook therefore is bleak, but not without hope.

But however wide the issues to be solved may be, the individual is not impotent in this power game and if greater personal responsibility is shown at all levels, despite the increasingly competitive nature of the world we live in, our planet would be a better place to live on and its future would, I think, be more secure.

The adequacies in Catholic social teaching, and for that matter in the social teaching of any church or religion, will ultimately depend on **realistic** propositions being put forward. Here John Paul has made a gentle start with his encyclical *Centesimus annus*. Whether his conviction of universal applicability of his encyclical and for that matter of Catholic social doctrine is correct, I am not entirely convinced. Each group of countries—the advanced economies, the nearly industrialised countries, the non-oil producing nations, the oil-producers themselves, not to speak of the Soviet Union and the East European countries—has its own problems, and within each group there are considerable differences. Pope Paul VI may well be right when in the face of such widely varying situations, he states in his encyclical *Octagesimo adveniens*[4] that "it is difficult for us to utter a unified message and to put forward a solution which has universal validity," implying that it is the task of local communities "to analyse with objectivity the situation which is proper to their own country." This view is also reflected by Peter Hebblethwaite when in the concluding sentence of one of his papers he states that "unless the present revival of Catholic social doctrine becomes a stimulus to local discussion of social morality, and is not regarded merely as a substitute for it, it will go the sad way of its predecessors." (Hepplethwaite, 1982, p.98) This surely has to be avoided at all cost in view of the gravity of the present world economic situation.

Notes

1. For a vital discussion of special aspects of political philosophy in *Centesimus annus*, and the process of its development, see Hebblethwaite (1991).

2. I am greatly indebted to Professor Aloysius Fonseca, S.J., for drawing my attention to the approach of the Ecclesiastical Authorities to various socio-economic problems at a meeting in Rieti (Italy) two days before his sudden death.

3. "The End of Laissez-faire", published as a pamphlet by the Hogarth Press in July 1926, was based on the Sidney Ball Lecture given by Keynes at Oxford in November 1924 and a lecture given by him at the University of Berlin in June 1926. The German text appeared under the title *Das Ende des Laissez-faire: Ideen zur Verbindung von Privat- und Gemeinwirtschaft.* (Munich/Leipzig: Dunker und Humblot, 1926, pp.40)

4. Keynes's essay entitled "The French Franc: An Open Letter to the French Minister of Finance(whoever he is or may be)" was first published in *The Nation and Athenaeum*, 9 January 1926. This essay was republished in France as part of a collection entitled *Réflexions sur le franc et sur quelques autres sujects* (1928).

5. Hamilton B. "Is it possible or even desirable that there should be a specifically Catholic social theory?" in Natale, McHugh, *Proceedings*. New Rochelle: Iona (College) 1991.

6. A Special Edition of Nigeria's weekly *Newswatch* on population explosion (22nd July 1991, pp. 38 - 39) drew attention to the fact that about 50% of Nigerians are below 20 years of age. Of the remaining 50% only 30% are capable of working. What they produce is minimal at the country's level of development. And even the present extremely limited resources would have to double every 25 years to maintain, at the present rate of population growth, at least the current, barely sufficient quality of life. This points to a desperate future if adequate measures are not adopted in time.

References

Boswell, J (1990) *"Community and the Economy"* (London: Routledge)

Davidson, G. and Davidson, P. (1988) *Economics for a Civilized Society* (London: Macmillan; New York: W. W. Norton & Co.)

Fonseca, A. (1988) "Are High Interest Rates Justifiable?", *Gregorianum*, Pontificia Universitas Gregoriana), vol. 69, no. 2, pp. 225-259

Frowen, Stephen (1991) *"Rerum novarum* and the World Economy Today", in Luciani, A. (ed.) *La "Rerum novarum" ei Problemi Sociali Oggi* (Milan: Editrice Massimo), pp. 75-92

Hebblethwaite, P. (1982) "The Popes and Politics: Shifting Patterns in Catholic Social Doctrine", *Daedalus, Journal of the American Academy of Arts and Sciences*, vol. 111, no. 1 of the *Proceedings of the American Academy of Arts and Sciences*, pp. 85-99

Hebblethwaite, P. (1991) *Centimus annus*, Europe and the Third World: or the Pastoral Care of Wolves (Paper presented at a Sedos, Rome Conference, 7 November 1991)

John Paul II (1991) *Centesimus annus* (Encyclical letter)

Keynes, J.M. (1919) "The Capacity of Germany to pay Reparations", from J.M.Keynes *The Economic Consequences of the Peace*, ch.5 "Reparations", in *The Collected Writings of John Maynard Keynes*, pt. I, ch.2, pp. 6 - 13 (London: Macmillan)

Keynes, J.M. (1926) "The French Franc: An Open Letter to the French Minister of Finance (whoever he is or may be", in *The Collected Writings of John Maynard Keynes*, vol. IX *Essays in Persuasion* (1931), pt. II, ch.3, pp. 76 - 85 (London: Macmillan for the Royal Economic Society, 1972)

Keynes, J. M. (1926) "*The End of Laissez-faire*," in *The Collected Writings of John Maynard Keynes*, vol. IX *Essays in Persuasion* (1931), pt.IV, ch.2, pp. 272 - 294 (London: Macmillan for the Royal Economic Society, 1972)

Keynes, J.M. (1929) "The German Transfer Problem", *The Economic Journal*, vol., March 1929.

Keynes, J. M. (1936) *The General Theory of Employment, Interest and Money* (London: Macmillan)

Leo XIII (1891) *Rerum novarum* (Encyclical Letter)

Marx, K. (1845) *Theses on Feuerbach*

Paul VI (1967) *Populorum progressio* (Encyclical Letter)

Paul VI (1971) *Octagesimo adveniens* (Encyclical Letter)

Pontifical Commission "Justitia et Pax (1986) *At the Service of the Human Community: An Ethical Approach to the International Debt Question*

Catholic Feminism's Contribution To The Church's Social Justice Tradition

Georgia Masters Keightley

This paper's thesis is a simple one, namely that Catholic feminism has a valuable contribution to make to the development of the church's social doctrine. This is so because feminism represents a perspective on the tradition that is at once critical and constructive.

My purpose is to show how and why this is the case. That is, I wish to indicate the manner in which a Catholic feminist perspective highlights certain ambiguities, inconsistencies in the church's social ethic, ones which ultimately stand in the way of a truthful account of social reality and thus prevent sound judgements as to what constitutes the morally good. On the other hand, I will argue that this perspective also yields up important insights about the sort of social transformation that members of the church ought to seek, that further, it suggests viable strategies for change. Because there is such a wide misunderstanding in Catholic circles as to what sort of reality feminism is, however, it is imperative to preface this study with some basic definitions.

A. *What is Feminism?*

Essentially, feminism is a matter of epistemology.[1] More exactly, it deliberately places woman at the center of inquiry: it considers her both as the subject and object of knowledge. For example, in feminist theory's initial phase, interested scholars observed that across the disciplines, women as the active agents of history had rarely, if ever, been made the object of empirical and theoretical scrutiny.[2] It was simply assumed that women's lives and experience were but variations on a basic common humanity.[3] Yet feminists also noticed that women were not only believed to be duplicate males; they were repeatedly judged to be naturally inferior ones, their lesser social position being but a manifestation of, even a legitimation of this. In light of these *a priori* assumptions about the sameness and/or interchangeability of men and women's lives, scholars then sought to determine if there were indeed any kinds of experiences that could be said to be gender-specific; in concluding that there were, they then went on to argue that henceforth, serious analysis could not legitimately dismiss or fail to take such differences into account.[4] In seeking a reason for "the absences, gaps, lacunae touching women and the feminine" in theory and history,[5] it was inevitable that feminists effect the Kantian turn and look to the horizon of the knower. As a result, feminist theory characteristically emphasizes that the knowing subject is always socially and historically rooted. Here it is axiomatic that context, environment and circumstances of life are determinative of what an individual can conceive and know. But especially it takes for granted that one's view of the world is affected by social status, such as this is defined culturally in terms of such variables as race, class and, of course, gender. Feminists argue that in the past, all public construals of reality, theory, frameworks of thought, etc., have been representative of the lived experience of society's dominant males.[6] Furthermore, the social system of patriarchy is identified as having been decisive to shaping cultural institutions and social life in the west.

Feminists also pay close attention to the relationship that exists between thought and language. In contrast to theories that view language as being merely the vehicle or conduit of ideas, feminists argue instead that language is actually constitutive, both of one's own self-understanding and that of the world.[7] That is, we are only able to make sense out of reality by means of the interpretive schemes encoded in language that are provided us by our immediate communities. Likewise, language is instrumental to creating the public roles and private self-understandings that give us identity; it makes available to us the accepted modes, ways of being in and negotiating the world.

With this in view, feminist analysis seeks to highlight "the complicity of discursive systems with oppressive social structures and the dependence of discourses on particular positions established by particular modes of language."[8] Research shows that woman's voice—expressive of her own lived experience—has historically gone unheard. Because of their control of the meaning-making organs of culture, men have been in a position to define who and what woman is, must be and do; feminists also observe that theory has "asked only the questions about social life that appear problematic from within the social experiences that are characteristic for men."[9] For this reason, feminist scholars seek to thematize the truth about women's lived experience, insisting that because classical definitions of women's place and status prove inadequate, women must now take responsibility for naming their own experience, for critiquing, defining and reshaping their own roles. Above all, they argue, women need to develop suitable language and categories for bringing to light those aspects of their lives which everyday discourse has heretofore rendered invisible, distorted and/or devalued.

In contrast to traditional approaches to theory, feminists also question that the knower either is or must be capable of transcending those more personal "feelings, emotions, passions, interests and motives, etc." that are actually constitutive of personhood.[10] As many of these scholars point out, a self disconnected from space, time or the complexity of social relations is a status usually attributed to disembodied spirits, i.e., to angels, alone! Feminists argue that, to the contrary, not only is the subject *not* free of social and political interests, she is of necessity implicated in them. Because "particular interests are served by every theoretical position," by every "textual or discursive system,"[11] the analyst's task then is to thematize and bring such predispositions to the surface. One must know how a particular worldview is structured; above all, one must take care to set out its working assumptions and in the process, become aware of its potential for bias.

All of this is not to say that feminist theory itself eschews questions of objectivity and truth. Most feminists prefer to view truth and objectivity as developmental and cumulative, rather than as being a permanent, once-for-all achievement. At the same time, they tend to downplay the subject/opinion—object/knowledge split. Rejecting the notion that a wide gulf separates the knowing subject and its object, feminist theory prefers to acknowledge the contiguity between them. That is to say, subject and object are not to be dichotomously divided into such mutually exclusive and mutually exhaustive categories as self\other, master/disciple, etc.; rather, the consensus is that these realities are best apprehended in terms of their continuities and/or differences.[12]

Some might prefer to describe feminism as being a critical and constructive strategy rather than a definite mode of abstraction and reflection. As theory, feminism is not only *not* disinterested: to the contrary, it is highly motivated by the goals and strategies necessary for creating an autonomy for women. As indicated, it deliberately places women's experience at the very center of analysis. And, at each phase of the investigation, feminist methodology poses the question of gender: it pays specific attention to the relation existing between the sexes and considers the symbolic framework in which the meaning of this comes to be articulated in practical and political life.[13]

B. *What is Catholic Feminism?*

Catholic feminism raises the question of gender within the context of Christian religious and ecclesial experience:

> If feminism is a primary movement toward human liberation, Christian feminists approach the struggle from a critical stance of awareness, analysis, and action amid enduring beliefs about the action of God in human life, and the meaning of the Gospel in the light of human experience (in this case, women's experience).[14]

While there is a tendency to assume that Catholic feminism's exclusive aim is critique of the church's internal life and discipline—but especially women's exclusion from the ordained priesthood—the fact is, its scope reaches far beyond this. Like their secular counterparts, Catholic feminists judge patriarchy to be "an essentially dysfunctional system." They offer in its place "an alternative vision for humanity and the earth," and actively seek "to bring this vision to realization."[15]

My interest is to show what results when Catholic feminism poses the gender question in reference to the church's social teaching. To borrow from the U.S. bishops, the Catholic feminist asks: what does this tradition do *to* and *for* women? Is Catholic social teaching inclusive enough, comprehensive enough so as to address the problems and dilemmas that are endemic to woman's situation? Such a query has obvious relevance in light of the church's conviction that it has a divinely given mandate to illumine all of human life and activity by the gospel's light, that it is obliged to challenge all those instances wherein personal dignity and human well-being come under assault.

As one feminist theologian has observed, however, statements about women are rarely to be found in the church's major documents on social justice or in the *Acta Apostolicae Sedis*. For a long period, what comments there were were confined to and took the form of informal papal addresses to groups of women visiting the Vatican.[16] While this has begun to change, most of the social documents nonetheless continue to assume masculine and feminine experience to be basically interchangeable; here too one finds the supposition that women's lives can readily be understood from the standpoint of the masculine or by the inclusive theological category, "common human experience."

But, influenced by and building upon the research of their secular counterparts, Catholic feminists have worked hard to establish the merit of gender analysis as applied to theology and ethics. The growing evidence is that until such time as the church's social doctrine begins to take the unique character of women's lives and experience into account, it can provide but a limited, even inadequate description of human social experience. And, because it leaves unexamined a significant segment of human reality, Catholic social teaching will finally be unable to effect the radical transformation it seeks.

C. *Experience as Public/Private*

In the space remaining, I want to examine a supposition central to Catholic social thought and that is the notion that human experience readily divides into the two spheres, "public," "private." Indeed, that the church has an entire body of teaching it overtly directs to such matters as politics, law, economics, peace, the development of culture, etc., confirms that the magisterium recognizes this to be a valid one.[17]

I will argue that incorporation of a critical feminist perspective could make a sizeable contribution to formulation of this dimension of church

337

teaching. Essentially, a feminist standpoint calls for magisterium and theologians to be cognizant not only of how the two categories "public/private" function; the former need to be aware of the importance of making explicit the contents and parameters of each. In doing so, it would become clear that in the interests of social justice, this basic framework of western life is deserving of some radical reform. Here is why:

In truth, scrutiny of the categories "public," "private" has been described as being "at the heart of the feminist enterprise"—this, for the reason that these terms have been central to the way in which human beings have "structured, guided, ordered and organized a life for themselves and others."[18] Theorists point out that images of public/private are tied to understandings of human nature, to "evaluations of human capacities and activities, virtues, and excellence," to assessments of moral agency.[19] Public/private are, above all, a means of defining and regulating social relations. They represent separate foci helpful to distinguishing the broad diversity of human activity as well as to delineating the modes of being associated with each. At the same time, each category represents "deeply felt imperatives," each proves to be "the repository" of humanity's most cherished dreams, interests and passions.[20]

As such, "public/private" represent two distinct moral environments.[21] That is to say, each category not only dictates its own norms of appropriate action, each also establishes the limits of what constitutes acceptable conduct. As indicated above, descriptions of public and private roles as well as their prescribed codes of behavior are linked to and embodied within a grammar of basic notions and rules, all of which are encoded in the language we appropriate from the different communities of which we are members.

Feminist scholars have established that historically the categories public/private as well as the boundaries separating them, the activities and codes of behavior appropriate to each have been defined primarily by men. Per classical thought, the term *polis* designated the public sphere wherein individuals by the deliberate exercise of intelligence and choice could achieve a capacity for self-direction and conduct their collective lives in an ordered, meaningful way. This world was seen to exist over

338

and against the private world of the household, the *oikos*, the realm of necessity whose single business was that of survival—here, life revolved around the indispensable tasks of production and reproduction.[22] Such a division automatically excluded women from the public world of power and action altogether, their activities being circumscribed to the private world of home and family. Yet even in this latter setting, women throughout history have found their existence subjected to male authority.[23] On these grounds, feminists today call for a reconstruction of both "public" and "private" and for revised definitions of women's relationship to each. For the secular feminist, a crucial question concerns the extent to which these categorizations either nourish or distort woman's capacity for purposive activity.[24] For her part, the Catholic feminist believes it also essential to ask: is the understanding of women's reality implicit to construals of public/private consistent with the gospel tradition's understanding of human dignity and worth?

I now want to consider two themes of Catholic social teaching which have been identified as representing "the major arguments of the tradition about the public and private."[25] I will indicate, from the vantage point of Catholic feminism, how allowing the categories public/private to go unexamined actually subverts the prophetic critique the church's social teaching proposes to make.

D. *Right to Equality and Participation*

A hallmark of the Catholic social tradition is its recognition of the right and duty of every person to participate in all aspects and at all levels of cultural and social life.[26]

In *Populorum progressio* for instance, it is emphasized that social involvement is indispensable to full personalization.[27] In *Sollicitudo rei socialis*, humanization is said to be an outright result of the collaborative work "of our personal and collective effort to raise up the human condition."[28] In the recently issued *Centisimus Annus*, John Paul II argues that the right "to make an active contribution to the common good of humanity" is "something due to man because he is man by reason of his lofty dignity."[29] The pontiff then directly links the securing of personal dignity to the effective engagement in political and economic life.

339

Despite such positive assertions, however, there is also to be found in the tradition a line of thought extending from Leo XIII to John Paul II that definitely limits, radically qualifies even, women's participation in public. For example, there are a sizeable number of texts stating that woman's proper sphere of activity is the private world of home and family. According to *Rerum novarum*, "woman is by nature fitted for home work."[30] To this Pius XII adds: "Now a woman's function, a woman's way, a woman's natural bent, is motherhood. Every woman is called to be a mother, a mother in the physical sense, or mother in a sense more spiritual and more exalted, yet real, nonetheless."[31] In 1961, John XXIII told a group of women: "We would also like to remind you that the end for which the Creator fashioned women's whole being is motherhood. This vocation to motherhood is so proper to her and so much a part of her nature that it is operative even when actual generation does not occur."[32] And out of his belief that child care is that pursuit most appropriate to women, that therefore all work outside the home has to be viewed as an impediment to her proper role as caretaker,[33] John Paul II calls for the restructuring of society so "that wives and mothers are not in practice compelled to work outside the home."[34]   Indeed, Catholic social documents regularly define the just wage in terms of that amount required to allow a man to be the sole support of his wife and children (e.g., *RN* #35; FC #23).

As the above texts reveal, the pontiffs assume woman's public activity to be defined as well as circumscribed by her nature. Other texts speak more explicitly about a fundamental difference between the sexes, a difference of ability in fact, that actually serves to place restrictions on what women may do in public. In his condemnation of coeducation, for instance, Pius XI cited the dissimilarity in organism, temperament, the disparity of abilities, that in his view makes it impossible to fashion women and men in "one and the same education."[35] In his turn, Pius XII argued that even though modern women are obliged to assume a more visible public role, he nonetheless insisted that woman's responsibilities remain distinct from those of men and are consistent with her natural dispositions:

Both sexes have the right and duty to work together for the good of society, for the good of the nation. But it is clear that while men by temperament are more suited to deal with external affairs and public business, generally speaking, the woman has a deeper insight for understanding the delicate problems of domestic and family life. . .It is not so much that each sex is called to a different task; the difference is rather in their manner of judging and arriving at concrete and practical applications. . .The sensibility and delicacy which are characteristic of the woman may perhaps bias her judgement in the direction of her impressions, and so tend to the prejudice of wide and clear vision, cool decision, or far sighted prudence; but on the other hand they are most valuable aids in discerning the needs, aspirations, and dangers proper to the sphere of domestic life, public assistance, and religion.[36]

Subsequently, Paul VI relies on the term "complementary" to convey his belief that woman's nature has qualities unique to it. Among these he includes "intuition, creativity, sensibility, a sense of piety and compassion, a profound capacity for understanding and love."[37]

Because woman's nature intends her for motherhood, because this qualification of her being (both physically and emotionally) disqualifies her for some public duties, several of the pontiffs go on to suggest that on these grounds, a certain inequality in the public realm as far as women are concerned is sometimes justified in order to maintain the common good. One finds this idea initially expressed in Pius XI's *Casti connubi*. Here the pontiff denounces those "false teachers" who attack "the loyal and honorable obedience of the wife to her husband" and who call for woman's social, physiological and economic emancipation. Pius identifies these as being but false freedoms:

> Physiological emancipation would free woman at will from the wifely and maternal responsibilities—and this as we have seen, is not emancipation but an abominable crime; economic emancipation would authorize the wife, without the knowledge of her husband and even against his will, to conduct and administer her own affairs without any regard to the welfare of children, husband or family; social emancipation, finally, would free the wife from the domestic cares of children and family, enabling her, to the neglect of these, to follow her own bent, and engage in business and even public affairs.[38]

Pius then cautions:

> "This is no true emancipation of woman... on the contrary, it is a degradation of the spirit of woman and of the dignity of a mother.[39]

When speaking of the changing status of women in the modern world in *Octogesima adveniens*, Paul VI also makes passing reference to "that false equality which would deny the distinctions laid down by the Creator Himself, and which would be in contradiction with woman's proper role."[40] Although Paul does not provide any actual examples of this, his remark indicates that he does not regard all public roles as befitting a woman.

This notion of a "false equality" reappears in the writings of the present pontiff. In *Christifideles laici*, for example, he notes that in contemporary culture, woman risks being confused by "what truly responds to her dignity as a person and to her vocation from all that, under the pretext of this 'dignity' and in the name of 'freedom' and 'progress,' actually militates against true values."[41] He suggests here that pursuit of these values will actually result in "the moral degradation of the person, the environment and society (*CL* #51)." In *Mulieris dignitatem*, his earlier meditation on the dignity and vocation of women, John Paul II again expresses the concern that women's pursuit of their rights must not end in their "masculinization."[42] That is, "in the name of liberation from male 'domination' women must not appropriate to themselves male characteristics contrary to their own feminine 'originality'(*MD* #10)." By way of remedy, the pontiff recommends the continuing evangelization of woman and the on-going illumination of her vision by faith (*CL* #51).

As is obvious, the texts just cited pose serious questions as to whether or not the magisterial documents actually mean what they say about equality and participation—as far as women are concerned, that is. Do they too have a God-given right to engage in social life as completely, as fully as men? Do women too have an equal responsibility for the common good? More importantly, these texts appear to doubt that woman is, of herself, capable of exercising genuine moral agency, of taking responsibility either for herself or for the welfare of the larger community. Then there is the suggestion that, by virtue of this natural debility, some measure of inequality in her case is even tolerable.

But for the Catholic feminist, because this material so clearly works to compromise what is said elsewhere—especially the magisterium's insistent call for respect for the person, his/her dignity and rights to equality and participation—the considerable ambiguity concerning women's own public role simply has to be addressed and clarified.

The urgency of such an undertaking becomes manifest, for example, when one considers the practical implications of the restrictions the above series of texts place on women. For as Catholic feminists point out, by consigning her to the private as these texts do, by making this the original, ultimate ground of her responsibility and identity, the pontiffs ineluctably consign woman to a state of perpetual political and economic dependence. Certainly those passages that equate a just wage with a family wage explicitly place the well-being of women and their children directly in the hands of men—both privately as husbands, fathers, and publicly as officials of government and leaders of industry.

Yet it is precisely economic independence that contemporary Catholic thought recognizes as being absolutely vital to dignity and personhood. This is certainly the thrust of the text from *Centisimus annus* given above. And, of course, it is this too that feminists cite as being an indispensable first step to achievement of woman's dignity and freedom today. For the fact of the matter is, at the present time and in almost every part of the world, women, bound by the norms of culture, find themselves in the very situation the pontiffs recommend: most women today continue to be in some way dependent on men.

To see how women fare under this type of social organization, it is useful to consider statistics provided by the recently published U.N. report, *The World's Women: Trends and Statistics 1970-1990.*[43] This study shows that:

1) between 1970-85, the number of illiterate women rose in the amount of 54 million while the number of illiterate men rose by only 4 million;[44]

2) across the world, women work as much as, or more than men everywhere—as much as 13 hours per week on average, even more in Africa and Asia;[45]

3) even in developed countries, the workplace continues to be segregated by sex; women fill over ½ the clerical and service jobs; men receive both higher wages and greater seniority and benefits than women.[46]

Another statistic included in the U.N. report—one also found to challenge church statements—has to do with those figures that show that approximately 60% of the world's women aged 15 and over are economically active.[47] When one consults church documents, however, one gets a strikngly different account of what women are doing. That is, the understanding implicit here is that all women are married, that they do not work outside the home, and that "the ideal is the so-called 'traditional family' with a father who is employed and a mother who takes care of the home and the children."[48] Here the worker is male and "productive work" is consistently equated with what "men do in the public arena." And, while man is here valued for his economic productivity, woman's value in contrast, is understood to reside in her social productivity.[49] But again, the picture provided by the U.N. report indicates something else entirely.

At the same time, Catholic feminists also stress that the failure to count all of the things that women do for home and family as having genuine monetary worth, economic value is a signal factor in disadvantaging women both politically and socially.

To explain: according to the U.N. report, women's home work, e.g., child care, food provision and health care, tending gardens and livestock, weaving cloth, etc. (and, all of which frees men for activity in the public domain) is either not considered by governments to be economically productive or else is way undervalued.[50] Because of this perceived lack of financial worth, governments are not inclined to invest in either women's education or health care. Neither are they inclined to formulate development policies supportive of "the internal economy of the household,"[51] the subsistence agriculture that is such a critical fact of life for women of the Third World. For the same reason the report suggests, governments do not "integrate the concerns and interests of women into mainstream policies"; neither is there much interest in creating or enforcing, where they do exist, laws that give women equality with men "in the rights to own land, borrow money and enter contracts."[52]

Yet the irony is that, again as the U.N. report makes clear, by investing in women, in their health care and education, by developing agricultural policies aimed at improving the production of household crops and small livestock, governments would not only enhance the overall well-being of women and children. They would at the same time improve the general standard of living across the board as well as increase the gross national product.

For the church's part, by allowing its traditional perceptions/biases about public/private to go unexamined, by its inability to see women's situation for what it truly is, the magisterium is unable, in this case, to read 'signs of the times' accurately. And, by not being able to see the truth of how, why, and under what limits women are presently allowed to participate in public life, the church also misses a privileged opportunity to be the prophetic voice it so earnestly desires to be. Above all, it misses the chance to mount a direct challenge to existing political,

economic and cultural structures in such a way as to relieve the increasingly perilous situation of the world's women and their children. In its bias, unfortunately, Catholic social doctrine remains unable to recommend viable strategies for change, ones able to address in an effective way the situation of women today.
Ms. her

E. *A Single Ethic for Public and Private*

A second theme of Catholic social thought addressed by feminist analysis is the claim that there exists a single overarching ethic for both public and private. In this section, I will identify some basic elements of feminist critique in this regard. In the course of this discussion, some of the creative proposals made by Catholic feminists for interpreting and/or reconstructing the categories public/private will become evident as will the implications such has for development of the church's social doctrine.

Regarding the morality of the public and private spheres, *Pacem in terris* states:

> The same moral law which governs relations between individual human beings serves also to regulate the relations of political communities with one another. This will be readily understood when one reflects that the individual representatives of political communities cannot put aside their dignity while they are acting in the name and interest of their countries; and that they cannot therefore violate the very law of their being.[53]

According to the feminist analysis discussed above, however, because public/private represent two different ways of structuring and giving coherence to experience, each category also represents a discrete moral environment which dictates "norms of appropriate or worthy action."[54] Furthermore, images of public and private are also said to be "necessarily, if implicitly" tied to different understandings of moral agency.[55]

In reality, scrutiny of church practise is found to support this feminist claim. On the one hand, study shows that the Catholic understanding of reality has long been framed in dualistic terms. And here, two sets of distinctions have been especially relevant: those of lay/cleric and church/world. Furthermore, these distinctions are conceived of as being essential, ontological in kind. Thus, *Lumen gentium* describes the difference between the ordained and baptismal priesthoods as being one "of essence, not degree."[56] Subsequently, *Christifideles laici* argues that laity are those Christians whose baptismal character is uniquely qualified in terms of their worldly situation, by the very context of their ecclesial activity (*CL#* 15). Indeed John Paul II makes use of the argument that "the secular functions are the proper field of action of the laity" to justify his prohibition against the involvement of clergy and religious in partisan politics.[57]

That these distinct ecclesial experiences implicate two different ethics, two different modes of Christian discipleship has also been present to Catholic understanding. In his classic, *Lay People in the Church*, Yves Congar takes note of Gratian's assessment, "*Duo sun genera christianorum*," and his notion that the lay state exists as a "concession" to human weakness.[58] Congar himself describes the difference between cleric and lay as originating in their different conditions of holiness, their different states of life. Thus the cleric/monk, concerned with "holy things," shapes his life following the way of perfection while the lay man, occupied as he is with the mundane, the affairs of the world, is obliged to pursue a more minimalistic ethic, the way of the commandments.[59] That clergy/religious live the higher, more demanding ethic has been reiterated by the present pope in this way: "Throughout her history the church has always defended the superiority of this charism [virginity] to that of marriage, by reason of the singular link it has with God (*FC* #16)."

But perhaps a greater challenge to *Pacem in terris* and its claim on behalf of a single ethic comes from the magisterium's own appropriation of natural law theory. As Richard Gula has observed, the natural law argument is increasingly used in two different ways. On the one hand, the magisterium has consistently followed a more conservative "order of nature approach" when evaluating personal sexual and medical moral matters. Yet when treating issues having to do with social ethics, the more liberal "order of reason approach" has become the methodological norm.[60] In agreement, moralist Richard McCormick goes on to add that "the different criteria and different methods" used in evaluating these moral questions not only seem arbitrary, this also evidences the presence of a "double standard," something he sees as seriously compromising recent efforts to present Catholic ethics as an exemplar of a consistent ethic of life.[61]

In showing the Catholic moral tradition to be inconsistent regarding the ethics of public/private, feminist theory also reveals it to be a limited, incomplete ethic because of its inability to give a sufficient account of either category, public or private. As suggested above, this stems from an initial failure to make explicit the presuppositions concerning the content and limits of these categories. What is lacking here, of course, is the vantage point of women and a specific attention to the particularities of their experience. In other words, what Catholic ethics neglects to take into account is that women's experience, too, is a constitutive, integral element of public and private and as such, functions both as a potential source of moral insight as well as reality open to and deserving of scrutiny and evaluation. This inadequacy has definite implications for the church's social doctrine insofar as deficient descriptions of public/private, the nature of their relationship, necessarily stand in the way of a correct reading of social reality on which in turn, good judgements as to what constitutes the morally good also depend.

To illustrate how the absence of woman's perspective affects Catholic social thought, both in terms of its method and content, I want to consider three important feminist theses:

a. *Some areas of experience escape moral scrutiny*

First of all, there is the feminist assertion that attention to women's experience opens up to moral scrutiny and evaluation areas of human experience that have heretofore gone unexamined. Thus Catholic women note that historically, theological ethics has had precious little to say about matters of direct interest and/or personal concern to women. Rarely does one find the magisterium concerned about such issues as physical violence against women and children, or condemning incest, rape or other forms

348

of sexual abuse.[62] And, until quite recently, neither has the magisterium spoken out against the specific burdens placed on women as a result of racial or ethnic discrimination.[63]

And, an issue central to women's lives today has to do with the disproportionate responsibility they bear for the business of family and children despite the fact that for economic reasons, they must also find employment outside the home. Yet Barbara Andolsen finds that Catholic social thought, "hamstrung by static notions of the nature of women and of the family,"[64] not only fails to grasp the actual situation of the world's women; it also fails to recognize that "any distribution of family responsibilities which leaves the wage-earning woman with the major share of household tasks violates the norm of justice."[65] She proposes that the church's social doctrine must advocate the restructuring of social patterns in such a way as to make "explicit provisions for domestic needs," she urges that church teaching propose formulae for change that make it possible "to integrate family and work in a structure humane to all parties."[66]

Finally, women's experience that life within the private world can also be one of oppression and subordination must stand as a cautionary note to those moral theorists who, in criticizing contractarian approaches to justice, put forward a model of community based on the types of relational patterns associated with family, neighborhood, nation.[67] Feminists point out that what these scholars tend to overlook is that, in addition to excluding outsiders, the practises and traditions of such groups have regularly been exploitative and oppressive toward some of their own members.[68] More exactly, such communities "have harbored social roles and structures which have been detrimental to women."[69]

And so, while feminists would not downplay the moral claims placed on us by these "communities of origin," they would also argue that the self-understandings of such groups may well "harbor ambiguities, ambivalences, contradictions, oppressions which complicate as well as constitute identity," that therefore the legitimacy of all such claims must first be subjected to stringent and careful critical evaluation.[70]

b. *The integral relation of the ethics of public/private goes unexamined*

A second argument made is that Catholic social thought, devoid of woman's point of view, is unable to recognize the reciprocal relation that exists between public and private and in consequence, also misses seeing that decisions made in private often have significant public consequences, and vice versa. In other words, the social implications of private ethics, but also, the impact of public morality on the private are not really attended to in magisterial documents. By way of illustration, feminist work presents the following two examples.

In First World countries particularly, as women enter the workplace at all levels and in increasing numbers, they bring with them a whole host of issues pertaining to family that heretofore have not been considered to be a matter of public concern. For example, women now question the ethos of careerism that "places personal achievement, security and satisfaction above any obligations to others," even those of children and spouse.[71] Women also call for "a humanizing of the workplace," advocating such innovative changes as shorter and more flexible work hours, parental leave, employer-sponsored daycare.[72] Research shows that what working women hope to achieve is "a life in which family and a public vocation" can be "satisfactorily integrated," and their belief that the two ought not to conflict but be "mutually enriching."[73]

What the experience of women brings to social ethics in this instance is the critical reminder that the individual is not just a worker, but a person belonging to a larger context and whose private commitments and connections to others are an integral factor determinative of his/her work life. To put it in another way, while calling attention to the fundamental interrelatedness of public/private, contemporary women strongly resist allowing the demands of the public realm to overwhelm or even obliterate the private and its own preferred values. Women's current struggle to create an acceptable balance between work and family undersores that, at bottom, for human beings to flourish, individuals and communities alike, some ideal of family life must be zealously guarded and protected, both by the public and for the public's own good.[74]

At the same time, woman's experience stands in counterpoint to those other tendencies that would overly romanticize participation in public life, noteably the world of work. Women's reality reveals that for some individuals, work is not always a matter of choice, that work's meaning is not always something intrinsic or that such effort always involves some measure of self-fulfillment, personal development. Rather the fact is, that work can simply be a necessary way of living out one's commitments to others. This truth finds expression in such diverse examples as the African woman who engages in petty trading to ensure the survival of her children; but it also includes the efforts of those American Catholic women, who by virtue of their education in the church's institutions, feel called "to stretch their loyalties beyond the domestic sphere to the sphere of public action on behalf of a wider good."[75]

A second instance where uncritical construals of public/private result in Catholic social thought's inability to deal with pressing social concerns is the area of human sexuality. Catholic feminists observe that the church has typically relegated questions about sexuality and reproduction to the private. They also emphasize, however, that to do so not only prescinds from and disregards the important differences that social context can make for moral truth and discernment;[76] it also tends to ignore the substantial way in which the institution of motherhood, as socially conceived and practised, can be determinative of a community's life. Thus Catholic feminists seek to reposition the discussion "by placing matters of 'personal' sexual and family ethics within a fabric of socially woven roles, expectations, pressures and consequences,"[77] insisting that only by so doing does sound moral analysis become possible.

Such repositioning not only raises questions for the current debate regarding public policy and the ethics of reproductive technologies.[78] It also dramatically underscores the church's failure to come to grips with the demographic problem in a satisfactory way. Maria Riley observes that while several of the social documents do acknowledge the relationship that exists between social and economic development on the one hand and population growth on the other, these stop short of investigating the myriad ways the absence of family planning impacts national well-being, the common good. As Riley stresses, "Population studies over the years have identified clear linkages between poverty, economic insecurity in old age, infant mortality and the number of children per family in developing countries."[79] She too argues that the population question must be

351

analyzed taking into account women's own experience of reproduction, i.e., "within the social, economic, political and cultural structures that shape women's lives, whether in the poor nations or in the so-called developed ones."[80] Finally she observes: "As long as the church continues to ignore the context of women's lives when it raises the issue of childbirth, its voice in this profound human concern will not be heard."[81]

At this juncture it is worth noting that when motherhood's public aspect is made integral to moral analysis, statistical evidence is available that makes clear that whenever women have access to safe methods of birth control and are able to control their own fertility, their lives change dramatically for the better.[82] Such however, is in striking contrast to church documents reflecting the magisterium's own understanding to the contrary, that woman's personal well-being actually depends on adherence to the dictates of her nature, of being open to and accepting of new life (e.g., *MD* #18).

c. *Limited understanding of moral agency, moral norms*

Besides this potential to provide a fuller, more adequate description of public/private, inclusion of a feminist perspective has other important methodological implications for Christian social ethics. As indicated above, public/private not only represent distinct moral environments, they also implicate discrete views of moral agency. In this regard, feminist theory represents a different vantage point from which to construe the moral problem. At the same time, it manages to present some basic norms in new light.

Moral theory has traditionally emphasized individual autonomy, it has stressed the values of equality, justice, reciprocity and rights. But in her study of women subjects, Carol Gilligan discovered a somewhat different understanding of the moral life, one emphasizing care, connection and a responsibility to one's relations with others.[83]

Those Giligan surveyed tended not to describe their relationships in either hierarchical or contractual terms. Rather, they saw themselves as part of an interdependent "network of relations created and sustained by connection and response."[84] Evident here was an ethic that went beyond

352

achievement of the *fair* solution to one aimed at *inclusivity*, a solution that "transforms identity through the experience of a relationship."[85]

Gilligan argues that this way of viewing moral experience gives significant new meaning to the term "dependence." While this condition is intrinsic to being human and usually calls to mind a state of helplessness, powerlesness, as being without control, Gilligan discovered that dependence (as attachment to others) may also be understood as an act of human agency. To deliberately place oneself in a situation of having to rely on others can be an acknowledgement that the interdependence of attachment can end in the empowerment of both self and other, not just one person at the other's expense. Once approached in this way, to act responsibly demands more than a simple fidelity to one's commitments and obligations; it also requires taking the initiative to gain awareness of the other's situation so as to be able to respond to his/her needs.[86] For this reason, activities of care,—e.g., listening, a willingness to help, understanding—take on a moral dimension; they reflect respect for "the injunction to pay attention and not to turn away from need."[87]

At the same time, this ability to aproach people on their own terms and to respond as they require inevitably generates the power both to help and to hurt; how this power is exercised then becomes the standard of responsibility and care in relationships. "In this active construction, dependence. . . denotes a decision to enact a version of love."[88] One cannot help but see in Gilligan's analysis a striking corollary to John Paul II's thesis that in certain instances, private values deserve to be made public ones, that indeed, mutuality is a norm as appropriate to social relationships as it is to personal ones.[89]

Women's way of construing moral problems also leads to seeing some classic norms in a fresh new way. For example, Catholic feminists assert that Christian love, *agape*, has been interpreted too narrowly as "self-less love." Not only have women been identified with this particular norm historically, they also know that this limited construal can actually result in an abuse of personal dignity, a debasement of the person.[90] In their efforts to re-value *agape*, feminist theologians emphasize that in relationships, love actually involves the kind of self-sacrifice that intends another's good; it is an expression of concern which aims at the establishment of mutuality between two parties. By retrieving these meanings of *agape*, feminists have successfully shown that self-sacrifice also has relevance for social ethics. For example, while such an attitude is not generally seen to be in a group's best interests, a willingness to yield to others can be seen as a realistic course of action when considered in the context of improving the quality of a community's relationships, both within and without.[91]

Similarly, feminists argue that achievement of formal equality alone has not proved the panacea for alleviating situations of oppression and discrimination as originally anticipated. Legally, equality implies that distinctions between men and women should be abolished so that practically women may not be treated differently than men. In practise, however, feminists now see that in the interests of achieving social justice, equality needs to understood in a much more complex way.

Practical experience, for example, has made feminists acutely aware that in some circumstances, formal equality can actually undermine rather than promote women's well-being.[92] Cases in point include the results of recent changes in U.S. alimony, divorce, and child custody laws. Today, heated debate centers on the issue of pregnancy and the workplace: because of their condition, are women entitled to special treatment and benefits from their employer, or are they merely deserving of what is available to any employee? [93] Studies also show that neither does achievment of formal equality address many aspects of social inequality experienced by women and minorities. For this reason then, feminists see need for and recommend as government policy affirmative action programs, comparable worth policies as a way of removing systemic inequities and for creating parity.

As becomes obvious, consideration of the feminist argument in this regard would enable the church to speak about equality in a more knowing, focused way in its discussion of human rights.

F. *Conclusion*

The purpose of this study has been to explore the thesis that Catholic feminism represents a critical as well as a constructive perspective on the church's social ethic. More exactly, its object has been to consider what happens when the question of gender is posed in respect to the church's social doctrine: what does this tradition do to and for women?

354

One must here conclude that while Catholic social teaching aims to be inclusive, it is not yet able to address the social experience of contemporary women in a satisfactory way. As I have attempted to show, this inability rests squarely on a failure to make explicit and reflect upon the content and parameters of a presupposition basic to western cultural understanding, namely that human experience is organized and structured on the basis of the two categories, public and private. Implicit to this classic construal of the private is a defective view of woman's nature that rather seriously qualifies those more positive statements made about the person's public rights and responsibilities. The sad irony is that this methodological failure appears to put the church in a position of actually impeding the progress of women, certainly as far promoting her freedom and autonomy as a public actor, a participation recognized to be so vital to her dignity and well-being. Then too there is a failure to recognize that women's experience itself proves worthy of moral scrutiny and evaluation, that it also represents a rich source of moral wisdom needing to be plumbed and interpreted.

At this point, one must judge that until such time as the magisterium is willing to see the true merit of the critique offered by the church's feminist scholars and theologians, it will be able to offer but an incomplete social analysis, a compromised ethic.

For the Catholic feminist theologian, the church's social tradition raises one last troubling question. Because of the latter's uncritical suppositions about women, their nature, can it be said then that this tradition views women to be capable of of acting as subjects of its teaching, to be its implementers, its agents? Or, is the most that women can hope is that their reality will at some point be made the specific object of this doctrine's attention and concern?

One presumes that the church's teaching on social matters is addressed to the entire church, i.e., to all of those baptized and in receipt of the Spirit and its grace. Yet on the basis of the understandings of public/private examined here, such very much suggests that even grace cannot overcome woman's nature, that ultimately and inevitably it is this that legislates her full meaning, her public duties and responsibilities.

But what then, for Christian women, Catholic women, is the meaning, the power, the very benefit of God's gracious favor?

ENDNOTES

1. A good summary article and critique of feminist epistemology can be found in Kenneth F. Gergen, "Feminist Critique of Science and the Challenge of Social Epistemology," in *Feminist Thought and the Structure of Knowledge*, ed. Mary McCanney Gergen (New York: New York University Press, 1988), pp. 27-48.

2. Elizabeth Gross, "What is Feminist Theory?" in *Feminist Challenges: Social and Political Theory*, ed. Carol Pateman (Boston: Northeastern University Press, 1986), p. 191.

3. *Ibid.*

4. Feminist historian Joan Kelly has argued that the history of women in no way coincides with that of men. Her research showed that during those periods of "so-called progressive change," "what emerges is a fairly regular pattern of relative loss of status for women." See her *Women, History and Theory* (Chicago: University of Chicago Press, 1984), p. 2.

5. Gross, p. 198.

6. One early articulation of the feminist thesis is to be found in Ch. 2 of Kate Millett's *Sexual Politics* (New York: Ballantine Books, 1978). Here the argument is presented that western social and cultural life has been organized—but especially the way human relationships have been structured and institutionalized—on the basis of patriarchy. This is a social system whereby males exercise dominance over women and children and hold power in all the significant institutions of the community's life.

7. Thus the Catholic feminist concern for inclusive language in liturgy, in interpreting scriture. This indispensable role of language is a thesis key to the sociology of knowledge. See Peter

356

Berger and Thomas Luckmann's *The Social Construction of Reality* (New York: Doubleday and Co., 1967), pp. 34-46.

8. Gross, p. 200.

9. Sandra Harding, "Is There a Feminist Method?" in *Feminism and Methodology*, ed. Sandra Harding (Bloomington: Indiana University Press, 1987), p. 6.

10. Gross, p. 199.

11. *Ibid.*, p. 201.

12. *Ibid.*

13. Gender analysis includes the examination of "class, property relations, change in modes of production and the relations between the domestic and public order." See Anne Carr, *Transforming Grace: Christian Tradition and Women's Experience* (New York: Harper and Row, 1988), pp. 81-2.

14. Andrea Lee, I.H.M. and Amata Miller, I.H.M., "Feminist Themes and *Laborem excercens*" in *Readings in Moral Theology No. 5: Official Catholic Social Teaching*, ed. Charles E. Curran and Richard A. McCormick, S.J. (New York: Paulist Press, 1986), p. 418.

15. Sandra M. Schneiders *Beyond Patching: Faith and Feminism in the Catholic Church* (Mahwah, N.J.: Paulist Press, 1991), p. 15.

16. Christine Gudorf, *Catholic Social Teaching on Liberation Themes* (Washington: Univ. Press of America, 1981), p. 255.

17.   Jean-Yves Calvez, S.J. defines Catholic social teaching as "the pronouncements of the official hierarchy of the Roman Catholic church in the social field (for example, the family, government, peace and war, the economy). . .[it includes all that written or spoken] in relation to social, economic, and political life." See his "Economic Policy Issues in Roman Catholic Social Teaching: An International Perspective," in *The Catholic Challenge to the American Economy*, ed. Thomas Gannon, S.J.,(New York; Macmillan, 1987), pp. 15-16.

18.   Jean Bethke Elshtain, *Public Man, Private Woman: Women in Social and Political Thought* (Princeton: Princeton University Press, 1981), p. xii.

19.   *Ibid.*, p. 4.

20.   *Ibid.*, p. 8.

21.   *Ibid.*, p. 5.

22.   *Ibid.*, pp. 11-12.

23.   In *Immortale Dei* Leo 13th reflects a commonly held view in the statement, "the authority of the husband is conformed to the pattern afforded by the authority of God." See *The Church Speaks to the Modern World: The Social Teachings of Leo XIII* (Garden City, NY: Image Books, 1954), p. 169.

24.   Elshtain, p. xv.

25.   Leslie Griffin, "Women in Religious Congregations and Politics," *Theological Studies* 49 (1988): 432.

26.   *Pacem in terris* nos. 8-21, 26-27 in *Seven Great Encyclicals*, ed. William Gibbons, S.J. (Glen Rock, N.J.: Paulist Press, 1963), p. 293; see also *Gaudium et spes* nos. 60, 68, 75 in *The Documents*

of Vatican II, ed. Walter Abbott, S.J. (New York: America Press, 1966), pp. 266; 276-77; 285-87.

27. *Populorum progressio* no. 14, in *The Gospel of Peace and Justice: Catholic Social Teaching Since Pope John*, ed. Joseph Gremillion (Maryknoll, NY: Orbis Books, 1976).

28. John Paul II, *Sollicitudo rei socialis* no. 31, *Origins* 17 no. 38 (March 3, 1988), p. 651.

29. John Paul II, *Centisimus Annus* #43, in *Origins* 21, no. 1 (May 16, 1991): 17.

30. Leo XIII, *Rerum novarum* no. 33 in Gibbons, p. 20.

31. *AAS* 37 (1945): 287; cited by Gudorf, pp. 273-74.

32. *AAS* 53 (1961): 611; cited by Gudorf, p. 304.

33. See *Laborem excercens* no.19 (Washington,D.C.: United States Catholic Conference, 1981), pp. 43-45.

34. *Familiaris consortio* no. 23 (Washington,D.C.: United States Catholic Conference, 1981), p. 21.

35. *AAS* 22 (1930): 70; cited by Gudorf, pp. 265-66.

36. *AAS* 37 (1945): 291-292; cited by Gudorf, pp. 290-91.

37. *A tutti*, Dec. 8, 1974, *Osservatore Romano*, Dec. 20, 1974; cited by Gudorf, p. 318.

38. *Casti connubi* (Washington,.D.C.: National Catholic Welfare Conference, 1969), pp. 25-26.

39. *Ibid.*

40. *AAS* 63 (1971): 410-11; cited by Gudorf, p. 315.

41. *Christifideles laici* no. 51, *Origins* 18 no. 35 (February 9, 1989): 586.

42. *Mulieris dignitatem* no. 10, *Origins* 18, no.7 (October 6, 1988), p. 269.

43. *The World's Women 1970-1990: Trends and Statisics*, Social Statistics and Indicators Series K, no. 8, New York, 1991.

44. *Ibid.*, p. 1.

45. *Ibid.*

46. *Ibid.*, p. 5.

47. *Ibid.*, p. 4.

48. Maria Riley, OP and Nancy Sylvester, IHM *Trouble and Beauty: Women Encounter Cathlic Social Teaching* (Washington, D.C.: Center of Concern Publication, 1991), p. 3.

49. *Ibid.*

50. See *Trends*, pps. 4-6, 89-91.

51. Rae Lesser Blumberg, "Toward a Feminist Theory of Development," in *Feminism and Sociological Theory* ed. Ruth Wallace (Newbury Park, CA: SAGE Publications, Inc., 1989), p. 189.

52. *Trends*, p. 2.

53. *Pacem in terris* nos. 80-81 in Gibbons, p. 307.

54. Elshtain, p. 5.

55. *Ibid.*, p. 4.

56. *Lumen gentium* no. 10 in Abbott, p. 27.

57. Cited by Griffin, p. 417.

58. Yves Congar, *Lay People in the Church* (Westminster, Md.: Christian Classics, Inc., 1985), pp. 9, 12.

59. *Ibid.*, p. 8. Congar points out here that over time, the original division of the church into lay, cleric and monk was reduced to two, "by a process of assimilation of clerics to monks and of monks to clerics" resulting in the double division of the community "into men of religion and men of the world." (p. 9.)

60. Richard Gula, *Reason Informed by Faith* (Mahwah, N.J.: Paulist Press, 1989), p. 237.

61. Richard McCormick, "The Consistent Ethic of Life: Is There an Historical Soft Underbelly?" in *The Consistent of Ethic of Life*, ed. Thomas G. Fuechtmann (Kansas City: Sheed and Ward, 1988), p. 103.

62. Mary D. Pellauer, "Moral Callousness and Moral Sensitivity" in *Women's Consciousness, Women's Conscience*, ed. by Barbara Hilkert Andolsen, Christine Gudorf, Mary D. Pellauer (Minneapolis: Winston Press, 1985), p. 33.

63. See Ada Maria Isasi-Diaz "Toward an Understanding of Feminismo Hispano in the U.S.A.," in *Women's Consciousness*, pp. 51-61.

64. Barbara Hilkert Andolsen, "A Woman's Work is Never Done," in *Women's Consciousness*, p. 13.

65. *Ibid.*, p. 3.

66. *Ibid.*, p. 15.

67. Marilyn Friedman, "Feminism and Modern Friendship: Dislocating the Community," *Ethics* 99 (1989): 277.

68. *Ibid.*

69. *Ibid.*

70. *Ibid.*, p. 285.

71. Rosemary Curran Barciauskas and Debra Hull "Other Women's Daughter's: Integrative Feminism, Public Spirituality," *Cross Currents* 37 (1988):45.

72. Andolesen, p. 16.

73. Barciauskas and Hull, p. 40.

74. Elshtain, p. 327.

75. Barciauskas and Hull, p. 47.

76. Lisa Sowle Cahill, "Notes on Moral Theology," *Theological Studies* 59 (1990): 61.

77. *Ibid.*

78. See the important discussion in Margaret Farley, "Feminist Theology and Bioethics," in *Women's Consciousness*, pp. 297-305.

79. Maria Riley, "*Sollicitudo's Blind Spots*" in *Center Focus* 89 (1989): 2.

80. *Ibid.*

81. *Ibid.*

82. *Trends*, pp. 3-4.

83. Her argument is presented in *In a Different Voice* (Cambirdge, Mass.: Harvard University Press, 1982).

84. Carol Gilligan, "Mapping the Moral Domain: New Images of Self in Relationship," *Cross Currents* 38 (1989): 55.

85. *Ibid.*, p. 56.

86. *Ibid.*, p. 54.

87. *Ibid.*, p. 61.

88. *Ibid.*

89. This thesis is argued in *Dives in misericordia, Origins* 10, no. 26 (Dec. 11, 1980) 413-14, nos. 141-48.

90. Christine Gudorf, "Parenting, Mutual Love and Sacrifice," in *Women's Consciousness*, ed. Andolsen *et al*, p. 183.

91. *Ibid.*, pp. 186-87.

92. Cass R. Sunstein, "Introduction: Notes on Feminist Political Thought," *Ethics* 99 (1989): 223.

93. For a good discussion of how this issue even divides feminists, see Lise Vogel, "Debating Difference: Feminism, Pregnancy, and the Workplace," *Feminist Studies* 16 (1990): 9-32.

Rerum novarum and its Critics on Social and Sexual Hierarchies

Barbara E. Wall

In celebration of the centennial anniversary of Pope Leo XIII's *Rerum novarum* this paper attempts to focus on the possibilities for dialogue between Pope Leo XIII, Karl Marx and contemporary feminists.[1] The dialogue with Marx concerns issues of the social hierarchy of class, the meaning of class in the medieval world and the modern state, the function of property in forming social classes, class conflict, and an examination of the conditions that would enable the flourishing of all persons and the creation of a more just, peaceful and responsible human community. The dialogue with contemporary feminists concerns the dilemmas of sexual hierarchy, a public/private hierarchy and an anthropology that might more adequately address the reality of productive labor for women and men in the modern world.

The turbulent changes and revolutions enacted at the end of the nineteenth century alarmed Pope Leo XIII, especially the revolutionary rhetoric of "class struggle" uttered by the socialists of his day. The first part of this paper attempts to contrast a concept of class that is central to the social theory of Leo, that sharply diverges from the socialists and Karl Marx. It is my contention that the concept of class that Leo uses is a product of a medieval world view and the concept of class articulated by Marx is a product of the modern state. In *Rerum novarum*, Leo articulates a concept of human nature and human dignity that is founded on natural law philosophy and a theology of Redemption—a theology that believes in reconciliation of the human community that transcends the immediate, temporal conflicts. Karl Marx offers a view of the human community that is grounded in an understanding that extant social structures preclude the flourishing of the human community and any attainment of the elimination of conflict is a product of transformed social structures. Both thinkers articulate a vision of society as a community but the foundation of their respective world views are dramatically different.

In the second part of the paper, I will address a concern of contemporary feminists regarding an understanding of human nature that assigns a "proper role" to women and the work they perform. When Catholic Social Teaching addresses the meaning of work, it focusses on the nature of the human person. What we find in Catholic Social Teaching, beginning with *Rerum novarum*, is a dualistic anthropology in which the nature of woman is distinct from man as evidenced in the kind of work each ought to perform. The dualistic anthropology of *Rerum novarum* is a product of a sexual hierarchy in Catholic Social Teaching.

In 1991, we celebrate one hundred years of Catholic social thought with the anniversary of *Rerum novarum*. The emergence of Catholic thought occurred at a time that historical change was much in evidence due to the rising revolution of capitalism. At this time, there was also the emergence of welfare states and the greater demands for universal suffrage which took place in Europe and in the United States.[2] The rise of capitalism brought many new problems to the fore. The meaning of work was changing rapidly from the craft guild model to the factory model. Industrialization brought a division between the agrarian worker and the urban worker as well as a change in the conditions of work with the introduction of the factory system. People worked in factories for wages predicated not so much on the quality of their work as on the quantity of time. For Marx, this revolution in the workplace was an instrument of levelling all workers to the same, exploitative level. No longer were people hired for their unique ability but solely for their time. A division of the public and private realms of work assigned the proper role of men to the public sector and the proper role of women to the private sector. Women were restricted to the private sector as domestic workers who gave birth to children and raised them. In a century that called itself "modern," women had a very little recognized role to play. In Leo's thinking, women no longer were included in the world of men's labor.[3]

In the pre-industrial world nature was most important. People in agricultural settings had a relationship with nature that gave direction and order to their personal and public lives.[4] The prevailing understanding of the old order of nature as articulated in a Natural Law theory was a patriarchal and hierarchical world order which was well regulated. Prior to the sixteenth century, western philosophy and theology privileged a world view that understood that human life developed in an immediate, organic relationship with a natural world which was regulated by a social hierarchy that was understood to be natural and interconnected. People lived in communities that were interdependent and cooperative, forming an organic whole. The community had a far more privileged status than the individual. The peaceful functioning of the community was understood as a product of the right ordering of people and animals within a social hierarchy that afforded each social station a "proper role" and rights relative to one's status in the social hierarchy. Central to such an organic theory was an identification with nature as essential for the ordered fulfillment and satisfaction of human nature. People knew by birth what station in life was theirs by virtue of the class they were born into. There were few chances for social and economic ascendancy. There is a security and order found in the Old Order that was to change rapidly with the New Order of the Industrial Revolution, the introduction of a market economy and the formation of the modern state.

The introduction of a market economy brought much social upheaval as well as conflicts over the traditional meaning of work and the traditional patterns of work and family life. According to Marx, more and more workers were becoming dependent economically on the factory systems as "wage-slaves."[5] The emerging Industrial Revolution was identified with capitalism and a market economy. Capitalism was a social revolution created from the waning feudal system. Social class is no longer controlled solely by birth right as it was in the feudal world. Through capitalism, more and more people achieved social ascendancy, and hence political power, through the accumulation of wealth. Society was now divided into the working class which provided all the labor, and hence wealth and the upper class which was dependent on the labor of others. There were numerous "workingmen's movements" in Europe and the United States in the early 1830's which challenged the exploitation of the workers. Leo and Marx were only children at this time of ferment but they both attempted to deal with the problems of nineteenth century Europe. At the end of the nineteenth century there was increased social, economic and historical upheaval, and Leo XIII attempted to address the

366

need for stability and opposed groups who attacked the prevailing order of authority. He feared social and moral chaos.[6]

The political world view of Leo XIII was hierarchical—he thought that human dignity could best be defended in such terms. Leo XIII's most notable achievement was in providing an argument for the sacredness and dignity of all human beings. With succeeding encyclicals there is the emergence of a more comprehensive treatment of the rights of the human person—rights which provide more adequately for the actualization and flourishing of humanity. In *Rerum novarum*, Leo placed great emphasis on human dignity, especially on the importance of work as a vehicle for the fulfillment of human nature.

Leo XIII's theological argument for human flourishing invokes a hierarchial order of nature. Human dignity is founded on a natural order ordained by God wherein the human person is defined by reason and the ability to self regulate according to the divine order of things. A view of human community emerges that is organic in nature. Because all people possess an inherent, God given dignity, they are all equal.

> What stands out and excels in us, what makes man and distinguishes him generically from the brute, is the mind or reason... since man by his reason understands innumerable things, linking and combining the future with the present, and since he is master of his own actions, therefore, under the eternal law, and under the power of God most wisely ruling all things, he rules himself by the foresight of his own counsel...Whence it follows that dominion not only over the fruits of the earth but also over the earth itself ought to rest in man, since he sees that things necessary for the future are furnished him out of the produce of the earth... Rightly, therefore, the human race as a whole, moved in no wise by the dissenting opinions of a few, and observing

367

nature carefully, has found in the law of
nature itself the basics of the distribution of
goods, and, by the practice of all ages, has
consecrated private possession as something
best adapted to man's nature and to peaceful
and tranquil living together.[7]

Leo's view of human nature is predicated on the belief that divine
order and tranquility will prevail if all members of society fulfill their
duties to the community. Within Leo's world there are legitimate forms
of inequality in existence. It is this question of inequality which is most
problematic and crucial in Leo's response to the notion of class struggle.
There is an implicit acceptance of the whole world order that is
homogeneous and ordered to the same end—tranquility. On the one hand,
all people possess an inherent dignity as persons and yet, on the other
hand, each is unique in natural endowments.

Leo argues that differences between people are natural and in fact
do exist within society. "...that in civil society the lowest cannot be made
equal with the highest...neither the talents, nor the skill, not the health,
not the capacities of all are the same, and unequal fortune follows of itself
upon necessary inequality in respect to these endowments."[8]

According to Leo, classes emerge naturally within society and are
integral to the completion of the social whole. Classes, as Leo
understands them are not by nature hostile to one another but flow from
a hierarchically unfolding world order. Leo is one of many thinkers who
accepted the reality of social classes as rightful and legitimate
determinants of social power and responsibility.

The concept of class used by Leo XIII and Karl Marx was not a
univocal concept, but one grounded in changing historical realities.
Classes exist in society. Are classes the product of a natural, harmonious
unfolding of society *or* are they the product of unjust social structures?
According to Iris Marion Young, without a critique of class, "many
questions about what occurs in a society and why, who benefits and who
is harmed, will not be asked and our theories are liable to reaffirm and
reify the given social reality."[9]

The concept of *class* was a significant issue in the emerging political debate of the 19th century. Marx and Hegel viewed class in exactly opposite ways. While for Marx classes represent a division of labor that has to be overcome because class functions as an economic determination of the political sphere, for Hegel they stand for the integration of this regrettable yet necessary division into a meaningful whole. For Hegel, classes reflect the various stages of consciousness, just as do periods in history. For Hegel, belonging to a class links one to a universal, hierarchical order. Class distinctions, according to Hegel, should represent ability and not inherited privilege. Leo, too argues that differences rest on unequal endowments that are natural and not based on social privilege. There are two political world views operative in attempting to understand the concept of class used by Leo, Hegel and Marx.

Marx argues that the human person is essentially a conscious, social participant in her/his species, i.e., "species being." According to Marx, the actualization of one's potential to be an authentic human being is achieved through awareness of oneself as "species-being," i.e., a conscious participant of the community.

> The atomism into which civil society is driven by its political act results necessarily from the fact that the commonwealth (*das Gemeinwesen*), the communal being (*das kommunistische Wesen*), within which the individual exists, is (reduced to) civil society separated from the state, or in other words, that the political state is an abstraction of civil society.[10]

For Marx, the political person is grounded in the existent social relations which comprise modern society. The political state, according to Marx, is grounded in lived social relations. Hegel had established a dichotomy between the individual and the citizen, between civil society and the political state. Marx acknowledged the dichotomy, but he posited "species-being" as the basis for unity of private and public life. The

369

individual alone, in abstraction, does not exist; the individual person is always many persons, a generic being, so each person by nature effects a unity of private, particular interests and universal, communal interests. It is Marx's doctrine of communal being that is the foundation for his analysis of the factors within the state that preclude the realization of genuine, universal community.

The criticisms Marx raises regarding Hegel's treatment of political agencies of the state are derived from the influence of Feuerbach and have import within Marx's doctrine of property. In Marx's view the real subjects of the state are the people. Political activity ought to flow from the very social nature of the people; therefore, the activities and agencies of the state are self-determinations of a people, not external sources separated from the social qualities of people. Marx's criticism indicates that in Hegel's analysis of the state the individual is deprived of his true social quality and instead is the predicate of the state, which is none other than an abstraction of the real subject, i.e., the real individuals.

The institution of private property, according to Marx, has its effect on the realization of the human community. The point is that private property determines the will of the individual in relation to the state. The sphere of private property is an exclusive sphere which establishes an antithetical relation to the internal exigence of will to determine itself as concrete, rational, universal will. Hence, the very institution of private property dialectically frustrates the individual will from self-actualization as "species-being." Private property is an institution that perpetrates exclusivity, separation, and distinctness within civil society. It is private property that determines the social class of the individual. The concepts of private property and class are inextricably intertwined. In the modern state, class does not mediate a person's relationship to the community but establishes that person in an exclusive sphere dependent for its very existence on the establishment of other classes.

In the Middle Ages, precisely because civil society was political society, the classes of civil society in general and the political classes were identical. To be a member of a class is to be determined socially according to an external property criterion. The classes of the modern state differ from former times in that the individual member of the class is not regarded as a communal being but rather as an individual with an externally determined relationship to the rest of society. The member of a particular class is placed in a relationship of exclusivity with regard to other members of the community. Marx indicates that private property is the external determination of class membership. The members of the state who do not own private property form a lesser class of civil society.[12]

The community becomes fragmented and divided in the modern state. The classes of the modern state do not exist as an objectification of communal being (*Gemeinwesen*).[13]

During the French Revolution, according to Marx, a separation between the political classes and social classes was completed, whereby the distinctions of civil society were transformed by the French Revolution which attempted to bring about political equality among the people. Civil society became separated from the political realm. According to Marx, "Class in the medieval sense remained only within the bureaucracy itself, where civil and political positions are immediately identical. Over against this stands civil society as unofficial class."[14] In the modern state, civil society is merely an arbitrary and unorganized mass of people separated from the political sphere. The actual citizen finds herself/himself in a two-fold organization: the bureaucracy of the political state or official class which exists as an external, formal determination of civil society and the social sphere or civil society which constitutes the realm of private judgement and private, particular will.

Civil society is not a unified whole, but a fragmented association of separate classes and social positions. Due to criteria such as money and education, rather than need and labor as in the Medieval world, civil society as "unofficial class" has membership in each of the distinct social classes.[15] "Class in civil society has neither need—and therefore a natural impulse—nor politics for its principle. It is a division of the masses whose development is unstable and whose very structure is arbitrary and in no sense an organization."[16]

The major criticism Marx raises against the notion of social class is that as a determination of an individual, social class emerges as an external determination and not as an objective determination of the individual's communal being.[17] Class also implies a notion of inferiority and superiority. One must recognize that Marx's analysis of class was predicated on his desire for the creation of a real, ethical community, and that he understands class as an historical, social, political and economic category that externally identifies each person in the social hierarchy.

> The present social class already manifests a distinction from the former class of civil society by the fact that it does not, as was formerly the case, regard the individual as a communal individual, as a communal being (*ein Gemeinwesen*); rather, it is partly chance, partly labor, etc., of the individual which determines whether he remains in his class or not, a class which is, further, only an external determination of this individual; for he neither inheres in his work not does the class relate to him as an objective communal being organized according to firm laws and related firmly to him.[18]

In contrast, Leo calls for the reconciliation of the classes which exist in a kind of natural symmetry with the state functioning as the natural mediator. He states:

> It is a capital evil with respect to the question we are discussing to take for granted that the one class of society is of itself hostile to the other, as if nature had set rich and poor against each other to fight fiercely in implacable war. This is not so abhorrent to reason and truth that the exact opposite is true; for just as in the human body the different members harmonize with one another, whence arises that disposition of parts and proportion in the human figure rightly called symmetry, so likewise nature

372

has commanded in the case of the state that the two classes mentioned should agree harmoniously and should properly form equally balanced counterparts to each other. Each needs the other completely; neither capital can do without labor, nor labor without capital. Concord begets beauty and order in things. Conversely, from perpetual strife there must arise disorder accompanied by bestial cruelty. But for putting an end to conflict and for cutting away its very roots, there is wondrous and multiple power in Christian institutions.[19]

Leo's defense of a social hierarchy is not without confusion. The strife referred to as setting the "rich" against the "poor" can be overcome by Christian institutions. In another passage, Leo claims that the rich have responsibilities toward the poor in terms of justice.[20] However, there is a tension between the expectation of the "Christian" rich to self regulate with regard to treating the poor justly and the claim that the state has the responsibility to protect each class justly and to insure the "well-being of workers" who are in a vulnerable position within the social whole.[21]

Is Leo's view of the political reality an extremely naive one? Does it assume a natural ordering that does not allow for a critique of the structures that produce classes? Is it enough to merely address the issue of distribution or rather do we need to raise questions of justice that include the social hierarchy of labor and class? Contemporary socialists, such as Iris Marion Young claim "oppression and domination... should be the primary terms for conceptualizing injustice."[22] Marx and Leo would perhaps share similar objections to liberalism's demand for "laissez-faire" economics and political determinants as constitutive of the development of human nature in the liberal world view. Ironically, Leo and Marx both argue for a coherent theory of community. Can community be established in a society that is rigidly class stratified and predicated on the notion that some classes are "higher" or "superior" to others which are "lower" or "inferior?"

373

Essential to Leo's understanding of human nature was the right to ownership of property. "To own goods privately, as we saw above, is a right natural to man, and to exercise this right, especially in life in society, is not only lawful, but clearly necessary. It is lawful for man to own his own things. It is even necessary for human life. But if the question be asked: How ought man use his possessions? The church replies without hesitation: 'As to this point, man ought not regard external goods as his own, but as common so that, in fact, a person should readily share them when he sees others in need'."[23]

What Marx could dialog with Leo about in Catholic Social Teaching is the notion that ownership of property is essential for human fulfillment, security and preservation of life. The ownership of property as defined in Catholic Social Teaching is limited by the demands and needs of the human community. Catholic Social Teaching has always emphasized the preferential protection of the poor. The needs of the poor have a claim on the goods of the community. "In protecting the rights of private individuals, however, special consideration must be given to the weak and the poor." [24]

What Leo and other proponents of Catholic Social Teaching could dialog with Marx about is an understanding that private property in the modern state establishes a relationship of exclusivity between the owner and object owned and the community as a separate and distinct reality incapable of making legal, ethical or economic demands on exclusive and excessive accumulation of wealth by one or few people, hence affecting the balance of wealth and human flourishing for the whole human community. Leo and John Paul II would have to be willing to investigate the social hierarchy that is perhaps responsible for the emerging conflict between classes.

In *Centesimus annus*, Pope John Paul II comments on the passage from *Rerum novarum* that addresses class conflict claiming that Leo XIII did not condemn all conflict but conflict that is not restrained by "ethical or juridical considerations."[25] Pope John Paul's claim is directed at the Marxist state as he experienced it in the twentieth century. "Therefore class struggle in the Marxist sense and militarism have the same root, namely atheism and contempt for the human person, which place the principle of force above that of reason and law."[26] There is a definite gap between John Paul II's concept of "class struggle in the Marxist sense" and class struggle which, according to Marx, will be transcended by a "classless society."

Marx's concept of the classless society is an ethical demand for the reconciliation of the interests of private individual good and the common good. Marx's argument for the classless society is not an argument for the elimination of classes, but for the elimination of all property qualifications, class structure and societal fragmentation which exist as *external determinations*.

In Marx's later writings, especially "The Jewish Question," the *1844 Paris Economic and Philosophic Manuscripts, The German Ideology*, and others, one finds a more elaborated concept of the essence of community that the "classless society" represents.

> ...every revolutionary struggle is directed against a class which until then has been in power...In all revolutions up till now the mode of activity remained unchanged, and it was only a question of a different distribution of this activity, a new distribution of labor to other persons. But the communist revolution is directed against the preceding *mode* of activity, does away with *labor*, and abolishes the rule of all classes along with the classes themselves, because it is accomplished by the class which society no longer recognizes as a class and is itself the expression of the dissolution of all classes, nationalities, etc....For the production of this communist consciousness on a mass scale and for the success of the cause itself, the alteration of men on a mass scale is required. This can only take place in a practical movement in a *revolution*. A revolution is necessary, therefore, not only because the *ruling* class

375

> cannot be overthrown in any other way but also because the class *overthrowing* it can succeed only by revolution in getting rid of all the traditional muck and become capable of establishing society anew.[27]

More and more, Marx moved away from a purely political analysis to one which is more economic in essence. The essence of the new community will be the fact that the person controls the process of her/his self-creation and her/his relationship to nature, all of which is part of Marx's concept of work.

As in the contrast between Marx and Leo on social class and property, we find distinctions and differences regarding social hierarchy and how such changes affect their theories of human dignity and human flourishing, so too, one will find that the dialogue concerning the notion of human work between Catholic Social Teaching and contemporary feminists is affected by differences in a sexual hierarchy that affects the understanding of the natures of women and men and the work they are expected to perform within the human community.

In this part of the paper, the focus will be on the concept of a dualistic anthropology that is evident in the defining characteristics of human work as it applies differently to men and women. In *Rerum novarum*, Pope Leo XIII refers to women in the section of child labor where he briefly describes the nature of work for women. "Certain occupations likewise are less fitted for women, who are intended by nature for work of the home—work indeed which especially protects modesty in women and accord by nature with the education of children and the well-being of the family."[28]

Catholic social thought as it emerges in the nineteenth century identifies workers as men and women as non-workers. The fact that women were not considered workers is a centuries old dualism between the public and private sectors of society. This ancient dualism is in large part a product of biology: women give birth to children, therefore it is assumed that women are the *natural* care givers or child rearers. The role and "proper place of women" was in the private sector, the home. Such acceptance is a product of a philosophical anthropology that relegates labor as dignified work which has rights attached to it, to the public sphere, as the work of men.

It is with the Second Vatican Council that Catholic Social Thought begins to change dramatically. With the Second Vatican Council, the discussion of how the person might best achieve personal growth and self-actualization begins to shift from a focus on withdrawal of the individual from a world that is "tainted" to finding one's fulfillment in relationship to God to a focus on the world; the messy socio-economic world is not a "tainted place," but the place wherein all peoples could fulfill their needs to be human. The world view of the Second Vatican Council is one that is a product of a much more democratic world, there is less hierarchy, less emphasis on a fixed natural order, and greater stress on the changing historical world in which humankind has a creative role to play.[29]

It is in *Pacem in terris* that women are first mentioned as workers in the public sphere. In describing the characteristics of the sixties there is a definite attempt to understand and effect the changing historical situation.

> Today, therefore, workers all over the world refuse to be treated as if they were irrational objects without freedom, to be used at the arbitrary disposition of others. They insist that they be always regarded as men with a share in every sector of human society; in the social and economic sphere, in the fields of learning and culture, and in public life. Secondly, it is obvious to everyone that women are now taking a part in public life. Since women are becoming even more conscious of their human dignity, they will not tolerate being treated as mere material instruments, but demand rights befitting a human person both in domestic and in public life.[30]

The worker, whether woman or man, is never to be treated as an instrument or as an irrational object. The workers are moral ends in themselves. However, there is another element in the above quote that needs commentary. The worker, according to Catholic Social Thought has the right to be treated with human dignity and ought to have a voice in determining the social and economic spheres in the creation of history and culture. It is intrinsic to the fulfillment of human nature that the person work, i.e., that work is constitutive of human nature. Do we also understand by the above statement of John XXIII, that human dignity is a product of the worker's self creation and self determination in the public sphere? One wonders if women would ever have been singled out here if they had not entered the public work sphere.

One might ask: does working in the public sphere bring with it a fullness of human nature, and if women now begin to enter this sphere do they share the same possibilities for fulfillment? Is human nature for men and women the same? In the Vatican Council II document on the *Pastoral Constitution on the Church in the Modern World*, there is an articulation of the "essential equality of all men and social justice." In this document, we find that discrimination of any kind is inimical to human dignity and the flourishing of women and men in society. Women are singled out as victims of such discrimination.

> True, all men are not alike from the point of view of varying physical power and the diversity of intellectual and moral resources. Nevertheless, with respect to the fundamental rights of the person, every type of discrimination, whether social or cultural, whether based on sex, race, color, social condition, language, or religion, is to be overcome and eradicated as contrary to God's intent. For in truth, it must still be regretted that fundamental personal rights are not yet being universally honored. Such is the case of a woman who is denied the right and freedom to choose a husband, to embrace a state of life, or to acquire an education or cultural benefits equal to those recognized for men.[31]

It is in this document that women are referred to as having a "proper role in accordance with their own nature." On the one hand, the document states that the rights and duties attendant on men, i.e., those rights that flow from an understanding of human nature, are the same for women. On the other hand, women have a distinct and "proper role" from men. Is this "proper role" intrinsic or accidental to human nature? If the "proper role" is intrinsic to distinguishing one kind of nature from another, then we have a dual nature. In St. Thomas, women's nature was defined by the activities of reproduction and the care of domestic life.[32] The "proper role" of women seems to be that of reproduction and her "proper" place is in the home.

The American Catholic bishops addressed the status of women in the draft pastoral, *Partners in the Mystery of Redemption A Pastoral Response to Women's Concerns for Church and Society*, 1988. The pastoral reiterates the concern for women evidenced in *Pacem in terris* and *Gaudiem et spes* for rights and freedom from discrimination. The pastoral identified the sin of sexism as "the erroneous belief or conviction or attitude that one sex, female or male, is superior to the other in the very order of creation or by the very nature of things...sexism is amoral and social evil."[33] One major difficulty in this definition as it relates to women's lives is that sexism is treated solely as a personal act, and there is no structural analysis regarding the institutionalization of sexism and the inequality of women. The unequal status of women and the discrimination afforded women are not solely products of personal acts, but also reflect the structures that promote and enforce unequal status for women.[34] In Sandra Schneider's analysis of this pastoral she addresses the issue of sexism as endemic to patriarchy. "Patriarchy is the correct technical term for a social system, a way of organizing social reality, that is both based upon and enforcing of the ideology of sexism itself which is the source of the discrimination against and oppression of women which the bishops decry."[35] There is a definite gender ideology within Catholic social thought that is the product of the uncritical acceptance of a sexual hierarchy that is predicated on difference and inequality which needs to be subjected to critical reflection. The acceptance of a sexual hierarchy is the foundation of a gender ideology that speaks of the dignity and sacredness of all people while at the same time reifying systemic inequality and injustices. The doctrine on "complementarity" is the justification for sexual hierarchy.

The pastoral also reinforces the concerns of feminists when the issue of "women's proper role" is addressed and woman's difference from man is spoken of as "complementarity." It is held, in Catholic social thought that women have natures that complement men. Complementarity has frequently been used to justify the religious form of sex role stereotyping. Under the guise of divine will, or "natural law," women are

379

portrayed as dependent, submissive, maternal and naturally suited to secondary roles. A doctrine of complentarity provides a justification for an understanding and affirmation that one sex is superior to the other within sexual hierarchy. It is woman's difference that relegates her to secondary status. There is something flawed in this analysis.

Catholic social thought is caught on the issue of a dual human nature: one for men and one for women. Women's nature seems defined by her sexual identity, i.e., the biological capacity for reproduction. One would also have to ask, could any woman fulfill her individual nature without childbirth? If the defining characteristic of woman is biological reproduction, are those women who choose not to have children less human? To the extent that woman's nature is defined by her reproductive work and domestic work, her potential for full participation in public life and attainment of the full range of social and political rights attendant human nature are continually frustrated. It seems that Catholic social thought has not moved away from a paternalistic, hierarchical view of woman's nature, and hence support the inequality of women in theory and practice.

To identify the dignity and wholeness of the human person with the action of productive work that takes place in the public sphere is highly problematic for feminists. There is this tendency to identify human dignity with productive work both in Catholic social teaching and Marxist thought. The concept of labor assumes a privileged status in defining the human person. According to feminists such as Jane Flax, such conceptions lack an uncritical assessment of labor and production. Flax argues that the "fundamental cause of gender arrangements in the organization of production or the sexual division of labor" is significantly flawed because "labor is still seen as the essence of history and the human being. Such conceptions distort life in capitalist society and surely are not appropriate to all other cultures."[36] Identifying the proper role of women by the biological category of sex denies the lived reality that the relationships between women and men in society are *gendered* relationships. The fact that men work outside the home and that the proper role for women is inside the home is not a product of sex or biology but of gender. Such a gendered perspective on work and the human perspective is also reflective of the kind of gendered relationships that perpetuate the domination of women.

The liberal political theories that emphasize the separation of the family and the state were a product of the eighteenth and nineteenth centuries. Such a philosophical anthropology is rooted in the separate sphere of productive labor. Even in Karl Marx, there is present a notion of productive labor that is involved in the creation of an object that is bought and sold. Linda Nicholson provides and insightful analysis of the nineteenth century emergence of the overriding importance of acquired economic power and profit and its concomitant effect on minimizing the value of life activities such as those that take place in the private sphere, the home.

Relying on the analysis of Karl Polanyi, Nicholson states: We might qualify Polanyi's argument by saying that it is not all labor that becomes subordinate to the laws of the market when the economy becomes a market economy; domestic labor does not, at least in any simple sense …Indeed, when we think of what is pivotal about industrialization it is that the production of goods ceases being organized by kinship relations and an activity of the household. The creation of goods by members of the household for the purpose of use by the household and organized primarily in accordance with family roles becomes replaced by the creation of goods by members of many different households for the purpose of exchange and organized in accordance with the profit motive. The commodization of the elements of production means not only, as Polanyi notes, a withdrawal of control on the part of the state over these elements but also a

381

> withdrawal on the part of the family. When
> labor remained at home, its content and
> organization was primarily a family matter;
> when it left, only its consequences, wages,
> remained such.[37]

It is assumed that men labor for wages and that their income is primary, whereas women who work at home receive no wages, and those who do work outside the home are considered "secondary income earners" or "supplemental income earners," which justifies paying only men a "family wage"—long a justification for paying women less. In the pastoral, *Partners in the Mystery of Redemption*, we find some confusion—on the one hand the American Catholic bishops argue that "work needs an expanded definition to include those who care for their family at home" and where they state "our heritage teaches that women should be free to choose to work or not to work outside the home." On this point, Pope John Paul II urged that employers pay a 'family wage' so that mothers have the opportunity, if they so choose, to devote themselves exclusively to their families."[38]

There is no such provision or recommendation for men, and more significantly women seem to work outside the home only because of economic necessity. There is no adequate recognition that a woman's work in the public sphere, as well as in the private sphere, may in fact be a free choice—a choice that contributes to the flourishing of her nature.

Another significant issue that emerges here concerns the assumption that reproduction and child care are divorced from the meaning of productive labor. Such dualism is appropriate and constitutive of the "role and ideology of the family in an industrial society."[39] It seems that Catholic social thought also reflects the ideology of an industrialized world view.

Another assumption that feminists question is the necessary identification of the child bearer which is a biological act with child rearing and nurturing which by culture and custom are associated with women. Child care is more a product of gendered relationships than of biology. One consequence of such an assumption is that men who have the capacity to care for and nurture children are told this is not their

382

"proper role." If nurturing and caring are not the proper role for men we are perhaps also saying that nurturing and caring are not normative behavior for humans.

Liberation for women within Catholic Social Thought must begin with a reevaluation of the nature of the human person. Feminists, defined as those who seek to end the subordination of women, are most concerned with the notion of human nature and the rejection of a dualistic conception of human nature. One argument is that women are identified by their biology and relegated to the domestic sphere. If the public sphere is identified with the work of men, and this work is normative for human nature, then by this very definition, the work of the private, domestic sphere is less than the norm and hence inferior to it, not just different from it, but inferior to it. A hierarchical view of human nature brings the consequence of two natures, one superior and one inferior. By this very definition the so-called noble work of child bearing and child rearing is not fully human. Any view of the two natures based on differences among humans serves as the ontological foundation for personal, social, economic and political domination. One must note that there is no analysis of race and its impact on understanding the meaning of human nature in Catholic Social Teaching. Gender ideology is inseparable from the ideologies of race and class in any systematic analysis.[40]

The nature of women as distinct from that of men is hierarchically defined by sex in Catholic Social Thought. Within a hierarchical definition of human nature, difference, whether biological or otherwise, is not celebrated but rather infers inferiority and superiority. It seems that the root of the problem is a flaw in our use of the meaning and nature of hierarchy. A hierarchical view of human nature has served to continue the subordination and domination of women. Social hierarchy and sexual hierarchy are serious problems for Catholic Social Teaching in our world today.

ENDNOTES

1.   Leo XIII. *Rerum novarum* (*On the Condition of the Working Classes*). The edition cited throughout is that of the Daughters of St. Paul, 1942. Hereafter *Rerum novarum* is referred to as *RN*.

2. Seth Koven, "'The Most Womanly of Woman's Duties': Maternalist Politics and the Emergence of Welfare States, 1880-1920." from *Gender and the Origins of Welfare States*, Seth Koven and Sonya Michel, eds. from Routledge. The term welfare states, Koven points out that the use of the term "is anachronistic for the pre-World War II period, but we have adopted it as a convenient shorthand" to refer "to public and statutory policies, programs, and institutions funded by and accountable to the state."

3. Carol Coston in "Women's Ways of Working," a paper prepared for the "100 Years of Catholic Social Thought Conference," held in San Francisco, June 1991, page 3, quotes Maria Montessori at an international women's congress in Berlin 1896: "I speak for the six million Italian women who work in factories and on farms as long as eighteen hours a day for pay that is often half of what men earn for the same work and sometimes even less."

4. Barbara Ehrenreich and Deidre English, *For Her Own Good: 150 Years of the Experts' Advice to Women* (NY: Doubleday), 1978, pp. 6-8, provides an analysis of the emerging, "masculinist world" of science and how it affected women in the nineteenth century. The authors refer to the Old Order (pre-Industrial) as *unitary*, *patriarchal* and *gynocentric*. By unitary is meant "life is not marked off into different 'spheres' or 'realms' of experience: 'work' and 'home,' 'public' and 'private,' 'sacred' and 'secular.'" "There is not yet an external 'economy' connecting the fortunes of the peasant with the decisions of a merchant in a remote city." Patriarchal refers to "authority over the family is rested in the elder males, or male...Under the rule of the father, women have co complex choices to make, no questions as to their nature or destiny: the rule is simply obedience." Gynocentric refers to "the skills and work of women are indispensable to survival. Woman is always subordinate; but she is far from being a helpless dependent...It was only women's productive skills which gave her importance in the Old Order. She knew the herbs that healed, the songs to soothe a feverish child, the precautions to be taken during pregnancy."

5.   Karl Marx, *The Economic and Philosophic Manuscripts of 1844* as cited in *The Marx-Engels Reader*, edited by Robert C. Tucker, 1978 edition, pp.70 ff. where Marx addresses the notion of estranged labor: p.73 "Thus in this double aspect the worker becomes a slave of his object, first, in that he receives an *object of labor*, i.e., in that he receives *work*; and secondly, in that he receives *means of subsistence*. Therefore, it enables him to exist, first, as a *worker*; and, second, as a *physical subject*. The extremity of this bondage is that it is only as a *worker* that he continues to maintain himself as a *physical subject*, and that it is only as a *physical subject* that he is a *worker*." *The Marx-Engels Reader* hereafter referred to as *MER*.

6.   *RN*, #5-6. Arthur McGovern, *Marxism: An American Christian Perspective*, (Maryknoll: Orbis Bks.), 1980, pp. 92-99 stresses the world upheaval that surrounded and church wanted to return to the monarchy and clashed with the French Republic over education, religious orders, and marriage. The German Church was still locked in battle with Bismarck and his *Kulturkampf*, and divided internally by the defection of Dollinger and the Old Catholics. In Italy, the recent loss of the Papal States was a festering wound, and Pope Leo would make efforts throughout his papacy to win them back."

7.   *RN*, #11, 12, 17.

8.   *RN*, #26.

9.   Iris Marion Young, *Justice and the Politics of Difference* (Princeton University Press, 1990), p.5.

10. *MER*, pp.31-2.

11. Marx defines the notion of private property in *On the Jewish Question*, *MER*, p.42: "The right to enjoy one's fortune and to dispose of it as one will; without regard for other men and independently of society. It is the right of self-interest. This individual liberty, and its application, form the basis of civil society. It leads every man to see in other men, not the *realization*, but rather the *limitation* of his own liberty. It declares above all the right to 'enjoy and to dispose *as one will*, one's

goods and revenues, the fruits of one's work and industry.' Marx understands private property as anti-thetical to a notion of community because of its claim to *exclusive* ownership of property."

12. Karl Marx, *Critique of Hegel's 'Philosophy of Right,'* (Cambridge University Press, 1970), translated by Joseph J. O'Malley, hereafter referred to as *Critique*, p.81.

13. *Ibid.*

14. *Ibid.*, p.80.

15. *Ibid.*, p.80.

16. *Ibid.*, p.81.

17. *Ibid.*, p.21. See John Maguire, *Marx's Paris Writings: an Analysis* (New York: Harper and Row Pub., Inc., 1973), p.37. Maguire asserts that "Marx is pushed to the analysis of the class structure because he believes it to be impossible to create a real community, a real universality of man, within the existing structure of society. Were we to assume that he started off with a theory of classes, we might well overlook the central importance of the idea of community and universality which lies behind this latter day theory." Maguire's treatment mentions the major problems Marx dealt with in the *Critique*, p.7, but does not cover the whole work in any depth. What this chapter adds to Maguire's analysis of classes in *Marx's Paris Writings* is the intellectual, logical foundation for such a theory of classes that Marx dealt with in the *Critique*.

18. *Ibid.*, p.81.

19. *RN*, #28.

20. *RN*, #32.

21. *RN*, #48-9. I am grateful to my colleague, William Werpehowski who makes this point more effectively in "Labor and Capitalism in Catholic Social Thought," *The New Dictionary of Catholic Social Thought*, edited by Judith Dwyer, forthcoming.

22. Young, p.9.

23. *RN*, #36.

24. *RN*, #54.

25. John Paul II, *Centesimus annus (On the Hundredth Anniversary of Rerum novarum*, May 1, 1991, NCCB publication, hereafter referred to as *CA*, #14.

26. *Ibid.*

27. *Writings of the Young Marx on Philosophy and Society*, edited by Easton and Guddat, (Anchor Books, 1967), *The German Ideology*, p.431; *MEGA* V, pp.27-8. In the classless society which was seen by Marx as the final phase of social development, the problem of bureaucracy is superceded together with that of the state. However, there is the transitional stage between the capitalist state and the completely classless society. Here there is still a state, the "class character" of which is defined by Marx as the "dictatorship of the proletariat." Marx was for a long time not clear about the political form which this dictatorship would take until he eventually thought he had found the answer in 1871 in the constitution of The Paris Commune which will be treated later in chapter six.

28. *RN*, #60.

29. *Pastoral Constitution on the Church in the Modern World*, from the Documents of Vatican II (Guild Press, 1966), pp.203-204, 261: "History itself speeds along on so rapid a course that an individual person can scarcely keep abreast of it. The destiny of the human community has become all of a piece, where once various groups of men had a kind of private history of their own. Thus, the human race has passed from a rather static concept of reality to a more dynamic, evolutionary one. In consequence, there has arisen a new series of problems, a series as important as can be, calling for new efforts of analysis and synthesis...Thus we are witnesses to the birth of new humanism, one in which man is defined first of all by his responsibilities toward his brothers and toward history."

30. *Pacem in terris* (Peace on Earth), #41; from *The Pastoral Constitution of the Church in the Modern World*, p.267, we find, "...women are now employed in almost every area of life. It is appropriate that they should be able to assume their full proper

role in accordance with their own nature. Everyone should acknowledge and favor the proper and necessary participation of women in cultural life."

31. *Pastoral Constitution on the Church in the Modern World*, pp.227-8. However, there seems to be concern over the changing relationships between women and men, especially as they reflect on family life. Cf. p.206. Maria Riley's *Transforming Feminism* (Sheed and Ward, 1989), pp.76-100 provides an excellent analysis of women in Catholic Social Thought that was most helpful to this author.

32. In Thomas Aquinas' view, woman's nature was defined by the activities of reproduction and the care of domestic life. cf. *Basic Writings of Saint Thomas Aquinas*, ed. by Anton Pegis (Random House, Inc., 1945) Questions 92-96.

33. *Partners in the Mystery of Redemption A Pastoral Response to Women's Concerns for Church and Society*, #39 (first draft)

34. The Center of Concern prepared quite thorough and systematic analysis of the second draft of the NCCB Pastoral Letter "One in Christ Jesus A Pastoral Response to the Concerns of Women for Church and Society." The twenty-one page document was submitted to NCCB Ad Hoc Committee.

35. Sandra M. Schneiders, "The Risk of Dialogue The U. S. Bishops and Women in Conversation," *The Journal for Peace and Justice Studies*, Vol. 2, No. 1, p. 58.

36. Jane Flax, "Postmodernism and Gender Relations in Feminist Theory," *Signs*, 1987, Vol. 12, No. 4, pp. 630-31.

37. Linda Nicholson, "Feminism and Marx Integrating Kinship with the Economic," *Feminism as Critique*, ed. by Seyla Benhabib and Drucilla Cornell (Univ. of Minnesota Press, 1987), pp. 22-23.

38. *Partners in the Mystery of Redemption*, #161.

39. Nicholson, p. 37.

40. Elizabeth V. Spelman's *Inessential Women Problems of Exclusion in Feminist Thought* (Beacon Press, 1988) p. 10 claims that there is a paradoxical problem in feminist theory when there is no mention of differences among women.

Theology After Modernity: Divinity, Difference and Social Justice

Phillip Blond

The interpretation of our contemporary spiritual, philosophical and moral situation as 'post-modern' is as controversial as it is pertinent. Pertinent, because this form of critique claims an unprecedented engagement with the contemporary loss of foundation and value; controversial, because critics decry its orientation as relativist and ultimately nihilistic and demand the reinstatement of self-certain truth and foundation. By the terms of this opposition it seems we must be consigned to a choice between ideological assertion or nihilistic relativism: either way, the forces of competition and power run amok. In the face of global terror and murder, enacted by those who claim to know the good, we must ask again the question of social justice, the question of difference; and the philosophical and theological status of those who differ.

The relationship between God and the Good has been understood as one of identity and correspondence. The task of philosophy and theology, then, is to represent the blinding light of the most high, providing the necessary foundations for the construction of the heavenly city on earth. As such, the duty of those enlightened by divine correspondence is to unveil the real and thereby determine the correct ethical stance within it.

The claim made by those thinkers who are characterised as post-modern is that this structure, moving from "revelation" to "the real" to "the right" does not discover the universal truth of Being; on the contrary, it creates it. Post-Modernity, arguing for the relativity of conceptual schemes, maintains a radical ontology of heterogeneity and primordial flux, a nominalist epistemology without universal subjectivity and a consequent ethical demand for the respect of difference as absolutely different.

From this perspective the claim to truth is inseparable from power; and power, manifested via universal truth—claims that necessarily occlude and repress the otherness of the other. Such a philosophical position regards the very structures of cognition and meaning as always already imperialistic, searching for ideological consensus as to the real in order to mask the illegitimacy inherent within the structures of knowledge.

Consequently, those thinkers wishing to break out of the hegemony of metaphysics institute a double moment of critique. A noumenal ontology of a world innocently beyond our reach is proffered, yet it is always already handed over for cognitive violation by the epistemic subject. The task of the post-modern is to liberate the object from the subject and the subject from self-objectification by breaking the epistemic relation that licences the handing over of the alterity of the world to consciousness.

Representation and alterity

Lyotard locates the theoretical source of totalitarianism in the epistemic model of knowledge as representation. This model of representation reduces the alterity of the other to what is meaningful for the structures of consciousness, hence the real becomes what is representable by that consciousness and the absent object drops out of the equation of meaning. Thus, representation mirrors capital's law of exchange and is, for Lyotard, its cognitive prerequisite. Knowledge as colonialism extends the law of value to all objects translating them into a market economy by denying them any localised use value, commodifying them instead as items of universal exchange value.

Lyotard attempts to refuse this moment of sublimation and translation by approaching a quality of resistance internal to an object of consciousness; he locates this resistance in a mode of temporal presentation which refuses translation into the universal language of exchange.

If objects of consciousness are the creations of cognition then language becomes for Lyotard the fabric upon which the objectification of the world takes place. This world fabric as a manifestation of linguistic construction is a shared public creation. However, there is no transcendental access to the full intelligibility of the whole. On the

390

contrary, the only ascending orders of identities that exist are the rules and codes of horizontal fabrication, the crucial point being that these overlap and conflict, restitching what was manufactured only seconds before. Lyotard, turning to Wittgenstein, attempts to break with the latter's subtle positivism by utilizing notions of conflict and contingent linkage. This ontology of conflicting sentences, language games and phrase universes, will for Lyotard 'break the bonds of necessity' (PR1), that demand the synthesis of sentences into the univocal presentation of meaning.

Sentences, ontology & linkage

Though Lyotard seems to fracture an essentialist ontology by positing a multiplicity of incommensurable language games, he still appears to concede the epistemic primacy of the cognitive model of representation. Consequently, the philosophical issue is for Lyotard one of epistemology; operating under the sway of identity thinking, we do not appear to be able to see the world for what is—a plethora of different conceptual objects and possibilities. So Lyotard attempts to find an epistemic term that will correspond to his ontology, but one which will not be assimilable by representational cognition.

The epistemological structures of representational meaning foreclose on ontological plurality by clustering into self-referential sentence clouds (phrase universes) which unconsciously predetermine what meaning they will derive from the world. If this predetermination remains unconscious, then the repression of alternatives will not only go unchecked but such phrase clouds, propelled by the trajectory of meaning, will undergo self expansion and proceed unabated to colonise the future, destroying other alternative constellations of meaning.

Lyotard claims to halt and fracture this process through the temporal formulation of the event. The event is the pure happening of an alternative sentence that challenges the very system that seeks to appropriate it. The event through exposing its otherness to that system via the epistemic "now" of its manifestation, becomes an alien term that vanishes even as representation reaches out to commodify it. As a future event which displaces the framework of reference that experiences it, this event of resistance cannot be grounded; there is no site upon which it can be represented and make sense. The event as the moment of difference can only be experienced as a present passing—away. Re-presentation as the gathering of past present moments to form them as meaningful for consciousness cannot convert the 'it happens' of the event in to the 'what is happening' of cognition. Time is for Lyotard the structure which postpones knowledge; temporality playing the role of a dynamic a priori provides the groundless ground of resistance to foundationalism. This temporal event always evades representational cognition. Assigned a political and ethical role by Lyotard the event provides the epistemic verification that the link between singular units of meaning bearing sentences is contingent upon an acknowledgement that otherness exists.

The Idea of Justice in Lyotard's eyes entails reference to linkage possibilities other than the mode of linkage pre-determined by the situated subject and judgement as to the justice of any such linkage. Such a formulation demands an epistemic space within which the temporality of the event can be acknowledged as other, without being converted into a object of meaning for anothers phrasing. Lyotard, turning to Kant, attempts to locate this epistemic space in the aporia between determinate and indeterminate judgement, a situation crystalised for him by the theory of the Sublime.

Lyotard & Kant—the infinite and the sublime

Determinate judgement is understood by Lyotard as one which stresses the superiority of reason over sensibility, the hegemony of the legislating faculties over the dumb intuitions. Such sensible intuitions are inchoate and blind until framed with meaning by concepts, which though empty without them were always already prepared for them. Knowledge structured thus, disempowers the external world, forcing its self-division into phenomenological expression and noumenal repression.

For Lyotard, the Kantian sublime was conceived of as that aesthetic moment when the infinite, overwhelming the faculties of consciousness, engenders the pleasure and the pain that grounds the finite as a universal self-legislating subject. The pain consists in being overwhelmed, the pleasure in the ability of the faculties to still make sense of the experience. Kant's response to this sublime experience was to use its cognitive marginality to maintain the finite as self-subsistent; the faculties could still provide the grounds for self-legislation even when presented with the Idea of the Infinite, for this Idea performed the regulatory role that limited knowledge in order to ground it. The Kantian use of the infinite to ground and maintain the finite, represses finitude because it internalises the response to difference and claims that the access to such difference is only through immanence, perpetuating the adequacy of the faculties to the intuitions.

In order to disrupt this synthesis of sense impressions into knowledge by concepts, Lyotard turns away from the 'determinate' Kant of the First Critique to the 'undeterminate' Kant of the Third. Here Lyotard identifies a mode of judgement without concepts. He writes: 'The ability to judge does not hang upon the observance of criteria. The form that it will take in the last Critique is that of the imagination. An imagination that is constitutive. It is not only an ability to judge; it is a power to invent criteria' (JG 17). Lyotard seeking to articulate the meaning of a faculty which has broken out of synthesis, finds it in the imagination which constitutes the criteria by which it judges. This mode of judgement, meaning derived without preexisting criteria, forces knowledge to become experiential and experimental; the prime experience of which, is once again the event.

Lyotard, inverting Kant, utilises the notion of the sublime in order to break the epistemic link which maintains the adequacy of the Idea to the intuition. Instead of containing the finite, the sublime is constructed as that which fractures the control of the faculties and liberates the finite, exposing it to the exteriority of the infinite. An effect which generates for Lyotard the possibility Qf the avant garde, the perpetual exposure to the new without inevitably subjecting the new to repossession by the old.

Lyotard, by collapsing the distinction between a priori Idea and a posteriori intuition, allows the event to be experienced as both intuition and Idea. The coincidence of intuition and Idea, the experience of the future anterior, undermines the sovereign mediation of the faculties which sought to police the response to the ineffable. Each Idea is present within the sensible intuition which presents the event, each event changes the conception of just by bringing with it, its own Idea of Justice.

Lyotard interprets the Kantian conception of the Idea as a regulator, as refering to a supersensible world comprising a totality of reasonable beings. Against this Lyotard opposes the sensible world of multiplicity. The heterogeneity of language games will not be oppressed by the Idea of the transcendental unity of Justice. Rather, they will be guaranteed in their multiplicity via reference to the epistemic event, a term bringing with it its own ineffable Idea of Justice. This prescriptive process of judging on the margins, employs a practice of judging without criteria, without reference to an overarching principal or discourse of justice for 'each situation is singular' (JG 7), presenting within itself the means for its own judgement.

Associating Kant's Idea of justice with finality, a convergence from the particular to the general, the subsuming of difference in abjection to the moral law of the totality. Lyotard's move is to deny the necessity of convergence, claiming that the sensible and the transcendent present together in the event provides us with the necessary means for judgement. 'If we abandon this Idea of congruence and we put in its stead the idea of discrepancy' (JG 4) then the horizon of Justice for Lyotard becomes an ever expanding multiplicity of incommensurable language universes.

Having provided the epistemological ground for acknowledgement of alterity, Lyotard introduces the ethics which demand orientation to the justice of this recognition. This ethics becomes one of unveiling, of showing the event as different in order to deny it to synoptic vision, as a result the ethical attitude becomes one of epistemological respect. For both Kant and Lyotard, the particularity of the sublime experience leads us to a moral state where we have access through *respect* to an Idea of universality; which is for Kant a moral necessity leading to law and Lyotard a moral demand asking for justice. Lyotard's injunction remains one of witness and testament not universalisable judgement, 'to find, if not' what can legitimate judgement, then at least how to save the honour of thinking' and 'bear witness to the different'(D).

Lyotard and relativism

The claim often made against those who try and make difference a principle of socialised communities is that of relativism and political irresponsibility. However, the demand for judgement in the absence of representable criteria is not a commitment to relativism. Rather as Bill Readings writes, 'to recognize the non-representability of law is to refuse undifferentiated relativism, which is the insistence upon the plural representability of law (the law is anything you say it is)'(IL,1-5). There is a distinction between the relativist refusal to judge and those who judge, but do so without the criteria of the self-certain. Relativists respect all things so respect nothing; whilst those who respect difference, respect the differences between things, and act in the name of these differences for the Idea of a just multiplicity. Justice is not a norm the truth of which can be re-presented unchanging throughout history. If circumstances not only objectively alter cases but also demand new ways of judging, then justice always waits in the future, called to act beyond the theatre of representation.

Remaining within identity thinking

However, there remain from a theological perspective, totalitarian possibilities hidden in the epistemology of the event and the ontology of the differend. Possibilities which seem to re-inscribe modernism and Platonic dualism even as Lyotard claims to have exceeded them.

The advent of the event claims to exceed metaphysics through relying on the opposition of presence to absence; against the ossification of meaning past, we are given the promise of a future meaning present. But in order to create this opposition a covert violent hegemony must be established, a pre-sorting of the world into simple dualistic categories which then must be policed, in order to be exceeded by an epistemology of shock, a vicious cycle of permanent rupture.

We can recall the claim to ontological innocence and Lyotard's demand for a non-instrumental relation with the object of cognition. Lyotard constructs this innocence as the purity of genres, an a priori structure presented through the ineffable idea of justice. But if, 'the language game which speaks of games is itself a language game whose stakes lie in establishing the ground rules and strategies of such games'; (PR1, 3-4). Then, upon what basis can one judge the justice of this characterisation of the world? For the initial premises of Lyotard's argument relies upon naming individual language games or phrase universes which occupy legitimate ontological positions, describing the world as it is. The role of justice then is to police these pre-set genres ensuring that one genre does not afflict another or try and usurp its place and space. But on what grounds can we determine the world as belonging to one genre or another, claiming that disagreements within genres are not the subject of the differend but are merely litigations between members of the same family?

Does not the claim to have derived the essential preset categories of the world correspond to a totalitarian gesture of metaphysics? Lyotard assumes these categories are present to consciousness through the Idea of justice. However, as the presentation of this frame is never questioned, there remains the question of the justice of this multiplicity of essences, who names the multiple and for whom do they name it?

If the multiplicity of genres are maintained in their irreducible singularity through the universal prescriptive Idea. The Idea that has no grounds yet the one which provides the grounds for its own operation. Then it is through the universal Idea that the purity of the genre is safeguarded, consequently the Idea of justice becomes that of law. The Idea predetermines what shall be its subject ~ the preset categories of genre and universe and then proceeds to enforce what it brought into Being. The Idea constructed as the manifestation of the ineffable ontology of heterogeneity, becomes an overarching transcendental onto-theology, which creates alternative universes in order to disguise its own hegemonic position.

For if 'there is no outside, there is no place from which one could photograph the whole thing' (JG,43), then how would the language game of Justice recognise each and every game in its absolute singularity through the haze of multiplicity? How would such an Idea of justice if it did not have an a priori knowledge of the multiplicity, be able to place the borders of each game in order to police them? To assume this is to hold that there is a primordial state of nature where pure language singularity proliferates, this essence is however, only accessible through the Idea of justice which brings them into Being and predetermines their categories. If 'the idea of justice will consist in preserving the purity of each game' and if 'it intervenes in as much as these games are impure'. (JG,96). Then the pure will be imposed on the impure and Justice will impose singularity on that which is not 'naturally' singular.

Lyotard, occupying the legislative vacuum of the totality he displaced, is forced by the logics of the occupied space to reconstitute a transcendental horizon. The concept of a supersensible world which legislates for the sensible is re-inscribed, the only exception to Kant being that diversity is enforced rather than conformity. The idea of a super-sensible world of singular multiplicity functions as a legislator which precipitates out language games from their intertwining world and preordains their relationship with one another. Lyotard contaminated by the idea of purity, essentialises difference, by containing and controlling the tendency of language to subvert identity through excess and he reconstitutes this excess as a 'creative movement' which merely furthers the identity of each universe.

If the yardstick of the post-modern is a value based not on static reference but on experimentation, then experimentation without reference becomes a monistic value whose intensity can only be measured by virtue of its differentiation from the norm. The norm then still remains the centre of the pagan world however much the pagan tries to escape from it. Difference by virtue of this model falls back under the sway of identity thinking, an epistemology of shock and rupture that perpetually traumatises what it claims to save by constantly normalising what went before in order to exceed it again.

The pluralism Lyotard sought becomes the repressive tolerance of capital. Under the guise of the free market, the perpetual commodification of objects always demands further resistance; but this resistance by continually retreating into the future, gives away the past and ensures the succession of capital through the proliferation of constrhcted singularities. As Marx pointed out, capital always changes in order to remain the same.

Such singularities are forced to construct their identities through war and struggle. Lyotard, through the Idea of purity, ensures that inter-generic communication is deemed as violent, for without conflict there would be no establishment of specific properties and domains. As each game is only what it is by virtue of what it is not, only battle produces identity. As this critique constructs justice through a war of equals it ensures political conflict. While this escapes the totalising move of dialectical resolution, it does so by locking incommensurable discourses into permanent struggle.

The relation to otherness as one of frustrated domination only succeeds in freezing the desire for subjugation; the commitment to maintenance of this position requires exactly those totalitarian powers that Lyotard sought to undermine. Lyotards war of identity presupposes what it seeks to usurp, namely the desire to dominate.

After Post-modernity

If the claim to break with modernity only re-inscribes the vicious powers of identity thinking, then how are we left? Modernism born of parricide, announced the death of God and the birth of man. 'Man' as a redemptive horizon claimed the powers of the creator God he displaced; God as an absence in the human power structure which maintained that structure was named as reason and transcendence became immanent. This violent logic of origin asserts an original presence which enslaves all those who subscribe to an identity they cannot recapture. After modernity and the death of man, the structure of origin and original truth becomes displaced by the violent logic of supplementarity. Which, in the absent space of transcendental presence, pathologically supplants moments of identity by moments of identity, seeking liberation in the intensity of rupture and its perpetual succession.

The question remains though, can we stand astride this opposition, which does not constitute an alternative, rather than be inscribed within it? Perhaps the alternative can be found beyond the terrain of identity and its pre/post/modern, a loci which exists otherwise than identity opposition. To claim this would be to maintain that the opposition of identity to difference is not an opposition at all. Not least because the opposition remains secular, trapped within the field of the finite, demanding that transcendence be thought in terms of immanence, lest the site of the powerful be exceeded beyond recovery.

Modernity and Post-modernity fail when both remain trapped within identity thinking, a form of thinking that divides subject from object in order to reunite them again under its rule. The dualisms of God and man, transcendental and elemental are opened up by those who wish to claim unique access to the divine in order to legitimate their power and authority over others.

The only form of difference that can fracture this thought, is one which is transcendental to the opposition; a mode of transcendence which avoids both Kant who maintained the finite by internalising the infinite and

Hegel, who essentialised the infinite in order to repress the finite. A form of infinity otherwise than the oppositional terrain of the representational lifeworld is required.

Such a form of 'difference' has to maintain itself as a 'presentable' other to representational consciousness without falling into the polarities of secular thought. Emmanuel Levinas, rather than denying the finite the possibility of contact with the infinite, argues that the very mode of cognition which conceives of this as an impossibility must be rethought. The finite must be shown to contain within itself the cognitive capacity to understand what has always already been given to it, the infinite. But this mode of experience conceived as that which exceeds the borders of self-interested ego-ology, is not representable or even presentable to thematizing consciousness. On the contrary the realm of human experience IS opened wide, into a space which does not divide and conquer the world, where knowledge as domination is no longer the mode of contact the sensible has with us. The possibility of a phenomenology without foundations is ordained and opened up, for us.

Levinas determines this mode as a pure sensibility, the initial sensing prior even to the first presentation of this sense to consciousness. Levinas locates this mode of experiental knowledge at the initial level, the first sensing, the first impingement of the world on the sensing corporeality of the body's skin. The touch of alterity, of difference, reaches out to us in a state of caress.

Though refractory to consciousness, this mode of sense is experienced, representation is undercut by a presence which is much closer to home, a relationship Levinas terms as proximity. This mode of experience cannot objectify, it cannot deduce itself as subject let alone the other as object, in Levinas's terms it is pure passivity. The passivity of this relationship which refuses to instrumentalise what it touches, is felt by the whole corporeal body as vulnerability, obsession and primordial openness.

In a state of experience, 'where birth is not yet sealed up in identity' (FL,34) is where for Irigaray, the infinity of this difference presents itself to us. In a moment when both revealed and natural theology collide, we stand in a state of unconditional agape, in a state of Being other than objectification, subject to a perpetual phenomenology of love.

399

This experience of being overcut and underrun dissolves the intentional object and the structures of totalitarian cognition, mirroring the experience of the female mystics who burn darkly the looking glass of philosophy. But in this encounter with alterity, there is no moment of fusion, sublimation and domination. The encounter is with an infinity which by virtue of its alterity remains always separate, indistinct and other, demanding a different form of cognition from the subject.

A gap and scission is created in material ontology, the space of the transcendent. This space maintains itself within the bi-polarities of identity by leaving behind its trace, which though refractory to consciousness imbibes within the given. In this radical embodied phenomenology, the given of philosophy is indeed given. The divine as that which fractures oppositional identity becomes the third that cannot be captured by representation. The third through creation, creates a world of identity and difference, a site in respect of which it is absolutely different, giving to us however an experience of 'a profusion, an excess a giving which asks for no return'. This gift of the given opens us to an experience of pure passivity, undermines the intentional ego such that 'subjectivity becomes sensibility'(OB,77).

This space of ethical fracture within the structure of representation, represents an irreversible past that is by definition irrecoverable by the self. This anarchic past is the trace of the passage of an absolute being, the trace left in totality by the infinite. 'As he and third person it is somehow outside the distinction between Being and beings. Only a being that transcends the world can leave a trace. A trace is a presence of that which properly speaking has never been there, of what is always past" (TO,3). The infinite through its self-division and evacuation denies itself the violence of origin and enforces its own disappearance and banishment, in order to bequeath to its subjects the possibility of peace and non-violence.

The status of the self-erasure of the third cannot be over-estimated. As the circumscribing beyond of evacuation it is both anterior and posterior to the relationship of self and other. However, this would seem to repeat all the cardinal errors of the past, placing an essence behind the other investing the world of self and other with meaning? But this relationship is not linear, the diachronic alterity of the past through the

400

modes of touch and trace is present in all dimensions and recoverable by none. God is in this sense already in myself, but divided from itself, unknowable by both me and you, in order to give us both a non-violent future, together, without power and knowledge.

By this reading, that which recedes beyond us, requests only that we forgo its representation in order that it can remain with us. The trace on this account remains with us as the mark of an absolute being that gave the world to me and you, by giving it away and denying participation in it to itself. However, this act is remembered and remarked by its traces and its most intimate touches, bequeathing to subjectivity "the impossibility of escaping God who lies at the base of me as absolute passivity" (OB, 177).

The divine difference beyond the power play of identity and difference is the only site that can make difference different enough. This divinity different from presence and its representation is not accessible to those who want to claim adequation with it, in order to give their private fantasies and schizoid prejudices, transcendental verification. This is not a privatised God for men and in and against women, in favour of the power hierarchy of representation: family church and State. Rather, this is the a priori pre-condition of resistance to such institutions; only God can give us the grace of alterity by virtue of which we can stand together in a state of non-indifference against those who persecute the differing in the name of a God that was never present to them.

Footnotes

PR:- Jean-Francois Lyotard, 'Presentations', tr. K. McLaughlin, *Philosophy in France Today*, ed. A. Montefiore, Cambridge, Cambridge University Press, 1983, pp. 1 16-135.

JG:- Jean-Francois Lyotard, Jean-Loup Thebaud, *Au Juste*, Paris:Christian Bourgois, 1979, *Just Gamin*, tr. W.Godzich, Minneapolis: Minnesota University Press, Manchester University Press, 1986.

D:- Jean-Francois Lyotard, *The Differend: Phrases in Dispute* tr., G. Van Den Abbeele, Manchester: Manchester University Press, Minnesota University Press,1988.

IL:- Bill Readings, *Introducing Lyotard: Art and Politics*, London: Routledge, 1991.

FL:- Luce Irigaray, 'The Fecundity of the Caress', tr. Carolyn Burke, in *Face to Face with Levinas*, ed. Richard A. Cohen, Albany: State University of New York Press, 1986.

OB:- Emmanuel Levinas, *Otherwise than Being: or Beyond Essence*, tr., Alphonse Lingis, the Hague: Martinus Hijhoff, 1981.

TO:- Emmanuel Levinas, 'The Trace of the Other', *Deconstruction in Context*, ed., Mark C. Taylor, USA: University of Chicago Press, 1986, pp. 345-360

The Threat of Postmodernism in Christian Theology

Margaret Archer

It is a truism that theology has always tracked philosophy. It is equally the case that attempts to express Christian truths through pagan or secular philosophical frameworks have always been a prime source of heresy and heterodoxy. Nevertheless there has to be a relationship between theology and philosophy for the simple reason that any theological exercise has to make use of some philosophical concepts and categories. However, the reasons for particular relationships have changed greatly over two millenia, and the main shift has been from involuntary entanglement to voluntary adoption.

Since the good news came down to the patristics in the classical idiom, they were constrained to elucidate the faith in terms of the philosophical exponents of its categories. This did not mean uncritical endorsement, or that Greek philosophy was homogeneous, only that they were unavoidably enmeshed in its toils until the end of the scholastic period. The difference today is that while any theologian has need of philosophical tools, there is a choice of tool kits. When a wide selection is available, the question why theology tracks the latest trends in philosophy is a very different one.

Some, of course, evade the question by presenting the theologian, like other thinkers, as the products of that very philosophical ethos. This has the twin difficulties of already conceding everything to relativism and of presenting the latest trend as commanding a philosophical consensus which eliminated choice. Others answer by stipulating some kind of theological imperative to engage with contemporary thought at its sharp point, but engagement can mean confrontation rather than accommodation.

Over the last two decades a sense of ending has grown amongst the European Intelligentsia, symbolized by the widespread use of the word 'post' to define the world into which we are moving. Specifically we are held to be or becoming post-modern: 'modernity' is felt to be done for.

'Postmodernism,' as a school of thought, is now enjoying a vogue in Western Europe and North America and already there are theologians pronouncing themselves to be postmodernists. This leads to three questions: Firstly, what exactly is 'modernity' which is being repudiated? Secondly, why does its supposed demise supposedly open up a new future for religion? Thirdly, what are the philosophical terms of this new deal for religious belief? The bulk of this paper will concentrate on the last question and argue that the costs of this permissive Concordat are too high for Christian theology to pay. However we need to address the initial question to understand how it is that willing signatories are coming forward. Put more bluntly; why is any theologian attracted to postmodernism?

Those who talk about the 'modern' and the 'postmodern' are announcing an epochal Great Break between them, which calls for a definition of the two socio-cultural orders. Yet requests for periodization or characterization are evaded in real terms in favour of an idealist emphasis on the sense of the relational move away. 'Periodizing' itself is rejected as a classical or modern idea. Instead, to one of the leading proponents, Lyotard, "Postmodern" simply indicates a mood, or better a state of mind. Characterization of the 'modern' is thus relational to post-modernist discourse, which generates its own concept of 'modernity' and thus swings free from historical reality. Thus the modernity which is condemned is an undated, unplaced, undifferentiated, under-analysed and over-thematized image of a homogeneous entity dubbed the 'modern world.' 'Post-modernity' is that which comes next. Already confusion is rife.

Nevertheless the thematics are evocative and can have a very special resonance amongst Christians. For what the main French postmodernists (Derrida, Foucault, Baudrillard, Lyotard) are denouncing as the axial principle of 'modernity' is the 'Enlightenment Project', where scientific rationality was to invade all domains and the steady progress of positivism was to be the mark of human progress. Thus the goddess of supreme reason is being rejected as the virago of instrumental rationality. Here lies the great attraction. After all the term 'modernity' does have a heavy history as a thoroughly secular concept with thorough-going secularized dynamics. To Marx it was the time when 'all that is solid

404

melts into air, all that is holy is profaned,' under the dynamic of historical materialism. To Comte it was the epoch when the zero-sum relationship between religious metaphysics and positivistic rationality decisively favoured the latter, according to the law of three stages—one version of historical idealism.

In short, postmodernists denounce modernity which to them is the embodiment of secular scientific rationalism, therefore some theologians feel an elective affinity with opponents of their enemy. Matters of course are more complex. The enemy of one's enemy is not necessarily one's friend. Yet postmodernists can seem to be very friendly indeed—offering rehabilitation to those in need, a reprieve from the secularization scenario and a philosophical warranty of a place in the third millenium for Christianity.

Their attack was not confined to positivistic objectivity (the idea of hard facts 'out there' which could be grasped by our senses) but assaulted any philosophical notion that we could gain direct access to reality and denied any objectivity to our talk about it. As reality became increasingly fugitive to postmodernists, they drew parallels between it and *deus absconditus*, present only in his absence. In other words, as they denounced scientific method as the way to truth they explicitly aligned with what they saw as its methodological antithesis—mystical theology. Hence the assertion of Jacques Derrida that 'The detours, locutions and syntax in which I will often have to take recourse will resemble those of negative theology, even to the point of being indistinguishable.' So the dark way of unknowing seemed to have acquired a new philosophy and friends amongst the earlier postmodernists. Yet as the notion of there being any reality 'out there' was itself challenged by these thinkers, then the question of where associating with them had led surely merits theological reflection.

The full blown postmodernism of those like Baudrillard and Lyotard had yet to flower in the mid-seventies, but the trouble was that considerable confusion already reigned amongst those appropriating the term to characterize their thought, a confusion due to the vagueness of the concept of 'modernity.' This was particularly the case amongst theological adherents. Basically there were some who denounced 'the shambles of modern culture' and promptly labelled their call back to the

405

faith as 'postmodern,' on grounds of an optimistic chronology. This is the position, for example, of G. W. Rutler in *Beyond Modernity: Reflections of a Post-Modern Catholic*. Yet the cultural features of 'modernity' which he denigrates turn out to be precisely those which the postmodernists celebrate. On the other hand, there are those who have grasped Derrida's olive branch and whose preoccupation with 'how do we tell the Christian story in a postmodern, pluralistic world' makes them welcome that in contemporary culture which rehabilitates our narrative. This is the position of the editor of *Postmodern Theology: Christian Faith in a Pluralist World, Frederic Burnham*, who exults in the following: 'The cultural hegemony of science has ended. The fundamental characteristic of the new postmodern era is epistemological relativism. A plurality of tongues now claims human allegiance. Though the language of the Bible is just one of many tongues, Christians no longer need be defensive.' The only way out of this confusion seems to be a closer scrutiny of postmodernist thought to determine the philosophical terms of the Concordat for theology. This will be done under three headings—the views of postmodernists on reality, reason and humanity and their implications for Christianity.

Postmodern Ontology

Postmodernism represents an extreme version of a current trend in the philosophy of science which denies reality itself or that we can have any access to it. This is part of anti-foundationalism, a movement which tries to pull the rug from under philosophy's claim to say anything true about the real, by undermining both terms. There have been excellent ripostes by Roger Trigg, *Reality at Risk* and Roy Bhaskar, *Reclaiming Reality*, some of whose arguments will be used here.

The most extreme exponent of this view is Baudrillard who asserts that in present society (dominated by informatics), conceptions replace reality, reality is transformed into images, simulacra constitute and count as the real, so that in short, 'T.V. is the world.' This constitutes a denial of any reality beneath simulated experience and a rejection of any attempt to get below the surface of things to discover what is really going on. Hence his approving quotation from Nietzsche, 'Down with all hypotheses which have allowed belief in a true world.'

406

The thesis is self-undermining. Baudrillard has denied reality, yet his writing presupposes access to the real because he purports to be telling us something new about it. If we do live in a simulated world, then Baudrillard is trapped in it like the rest of us. So how can he reach outside it to characterize it as imagery and to discuss the transition from the real to the hyperreal? Consistently he cannot, so he is faced with the choice of either giving up his anti-realism in favour of 'belief in a true world,' or abandoning consistency. He takes the latter path by collapsing philosophy into literature, where the avoidance of contradiction is (said to be) subordinated to the primacy of aesthetic demands.

The pathway into aestheticism is shared by postmodernists and particularly by Derrida's influential 'textualism.' His version is less concerned to deny reality itself than to assert that it cannot be represented because we cannot have direct access to it. The assertion is based on his theory of language. While most of us hold no brief for the atomist theory of language which claims a straightforward correspondence between words and things, and most too accept that knowledge of things is theory-dependent (that there is no return to the doctrine of immaculate perception), we neither conclude that the nature of reality makes no difference to our observations nor that there are no means for saying that some theoretical languages capture reality better than others. Derrida goes to the opposite extreme and argues that language stands in no immediate, determinate or systematic relation to reality and yet everything comes to us mediated through linguistic 'discourse.'

Appropriately this view has been dubbed as 'textualism.' Our world is the world of texts and *il n'y a pas de hors texte* ('there is no outside-text'). This does not actually mean that there is 'nothing' (ontologically) outside the text. It states that just as the text makes no authoritative reference to 'what is,' neither does it stand in a symmetrical relationship to what is absent from it. Nevertheless, if textualism does not deny the existence of a reality outside discourse, it does deny our ability to know it. Consequently we are prisoners of a textualism whose discourse is denied any relationship to reality.

All of this is of considerable significance for science and religion. Since neither can make authoritative reference to 'what is,' even with the caveat 'to the best of our knowledge,' the cognitive content of their texts is denied. Both are reduced to rhetorical devices and we are enjoined to treat them as literary genres. Such aestheticism can only have appeal for those who simply endorse the Bible-as-great-literature (or 'Einstein makes good reading' for that matter). It stands in direct contradiction to Christian belief in at least four important respects:

Firstly, although some fundamentalists might covertly welcome this dethronement of science and reinstatement of Scripture on terms of equality, the terms themselves are unacceptable. In fact, scientists and Christians should be standing shoulder to shoulder repudiating what is a totally anthropocentric view of both science and religion. For by denying any access to a self-subsistent reality (nature or divine), our texts become exclusively dependent upon our thoughts. God and gravity suffer the same fate at postmodernist hands. Neither subsist outside of texts, which attempt to disclose them or are in any way regulated by them. Instead, both become man-made textual creations to all intents and purposes, for even if they are not we have no way of knowing it. Science then is the practice of scientific communities and religion the practice of religious communities only because different literary genres appeal to them and are produced by them. Secondly, the verb 'to believe' has been abolished in postmodernism. Since the test makes no authoritative reference to 'what is,' then to say that I believe in something which I hold to be non-authoritative, is a contradiction in terms. Fidelity is merely long lasting aesthetic satisfaction. It witnesses only to a powerful tradition of rhetoric. Since reality is inaccessible, no 'evidence' can ever supply grounds for faith or for disturbing it. Take, for example, new material which either substantiates or casts doubts on the Resurrection: claims by the authors to be eye witnesses and truth tellers go for nothing for they too are prisoners of discourse. All that could be forthcoming are new texts to be evaluated by their stylistic persuasiveness. The postmodern Christian would thus be someone who was agnostic about what, if anything, happened, but admits to being moved by stories about a God-man.

Thirdly, it might appear at first sight that those who interpret Scripture as mythical literature occupy a position which is compatible with textualism of the postmodern variety. Yet such thinkers generally assume that the myths are indeed saying something about reality—a reality different from that of their surface story, but still real and worth taking seriously. They thus want to make a move forbidden by Derrida of appealing to the concept of reference, this time not to the facts of the case or evidence about it, but to 'pure concepts' which are somehow transcendentally present to the consciousness without discursive mediation. However, in textualism the concept of 'evil,' for example, is treated in exactly the same way as 'evidence of evil doing.' Both are irremediably embedded in the telling but open to endless rhetorical revision in the retelling. There is no fixed point then to any Biblical story (they are not really about anything determinate) and we can only 'take them seriously' in the same sense that we take novels seriously—that is variably on their aesthetic merits.

Finally, because reference, representation and reality itself have been rendered problematic so has the very idea of being serious. Since we cannot make out reality and cannot know anything to be true, then the best we can do is to make 'art' and make it ironically. The postmodernist has to settle for producing superficial, shocking, arresting and incongruous effects spontaneously in obedience to their own veto on representation, truth or lasting meaning. Life in the ironic mode of postmodernism is impoverished in Christian terms—joy becomes impishness; contrition, flippancy; ecstasy, titillation; glory, glamour; faith, faddism; hope, nihilism and love degenerates into the most banal form of liking, taste.

Postmodernist Epistemology

In their discussion of knowledge and how we come by it, postmodernists add their voices to those philosophers who attack the idea that reason is indispensable for arriving at truth. To them rationality is far from benign: it is the servant of terrorism who comes disguised as the handmaid of truth. Indeed the main villain of 'modernity' was to them Enlightenment Rationality. Such rationality was universalistic—under-pinning the idea of universal science, fostering 'grand narratives' which explained social progress universally, and advancing reason itself as the universal goal of human development. All of this is condemned as 'totalizing,' that is riding roughshod over cultural diversity, pluralistic traditions and communal variations, for purposes of efficiency, domination and power. Hence they arrive at what is effectively the syllogism of postmodernism: totalizing efforts are terroristic/rationality is totalizing/therefore rationality is terrorism. (Not that any postmodernist would go in for syllogisms but they need their rhetorical equivalent to get from the Enlightenment to Auschwitz). This attack may have some appeal to theologians who see 'faith' and 'reason' as opposed and view reason as hostile to religious truth rather than necessary to it.

However, what postmodernists are doing is making capital out of conflating Rationality (as a goal or end-state) with reasoning (as a process or tool). I want to separate the two very clearly and to argue that reasoning is indeed indispensable to the statement, communication and justification of religious belief. The key point is that any linguistic communication whatsoever is based upon obedience to the laws of logic. Without the law of non-contradiction being observed nothing can be communicated, within a language or between languages, publicly or privately. If others cannot see that the truth excludes the truth of its denial, how could they ever communicate truths to one another and reason from them to other truths? The invariance of the law of contradiction, which is the touchstone of intelligibility itself, is a prioristic to language, and not optional, and therefore is universal and not conventional.

What the postmodernists are doing is to elide this transcultural reasoning with Enlightenment Rationality and to beat them both with the same stick. Yet what distinguished the Enlightenment was not 'reasoning'; for if this were an eighteenth century invention, on what did the scholastics, patristics and classical thinkers get by? It was atheism. Comte's vision and our nightmare of Positivistic Rationality as the summit of human progress—the Goddess of Supreme Reason with the Sociologist as High Priest.

On the contrary, reasoning is never a target, but a necessary condition of articulating one's own beliefs and finding those of others intelligible if unacceptable. Without it, religious commitment becomes a matter of irrationalism or social determinism. Those who settle for this automatically debar themselves from recommending their faith to others or justifying it to themselves. For if it is held arbitrarily, there are no reasons for adhering to it, and if it is socially determined, then one belief is caused in one group and other beliefs in other groups where different

410

social determinants are at work. In neither case can the question of justification arise.

Those who do not regard their commitment to Christianity as irrational or determined do accept that they have reasons (not proofs) for their beliefs. Confronted with non-Christians, they can discuss their reasons for their belief and what constitutes a good reason for making a commitment—an option closed to the irrationalist. Since we do indeed have a 'grand narrative' (Covenant history as the Narrative of narratives), it is the Christian irrationalist who could be tempted to universalize it 'terroristically,' since an arbitrary choice can only be extended to others by imposition. Those with reasons for their commitment will use them to recommend it and the same reasons justify the attempt at recommendation. We will doubtless find that our reasons are not compelling. Faith cannot be reduced to reason, but while faith does go beyond reason, it does not go against it.

By rejecting the universality of reasoning, thrown out with the bath-water of Enlightenment Rationality, the postmodernist immediately falls back on relativism. Thus to Lyotard, 'there is no reason, only reasons,' reasons which are not transculturally undergirded by common reasoning. Different communities, localities or 'forms of life' are playing their own language games governed by different criteria of reason and truth. But if cultural beliefs are fundamentally contextual and radically incommensurable, then all the arguments against relativism surface in full force. Basically these go as follows. Interpretation of the beliefs of others depends upon being able to identify them and understanding relies upon intercommunication about them. Both of these are predicated upon us all reasoning in much the same way, even though we reason about different things on the basis of different information. Since relativists deny this, we can neither understand the beliefs of others nor discuss ours with them; theirs cannot challenge ours and we cannot recommend ours to them.

Consequently, to Lyotard, 'all we can do is to gaze in wonderment at the diversity of discursive species,' respecting the permanent and irreducible cultural diversity manifested in different forms of life, communal traditions or language games. In gazing at such diversity of beliefs, postmodernism supposedly 'refines our sensitivity to difference

411

and reinforces our ability to tolerate the incommensurable.' It is a formula for mutual tolerance of what is mutually incomprehensible.

Confronted with this irreducible diversity, all we can do is to enrich our own 'game' through incorporating immediate experiences of other 'games' (superficial ones because there is no access to what they are really about) and we can only incorporate them aesthetically (since without common reason they must remain unintelligible). Hence, enrichment is not about communication but sensation, not about understanding the beliefs of others but about expressive reactions to the aesthetic form of that which is expressly not understood.

The accompanying tolerance is premised on the assumption that no particular language game is to be privileged, that none can be assessed as superior to others in any terms whatsoever since they lack common terms in which to do so. Yet here is the catch. Lyotard want to privilege precisely this plurality of language games itself. This is to assume a priori that all validity claims are on a par, that there are no true and false beliefs. Instead all beliefs are true to the communities which hold them. These are the terms on which postmodernism recognizes Christianity—it is perfectly welcome to remain part of the pluralistic array of truth contenders and the postmodernists pronounce their permissive blessing on the lot.

Postmodern Ethics

Theories of ethics have traditionally been founded upon a theory of human nature. What is good for humankind has been derived from the attributes essential to or in humanity, such as happiness, pleasure, or in Christianity—love. However, the postmodernists deny the unicity of human nature. They reject the notion that humankind has any fixed properties across time and space, whether this essence is conceived of metaphysically, biologically or sociologically. Because we participate in so many variegated language games and are formed by such diverse types of discourse, we cannot talk of humanity as one for all time, least of all now.

Because it affirms the superordinate status of culture over humankind, such that it makes, and remakes and unmakes what human beings are, there is a dangerous anti-humanism in postmodern thought.

412

Thus to Baudrillard, humanity becomes 'that spongy referent, that opaque but equally translucent nothingness,' whilst to Lyotard 'a self does not amount to much,' merely a nodal point through which multifarious cultural messages pass. Foucault is brutally clear: 'man would be erased, like a face drawn in sand at the edge of the sea,' given the cultural changes he has described, 'Man has come to an end.'

This notion is adopted wholesale by Richard Rorty who has been responsible for articulating a postmodern ethics from it. Instead of our having a coherent essence as particular people (an identity which we know as our true self) we are a compound of 'quasi persons' composed of 'incompatible systems of belief and desire' which are the product of 'a host of idiosyncratic, accidental episodes.' We have no stable core, no coherent personality, the self is 'centreless.' Anti-foundationalism in the ethical field rests on this denial of any essence to humankind and an aestheticization of ethics follows.

Strictly, this is not a logical derivation. If humanity lacks any unifying essence, this implies no determinate ethic for it and cannot therefore imply an aesthetic one. Yet as a recent commentator argues, 'it still may be said to lead to an aesthetics of taste, since in the absence of any intrinsic foundation to justify an ethic we may reasonably be encouraged to appeal to one that most appeals to us; and it is plausible to think that such an appeal is ultimately an aesthetic question, a question of what strikes us as most attractive or most perfect.' In this vein, Rorty explicitly advocates the 'aesthetic life' as the ethically good life.

Of course, to say that aesthetic considerations should have primacy in deciding how we lead our lives or defining what constitutes a good life, does not determine which aesthetic criteria we should adopt. Traditional and ascetic aesthetics make strong appeal to criteria of purity, harmony and restraint. But the postmodernists are too engrossed in their novel kaleidoscopic culture to consider such alternatives as other than already outmoded.

Consequently with no true self to discover, the good life becomes a project of 'self-creation' from the endless experiences, narratives and encounters which postmodernist culture offers. Ethics are private matters, motivated to Rorty by the 'desire to enlarge oneself,' through embracing 'more and more possibilities,' all of which is expressed in 'the aesthetic

413

search for novel experiences and novel language.' Making one's life work of art is the ethical injunction of all postmodernists, one rooted in Nietzsche's notion that men should invent themselves—in his *Ecce Homo* as man's own achievement. The first objection to this aesthetic ethic concerns its basic incoherence. How can there be a quest for 'self-enlargement' in the absence of a 'self' which integrates the welter of incoming fragments? Without a consistent identity, there is no self which is capable of self-enrichment. There is a basic contradiction involved in exhorting to 'self-enlargement' whilst denying that there is a self to enlarge. The only constant element is changeability, the inconstant adoption of novel self-descriptions and new subjective narrations taken up by the 'plurality of persons' who share the same proper name. This seems to be more of a formula for the fragmentation of the individual than for his or her creation.

The second difficulty is that if we abandon any foundationalist view of human nature and deny any unity to the self, then the individual personality can only be 'created' in terms of narratives from without. In consequence the project of 'self-creation,' presented in glowing hyperactive terms, turns out to be a rather passive and culturally dependent process. Moreover any unity and coherence that can be incorporated to constitute the self will rely exclusively upon the unity and coherence of the narratives available. Yet as was seen in the previous section, the narratives themselves are incommensurable: they lack common terms by which to integrate them, and through them, ourselves. The power of tradition to bind is broken and what is postmodern is the refusal to mourn. On the contrary, to Lyotard, the postmodernist celebrates our inability to experience reality as an ordered and integrated totality. But who can do the celebrating remains a mystery after this new fatality—the Death of the Self.

Thirdly, there are a range of moral objections, some of which would be voiced by Christian and humanist alike. The aestheticization of ethics in which the good becomes that which enriches me, is a license for self-indulgence. 'Self-creation' and 'self-enlargement,' in so far as sense can be attache to them, are the diametrical opposites of Christian 'self knowledge,' 'self purification' and 'self emptying.' Ethics becomes a private domain preoccupied with instant gratification. This might be capable of embracing the novel experience of liturgical glitter, but it could never prompt a desire to enlarge oneself through the sacrificial imitation of Christ. Self-creation is at bottom unredeemed selfishness.

It is a narcissistic project and Rorty's privatized morality confronts further problems when he appeals to social solidarity as something which can enhance the 'aesthetic life.' It supposedly does this because the personal narrative intertwines with other people's and is embedded in some larger narrative or tradition. The trouble with this is that we are all in the same boat. Where are the bastions of tradition if we are all frenetically sitting-in on as many language games as possible for enriched? How can we reach out in genuine solidarity with others without a unified self which will still pay the price when group welfare has no appeal? In what way can human relations be anything but fleeting contacts, in which 'quasi selves' gain momentary satisfaction, if there is no self firm and unified enough to commit itself to another? The desire to 'enlarge oneself' can only be at the expense of others who are reduced to being possible objects of self-enrichment, never subjects of concern.

The Death of God, of Reality, of Reason, of the Person is joined by the death of Concern. Baudrillard is quite willing to draw that conclusion: 'All that remains to be done is to play with the pieces. Playing with the pieces—that is postmodern.' But the pieces are human beings and there is a pernicious anti-humanism in this notion of playfulness. The Christian cannot be prepared to endorse an ethical system which the secular humanist would deplore. There is no way of blunting the antithesis between the 'Denial of Self' in postmodernism and the self-denial which is taking up the Cross.

CONCLUSION

To dislike and deplore many features prominent in 'modernity' should not precipitate Christians into an alliance with Postmodernism. The terms of the Postmodernist Concordat are unacceptable for the simple reason that 'Postmodernist Christianity' is a contradiction in terms. The anthropocentricism, relativism and anti-humanism of the postmodern philosophers are the direct antitheses of Christianity's Way, Truth and Life.

415

MAIN REFERENCES

J. Baudrillard, *Simulations*, New York, 1983.
J. Derrida, *Writing and Difference*, London, 1978.
M. Foucault, *The Order of Things*, London, 1970.
J-F. Lyotard, *The Postmodern Condition*, Minneapolis, 1984.
R. Rorty, Contingency, *Irony and Solidarity*, 1989.

A Modest Proposal:
Keep Holy the Sabbath

John G. Driscoll

The invitation to participate in this conference was resisted at first, and the resistance turned into intimidation when I studied the list of speakers that would participate and when I read the abstracts of their contributions. I knew I had nothing to offer on the subject of *Rerum novarum* that had any historical, technical, philosophical, or scholarly interest. My anguish was relieved, however, when (after a lapse of many, many years!) I again read the encyclical, especially paragraphs 57 and 58 which speak of the need for Sabbath in the schedule of work.

It has been noted that there are over 4,000 conferences being held this year on *Rerum novarum*. I wonder how many of the presentations address the topic of rest instead of labor! However, I have determined to speak of Sabbath, the law which, when given, incorporated the law of work.

Hebrew and Christian scriptures from beginning to end recognize that work is good. In the book of Genesis we read of God at work and God saw that the work was good. In John 5:17 we read, "My Father is working still." And in Revelations 15:3 we read, "Great and wonderful are your works, Lord God Almighty."

In fact, ten years ago Pope John Paul II wrote in the encyclical *Laborem exercens*, on the ninetieth anniversary of *Rerum novarum*, that "...work is a fundamental dimension of human existence on earth..." After the example of God the Creator—in whose likeness we are made—we bring the earth under control by our labor, by our work.

In my presentation today there is a decided insistence on Sabbath, but I need to forewarn you that it is myself to whom I address this insistence. My remarks are by way of a confessional reflection and what may sound like an indictment, or even a lack of understanding about "the real world" today, comes out of a personal awakening which has, in effect, prompted my participation in this conference.

I need to be somewhat autobiographical in order to establish my ground. I am the president of Iona College, a university of 7,500 students, and one which must develop its operating budgets through fees paid by students and money raised by solicitation from business, government, and friends. Last year I completed nineteen years as President, in what I used to describe with a certain pride as being a seven days a week job. Then, having accepted an extension of my contract for another four years, I decided to spend seven weeks in Israel where I did some studying of the Gospel of Mark, some of the writings of the prophets, and a number of the psalms. Part of the time was spent atop Mt. Sinai where my instructor dialogued with me about the Torah and, in particular, asked me about my observance of Sabbath. At the beginning, I thought that the question was somewhat facitious, given "how hard I work every day of the week." Then my instructor challenged me with another question: did my position as president of a university exempt me from any other of the Lord's commandments, or the law! It was clear that we were onto serious grounds and I was told to go apart for some hours and reflect on my life, my health, my condition of soul and spirit; to see, in effect, if my lack of observance of this law of Sabbath was not having negative consequences in my life.

Let me share with you now some things from the stream of reflections which I confronted through a long and cold July night on top of Mt. Sinai: I have become a slave to work and this enslavement is having a serious negative effect on family and friends. No one is going to interfere with my compulsion. Why should "they?" The more I do the better off "they" are. And then, "they" ease off even more and I work harder, and the anger mounts. Hobbies, golf, reading, music, theater are all going, going, gone. The pathology of my weekend sinfulness is also visited upon my colleagues and staff each Monday. A sense of isolation grows and personal imprisonment mounts. There are claustrophobic episodes. Resentment builds. It is clear that I can never get everything done anyway, but the obsession takes hold, like anorexia. I am going faster and going harder, and becoming possessed by my work and upset at "them" for not appreciating me and my hard work. And the downward spiral begins which ultimately involves the body in stress and the soul in shadow.

But suddenly there is a grace, there is an awakening—*ani la dodi va dodi li*—I to my Beloved and my Beloved to me—the Sabbath is for you, not you for the Sabbath. The Sabbath is a wedding ring of the eternal covenant which binds me with the Sovereign Lord God who fashioned all things in six days and on the seventh day rested.

I take my theme from paragraph 41 of *Rerum novarum*: "In the case of decaying societies it is most correctly prescribed that if they wish to be regenerated they must be recalled to their origins." I was such a decaying society. And so this awakening to Sabbath is a recall to origins for me, which I wish to share with you.

Obviously my remarks are made in the context of a faith tradition, a belief that affirms the fact that "I am" is more important than "I do." My faith tradition begins with a creation story and a paradise--one which involved a cycle of labor and rest. I refer you to the Book of Genesis, that poetic chronicle of the days of creation. It is unfortunate that the person who originally divided the text into chapters and verses separated the seventh day from the other six by using the creation of the seventh day as the opening verses of Chapter 2. In point of fact, we must read these seven days together. God worked for six days and on that seventh day God rested. But not because God was tired! The human person and the Sabbath were in God's mind before the work of creation began; this is an insight from Jewish mysticism. The Sovereign Lord God rested from work because there is more to do than *doing*, there is more to being than *working*.

And in the beginning the cycle of mastering creation and resting followed the right order; God's order prevailed. But at some point there was a fall from grace, an indiscretion of catastrophic proportions such that we are still dealing with its consequences: a maldistribution of resources, painful imbalances, humans oppressing other humans, a disorganization crying out for a redemption, for the Messiah who will restore God's order.

My contribution to the conference is by way of a reminder, principally to myself, but gladly shared with you, that the observance of Sabbath is a necessary and principle vehicle for the restoration of the Lord's right order in creation—the hungered-for opportunity to see, hear, taste, smell, touch as we were meant to—the yearning to rebalance, at least individually, the scales of justice and harmony as the Sovereign Lord God meant these to be—in a faith-founded confidence that paradise will be restored by an endless chain of goodnesses, and a final Coming/Call to right order, a last summoning to justice and peace, to eternal life, to LIFE restored.

Now is all of this "Alice in Wonderland" stuff? No. It is of faith, hope and love. The great temptation is to moral fatigue, to renounce the personal challenge, to grab and take for one's own self. Or, through some other construct or denial, either to dissociate from reality pathologically, or—as in a shoah—to attempt to purify the world of its "weaker elements" through the purges of power.

A critical strategy for healthy restoration for which we yearn authentically is the law of Sabbath. I am called to be *in* the world, assisting, in my own time and with my own gifts, in the restoration of the balance of right order. The Sabbath is part of God's creation which is a principle vehicle for the reinstitution of peace and justice, for the experiencing of personal harmony.

How is Shabbat observed? How is the Sabbath exercised? By an act of imaginative will I construct in time, and live within that construction, the world as it was, as it was meant to be, and as it will one day be. Although I recognize that there is so much work still to be done, I live one day out of seven in faith, and do not do the work. I just let it all be. I behave this way trusting in the power of the strong arm of the Lord who has already acted more than once to save Israel, to save me, who has been a slave.

> Observe the day of the Sabbath to sanctify it,
> as the Lord your God has commanded you.
> Six days shall you labor, and shall you do all
> your works.
> The seventh day is the day of the Sabbath,
> that is, the rest of the Lord thy God.
> You shall not do any work therein;
> You nor your son nor your daughter;
> Nor your man servant nor your maid servant;
> Nor your ox, nor your ass, nor any of your beasts;

Nor the stranger that is within your gates;
That your man servant and your maid ser-
vant   may rest, even as yourself.
Remember that you also did serve in Egypt,
And the Lord your God brought you out
from there with a strong hand,
And a stretched out arm.
Therefore has the Lord commanded you,
that you should observe the Sabbath day.
(Deut. 5:12-15)

Sabbath is a testimonial day. *Adonai sefati teeftah yaqid tehillah tahah.* (Lord open wide my boundaries and my lips will announce your praise.) Sabbath is for celebration and ritual, with clean bodies, with best clothes, good food, joyful songs, mutual loving. "Six days a week you shall work, and do all your creative labor, and the seventh day is Shabbat to the Lord your God." (Ex: 20:9-10)

In creating and celebrating the Sabbath the human person becomes even more luminously in the image of God. Put aside the acts of work and doing, the artifacts and tools of labor, and focus on the sacredness of being, not the obligation of doing. You are more than your accomplishments. "I have made you a little less than the angels." Consider the ancient paradox: The law is given for my freedom, but I am not to be enslaved by the law.

To work seven days a week, workaholism, is a slavery. It is worse: it is an idolatry where I make myself into a false god and take pride in it. Control is self mastery. To stop is to be in control. Stopping is an act of freedom, independence. Just because we *can* do doesn't mean we *must* do!

Sabbath is an act of independence from work, but it is more than leisure from labor. It is a time for inner discovery, tranquility, unfolding. It is a day spent in heaven. It is an oasis in the desert. It is a cathedral built in time, not in space. It is more than "not toiling." It is the time for living within that cathedral, a time for all the modes of personal development that the call for reconciliation, the call for teshuvah, illuminate: reconciliation of me with my God, me with my neighbor, me with myself, me with creation. All these learnings, all these developments of relationships, these are the major activities of Shabbat. My love grows through reflection on these considerations of reconciliation, and the greatest of all these things you could ever do is *to be* in love.

Sabbath is a recognition that life is rooted in the divine and all life shrinks and dies if separated from this rooting. And so prayer is a necessary part of the day of rest from toil. Scripture, psalms, Torah, hymns, meditation, contemplation, personal prayer, communal prayer, liturgy—whatever the form, there must be prayer.

Sabbath also calls me beyond myself, to neighbor—sharing—not just with family and intimates, but with strangers, either directly, or indirectly through charity. Sabbath is for all. Paraphrasing an Irish song: "Both man and master in this day are one; All things are equal till this day is done; The prince, the ploughman, the slave, the free man— "all find their comfort in the Sabbath. Sabbath is for all workers and even for animals. I need to spread my Sabbath reach well beyond my grasp because the paradise that my Sabbath efforts seek to restore is a paradise of community, not a cathedral for me alone. Male and female He created them and told them to fill the earth, and be responsible for all of it. This Shabbat oasis is not a one-person rest stop!

And then, at the end of the day, in some ritual moment or sign, Shabbat is ended and I must reenter the space outside the cathedral built in time and begin again to labor, to work, and toil in space. One day of every seven I stop and take the endless progression of time and fashion a special rest out of it; the other six days I observe the law of work.

Is the Sabbath an "all or nothing" experience? Can there be a part-time Sabbath? Can Sabbath be a Saturday or Sunday? Or can it be Friday as in Islam? What exactly is work? What can I do, and not do? Is sewing work if it is my hobby? Can there be a pluralist approach to the observance of Sabbath? What about the need to pay bills, for "two income families," for part-time work, etc.?

There are volumes written on Sabbath—poetry, prose, laws, interpretations, conference proceedings. My offering today does not deal with these complexities. Rather it is a reminder to me that on the seventh day the omnipotent Lord created rest and gave soul to God's work. God "souled" creation on the Sabbath. Labor is not enough. Camus wrote,

"When work is soulless, life stifles and dies." Oscar Wilde added, "We know the price of everything and the value of nothing."

It is difficult to Sabbath because for most us it will involve a change in behavior, and to do it well and faithfully—like diets, and skiing, and golf, and piano—requires a commitment that draws energy from a deep belief. I must believe firmly that the effort is worth it.

Anything worth doing is worth doing poorly—at least at the beginning—like expressing love—but with attention, and effort, and practice I will get better at it.

It might even be true that if we haven't faithfully practiced Sabbathing in this life, we will not yet be ready for the eternal Sabbath. And how we long for the everlasting Shabbat.

At the beginning there was a paradise, with the Lord's right order, with the cycle of work and rest, of striving and reflection, of mastery of the created world and resting with the Lord. Then something happened: expulsion, earning bread by the sweat of one's brow, oppression, stealing, robber barons, seven days of consumerism, production, buying, selling, tilling, toiling, advertising, marketing, desiring, acquiring—seven days so unredeemed that I could lose the hope of even seeing an alternative, never mind experiencing one.

This is not an indictment of anyone, but a personal effort to call myself to observance of the law.

> And the Lord spoke to Moses saying
> Tell the children of Israel what I have said to you:
> See that you keep my Sabbath
> because it is a sign between me and you for your
> generations that you may know that I am the Lord who
> sanctifies you.
> Keep my Sabbath for it is holy unto you.
> Anyone who shall profane it shall be put to death.
> Anyone that shall do any work in it, that person's soul shall
> perish out of the midst of the people.
> Six days shall you work,
> But on the seventh day is the Sabbath, the rest which is
> holy to the Lord.

Everyone who shall do any work on this day shall die.
Let the children of Israel keep the Sabbath and celebrate it
in their generations.
It is an everlasting covenant between me and the children
of Israel,
And a perpetual sign.
For in six days the Lord made heaven and earth
And in the seventh God ceased from work.
And the Lord, when these words were ended
at Mount Sinai, gave to Moses two stone
tablets of testimony, written with the finger
of God. (Ex. 31:12-18)

This is the modest proposal made to me, *but* from an Infinite Source. I am part of the pilgrimage that began with an exile from paradise; a long line of faithful marchers who stop weekly—not because our work is done, but *as if* our work were done—a procession of covenanted people who wear Sabbath as a wedding ring; people of the law who even if because of extenuating circumstances may not be able to rest from toil still yearn for the experience of Sabbath which they deeply miss.

Is all of this idealism? Is it crazy to hope that the world should behave this way? Perhaps. But *I* can. You might want to try it too. And then somebody else might copy you. Or copy me. And then another might. Who knows: we might create a critical mass of observers, here and there, and a shop owner might decide to close the premises on Sabbath to allow some people to "not work."

Or some few people might want to learn what else is in God's law that is gift to us for the right ordering of the world.

Or the naked might be clothed and the sick might be visited because of the love that derives from reflection on the Torah, on the teaching of the Lord.

Somewhere it is written that if every person celebrated Sabbath at the same time, then the Messiah would *have* to come, because paradise would have been regained.

REFERENCES

Fisher, Eugene: *The Jewish Roots of Christian Liturgy*. Paulist Press, 1990.

Fritz, Maureena: "Rediscovering the Sabbath." *In Review for Religious*, vol. 41, 1982.

Greenberg, Irving: *Guide to Shabbat*. CLAL, 1981.

Heschel, Abraham: *The Sabbath*. Noonday Press, 1951.

Contributors

Margaret Archer, Professor of Sociology at the University of Warwick, England.

Philip Blond is a post-graduate student and Research Fellow at the New School for Social Research, New York.

Jonathan Boswell, B.A. in PPE (University of Oxford); Doctorate from the City University of London. Work experience in Industry and Commerce. Gras Research Fellow at Harvard Business School, 1979. Senior Associate Member of St. Anthony's College, Oxford, 1988-90. Currently Senior Research Associate of the Von Hugel Institute, St. Edmund's College, Cambridge. Author of the much acclaimed *Community and the Economy: the theory of public co-operation*. Routledge, 1990

Bernard Brady, Ph.D. is an assistant professor of Moral Theology at the University of St. Thomas,
St. Paul, MN.

Jonathan Chaplin, Lecturer in Political Theory at Plater College, Oxford.

John G. Driscoll, C.F.C., Ph.D., President, Iona College, New Rochelle, NY.

Joseph W. Ford, Ph.D. Chairperson, Finance and Business Economics Department, Hagan School of Business, Iona College, New Rochelle, NY.

Stephen F. Frowen, Ph.D., Professor of Economics, University College London, and Von Hugel Institute at St. Edmund's College, Cambridge University.

Kenneth E. Goodpaster, Ph.D., Professor of Ethics and Business, St. Thomas University. St. Paul, MN.

Peter Hebblethwaite, scholar and reporter. He is presently completing his book *Paul VI, the First Modern Pope* to be published in the United States.

Georgia Masters Keightley, Ph.D., assistant professor of Theology, Trinity College, Washington, D.C.

John E. Kelly, Ph.D., Chairman of the Department of Philosophy at Canisius College, Buffalo, NY.

Robert Kennedy, Ph.D., is an assistant professor of Management at the University of St. Thomas,
St. Paul, MN.

Christopher Knight, Ph.D., is a priest of the Anglican Communion and present Chaplain, Fellow and Director of Studies in Theology at Sidney Sussex College, Cambridge University.

Francis P. McHugh, Ph.D., Fellow of St. Edmund's College and Director of the Von Hugel Institute at St. Edmunds College, University of Cambridge, England.

John Milbank, Lecturer in the Faculty of Divinity of the University of Cambridge. Author of *Beyond Secular Reason: theology and social theory*. 1991

Samuel M. Natale, D. Phil. (Oxon.), is Professor of Studies in Corporate Values, Iona College, New York and Senior Research Associate, Von Hugel Institute, St. Edmund's College, University of Cambridge, England.

Michael Novak is a theological author and U.S. ambassador. He holds the George Frederick Jewett chair in Religion and Public Policy at the American Enterprise Institute, Washington, D.C.

427

Charles F. O'Donnell, Ph.D., Professor of Economics, Dean, Hagan School of Business, Iona College, New Rochelle, NY

Sebastian A. Sora, DPS, Associate Professor, Montclair State College, New Jersey and Consultant to Promotional Systems Application Development, IBM, White Plains, New York.

Barbara Wall, O.P., Ph.D., Assistant Professor of Philosophy at Villanova University, Pennsylvania.

Acknowledgements

For the prepartion of the text thanks are due:

Mrs. Mary Bruno, Director, Secretarial Service Center of Iona College; the staff: Teresa Alifanti, Patti Besen, Nancy Girardi, Teresa Martin, Máirín McSweeney, and the members of the Duplicating staff: Terry Semenza, Charlie Taylor and Elinor Torelli.

Special thanks to Richard Perna and Rebecca Dunn Chowske for their continued assistance with the text.

429